D1649018

KNOWING THE AMOROUS MAN

Harvard East Asian Monographs 355

KNOWING THE AMOROUS MAN

A History of Scholarship on
Tales of Ise

Jamie L. Newhard

Published by the Harvard University Asia Center
Distributed by Harvard University Press
Cambridge (Massachusetts) and London 2013

Printed in the United States of America

The Harvard University Asia Center publishes a monograph series and, in coordination with the Fairbank Center for Chinese Studies, the Korea Institute, the Reischauer Institute of Japanese Studies, and other faculties and institutes, administers research projects designed to further scholarly understanding of China, Japan, Vietnam, Korea, and other Asian countries. The Center also sponsors projects addressing multidisciplinary and regional issues in Asia.

Library of Congress Cataloging-in-Publication Data

Newhard, Jamie L.
   Knowing the Amorous Man : a history of scholarship on Tales of Ise / Jamie L. Newhard.
        pages cm. — (Harvard East Asian monographs ; 355)
   Includes bibliographical references and index.
   1. Ise monogatari—Criticism, Textual—History.   I. Title.
   PL787.I83N49 2013
   895.6′11—dc23
                                                    2012039299

Index by the author

∞ Printed on acid-free paper

Last figure below indicates year of this printing

22 21 20 19 18 17 16 15 14 13

For my parents

Contents

Reference Matter

Acknowledgments

I am grateful to many individuals and institutions for their support during the research and writing of this book. I do not have adequate words to thank Haruo Shirane, without whom I might never have found my way into the field of premodern Japanese literary studies in the first place, and whose guidance and encouragement have been invaluable at every stage. I owe special thanks to Lewis Cook, who read the entire manuscript, some parts several times, and has also helped me out of many a tight spot when dealing with difficult passages from commentaries. I have learned a great deal in the course of many stimulating discussions with him. I am also indebted to Araki Hiroshi, Ii Haruki, the late Kawahira Hitoshi, David Lurie, Joshua Mostow, Young Kyun Oh, Tomi Suzuki, Unno Keisuke, Yamamoto Tokurō, and Jonathan Zwicker for their insights, advice, and encouragement.

I owe much to my colleagues at Washington University in St. Louis, particularly to Rebecca Copeland, Letty Chen, Beata Grant, Bob Hegel, Ji-Eun Lee, Pauline Lee, Marvin Marcus, Ginger Marcus, and Lori Watt. I could not ask for a more stimulating, supportive environment in which to teach and write. I am also grateful to my former colleagues at Arizona State University, especially to Tony Chambers.

Research in Japan was made possible by a Japan Foundation Dissertation Research Fellowship in 2000–2001 and a Japanese Ministry of Education, Culture, Sport, Science and Technology Research Student Scholarship in 2001–2002. Portions of the translations in Appendix 2 appeared in slightly different form in *Traditional Japanese Literature: An Anthology, Beginnings to 1600*, edited by Haruo Shirane (copyright (©) 2007 Columbia University Press). I am grateful to the publisher for permission to reprint them. Lewis Cook gave valuable feedback on the whole appendix, but all errors and infelicities that remain are mine. I also thank the staff at the General Library of the University of Tokyo for their assistance in acquiring the images of woodblock-printed books that appear in Chapter 4, and Marta Fodor and Ellen Takata at the Museum of Fine Arts, Boston, for their generous help in finding and securing permission for the beautiful image on the cover and the image of the *Saga-bon* that appears in Chapter 4.

I am grateful to the anonymous readers for Harvard University Asia Center for their helpful suggestions; to William Hammell and Deborah Del Gais for steering me through the publication process; and to Wendy Nelson for her assistance with the copyediting.

Finally, I thank my parents, Dave and Linda Newhard, and my brother Chris Newhard for their love and support throughout the years that I have been working on this project.

Tables and Figures

Tables

Figures

Note on Names, Dates,
and Periodization

Japanese names are given in the traditional order, surname first, but following convention, after the first mention premodern scholars are generally referred to by their given or clerical names.

When dates are given, years have been converted to their Western equivalents, but months and days are given according to the Japanese lunar calendar. Since the Japanese lunar month falls a month or two after the Western equivalent, the reader should understand that something that happened in the twelfth month of Genroku 1 (1688) would have occurred in early 1689 by the Western calendar rather than December 1688.

Although I use standard period names throughout, I often use general terms like "early medieval," "late medieval," and "early modern" as well; for reference these are paired with specific period names and dates in the following chronology. I am fully aware that these labels and my use of them have many inadequacies, forcing an unwarranted, perhaps reductive precision on phenomena or transitions that were in reality messy and complex, and evoking Western categories that do not always fit comfortably with the Japanese case. Given that none of these labels can likely be defined in a way that will find universal acceptance, I use them simply as convenient approximations and intend them to apply specifically and narrowly to the progress of literary history, or even more narrowly, to the history of literary scholarship, without regard for how well or badly they fit in terms of political history.

Ancient	Nara period (710–84)
Classical	Heian period (794–1086)
Early medieval	Insei (rule by retired emperors; 1086–1185) Kamakura period (1185–1333) Nanbokuchō/early Muromachi period (1333–1467)
Late medieval	Late Muromachi or Warring States period (1467–1573) Azuchi-Momoyama period (1573–1603)
Early modern	Tokugawa or Edo period (1603–1868)
Modern	(1868–present)

CHAPTER I

Literary Knowledge in Sociohistorical Perspective

In 1912, a little-known book titled *Zaigo chūjō Narihira hishi* was published in Tokyo. The title might be translated as "The Secret History of the Ariwara Middle Captain Narihira," but upon opening the book to the title page, one finds that the author, Kimura Takatarō, has given it his own rather extraordinary English rendering: *The Nestorian Priest of Ariana, or 'The Word Sent From God' in Japanese History.* Kimura uses a linguistic analysis of *Ise monogatari* (Tales of Ise), the tenth-century classic of Japanese court literature, to prove that the work's ostensible protagonist, the ninth-century poet-courtier Ariwara no Narihira (825–80), hailed originally from what is now Afghanistan, integrated Nestorianism with worship of the sun goddess Amaterasu, traveled through Asia from Taiwan to the Arabian Peninsula spreading his own "Narihira movement," and brought the New Testament to the West from Japan.[1] The reader who stumbles across a gem such as this in a used bookstore might find herself barely able to flip the pages as her astonishment at the proceedings and their perversity increases. And yet, in his recondite approach to *Ise monogatari*, Kimura is in excellent company: his effort is merely one of the more outrageous examples in an eight-century-long exegetical tradition that is often inventive to the point of puzzling, rather than enlightening, a modern reader.

---

1. Kimura, *Narihira hishi*, pp. 1–4, 22–23, and passim.

Ise monogatari was established as a central text in the classical Japanese literary canon as early as the eleventh century and has remained one of the most widely read and highly influential texts in the tradition ever since. It has inspired generations of poets and artists, formed the basis of Noh and kabuki plays, been translated, adapted, and parodied in popular narrative, and exerted a great impact on Japanese aesthetics. However, the text has never lent itself to easy solutions to the questions of what it is and how it should be read. Forced to grapple with its numerous variants, mysterious origins, and idiosyncratic form—125 loosely connected episodes, each a taut balance of poetry and brief prose context, recounting the life and loves of an anonymous middle-ranking courtier who persistently evokes Ariwara no Narihira—successive generations of commentators have spilled staggering quantities of ink trying to aid others in understanding the text: along with *Genji monogatari* (The tale of Genji, ca. 1008) and the *Kokinwakashū* (Collection of old and new Japanese poems, 905; informally known as *Kokinshū*), it is one of the three most extensively studied and commented-upon works in Japanese literary history. But definitive solutions to its puzzles and readings of the text as a whole that are both compelling and comprehensive remain elusive.

I do not attempt to put forth a reading of *Ise monogatari*, definitive or otherwise, in these pages. Nor is it my goal to assess the persuasiveness or credibility of others' views. Rather, the object of this study is to trace scholars' use of *Ise monogatari* as a vehicle for advancing a variety of personal or institutional agendas that go beyond interpretation of the text. I am interested in how these scholars' efforts serve to construct, transform, and transmit the literary and cultural value of the text, and shifts in those values over time, but the larger goal of my research is to define the contexts for these changes: to give a more comprehensive picture of the social networks and institutions within which literary scholarship was conducted and circulated, to identify the ideological and literary issues that drove and shaped scholars' work, and to trace how scholastic institutions and methodologies evolved as the audience for classical literature expanded beyond aristocratic circles to include other social groups.

Focusing on *Ise monogatari* provides uniquely rich possibilities for a study of these phenomena. First, the difficulties that plague the text served to render it an all the more appealing playground within which commentators of various persuasions might ride their hobby horses with abandon. The laconic ambiguity of *Ise monogatari*'s style and the obscurity in which its origins are shrouded engender a sometimes lavish inventiveness in the interpretations, in the course of which commentators tend to reveal more of what drives them than might otherwise be the case. Furthermore, the text's relative brevity permits a thorough examination of a larger number of commentaries than would be possible with *Genji monogatari* or the *Kokinshū*, the other pillars of the premodern literary canon. Finally, the ambiguous generic status of *Ise monogatari*—a hybrid of fact and fiction, of poetry and prose—highlights the significance of genre to the conduct of literary scholarship and production of ideological value. Commentators' perceptions of *Ise* as either factual or fictitious, and of the genre with which it is most closely aligned (history, fiction, or poetry collection), exerted a profound influence on the details they singled out for attention, their interpretation of those details, and their sense of *Ise*'s larger significance. Fiction was initially regarded with disdain or suspicion compared to more "serious" genres like history and poetry, and was criticized (particularly in the case of works like *Ise* and *Genji* that depict illicit amorous encounters) for its potential to lead readers into immoral behavior. Tracing shifts in the strategies through which early scholars grappled with issues of fictionality and moral value reveals the complex interactions among genre, ideology, and hermeneutics as these relate to assessments of the work's value and to its status within the literary canon.

Commentary was the dominant mode of literary scholarship practiced on *Ise monogatari* in medieval and early modern Japan, and surviving commentaries are key sources through which to reconstruct the processes by which the value of *Ise monogatari* was produced and transmitted. Commentaries are valuable for their overtly dialogic quality: new commentaries were always produced with old commentaries on hand, and commentators defined themselves against the past, alternately confirming, expanding upon, and challenging earlier views in a way that renders both shifts and continuities easily discernible. Commentaries are also a site where the intersection of ideology and hermeneutics is clearly visible, where one can observe not only the impact ideology has on interpretation but also how commentators deliberately call attention to their methodological and interpretive innovations as a means of claiming legitimacy for themselves and contesting their predecessors' or rivals' authority.

Scholars generally divide premodern commentaries on *Ise monogatari* into three groups.[2] The Old Commentaries (*kochūshaku*) are secret transmissions compiled by Kamakura and early Muromachi-period *waka* poets who viewed *Ise monogatari* as disguised historical fact, the life story of the ninth-century poet and courtier Ariwara no Narihira couched in various fictions, and who saw their task as recreating the "truth" behind the fiction even where there was no truth to be found. The Transitional Commentaries[3] (or "Older Commentaries," *kyūchūshaku*), beginning with Ichijō Kaneyoshi's *Ise monogatari gukenshō* (1460), are the work of fifteenth- through seventeenth-century *waka*, *renga*, and *haikai* poets who rejected the more fanciful excesses of their predecessors but persisted in viewing *Ise monogatari* as at least partly rooted in the facts of Narihira's life. I divide the Transitional Commentaries further into an early (late medieval) group and a late (early modern) group, with the beginning of the seventeenth century as the dividing line. This mark corresponds not only to the political shift that took place with the establishment of the Tokugawa shogunate; it is also the point when manuscript culture gave way to a combination of manuscript and print, as well as the starting point for other substantial social and cultural changes that altered the ways in which commentaries were produced and packaged, even though the interpretations put forth in the commentaries changed little until the late seventeenth century. Finally, the New Commentaries (*shinchūshaku*), beginning with Keichū's *Seigo okudan* (1693), are mostly the work of scholars associated with the *kokugaku* (national learning, or nativism) movement of the mid to late Edo period, who viewed earlier commentaries skeptically and brought more rigorous scholarly methods to bear on the text, opening it to fresh interpretations.

A handful of studies that deal partly with premodern *Ise monogatari* commentaries have already appeared in English. Richard Bowring's sweeping "The *Ise monogatari*: A Short Cultural History," a journal

---

2. See Ōtsu, *Ise monogatari kochūshaku*, p. 25. Ōtsu, one of the pioneers in studying the commentaries on a large scale, is the first to make the division this way. Although some refer to the commentaries by political period (Kamakura, Muromachi, Edo), Ōtsu's scheme has the distinct advantage of grouping the commentaries by shared approach as well as approximate chronology, thereby accommodating the fact that *kochū*-style commentaries continued to be produced through the mid-Muromachi period, and *kyūchū*-style commentaries well into the Tokugawa.

3. I am borrowing Susan Klein's usage here.

article published in 1992, discusses premodern *Ise* scholarship together with the text's transformations in illustrations, in Noh, in *otogizōshi*, in Edo-period parodies, and so on. More recently, Susan Klein's *Allegories of Desire: Esoteric Literary Commentaries of Medieval Japan* (2002) gives a meticulous treatment of key Old Commentaries on *Ise* as well as on the *Kokinshū*, analyzing their use of allegoresis as an interpretive strategy and placing them in historical context. She has also produced a full translation and introduction of *Ise monogatari zuinō* (1997–98), a work that is closely related to the Old Commentaries, and her Ph.D. dissertation, "Allegories of Desire: Kamakura Commentaries and the Noh" (1994), describes the impact of the Old Commentaries on several Noh plays based on sections of *Ise*.[4]

These studies rely on the work of Katagiri Yōichi, whose seminal *Ise monogatari no kenkyū* (1968–69) inaugurated in-depth study of the commentaries, principally the Old Commentaries, as a window on *Ise monogatari's* reception. Two additional book-length studies had appeared earlier. Ōtsu Yūichi's indispensable *Ise monogatari kochūshaku no kenkyū* (1954; updated in 1986) introduces 138 commentaries, ranging from the Kamakura period through the end of the Tokugawa period, with information about the authors and variant texts as well as brief samples from each commentary. The approach is bibliographic rather than interpretive, but the book serves as an excellent guide nonetheless. Tanaka Sōsaku's *Ise monogatari kenkyūshi no kenkyū* (1965) is valuable for its focus on Tokugawa-period commentaries (both late Transitional Commentaries and New Commentaries), including discussion of many that are not available in modern printed editions.

Despite this activity in the 1950s and 1960s, though, and a subsequent "commentary boom" that developed in the 1970s and 1980s and continues to this day, making many more texts available in printed editions and yielding numerous articles on textual problems that surround individual commentaries, it is only in the past twenty-five years or so that analytical or critical articles about the commentaries have begun to appear with any frequency, and, no doubt owing to Katagiri's pathbreaking work, the coverage has tended to be slanted toward medieval

---

4. In addition to these, see Vos, *A Study of the Ise-monogatari*, pp. 101–15, for a helpful survey in English of important premodern commentaries.

commentaries. Yamamoto Tokurō and Aoki Shizuko have both produced significant bodies of work, particularly on the mainstream Transitional Commentaries, on which my discussion will rely heavily,[5] but apart from Tanaka, scholars in Japan have tended to ignore or dismiss later Transitional Commentaries, many of which were produced for unsophisticated nonscholarly audiences after the advent of commercial publishing in the seventeenth century,[6] and no fully integrated account of even the mainstream commentaries of this group has yet appeared. By the same token, there is relatively little scholarship on the New Commentaries of nativist scholars (again, with the exception of Tanaka's work), partly because study of *kokugaku* in Japan is dominated by historians rather than *kokubungaku* (national literature studies) scholars, partly because nativist scholars' work on *Ise* appears tangential or secondary within their respective corpuses, and partly, I believe, because these commentaries seem either too accessible—a number of them were still found to be as useful as contemporary commentaries well into the modern period—to merit study at arm's length or, conversely, too far out in ideological left field to be treated as more than idiosyncratic tirades. But whatever the reasons, research on nativists' work on *Ise*, when it exists, is most often undertaken as part of the study of the respective nativist scholar's work as a whole, not as part of a study of *Ise* commentaries or of *Ise*'s reception generally. My work seeks to bridge some of these gaps, by providing a more comprehensive, integrated history of the Transitional and New Commentaries, with particular attention to shifts in the way the study of literary texts is conceptualized, to issues of openness and secrecy, to the forms in which works of scholarship circulated, and to the genre issues that very often drive the commentators' interpretations.

---

5. Much of Yamamoto's earlier work is conveniently gathered in Yamamoto, *Ise monogatari ron*, and he has also very recently spearheaded a number of edited volumes gathering together new work on *Ise* reception (not limited to discussion of commentaries) by a wide range of scholars. See particularly Yamamoto, ed., *Ise monogatari: Kyōju no tenkai*, and Yamamoto and Mostow, eds., *Ise monogatari: Sōzō to hen'yō*.

6. Yamamoto has taken the first steps toward rectifying this gap as well, in the form of *Ise monogatari hanpon shūsei*, a large volume of photographic reproductions of popular early modern woodblock-printed books together with vast amounts of bibliographical information. Unfortunately, because this book appeared as the present volume was in the final stages of preparation, it has not been possible to incorporate the wealth of new information here.

Literary Knowledge

The title of this book, *Knowing the Amorous Man*, is intended to evoke both the central questions about *Ise monogatari* that taxed medieval and early modern exegetes, and the framework that supports this study. As the strange case of Kimura Takatarō suggests, the figure of Ariwara no Narihira, *Ise's* presumptive protagonist, very often becomes the bearer of larger burdens of meaning, such that knowing what *Ise monogatari* means becomes an extension of knowing Narihira—reconstructing what is true of him historically or biographically; explicating what is true of him literarily, as he is presented in *Ise monogatari*; accounting for (or effacing) gaps between these two Narihira-constructions; and at the same time, elucidating the significance of his supposed "amorousness." In the course of tackling these issues and others, commentators produce and transmit not only new knowledge, but new strategies of knowing. Devising appropriate, effective ways to conduct historical inquiries, to analyze and interpret the text and its language, to create coherence, and to extract moral lessons or aesthetic principles—all of these are deeply implicated in commentators' activities.

To underscore these strategies, throughout this study I view the material put forth in commentaries on *Ise monogatari* as sociohistorically situated instantiations of "literary knowledge." I take literary knowledge to be just one specialized type of knowledge among the plurality of knowledges that might, in Norbert Elias's phrase, function as a "means of orientation" in a given society or group,[7] and that range from practical everyday knowledge to abstract, theoretical scientific or philosophical knowledge. As I am interested in how literary knowledge changes over a long period of time, my working definition is necessarily loose: transmitted, more or less systematized information considered necessary to appreciate or utilize a belle-lettristic piece of writing in a particular sociohistorical setting; in other words, the information or competencies beyond mere literacy that a reader needs in order to perform as a skilled reader within a particular milieu. Needless to say, there is considerable overlap between literary knowledge in this sense and other kinds of knowledge. To enable readers to engage "correctly" with *Ise monogatari*,

---

7. Elias, "Knowledge and Power," p. 204.

for example, commentators introduce historical knowledge, knowledge of Heian-period customs, Buddhist and Confucian knowledge, and so on, but insofar as these other knowledges are being applied to or extrapolated from *Ise monogatari*, in the context of an *Ise* commentary they function concurrently as literary knowledge.[8]

As the terms of the foregoing definition suggest, I am construing literary knowledge from a specifically, perhaps narrowly, social, transactional point of view, involving a party (or text) who produces, packages, and transmits knowledge, and a second party, implied or actual, who receives it. I am not, for current purposes, interested in epistemological questions, such as how we can know what a literary work means or determine what interpretations are valid, what special kinds of knowledge (about the human condition, about language, and so on) are extricable from literary works and how they may be retrieved, or what constitutes a work as "literary" in the first place. Although these are certainly valid and fascinating lines of inquiry, they fall outside the purview of this study. My own concerns are in the following questions: How was literary knowledge conceptualized in medieval and early modern Japan? How was it produced and controlled, and by whom? On what did its producers base their claims to authority? Who wanted literary knowledge and for what purposes? Through what channels and in what forms did literary knowledge circulate?

At any particular point in time, the answers to these questions are closely interrelated and may be thought of as forming a complex structure, what we might, following Pierre Bourdieu, view as a distinct area within the larger field of cultural production. In Bourdieu's work, a field is a social space wherein agents (in this case, producers and disseminators) vie to maximize their reputations, influence, and authority, changing the structure of the field itself with every move they make in relation to each other. In Bourdieu's own words,

> the initiative of change falls on the newcomers . . . who are also those least endowed with specific capital; in a universe in which to exist is to differ, i.e., to occupy a distinct, distinctive position, they must assert their

---

8. By the same token, one might find aspects of literary knowledge deployed in commentaries on other kinds of texts, as when metaphor or parables are discussed in a commentary on a Buddhist sutra.

difference, get it known and recognized, get themselves known and rec- ognized ("make a name for themselves"), by endeavouring to impose new modes of thought and expression, out of key with the prevailing modes of thought and with the doxa, and therefore bound to disconcert the orthodox by their "obscurity" and "pointlessness." The fact remains that every new position, in asserting itself as such, determines a displace- ment of the whole structure and that, by the logic of action and reaction, it leads to all sorts of changes in the position-takings of the occupants of the other positions.[9]

At the same time,

> When the newcomers are not disposed to enter the cycle of simple repro- duction, based on recognition of the "old" by the "young"—homage, celebration, etc.—and recognition of the "young" by the "old"—prefaces, co-optation, consecration, etc.—but bring with them dispositions and position-takings which clash with the prevailing norms of production and the expectations of the field, they cannot succeed without the help of external changes. These may be political breaks, such as revolutionary crises, which change the power relations within the field . . . or deep- seated changes in the audience of consumers who, because of their affin- ity with the new producers, ensure the success of their products.[10]

The model is thus particularly useful for elucidating the changes that took place in the production, consumption, and circulation of premod- ern Japanese literary scholarship across critical historical junctures such as the Ōnin War and the establishment of the Tokugawa shogunate— times when social and political upheaval led to new relationships between producers and consumers and new patterns of dissemination.

Conceptions of what literary knowledge entails also change over time, hand in hand with the methods employed to produce it. Some is- sues that were of particular, pervasive interest to the commentators dis- cussed herein include:

- explanations of a work's title
- attempts to identify authors and the time of writing
- textual history and evaluation of variant texts
- glosses of obscure vocabulary

---

9. Bourdieu, *Field of Cultural Production*, p. 58.
10. Ibid., pp. 57–58.

- identification of omitted grammatical subjects
- tracing allusions to earlier works, particularly to poetry, or discussion of later poems that refer back to the text under discussion (*hikiuta*)
- explanations of relevant court protocol and precedent (*yūsoku kojitsu*)
- identification of anonymous characters or poets as historical personages
- reading conventions (*yomikuse*)
- explications of poems
- critical evaluation of poems, or of prose passages
- acceptance or rejection of previous or other schools' interpretations
- discussions of genre
- narratological observations (regarding narrators' intrusions, and so on)
- extraction of moral lessons, with or without support from secondary sources
- methodological issues and assertions
- conventions or practices pertaining to the transmission of information (how to begin or end a lecture; references to the existence of secret teachings; etc.)

Many of these concerns, of course, persist to this day. Open any volume of one of the standard modern editions of a premodern classic, and one of the first things to appear in its *kaisetsu* (explanatory essay) will be a discussion of the title and author, while the notes brim with allusions, definitions, and historical background. However, even when the conclusions are similar, differences in the methods employed to arrive at them and the sources of their authority (distinct but often related questions) can lead to fundamental differences in their significance. Something as simple as a statement about whether a particular consonant should be voiced or unvoiced, for example, may prove to have very different implications when it is made by a late medieval scholar versus an early modern scholar. The late medieval scholar's assertion will very often derive from a traditional reading convention handed down from some past luminary in the poetic tradition, acceptance of which identifies the receiving party as an adherent of a particular school. An early modern scholar, meanwhile, would more likely base his conclusion on philological research that he is at pains to explain in his commentary as a means of justifying the break he makes with the views of earlier, established commentators.

Literary knowledge has significance beyond its content (the specifics about which producer-agents contend and the methods through which they justify their conclusions), however. It also functions as a form of cultural capital for both producers and consumers, albeit in different ways. Producers rely on other forms of symbolic capital—designation as heir in a scholarly family, possession of or access to authoritative texts, initiation into secret teachings, connections with well-placed (wealthy or powerful) students, acquisition of a popular following, possession of an advanced degree, to name a few possibilities—to legitimize their status as producers and disseminators of knowledge, while possession of legitimate status in turn "consecrates" the knowledge itself and reconstitutes it as yet another source of symbolic capital for the producer. Although their methods, practices, and sources of authority vary widely, a fifteenth-century *renga* master, an eighteenth-century nativist scholar, and a twenty-first-century Japanese literature professor are all engaged in this process of converting their own acquired capital into knowledge and thence into new capital for themselves and for others. The output of each is inextricably linked, on one hand, to the institutional configurations in which they operate and the positions they take in relation to other players in the field, and on the other hand, to the specific character and needs of their target audiences. Consumers, meanwhile, come to desire literary knowledge based on the possibility of converting it into other kinds of capital (social, economic, political, and so forth). A medieval courtier might seek to be recognized as a skilled poet, and thence to attract the attention or patronage of superiors. An early modern woman might wish to demonstrate cultural literacy and sophistication in order to enhance her marriage prospects. And a twenty-first-century student might seek no more or less than to pass a college entrance examination, or to fulfill requirements for a degree that will lead to gainful employment. A principal goal of this study is to trace the history of premodern Japanese literary scholarship, as revealed specifically in scholarship on *Ise monogatari*, with attention to the interconnectedness of consumers' needs, producers' distinguishing strategies, and the content of literary knowledge in a complex, constantly shifting structure.

Secrecy and Openness

A distinctive feature of premodern Japanese literary scholarship and another broad concern of this study is the use of secrecy to manage the circulation and thence the value (social, economic, and otherwise) of literary knowledge. Medieval scholars, taking their cue from esoteric

Buddhism, maintained more or less elaborate systems of teachings that were made available only to select initiates. During the early modern period, however, these practices fell into disuse outside court circles: the "culture of secrecy" gave way to one of increasing openness, and to dramatic changes in the way literary knowledge was produced and consumed. The beginning of the shift corresponds loosely to the advent of commercial publishing in the seventeenth century, but it is a great oversimplification to imagine that publishing alone destroyed the authority or prestige of secret knowledge. Residual interest in secret teachings persisted to the end of the early modern period, and proponents of "openness," such as nativist scholars, as newcomers to the field, were by no means in a position to create new norms without considerable struggle.

Although Chapter 3 below examines in some detail the content of a particular set of secret teachings on *Ise monogatari*, I am more generally interested in secrecy as "essentially a boundary mechanism separating members of different social categories or groups. . . . the content of the secret is often insignificant compared to the rights, obligations and privileges generated by the fact of secrecy."[11] For medieval Japanese literary scholars and poets, possession of legitimately obtained secret knowledge served to distinguish insiders from outsiders and at the highest levels conveyed the authority to reproduce and transmit knowledge within a school, as well as to earn money from doing so. Therefore, even when the specifics of the secrets remain unknown, as is the case with many late medieval secret teachings about *Ise monogatari*, the fact of a commentator having occupied a position in a transmission lineage implies a great deal about that commentator's status and modus operandi:

> Secrecy . . . is better understood, not in terms of its content or substance . . . but rather in terms of its *forms* or *strategies*—the tactics by which social agents conceal or reveal, hoard or exchange, certain valued information. In this sense, secrecy is a discursive strategy that transforms a given piece of knowledge into a scarce and precious resource, a valuable commodity, the possession of which in turn bestows status, prestige, or symbolic capital on its owner.[12]

---

11. Murphy, "Secret Knowledge," p. 193.
12. Urban, "Torment of Secrecy," p. 210.

Secrecy thus becomes an effective method to manage the value, economic and otherwise, of knowledge. Late medieval scholars might lecture on a particular text and allow notes (*kikigaki*) to be taken, but they maintained parallel stores of secret knowledge (*hiden* or *denju*) that were transmitted only orally (*kuden*) or in separate memoranda (*kirigami*). It is important to note that knowledge, whether secret or widely known, does not function exactly as a commodity.[13] Unlike a measure of rice, knowledge does not cease to be possessed by whomever transmits it, even after it has been transferred to another party—it is capable of being transmitted repeatedly, and attempts to control its transmission may be necessary to preserve its value. Access to secret knowledge typically required the consent and cooperation of the scholar who held it, as well as the signing of oaths forbidding retransmission, and perhaps participation in an initiation ceremony. If acquired without involvement in the full process, the knowledge was essentially valueless. Mark Teeuwen makes a helpful distinction in this regard between "knowing" a secret and "owning" it:

> Secrets are a function of a complicated set of official rules of transmission. These rules signalize that the secret in question is the property of a specific lineage. "Secret" appears here to mean "that which is to be transmitted within a lineage," rather than "that which is to be hidden." Even when the knowledge that is declared secret is not physically removed from the public realm, it still retains a special status in the sense that only those who have gained it in the "proper" way, through an initiation within the right lineage, have the authority to use it. A person who has studied the Tōmitsu secrets in the library, or who has overheard them in a temple, has no legitimacy as a priest—just as a person who has read a medical handbook is not allowed to practice as a doctor.[14]

The content of secret knowledge is thus only one component of the arrangement that ensured the authority of both the producer-transmitter and the knowledge itself.

Early modern thinkers famously deplored the existence of secret teachings and initiated the movement toward openness. Matsunaga Teitoku (1571–1653), for example, a commoner who had studied under several aristocrats but who had not been permitted to receive secret teachings,

---

13. Stehr, "Knowledge Societies," p. 304.
14. Teeuwen, "Knowing vs. Owning," p. 173.

gave public lectures on *Tsurezuregusa* (Essays in idleness, ca. 1331) as early as 1603, much to the consternation of his patrons. Teitoku was no revolutionary—he initiated the transmission of the so-called *jige denju* (commoner *denju*) based on what he had learned from courtiers—but the concern he evinced throughout his long career for educating members of his own class who sought knowledge of the classical literary tradition makes him a key transitional figure. Nativist scholars' hostility to secret teachings, particularly to the *kokin denju* (secret teachings of the *Kokinshū*)[15] was far less equivocal. In *Kokka hachiron* (Eight theses on national poetry, 1742), Kada no Arimaro expresses a typical nativist view:

> Approaching recent times, something called the *kokin denju* came into being. To understand writings, one compares them to other writings and adds one's own ideas. There is no other method. What sort of transmission could there be? Moreover, since the *Kokinshū* is simply a collection of poetry, how can there be meaning created from anything beyond the words of the poems? Therefore, from antiquity onward, there was no field in the study of poetry known as the *kokin denju*. It was probably created spuriously by Tō no Tsuneyori and spread by the monk Sōgi. Sōgi, who supposedly received the transmission, lectured on the *Kokinshū*, and when you look at the works of Hosokawa Yūsai,[16] who explicated *Ise monogatari, Hyakunin isshu,* and *Eiga no taigai,* from beginning to end there is not a single word among the explanations that one should look up to and accept. With their scanty knowledge they arbitrarily believed groundless ideas.[17]

Arimaro rejects the *kokin denju* essentially on methodological grounds. Knowledge about poetry must in his view be generated directly from examining texts; tradition and transmission lineage become irrelevant

---

15. The *kokin denju* is a body of secret knowledge pertaining to the *Kokinshū* (and to some extent to *Ise monogatari* and other texts) that originated in lectures given by Tō no Tsuneyori to the *renga* master Sōgi in the fifteenth century. Sōgi subsequently transmitted the teachings to courtiers of the Sanjōnishi and Konoe families, as well as to his disciple Shōhaku. The teachings continued to be transmitted in court circles through the end of the Tokugawa period.

16. A warrior and poet with close ties to the court, Yūsai (1534–1610) received the *kokin denju* from the Sanjōnishi family and became a key figure in the establishment of both court *denju* and commoner *denju* in the Tokugawa period.

17. Hashimoto, et al., *Karonshū*, pp. 560–61.

as a basis of authority. The argument is part of a larger project of discrediting the court-associated scholars for whom a monopoly on literary knowledge was a birthright and of creating a space wherein commoners too might be accepted as legitimate interpreters of the classical literary tradition.

Secret teachings nonetheless retained a powerful hold on the popular imagination, and some of Arimaro's and other nativists' vehemence can perhaps be attributed to the fact that they were fighting a decidedly uphill battle. From the Genroku period (1688–1704), continuing through the eighteenth century, a truly astounding array of supposedly secret knowledge begins to appear among booksellers' wares. Many had to do with poetry, but books were also published on secrets of cooking, Noh chanting, *go* playing, letter writing, and, separately, letter folding. There are published secrets of medicine, military strategy, feminine deportment, China, bureaucracy, carpentry, good health, acting, *biwa* playing, *kana* usage, incense making, sericulture, archery, *jōruri*, drumming, dance, and moxabustion. There are books identified as "mirrors" of secret transmissions, "pillows" of secret transmissions, "bags" of secret transmissions, and "illustrated bags" of secret transmissions. The titles of these books echo the language of medieval *denju* culture, using words like *hishō, hiden, kikigaki,* and *kirigami.* But even in cases where "real" secrets were being published, there is a crucial difference: there is no master-disciple relationship, no transmission ritual. The knowledge might for all practical purposes have been bought and sold earlier, but never would a serious secret have been transmitted outside a personal relationship, without lectures exchanged and oaths signed, and so on. In the early modern period, however, this knowledge did in fact become merely a commodity: the supposedly secret knowledge was displayed openly on the shelf, accessible to anyone who had the necessary cash. With the practices stripped away, an essential part of the value is lost, and all that remains is rhetoric, a marketing strategy.

Commentaries, Canons, and Books

Commentary is the dominant form in which exegesis was practiced not only in premodern Japan, but in premodern societies across the globe—the most common scholarly response to the problems inherent in interpreting and assimilating a valued classic in a time long enough after its formation that it cannot be understood as is.[18] Although we might view a wide range of texts and genres as "commentaries" on other works—a Noh play, a parody, a translation, even a painting may serve as a "comment" on *Ise monogatari*—in this study I use the term in the restrictive sense of writing that attempts to clarify a particular base text section by section, line by line, sometimes even word by word, often, though not always, sharing the written or printed page with the base text. Because the structure of a commentary derives from the structure of the base text, dealing with problems as they come up, commentaries do not typically present an organized, coherent argument about a given text. Rather, larger agendas must be reconstructed from an examination of patterns in the scattered annotations, adduced from extratextual evidence, or glimpsed in seemingly offhand remarks. Even when a commentary includes a preface addressing general matters, one often finds that what the author of a commentary says he is going to do diverges significantly from what he actually does.

John Makeham, writing of Confucian commentary, describes a pervasive weakness in the way commentaries tend to be approached:

> I would suggest that most readers today tend to regard the commentary as an accessory, supplement or even vestige, the significance of which is defined by that of the text and subordinate to it. We accept the text as an integral whole but we pick and choose which passages of commentary to adopt and ignore the rest. . . . Consequently we have tended not to appreciate sufficiently that many commentaries do more than simply comment on a text: often passages of text serve as pretexts for the commentator to develop and expound his own body of thought.[19]

Despite what might initially appear to be a sort of formal rigidity deriving from the inseparability of a commentary from its base text, the commentary form is actually extremely fluid: the lack of any imperative to produce a coherent, overarching argument makes the form very amenable to digressions and detours, and it is often these junctures, seemingly tangential to the task at hand, that reveal the most about what underlies the commentators' readings. Commentaries are thus an unparalleled

---

18. Henderson, *Scripture, Canon and Commentary*, p. 4.
19. Makeham, *Transmitters and Creators*, pp. 2–3.

source of information not only about history of a particular text's reception—a rare opportunity to see readers of bygone ages in action—but also about the broader issues and conventions that motivate commentators' reading practices and shape their conclusions.

Among the things that dictate how commentaries work, perhaps the most basic derive from beliefs about the nature of canonical texts and of canons as a whole. In his comparative study of Confucian commentary and various Western commentarial traditions—Christian biblical exegesis, Qu'ranic exegesis, and rabbinical Judaism, as well as Vedānta—John Henderson identifies a number of "commentarial assumptions" that govern how canonical texts are approached in these otherwise divergent traditions:

1. The canon is comprehensive and all-encompassing.
2. The canon is well-ordered and coherent, arranged according to some logical, cosmological or pedagogical principle.
3. The canon is self-consistent; internal contradictions in it are only apparent.

These coexist with assumptions about the works that comprise the canon:

a. The classics are moral.
b. The classics are profound.
c. The classics contain nothing superfluous or insignificant.
d. The classics are clear and accessible.[20]

These assumptions are reflected not only in commentaries on scriptural canons, but also on some literary canons or works.[21] Differences may arise, however, according to the nature of the particular canon. As Haruo Shirane points out, although scriptural canons are generally stable and closed, literary canons are in constant flux.[22] Thus, they are less likely to be subject to assumptions about comprehensiveness, for example. We do

---

20. For detailed discussion of each of these propositions, see Henderson, *Scripture, Canon and Commentary*, pp. 89–138.

21. Henderson discusses commentary on Homer, though he identifies the epics as quasi-scriptural. Other literary examples may be found in Baswell, *Virgil in Medieval England*, and Parker, *Commentary and Ideology*, showing that commentaries on *The Aeneid* and *The Divine Comedy* have characteristic encyclopedic qualities and appear to approach the texts with the assumption that they are moral, profound, and so forth.

22. Shirane, "Introduction: Issues in Canon Formation," p. 3.

not generally find late medieval scholars in Japan mining *Genji* and *Ise* for information about how to govern a state or what happens after death (though we do find broader concerns in the work of Confucian and nativist scholars). Many of the other assumptions, however—that the canon is somehow orderly, that apparent inconsistencies in it can be resolved, that classics are moral, that they are deeply and entirely meaningful, that (with the aid of a commentator) they are accessible—hold in the case of *Ise monogatari* commentaries of all periods and go a long way toward illuminating the sometimes strenuous gymnastics commentators engage in to reconfigure aspects of the text that seem to defy these assumptions.

On the other hand, there are important issues for which Henderson's analysis does not entirely account. Commentaries do not arise in a closed room containing just a text and a commentator; external political and social pressures influence their production and content as well. A particular commentator's sense of morality, for example, may derive from sources other than the canon itself or may rely upon a reconstitution of the canon. At the same time, commentaries can themselves become canonized and thereby set or restrict the agendas of subsequent commentaries.

It is also essential to consider the social aspects of commentaries. I would argue that commentaries, in all cases, are not merely collections of an individual's or institution's interpretations; they are traces of interpersonal transactions wherein a party with some claim to authority, stated or implicit, attempts to enlighten, persuade, or indoctrinate a reader or group of readers (or auditors), while shoring up and sometimes ritually transmitting that authority. In short, commentaries are intimately connected to the power relations within or among various scholastic institutions, by virtue of both the distinctive knowledge they contain and the practices surrounding their production and transmission. Commentaries must thus be considered not only as part of the reception of the base text, but also in terms of their own reception history, their projected and actual effects on their intended (and unintended) audiences.

This history is inseparable from the material form of the commentary. In the simplest case, a commentary may consist simply of notes jotted in the margins or between the lines of a previously existing copy of the base text, representing either the jotter's reactions to the text itself or the results of his or her engagement with another commentary. In other cases, a commentary may begin as a student's notes on lectures given by some authority, which may later be recopied and certified by the lecturer as a faithful transcription of the lecture, and then be circulated selectively to others. Alternately, authorities may produce commentaries of their own, with preconceived intentions regarding the breadth of the texts' circulation. Commentaries may be prepared in manuscript for the sake of having them printed but might also come to be printed irrespective of the original intention. In short, the form the commentary takes on the written or printed page and the process through which it attained that form contains its own wealth of information that must be accounted for when attempting to situate its interpretations of the base text.

Such information often appears prominently in what Gerard Genette calls "paratexts," defined as "what enables a text to become a book, and to be offered as such to its readers," or more specifically,

> verbal or other productions, such as an author's name, a title, a preface, illustrations. . . . although we do not always know whether these productions are to be regarded as belonging to the text, in any case they surround it and extend it, precisely in order to *present* it, in the usual sense of this verb but also in the strongest sense: to *make present*, to ensure the text's presence in the world, its "reception" and consumption in the form (nowadays, at least) of a book.[23]

Of course, commentary can itself be viewed as a paratext of the work it elucidates, depending on its presentation—as a secondary appendage to the base text, as in the case of popular early modern printed commentaries on *Ise monogatari*, rather than as the primary focus of the book or manuscript that "presents" it, as in the case of most of the other commentaries considered below. But other paratextual features, such as prefaces, colophons, publisher's postscripts, and such, some of which attract scant attention when commentaries are analyzed and discussed, will be examined closely in this study for what they reveal about the commentaries' origins and intended uses. Issues of material form and composition will be particularly prominent in my discussion of early modern Transitional Commentaries, but this entire study is informed by a view of commentaries as objects whose material (or in the case of oral transmissions,

---

23. Genette, *Paratexts*, p. 1.

virtual) form, including its paratexts or "presentation," is determined by, and therefore reveals, distinctive social or institutional relations.

Genre and Interpretation

Because genre issues are central to a consideration of *Ise monogatari*'s place in Japanese literary history and appropriation for various purposes by literary scholars, a few words are in order about the concept as it will figure hereinafter. The generic classification of a literary work is both a precondition for and a consequence of critical intervention. Such classification may be considered a sub-operation (or super-operation) of the hermeneutic circle whereby one cannot understand a work as a whole without understanding its constituent parts, yet cannot understand the parts without knowledge of the whole. A commentator reasoning about a text, whether in broad outline or in fine detail, is hard-pressed to avoid making generic assumptions, even if these assumptions remain implicit. At the same time, genre classifications are closely linked to a work's canonicity or lack thereof.

In the simplest case, genre may be defined from a productive or normative point of view, as a set of existing conventions or rules to which a writer adheres or that he or she flouts. Though the reasons may differ, this definition is valid for both traditional genres and contemporary popular genres: a classical *waka* poem, for example, must have 31 syllables arranged in phrases of 5, 7, 5, 7, and 7; it must use a limited range of classical diction, it is composed on a limited range of appropriate topics, and so on. A mass-market romance novel is typically a prose narrative that proceeds from a meeting of two members of the opposite sex through a set of complications to a happy ending, usually in the form of wedding. The conventions may change over time as tastes change—a waka from the *Shinkokinshū* (New collection of old and new poetry, 1205) uses self-consciously decorous diction, but one from the *Man'yōshū* (Collection of ten thousand leaves, after 759) does not necessarily do so; a short paperback romance from the 1970s is likely to be set in an exotic location, whereas one from the 1990s is not—but at any particular moment in time, the rules exist within a particular range, driven, explicitly or not, by the community of producers (including compilers, publishers, and such, as well as writers), and sometimes influenced by their sense of audiences' tastes. Deviations that fall wildly outside that range (a *waka* with 37 syllables; a romance novel that ends with a nasty divorce) effectively exclude the work from the category.[24]

Such categories also have distinct implications for readers and critics: they provide a scheme against which the work might be read and evaluated. As Fredric Jameson notes,

> Genres are essentially literary *institutions*, or social contracts between a writer and a specific public, whose function is to specify the proper use of a particular cultural artifact. . . . Still, as texts free themselves more and more from an immediate performance situation it becomes more difficult to enforce a given generic rule on their readers. No small part of the art of writing, indeed, is absorbed by this (impossible) attempt to devise a foolproof mechanism for the exclusion of undesirable responses to a given literary utterance.[25]

Jameson is writing specifically about modern genres, but his observation has important implications for genres approached at a significant temporal remove from the "immediate performance situation." A modern reader might recognize a *waka* as such immediately because of its prosody, but a historicized reading is dependent upon understanding and accepting the other conventions that originally governed their composition.

However, not all works in the universe of writing are susceptible to normative, producer-oriented classification. Other generic classifications are imposed on works long after they are written, in ways that the writer would not likely have anticipated, and these are necessarily fluid. Sei Shōnagon was not in a position to know that she was writing a "miscellany" (*zuihitsu*) when she wrote out her stories, observations, and lists in *Makura no sōshi* (The pillow book, ca. 1000), and as far as Daniel Defoe was concerned, *Moll Flanders* was a (fraudulent) "history"; only later would it be considered a novel, or not quite a novel, depending on the critic. Even though *Ise monogatari*'s poetry is naturally interpretable according to the norms of the (producer-oriented) *waka* category, the work as a whole emphatically does not fall into such a category. We have no idea what *Ise*'s authors thought they were producing, and indeed, reading it is in many ways no more or less than a process of trying to pin it down to some, or any, generic baseline for interpretation.

---

24. See Radway, *Reading the Romance*, p. 99, for evidence pertaining to the latter case.
25. Jameson, *Political Unconscious*, pp. 106–7.

Needless to say, reader- and critic-generated classifications are informed by agendas that diverge significantly from producer-generated ones—the former classifications are not "social institutions," or contracts between writers and their audiences. The critic generally classifies in order to produce a narrative of some sort, or to fit a work into an existing narrative, to establish resemblances and distinctions among the works in a given set (canon) or to trace the development of forms over time. The implications become clear when, for example, instead of accepting that some sort of miscellany-ness is immanent in *Makura no sōshi*, one wonders, would we have needed to specify that Sei Shōnagon wrote a miscellany if Yoshida Kenkō had not adopted a similar form for his *Tsurezuregusa* after her, or would we be content to say she had written a pillow book? Or would we think of it as a literary diary (*nikki*) plus alpha? Without *Tsurezuregusa*, forming a bridge between recluse writing and fragmentary prose writing, would it have occurred to anyone to put the far more coherent, essayistic *Hōjōki* (An account of a 10-foot-square hut, 1212) in the same category as *Makura no sōshi*?[26]

Thomas O. Beebee makes a valuable observation that encompasses both producer- and critic-oriented genre designations, namely, that contrary to appearances, "genre is a system of differences without positive terms."[27] His analogy is to Saussurean principles of linguistics, whereby sounds and words can be understood only in opposition to similar sounds or words.

> Rock and not country, folk and not rock: to say a work's genre is to say what it is not. Rather than seeing fiction as something in and of itself, we judge it by its nonrelatedness to the world, by the nonillocutionary force of its speech acts. The novel is a kind of biography which does not allow us to sue. Oddly, though, when we go to name fiction's opposite, the only general term we have for it (in English), "nonfiction" also denotes a lack. It is this lack, rather than a presence, which "establishes" the genre, like the double lack that established the genre of the prose poem. The systemic nature of genre foils formalist studies, because formalism is limited to describing what is "there" in the texts, whereas any generic

---

26. See Chance, *Formless in Form*, pp. 25–35 and 176–79, for a useful discussion of these issues.
27. Beebee, *Ideology of Genre*, p. 256.

reading of a text is based equally on what is not there, on what the text does not say, and ultimately on what cannot be done with it.[28]

This observation proves to be of great consequence in the case of *Ise mo-nogatari*, poised as it is in the borderlands of better established genres. Premodern scholars almost always performed the operation of fixing it on one side or the other of the divide between fact and fiction by referring to other works: many note that it is not factually trustworthy like the *Kokinshū* (which itself is viewed not merely as a collection of poetry but also, to the extent that it gives the names of poets and occasions on which poems were composed, as a historical record, as well as a repository of what we might call "poetic truth"), whereas others note the way it resembles, yet does not resemble, the more unambiguously fictional *Genji monogatari*. Even the *uta monogatari* (poem-tale) category devised to give *Ise monogatari* a home of its own in the Meiji period does not positively single out *monogatari* that include poems—all classical *monogatari* include poems—so much as it identifies *Ise* and the other works in the category as *monogatari* that lack narrative continuity, and instead proceed as a collection of at best loosely connected vignettes or episodes.[29]

The term *monogatari* poses considerable problems of its own. Typically translated as "tale," in itself the word means simply "talking about things"; it identifies a work as a vernacular (*kana*) narrative, but nothing further. Later scholars and critics established a variety of subdivisions. The *Nihon koten bungaku daijiten* (Dictionary of classical Japanese literature), for example, identifies seven subtypes: *denki monogatari* (tale of marvels), *uta monogatari* (poem-tale), *tsukuri monogatari* (fictional tale), *rekishi monogatari* (historical tale), *gunki monogatari* (military tale), *setsuwa monogatari* (exemplum), and *giko monogatari* (tale written in imitation of older tales). This classification scheme is far from systematic or

---

28. Ibid., p. 263.

29. Submerged within the definition and complicating it is the notion that, unlike *Genji* and other purely fictional *monogatari*, *uta monogatari* contain truth or fact, ostensibly because many of the poems in *Ise monogatari*, *Yamato monogatari*, and *Heichū monogatari* can be found in other sources and/or associated with real people. At the same time, because their content cannot be pegged to chronologically arranged dates and events in a life story (or because they were not, as far as we know, written by individual women or men posing as women), they are not *nikki*.

logically consistent, with subtypes based variously on content (*denki monogatari, gunki monogatari*), form (*uta monogatari, setsuwa*), relation to earlier types (*giko monogatari*), and fictionality/factuality (*tsukuri monogatari, rekishi monogatari*), sometimes with significant overlap between categories (*rekishi monogatari, gunki monogatari*, and even *uta monogatari* may contain *setsuwa*, for example). There are ambiguities deriving from the fact that terms such as *setsuwa monogatari* or *uta monogatari* may refer either to single, brief anecdotes or to compilations of such anecdotes. In this scheme, *otogizōshi* and *kanazōshi* are not considered to be *monogatari* at all, even though the titles of individual works in these categories often contain the word, and *otogizōshi* as a group are sometimes referred to as "Muromachi *monogatari*." Arguably, the *tsukuri monogatari* (and particularly *Genji monogatari*) serves as the prototype in this system, from which the other genres are merely deviations—in the *Nihon koten bungaku daijiten*, *tsukuri monogatari* is defined under *monogatari* and does not have an entry of its own.

For modern scholars, the *uta monogatari*, *Ise monogatari*'s designated genre, is closely connected to the term *utagatari*, a term that (unlike *uta monogatari*) is attested in premodern sources, and refers to conversation about poems, particularly about the circumstances in which their authors composed them.[30] Of the three surviving works typically categorized as *uta monogatari* (*Ise monogatari, Yamato monogatari* [Tales of Yamato, ca. 951], and *Heichū monogatari* [Tales of Heichū, ca. 965][31]), *Yamato monogatari* seems most fittingly and comprehensively explained in terms of *utagatari* origins. The text consists of some 170 brief narratives that give the "back story" of individual poems or exchanges of poems. Most of these poems were written by historical figures who served at court in the first half of the tenth century and are placed in realistic-seeming contexts of court life at the time, whereas others are given more elaborate legendary contexts. However, though *Ise monogatari* shares *Yamato monogatari*'s approach to placing poetry in narrative context, the work as a whole is unmistakably the product of a sophisticated agenda that goes beyond explaining the origins of

---

30. Insofar as *utagatari* are viewed as oral in origin, there are further affinities here to *setsuwa*.

31. *Heichū monogatari* is also referred to as *Heichū nikki* or *Sadafumi nikki*. And the dictionary *Kōjien* muddies the waters further by defining it as a compilation of "love *setsuwa*" about Taira no Sadafumi.

poems. For all its elusiveness, *Ise monogatari* quite clearly gestures in the
direction of giving the life story of its anonymous, fictionalized protagonist
via his poetry. Given that poems known to have been written by other poets in irrelevant contexts are attributed to *Ise*'s protagonist in order to develop his character, *Ise monogatari,* unlike *Yamato monogatari,* cannot be
explained adequately in terms of *utagatari.* Placing *Ise, Yamato,* and *Heichū*
together in a group serves to highlight the importance of context to appreciating Heian-period poetry and the importance of contextualized poetry
within subsequent *monogatari.* But doing so at the same time downplays
and obscures important commonalities that *Ise monogatari* has with other
genres, such as poetry collections and poetic diaries.

In any event, I borrow and emphasize Beebee's notion of genre as a
system of differences in order to suggest that designations such as *uta
monogatari,* laden as they are with distinctly modern baggage, must be
discarded before a consideration of premodern scholarship on *Ise* can proceed. Like any text that cannot be categorized from a normative point of
view, *Ise monogatari* contains elements drawn from the range of genres
that existed at the time of its composition, and possible defining elements (or defining deficiencies) are identifiable only when the work in
question is reflected back in a mirror constructed of other works. The
selection of defining elements versus nondefining elements in this or any
specific case is entirely dependent upon the critic or commentator who
fashions and peers into that mirror, as well as the time and place of the
peering. As John Frow argues,

> The order formed between and among genres should be regarded as a
> historically changing system rather than as a logical order. Such an ap-
> proach makes it possible to bring together the categories of a poetics with
> those of the historical event: if genres are actual and contingent forms
> rather than necessary and essential forms, they are nevertheless not arbi-
> trary. And this in turn means that the "internal" organization of
> genre . . . can be understood in terms of particular historical codifica-
> tions of discursive properties.[32]

The genre system described above, which (more or less) holds sway now,
bears little resemblance to the one within which premodern commentators
worked. Although these commentators initially took *Ise* up as an object of

---

32. Frow, *Genre,* p. 71.

study because of its poetry, in their attempts to categorize it or position it vis-à-vis other works they were far less concerned with its disjointedness or the prominence of poetry within it than with their sense of it as a work of fact, a work of fiction, or a hybrid of the two. Thus, the shifting status of fiction in the canons of Japanese literature over the last 1,000 years is one of the keys to understanding *Ise monogatari*'s reception, and a final issue to be explored in this study.

The remainder of this book is divided into five parts. Chapter 2 gives background information on Ariwara no Narihira and *Ise monogatari* and its initial formation, then considers early medieval *Ise* scholarship in contrast to scholarship on poetry in an attempt to put the idiosyncrasies of the Old Commentaries on *Ise* in perspective and to provide more context for the emergence of the Transitional Commentaries.

Chapter 3 examines commentaries produced during the chaotic times between the beginning of the Ōnin War in 1467 and the early years of the Tokugawa shogunate (in other words, the early Transitional Commentaries). This period saw the beginnings of the commodification of learning, as courtiers, reduced to poverty during the violent upheavals that swept the capital, turned to scholarship to support themselves, selling off prized family texts, commentaries, and expertise to elite warriors and eventually wealthy townsmen who were eager to elevate themselves (and in the case of warriors, to legitimize their claims to authority) through participation in the courtly literary tradition. Itinerant *renga* masters formed another group of key players, both instructing and receiving instruction from courtiers, giving lectures and producing commentaries of their own at the request of warriors, and serving as couriers, facilitating exchanges of texts and money between the other groups. Commentators of this period rejected in strong terms the earlier esoteric commentaries that had sought out historical facts and personages behind every incident in the *Ise monogatari* and began to view the text as at least partly fictitious. However, a closer examination reveals that opportunistic use of old, pseudo-historical interpretation persists in these commentaries, a phenomenon that is in some cases related to value-enhancing stratification policies whereby certain interpretations were reserved for disciples of highest standing in the school, and alternate views disseminated more widely.

Chapter 4 focuses on the rise of printing and commercial publishing in the early modern period and its impact on the production and circulation of *Ise monogatari* and its commentaries. Although the earliest printed commentaries were simply reproductions of late medieval scholars' Transitional Commentaries, by the second half of the seventeenth century a new range of people without court connections—*haikai* poets, Confucian scholars, and even writers of popular fiction—began producing commentaries intended to introduce the classics to a broad audience, mostly repackaging the still-authoritative interpretations of late medieval courtly scholars in new, user-friendly formats. The pursuit of new audiences led to a radical transformation in the semiology of the printed page: commentary that had originally been presented as an undifferentiated mass of exegesis flowing seamlessly out of a base text too minutely divided to be read on its own, began to fragment into headnotes, interlinear notes, and vernacular glosses, and, in some cases, to be accompanied by illustrations, summaries of important points, and other features, framing rather than carving up the base text and reconfiguring it as an object of reading as well as of study.

Chapter 5 discusses further transformations in the conduct of literary scholarship that accompanied the rise of *kokugaku*, or nativism, in the eighteenth century and with it the development of the New Commentaries. Nativist scholars, who were mostly commoners or Shinto shrine affiliates, are thought of as having promoted the study of the native tradition as a repository of national identity, a project that required them to challenge not only the Confucian scholars who dominated the intellectual world at the time, but also the court-centered aristocrats who had controlled the classical poetic tradition since the medieval period. In the New Commentaries, they pursued this aim through pointed criticism of medieval scholars' secretiveness, conservatism, and lack of philological rigor, and in the process developed new approaches to fictional narrative.

I close with an epilogue discussing the creation of the genre designation *uta monogatari*, or "poem-tale," to classify *Ise monogatari* in the Meiji period. This category grew out of negotiation with Western notions of genre, which dictated a separation among drama, poetry, and narrative, and out of attempts to create genealogies of narrative kinds that led smoothly to the modern novel (*shōsetsu*). The mid-tenth century came to be characterized as the age of the *uta monogatari*, an intermediate stage between an age of poetry and the age of *tsukuri monogatari* (fictional tale), the pinnacle of which was *Genji monogatari*. From the 1910s, the *uta monogatari* came to be viewed as a genre that emphasized love and lyricism (important concerns in the literature of the time), leading to new conceptualizations of *Ise monogatari*'s significance in the classical literary canon.

I also include, in Appendix 1, a diagram showing the relations between characters who appear in *Ise monogatari*, and in Appendix 2, translations of sections of *Ise monogatari* that come up for discussion in the body of the book. The latter are provided purely as a convenience to readers who may not be familiar with *Ise monogatari* and are not intended to represent a definitive reading of it. Throughout this book, I have tried to render passages from *Ise monogatari* in ways that reflect the concerns of the commentators under discussion, but, unavoidably, I have my own understanding of what this extremely spare and often ambiguous text means, an understanding that sometimes differs from that of other available English translations.[33] These translations may therefore serve secondarily to make some of my biases visible. Nevertheless, Appendix 2 should be understood and used with acknowledgment of the purely provisional spirit in which it is included.

---

33. Four full translations have been undertaken to date: Vos, *A Study of the Ise-montagari* (1957); H.C. McCullough, *Tales of Ise* (1968); Harris, *Tales of Ise* (1972); and Mostow and Tyler, *The Ise Stories* (2010). The very useful commentary sections in the last of these include frequent references to premodern scholarship on *Ise*.

CHAPTER 2

Ise monogatari *in Heian and Early Medieval Literary Thought*

Histories of scholarship on *Ise monogatari* typically begin with an account of the *kochūshaku*, or Old Commentaries, which employ metaphorical readings to unearth historical facts behind *Ise*'s stories, often inventing spurious sources to support their rather eccentric contentions. Despite their idiosyncrasies, these commentaries are indisputably important, both for what they reveal about esotericism and early medieval literary thought and because their interpretations of *Ise* achieved wide currency in Noh and Muromachi fiction. However, the Old Commentaries, the first of which appeared in 1265, some three centuries after *Ise monogatari* came into being, do not give a full or representative picture of early readers' and scholars' approaches to the text. References to *Ise* appear with some frequency in late Heian and early Kamakura treatises on poetry and poetry contest judgments and suggest views both of *Ise monogatari* and of the enterprise of literary scholarship that diverge significantly from those that predominated in the Old Commentaries. In addition to giving background information on *Ise monogatari*'s initial formation and the challenges it posed for commentators, this chapter will examine references to *Ise monogatari* that appear in the work of such court poet-scholars as Fujiwara no Kiyosuke (1104–77), Kenshō (ca. 1130–ca. 1210), Fujiwara no Shunzei (1114–1204), and Fujiwara no Teika (1162–1241), with a view to placing the Old Commentaries in perspective and explaining the emergence of the late medieval Transitional Commentaries more fully.

Ariwara no Narihira and the Formation of *Ise monogatari*

As discussed above, the first problem that confronted most premodern scholars who sought to engage with *Ise monogatari* was the question of how the text is related to Ariwara no Narihira, whether as its protagonist, as its author, or both. The text of *Ise* most commonly used today consists of 125 loosely connected sections, called *dan*, that center on the activities and poetry of an anonymous middle-ranking courtier from his coming-of-age until his death, depicting his secret affair with the Nijō empress (Fujiwara no Kōshi, or Takaiko, 842–910), his exile to the eastern provinces (the so-called Azumakudari), his affairs with various unnamed women, his involvement with the high priestess of the Ise Shrine (Princess Tenshi, d. 913), also known as the Ise virgin, his friendship with Prince Koretaka (844–97), and his frustrations in public life along the way. There is good reason to associate *Ise monogatari* with Narihira: it contains all thirty of the poems attributed to him in the *Kokinshū*, often with prose contexts that closely resemble the *Kokinshū* headnotes. It also points to him frequently, even where his own compositions are absent, by means of allusions to court positions he is known to have held, occasional use of humble or self-deprecatory language to suggest that he wrote it himself, and references to historical figures he was known to have associated with, such as his brother Yukihira (818–93) and his father-in-law, Ki no Aritsune (815–77). Some of the references to historical personages occur within the stories that give context to the poetry (for instance, "In the past, there was a man named Ki no Aritsune"); others are given in appended comments that follow stories ("This was when the Nijō empress was still a commoner.") These appended comments typically identify characters that go unnamed within the stories themselves and are thought to be notes made by early readers that subsequently came to be incorporated into the text—in a sense, then, these interpolated notes constitute the very earliest commentary on *Ise monogatari*. But despite these pointed gestures in Narihira's direction, the protagonist of *Ise monogatari* himself is, with two exceptions,[1] referred to only as "a man," rather than named outright as Narihira, and the vast majority of the 125 episodes cannot, in

---

1. In Section 63 he is referred to as Zaigo Chūjō, "the fifth-son Ariwara Middle Captain," whereas in Section 65 he is referred to as "a man of the Ariwara clan."

fact, be linked to Narihira reasonably by an examination of the poetry or of known historical facts.

The most neutral external source of information about Narihira that is approximately contemporary with him, relatively free from the influence of *Ise monogatari* itself, is an entry in the *Nihon sandai jitsuroku* (True records of three Japanese reigns, 901), an official history written in classical Chinese covering the reigns of emperors Seiwa (r. 858–76), Yōzei (r. 876–84), and Kōkō (r. 884–87), which records the poet's death in 880.

> 28th [of the fifth month]. Lord Ariwara no Narihira of the Junior Fourth Rank, Upper Grade, Provisional Middle Captain of the Right Bodyguards[2] and Provisional Governor of Mino, passed away. Narihira was the fifth son of the late fourth-ranked Prince Abo, and the younger brother of the Senior Third Rank Middle Counselor Yukihira. Prince Abo married Princess Ito, the daughter of Emperor Kanmu, and she gave birth to Narihira. In the third year of Tenchō [826], the prince made a petition to the throne, saying, "The sons and daughters of unranked Prince Takaoka have previously abandoned the royal title, and have received the title Asomi [indicating commoner status]. My children have not yet been granted the changed title. Since they are all the children of brothers, why should there be this difference in their arrangement?" Therefore, the emperor decreed that Nakahira, Yukihira, Morihira, and the others should receive the title [and surname] Ariwara no Asomi. Narihira was handsome and elegant in appearance, self-indulgent and unreserved, generally lacking in aptitude for learning,[3] and composed Japanese poetry well. In the third month of the fourth year of Jōgan [861] he was granted the Junior Fifth Rank Upper Grade; in the second month of the fifth year [863] was appointed Assistant of the Right Military Guards. In several years he became Provisional Lesser Captain of the Left Bodyguards. He became Director of the Right Imperial Stables, and reached the Junior Fourth Rank Lower Grade. In the first year of Gangyō [877] he became Provisional Middle Captain of the Right Bodyguards. In

---

2. For translations of ranks and titles, I follow the appendices in McCullough and McCullough, *Tale of Flowering Fortunes.*

3. Note that this line (*ōmune saigaku nashi*) became a matter of some dispute in the Edo period—scholars such as Kamo no Mabuchi doubted that a courtier could succeed without Chinese learning and suggested that *nashi* had somehow displaced *ari*—but modern scholars see no particular reason to doubt that Narihira was a lackluster scholar.

the next year along with this office he became Provisional Governor of Sagami and later became Provisional Governor of Mino. When he died he was fifty-six years old.[4]

Although the details regarding Narihira's parentage and his progress through the court bureaucracy are fairly standard, the mix of personal information given in the obituary is somewhat unusual—as Helen Mc-Cullough observes, official histories do not often comment on individuals' physical appearance.[5] The seventeenth-century scholar Keichū notes further that Narihira is the only figure in the national histories whose talents as a *waka* poet are mentioned.[6] Although two of the court titles, Director of the Imperial Stables and Middle Captain, are used in *Ise monogatari* to identify its protagonist, and the image of Narihira we glean from those four little phrases "handsome and elegant in appearance, self-indulgent and unreserved, generally lacking in aptitude for learning, and composed Japanese poetry well" does conform closely to that of the amorous, peripatetic poet-hero of *Ise*, this is all we have to go on. No reliable historical records confirm, for example, the exile to the eastern provinces or the affair with the Nijō empress.[7]

Even independent of confirmation in historical sources, the text of *Ise* presents other problems that work against attempts to read it as a factual biography, let alone as autobiography. Some are chronological: Section 114, for example, describes an imperial progress to Serikawa that took place in 887, seven years after Narihira's death, while Section 11, part of the "Azumakudari" sequence (Sections 7 to 15), places in the mouth of the protagonist a poem attributed in the *Shūishū* (Collection of gleanings, ca. 1005) to Tachibana no Tadamoto, who flourished in the mid-tenth

---

4. Kurosaka and Kokushi Taikei Henshû kai, *Nihon sandai jitsuroku*, pp. 475–76. A *yomikudashi* of the entry can be found in Katagiri, *Tensai sakka*, pp. 18–19.

5. McCullough, *Tales of Ise*, p. 43.

6. Hisamatsu, et al., *Keichû zenshû*, 9:5.

7. See Katagiri, *Tensai sakka*, pp. 69–100, for details. Although poetry from various sections involving the Nijō empress does appear in the *Kokinshû*, and headnotes to other poems indicate that she might have been the center of a literary salon in which Narihira took part, she is not named in the *Kokinshû* in connection with the relevant, more suggestive episodes, and there is certainly no evidence to suggest he abducted her. The bulk of the "Azumakudari" is also somewhat suspicious. Katagiri suggests that Narihira may have composed even the poems that are securely attributed to him as fiction.

century; and there are many other examples of poems that postdate Narihira, that are attributed to other poets, or that predate him substantially,
including a number that can be found in the *Man'yōshū*. The text also
contains several instances of conflicting variations on similar themes, such
as an abduction story in Section 6 that seems to take place simultaneously
in Settsu province and in the capital, versus one in Section 12 that takes
place in Musashi province; or the self-imposed exile to the eastern provinces in the "Azumakudari" sequence versus one to provinces sufficiently
nearby that the man is able to sneak back into the capital nightly (there is
no province that served as a place of exile in the Heian period from which
this would have been possible) instigated by the emperor (Section 65). Finally, there are sections that seem to have nothing to do with the *Ise* protagonist (or with Narihira) as he is portrayed in the bulk of the *monogatari*, such as Section 23, which tells of a courtship and marriage between a
man and woman described as "children of people who made their living
in the provinces" as opposed to people of the capital.

To some degree the contradictions and inconsistencies can be explained
by the way the text was written. Modern scholars generally agree that *Ise
monogatari* assumed a shape resembling its current one over a period of
fifty to one hundred years, from sometime prior to the compilation of
the *Kokinshū* in 905 to sometime between 950 and 1000, and that multiple
authors were involved in producing it. The details of this process are unre-
coverable, but certain conclusions can be drawn based on internal evidence
and comparisons with other texts in which the same poems appear. The
prevailing theories hold that Narihira had a personal poetry collection, no
longer extant, that was used as a source for both the earliest version of *Ise
monogatari* and some of Narihira's poetry in the *Kokinshū*, and that additional sections were added to this core group of stories much later.

Katagiri Yōichi posits three stages in the formation of the text, supporting his theory both with an examination of *Ise* poetry that appears
in later anthologies (including variants of a *Narihira shū*, or personal
poetry collection, compiled in the mid-tenth century) and with an analysis of deictics, emphatic particles, and interpolated comments, which
indicate the presence of a narrator and the variable distance of that narrator from the substance of the story. In his view, the amount of material
drawn from Narihira's original poetry collection would have been quite
small, limited to eleven or twelve sections with parallels in the *Kokinshū*
that depict, for example, the man's relationships with his mother, with

Prince Koretaka, and with the Ise high priestess, as well as part of the "Azumakudari" and some of the sections associated with the Nijō empress, and sections that seem to be set before Narihira's time.[8] The second stratum would have taken shape between the compilation of the *Kokinshū* in 905 until shortly after the compilation of the *Gosenshū* (Later collection) in 951. This group of sections are set in Narihira's time and include most sections that show the man, often identified with Narihira's court titles, interacting with historical personages (Ki no Aritsune, Minamoto no Tōru, et al.) or that suggest him in decline in old age. These sections constitute a relatively faithful amplification of the image of the protagonist put forth in the first stratum, an elegant, romance-seeking, but sincere man who encountered frustrations, first in his pursuit of women beyond his station and then in various aspects of his public life. The third stratum, then, is composed largely of variations on themes introduced in the first two strata, but with a notable shift in the nature of the protagonist: in general the man of this stratum is increasingly distant from the historical Narihira, becoming more of a Narihira "type," much closer to the amorous, playboy-Narihira image that predominated in subsequent centuries, and sometimes approaching caricature by comparison with the sincere but perpetually frustrated man of the earlier strata (for example, in his philandering with women who are in some way inferior, such as the old woman of Section 63 or the impossibly rustic woman of Section 14).

This is not to say that the early strata are "true" and the last one "false," however. Katagiri suggests that even parts of Narihira's personal poetry collection were composed by him as fiction, notably those dealing with his secret affairs with the Nijō empress and the Ise high priestess, two of the episodes most central to the Narihira legend.[9] In view of this, it becomes very difficult to say that anything at all in *Ise monogatari* can be viewed as unequivocally biographical.

---

8. For example, Section 2, which is set shortly after the move of the capital to Kyoto in 794. Katagiri argues that Section 69, the Ise priestess story, is also "historical fiction" because no imperial huntsmen were being sent to Ise in Narihira's time. This summary of Katagiri's account of *Ise monogatari*'s formation is taken from Katagiri, *Ise monogatari, Yamato monogatari*, pp. 11–23.

9. Katagiri, *Ise monogatari no shinkenkyū*, pp. 103–13. In addition to pointing out discrepancies between *Ise*'s stories and known historical facts, Katagiri identifies parallels between these episodes and Tang-dynasty *chuanqi*, such as *Yingying zhuan*, suggesting that Narihira might have been inspired by and reworking them.

Whether or not one agrees with the specifics of Katagiri's hypothesis, it serves to highlight some sources of the unusual problems *Ise monogatari* presents to would-be interpreters. The existence of multiple, anonymous authors whose intentions and view of the hero diverged in significant ways results in a text that is ultimately multivoiced but lacks the kind of pointed cues that would make that fact and its implications immediately evident to the reader. Absent this piece of the puzzle, premodern commentators were often hard-pressed to reconcile *Ise*'s internal inconsistencies with its superficial appearance of giving a single life story. Their response, most often, was to manipulate the fuzzy boundary between fact and fiction (or the very definition of fiction) in ways that served to lend some sort of overarching coherence to the text and its protagonist and to support in the most advantageous ways they could contrive whatever agendas led them to be studying the text in the first place.

Early Views of *Ise monogatari*'s Genre

As suggested in Chapter 1, generic classification is closely related to canon formation insofar as canons identify some genres as important and others as unimportant. In the Heian period, *monogatari* were clearly unimportant as a rule, as attested by authors' disinclination to have their names attached to them and how few of them survive. The *Sanbōe* (The three treasures, illustrated; 984) by Minamoto Tamenori gives the following disparaging characterization of them:

> They flourish in numbers greater than the grasses of Ōaraki Forest, more countless than the sands on the Arisomi beaches. They attribute speech to trees and plants, mountains and rivers, birds and beasts, fish and insects that cannot speak; they invest unfeeling objects with human feelings and ramble on and on with meaningless phrases like so much flotsam in the sea, with no two words together that have any more solid basis than does swamp grass growing by a river bank. *The Sorceress of Iga*, *The Tosa Lord*, *The Fashionable Captain*, *The Nagai Chamberlain*, and all the rest depict relations between men and women just as if they were so many flowers or butterflies, but do not let your heart get caught up even briefly in these tangled roots of evil, these forests of words.[10]

---

10. Kamens, *Three Jewels*, p. 93.

The main objection here is to the unrealistic elements of *monogatari*. The author of the *Kagerō nikki* (Gossamer diary, after 975), known only as Michitsuna's mother, records similar objections in the opening passage of her work, dismissing old *monogatari* as "copious fabrications" and offering her life story as a corrective, a more realistic portrayal of an aristocratic Heian woman's life.[11] Sometime later we also find *monogatari* explicitly designated as the least-esteemed form in a hierarchy of genres set out in the *Genji ippon kyō* (Genji one-volume sutra, 1166), after Buddhist scripture, works in the Confucian canon, Chinese histories, the works of Chinese literati, and Japanese poetry. The perspective here is pointedly Buddhist, highlighting again the falseness, frivolity, and seductively corrupting potential of *monogatari*. Like a number of other texts of the same period, however, the *Ippon kyō* goes on to suggest that although the writing of *Genji monogatari* was a grave enough sin to have led its author to be reborn in hell, and that reading it was no better, one might atone for one's preoccupation with immoral fabrications by copying out the Lotus Sutra and writing the names of *Genji*'s chapters on it: thus even a lowly *monogatari* might become an aid to enlightenment, and there is perhaps an opening to read some ambivalence into the *Ippon kyō*'s condemnation of them.[12]

However, *Ise monogatari* does not appear to have been subject to the same kinds of concerns that dogged *Genji* and other Heian *monogatari* in the early medieval period, perhaps because, despite its title, *Ise monogatari*'s status as a member of the *monogatari* category seems to have been ambiguous in the first centuries after its appearance. Indeed, *Ise*'s title itself may well have been in flux in the earliest stages. The title *Ise monogatari* is first attested in the "E-awase" (A picture contest) chapter of *Genji monogatari*, but it is also referred to as *Zaigo ga monogatari* (The tale of the fifth Ariwara son) in the "Agemaki" (Trefoil knots) chapter, simply as *Zaigo* in a list of *monogatari* given in *Sarashina nikki* (Sarashina diary, after 1058), and, perhaps most tellingly, as *Zaigo ga nikki* (The

---

11. Hasegawa, et al., *Tosa nikki*, p. 39.

12. Abe, et al., *Genji monogatari jō*, p. 37. Translation of a key passage of the *Genji ippon kyō* and further helpful information about medieval Buddhist views of *Genji monogatari* and its potential both to obstruct and to lead to salvation can be found in Shirane, "*The Tale of Genji*," pp. 17–19.

diary of the fifth Ariwara son) in *Sagoromo monogatari* (Tale of Sago-romo, 1070s).[13]

The reference in "E-awase," which depicts a contest wherein court ladies divide into two sides and argue the merits of paired *monogatari* illustra-tions, does appear to place *Ise* firmly amid the ranks of other well-known fictional *monogatari*. After a round that matches *Taketori mo-nogatari* (The tale of the bamboo cutter, ca. 895) against *Utsuho monogatari* (The tale of the hollow tree, late tenth century), *Ise* is matched against *Jōsanmi monogatari* (The tale of Jōsanmi, no longer extant). The *Jōsanmi* illustration, described as "a bright, lively painting of contemporary life with much, including details of the palace itself, to recommend it," appears to have the edge and provokes a somewhat desperate-seeming appeal in the form of a poem from the *Ise* side ("Shall we forget how deep is the sea of Ise/Because the waves have washed away old tracks?"), along with the statement, "Are the grand accomplishments of Lord Narihira to be dwarfed by a little love story done with a certain clever-ness and plausibility?"[14] What the *Ise* side evidently cannot argue on ar-tistic grounds (the *Ise* painting is never actually described), they attempt to offset by arguing for the superiority of the work on which the painting is based, relying on its status as something venerably old and its associa-tion with the highly esteemed poet-protagonist Narihira. In the end, despite the fact that *Ise* appears here as just another *monogatari*, keeping company comfortably with the thoroughly fantastic *Taketori monoga-tari*, it seems that a consideration of its rootedness in reality, in Narihi-ra's historical existence and continuing reputation, was also an unavoid-able component of its reception.

---

13. It is possible that the *Sarashina nikki* reference is not to *Ise monogatari* at all; be-cause no context is given, it is difficult to judge. In *Sagoromo monogatari*, however, the reference is to the same section of *Ise* that is at issue in the "Agemaki" chapter of *Genji*, corresponding to Section 49 of the texts used today.

14. Seidensticker, *The Tale of Genji*, p. 312. Fujitsubo, serving as the judge in the contest, seems to find such arguments at least a little compelling, saying, "However one may admire the proud spirit of Lady Hyōe [presumably the protagonist of *Jōsanmi*], one certainly would not wish to malign Lord Narihira," and adding a poem of her own: "At first the strands of sea grass may seem old/But the fisherfolk of Ise are with us yet." The concern with the relative merits of old and new throughout this episode is noteworthy.

Another fictional gathering of court ladies engaging in informal *monogatari* criticism, penned about 200 years later, offers an intriguing contrast to the view of *Ise monogatari* suggested by *Genji monogatari*'s picture contest. *Mumyōzōshi* (Unnamed book, ca. 1201), attributed to the daughter of Fujiwara no Shunzei (who was actually his granddaughter), depicts a group of women conversing at considerable length about *monogatari*, focusing particularly on characters, incidents, and poems that they find moving or otherwise impressive or striking. Discussion of *Genji monogatari* consumes about a third of the work, with *Sagoromo monogatari* and other *monogatari* that followed *Genji* occupying another third, and discussions of poetry collections and notable women writers comprising the last third. Wedged between the sections on *monogatari* and on poetry collections, there is a brief but telling discussion of *Ise monogatari*:

> The usual young voice said, "When I think about it, all of these works are lies and fabrications. Please talk about those that relate things that really existed. When I hear that *Ise monogatari* and *Yamato monogatari* relate actual events, I am endlessly impressed. Please talk a little about those."
>
> "*Ise monogatari* is just material intended to show the amorous heart of Narihira. Among all the people living in this world, high-ranking and low, everyone who has even a little understanding, is there anyone who is not familiar with *Ise monogatari* and *Yamato monogatari*? So there is no need to discuss these in detail. Wandering far from the capital, Narihira asked something of the capital bird on the bank of the Sumida River, and longed for his beloved wife at a place called Yatsuhashi, and so on[15]—it all appears to be just a record of his philandering acts. *Yamato monogatari* tells the same kinds of stories, so we needn't discuss it. It's something everyone can understand by reading it. As for the good and bad of the poetry in these works, just look at the *Kokinshū* and such. The poems that are thought to be good should be included there."[16]

---

15. These are references to Section 9 of *Ise monogatari*, which depicts the protagonist's journey to the eastern provinces. The Sumida River is in modern-day Tokyo, while Yatsuhashi is near modern Nagoya. The implication in the phrase that follows (*tada ka no itaranu kumanaki shiwaza*, with *ka no* ostensibly referring back to Narihira's "amorous heart") is that there is nowhere Narihira would not go in pursuit of women.

16. Kuwabara, *Mumyōzōshi*, pp. 99–100.

This time *Ise monogatari* is explicitly and definitively excluded from consideration alongside *Genji, Sagoromo*, and the rest. The fact that *Ise* is paired with *Yamato monogatari* here, and the position of this passage between the sections on *monogatari* and on poetry collections, might incline a modern reader to conclude that these works have been bracketed because they are *uta monogatari* rather than *tsukuri monogatari* or *giko monogatari*, and indeed, both the editor of the Japanese edition of *Mumyōzōshi* and the translator of the English version label this passage with the inserted subheading "*Uta monogatari*" or "Poem-Tales."[17] But for the author of *Mumyōzōshi* a category midway between prose narrative and poetry did not exist, and her focus is instead on *Ise*'s perceived status as a record of "things that really happened."[18]

The foregoing references to *Ise monogatari* suggest that early readers did not have a uniform sense of how or where *Ise* fit into the universe of vernacular narrative; the dominant impression is rather that it fits imperfectly, and this state of affairs continued on for many centuries. However, *Ise*'s most conspicuous claim to importance in the early medieval period, and the one that would exert the greatest influence on its reception subsequently, did not in fact have to do with its status as narrative. Instead, it came to occupy a prominent place in the canon for poetic studies, which in turn led it to become the target of scholarship for the first time.

Ise monogatari in the Work of Rokujō Family and Mikohidari Family Poet-Scholars

In the twelfth century, "The Way of Poetry" had come to be a kind of hereditary profession, dominated by "those families which sought . . . to establish and pass on their fortunes by serving the imperial household and the court as sanctioned purveyors of expertise on matters of poetry. In practice, this would entail duties such as officiating as judges in formal

---

17. Ibid., p. 99; and Marra, "*Mumyōzōshi*, Part 3," p. 418.

18. Although they do not explicitly discuss *Ise monogatari* as a work, the handling of material from *Ise* that one finds in *Yamato monogatari* and *Ōkagami* (The Great Mirror, ca. 1090), both of which conflate multiple sections of *Ise* into unified stories that name Narihira and other characters outright, suggests that here too *Ise* is viewed as "things that really happened." For a detailed discussion, see Bowring, "*Ise monogatari*," pp. 415–17 and 423–28.

poetry matches, presiding over 'poetry meetings' . . . , editing imperially commissioned anthologies or other collections, etc."[19] The two most prominent poetic houses in the twelfth century were the Rokujō family, founded by Fujiwara no Akisue (1055–1123)[20] and carried on by his son Akisuke (1090–1155), his grandson Kiyosuke, and Akisuke's adopted son Kenshō; and the Mikohidari family, founded by Fujiwara no Shunzei and his son Teika. Although none of these individuals left full-blown commentaries on *Ise monogatari*, suggestive mentions of *Ise* may be found in some of their work on the *Kokinshū* and in their poetics treatises, and it becomes clear that at this stage familiarity with *Ise* was considered essential for aspiring poets. In *Waka shogaku shō* (Excerpts on *waka* for beginners, before 1169), Kiyosuke notes that a poet must "choose from those old words that are pleasing and make them continue fluently." He then mines *Man'yōshū*, *Kokinshū*, *Gosenshū*, *Shūishū*, *Goshūishū* (Later collection of gleanings, 1086), *Ise monogatari*, and *Yamato monogatari* for examples of appropriate old diction.[21] Earlier, in a collection of poetic lore titled *Fukurozōshi* (Book of folded pages, ca. 1157) that he compiled for Emperor Nijō (r. 1158–1165), Kiyosuke had also included a description of *Ise monogatari* amid descriptions of poetry collections. His comments are as follows:

> *Ise monogatari.* 250 poems (but, the number varies according to the text).[22] This is the work of Lord Narihira. It does not consist exclusively of poems made by him. Perhaps interesting poems from among those in the *Kokinshū* were written down. Furthermore, without regard for whether they were his own or others' poems, they are written in succession as though they are the work of the same person. Perhaps this is because there are illicit matters mixed in. Many *Man'yōshū* poems are included. Regarding the title, there are two explanations. Because there are illicit matters, in order to label these as false, it was called *Ise monogatari*. There is a saying that "people from Ise tell tales." The other view is that it

19. Cook, "Discipline of Poetry," p. 63.
20. See Klein, *Allegories of Desire*, pp. 79–89, for details on Akisue's activities, particularly those surrounding the invention of the Hitomaro *eigu*, a ceremony held to venerate the *Man'yōshū* poet Kakinomoto no Hitomaro and that served as a sort of prototype for subsequent poetic initiation ceremonies.
21. Sasaki Nobutsuna, *Nihon kagaku taikei*, 2:172–86.
22. The texts in use today have 209 poems.

is called *Ise* in order to make the matter of the Ise priestess the ultimate point. Perhaps this is the correct explanation. The Izumi Shikibu text begins with the matter of the Ise priestess.[23]

Kiyosuke's remarks are brief but revealing. First, the fact that *Ise* is described in the thick of a list of poetry collections gives evidence that for Kiyosuke it is principally significant for its poetry, rather than as a *monogatari*. Given that Kiyosuke writes as the head of Rokujō house (succeeding his father, Akisuke, who had died two years earlier), it is unsurprising that his concern is with poetry. The association of *Ise* with Narihira is of course clear in Kiyosuke's remarks as well, but the identification of the two is much less complete than what appears in other late Heian and early medieval sources. Kiyosuke's remarks reveal ample awareness that *Ise* contains much that cannot, in fact, be associated with Narihira, and his language suggests the possibility that he views *Ise*'s anonymous protagonist as separable from Narihira—the poetry, irrespective of who wrote it, is described as the poetry of "the same person," possibly the (fictional, anonymous) "man of the past," rather than Narihira. As will be discussed below, this view is extremely unlike the one that would drive the Old Commentaries in the next century and beyond. Obliquely, Kiyosuke also reveals a distinctive take on questions of the relationship between fiction and morality. Rather than put the matter in the Buddhist terms that were more typical of the age (that is, suggesting that fiction is a species of lying that may lead readers into immoral behavior), his remarks suggest that acknowledging *Ise monogatari* as at least partly fictional ("people from Ise tell tales") serves in a sense to neutralize the illicit matters depicted therein—they are mere stories, rather than indicators that various historical figures were given to indecent behavior.

Fujiwara no Shunzei's remarks in *Korai futeishō* (Poetic styles of the past, 1197), a poetics treatise written at the behest of Princess Shokushi, also give subtle hints about *Ise*'s fictionality, this time as it relates to poetry. The reference to *Ise monogatari* follows Shunzei's recounting of a

---

23. Fujioka, *Fukurozōshi*, p. 66. Today the text Kiyosuke mentions is referred to as the *Koshikibu no Naishi-bon*, for Izumi Shikibu's daughter, who supposedly copied it, or simply as the *Kari-no-tsukai-bon* (the imperial huntsman text, so called because it opens with Section 69, wherein the protagonist serves as imperial huntsman and visits the Ise Shrine).

story where an aged monk unexpectedly makes an allusion to a *Man'yōshū* poem during an interaction with a high-ranking court lady of the late ninth century. An earlier commentator had said, "Since this poem is in Book 20 of the *Man'yōshū*, this story must be completely made up, but in the good texts of the *Man'yōshū* around 40 poems are missing. This poem [the one to which the old monk alludes] does not appear in that text. What does it mean? It is unclear." Shunzei, by contrast, is unconcerned with the sourcing of the poem and notes, "Whether or not the poem is in the *Man'yōshū*, it certainly appears to be an old poem. And do not people of the present recite old poems when they are in accord with present circumstances?"[24]

Shunzei goes on in the same vein to discuss Section 23 of *Ise monogatari*, where the man ceases to visit a woman in Kawachi province in favor of staying with his wife, citing the following poem, composed by the woman in Kawachi:

> *kimi ga atari*   I shall continue
> *mitsutsu o oramu*   to look in your direction.
> *Ikomayama*   Do not hide Mt. Ikoma,
> *kumo na kakushi so*   O clouds,
> *ame wa furu to mo*   even if it rains.

Shunzei remarks:

> This too is a poem in Book 12 of the *Man'yōshū*. In *Ise monogatari*, things that really happened are written about. At the same time, the condition of people from the countryside is also written about in terms of things that did not happen in order to make it more interesting. They are made to say things and compose poems, and at times when there is an old poem that matches [the situation], they are made to say that old poem. Also, even if they do not actually know an old poem, there are times when the people from the countryside compose something that matches an old poem.[25]

Beyond the possibility that a person may recite an existing old poem when circumstances call for it, whether in fiction or in real life, Shunzei

24. Hashimoto, et al., *Karonshū*, pp. 366–67.
25. Ibid., pp. 367–68. He cites the poem composed by the rustic woman in Section 14 in the same vein, as well as a section of *Yamato monogatari*.

sees a link between old poetry, identifiable as such via its diction[26] or the relative straightforward simplicity of its sentiments, and the people of the provinces who make intermittent appearances in *Ise monogatari*. In some cases, the link is so organic that a character who might not be expected to be attuned to the poetic tradition, and thus to the fact that there are allusions to be made, just happens to compose something that resembles an old poem. But in other cases Shunzei clearly sees the inclusion of extant poems as calculated fabrications on the part of the author—the creation of new contexts and new speakers for old artifacts, intended to lend interest to the stories, or perhaps to give texture to characters the protagonist encounters. Given that Shunzei operated in a milieu where composition on set topics (*daiei*) was a fundamental poetic activity that frequently involved the adoption of a different persona (as, for example, when a man composed a love poem from the perspective of a woman), it seems only reasonable that he would be fully conscious of and unperturbed by *Ise monogatari*'s fictional elements as they relate to composing poetry.

In general, Rokujō family scholarship, particularly that undertaken by Kiyosuke's adoptive brother Kenshō, who succeeded him as head of the house, was marked by wide-ranging philological inquiry aimed at clarifying the meaning of poetic language. David Lurie suggests that the rise of this kind of scholarship can be linked to the development in this period of "truly competitive *uta-awase* as a major venue for contesting poetic authority. The judgments of such competitions focus on distinguishing between acceptable and unacceptable uses of language and this must have spurred more rigorous attention to the nature of poetic usages."[27] Kenshō's lexicographical work incorporates evidence from texts ranging back to *Man'yōshū* and *Nihongi* (Chronicle of Japan, 720), and includes Chinese material as well. Mikohidari family scholars, on the other hand, seem to have been much less intent on resolving obscurities for their own sake, in favor of establishing a foundation for contemporary poetic practice—for example, defining proper or aesthetically pleasing uses of old poems as the basis for allusive variations (*honkadori*).

---

26. Again, he gives the woman's poem in Section 14 of *Ise* as an example of this.
27. Lurie, "Digesting Antiquity."

The *Roppyakuban utaawase* (Poetry contest in 600 rounds, 1193) offers an opportunity to see Kenshō and Shunzei tangling directly about *Ise monogatari*. By this time the Mikohidari family was ascendant in poetic matters, and Shunzei was the judge in this contest while Kenshō was a poet for the left. But Kenshō can be found offering a spirited defense of his own brand of scholarship both during the contest and in a rebuttal to some of Shunzei's judgments that he penned five years later, in 1198.

Winter, round 24: Sleet. A tie.

Left (Kenshō):

Utsu no yama	Sleet falls
yū koekureba	As I cross Mt. Utsu
mizore furi	in the evening—
sode hoshikanetsu	I cannot dry my sleeves
aware kono tabi	so sad is this journey.

Right (Tsuneie):

kyō mo mata	Today, again
Katano no mino ni	it is sleeting
mizore shite	in the fields of Katano,
kawaku ma mo naki	leaving my hunting robe
karigoromo kana	no time to dry.

The right had no criticism of the left's poem. The left said the right's poem was old-fashioned.

The judge said: The left's "I cannot dry my sleeves, so sad is this journey," gives a lonely feeling, but is there a precedent for this use of Mt. Utsu? In the place in *Ise monogatari* where it says "In the area near Mt. Utsu/in reality"[28] falling sleet does not appear. Even if that were not the case, there are many mountains where sleet can be expected to fall and about which one might say "so sad is this journey." There is no reason to use Mt. Utsu, and no precedent. As for the right's poem about "The fields of Katano," too, there is hail [not sleet] in the poem that says, "since there is no one who will lend me lodging where I will not get

---

28. See Kenshō's rebuttal below for a full citation of the passage in question, from Section 9 of *Ise monogatari*.

wet,"[29] and the idea of hunting there now sounds a bit strange.[30] Both the left's poem about "Mt. Utsu" and the right's about "the fields of Katano" sound as though they could be set anywhere. I must call it a tie.[31]

Kenshō's objection to the judgment is as follows:

> Because sleet is something that falls anywhere, one should not hesitate to compose about it falling at any field, mountain, sea, or river. When rain or snow falls and mist or haze settles, it is the same thing. However, as for my associating it with travel, in *Ise monogatari* it says:
>
> > "Entering Mt. Utsu in Suruga province, they were troubled to find that the road they planned to take was very dark and forbidding, with dense growth of ivy and maples. As they were thinking what unexpected and difficult experiences they were having, they met with a pilgrim. 'What are you doing on such a road as this?' he asked them, and the man recognized him as someone he had met before. He wrote a letter and asked the pilgrim to take it to the lady he had left in the capital.
>
> > | | |
> > |---|---|
> > | *Suruga naru* | Near Mt. Utsu |
> > | *utsu no yamabe ni* | in Suruga |
> > | *utsutsu ni mo* | I can meet you |
> > | *yume ni mo hito ni* | neither in reality |
> > | *awanu narikeri* | nor in my dreams." |
>
> Since one can see this situation before one's eyes, forlorn and sad, I specifically composed the poem about that mountain path. As for mountain paths on the road to the east, there are the Ausaka and Fuwa barriers, Futamura, Takashi, Mt. Utsu, Ashigara, and Hakone—these are all commonly composed about. It is when one deliberately composes a poem about an unexpected place, one that is not usually composed about, that it sounds strange and one wonders what the association is. In [*Ise*] *monogatari*, Mt. Utsu is accompanied by the word "reality" [*utsutsu*]. Since my

---

29. A poem in the *Shikashū* (1144) by Fujiwara no Nagatō.

> | | |
> |---|---|
> | *arare furu* | On the fields of Katano |
> | *katano no mino no* | where hail falls, |
> | *karigoromo* | my hunting robe |
> | *nurenu yado kasu* | is wet, since no one |
> | *hito shi nakereba* | will lend me lodging. |

This poem itself recalls Section 82 of *Ise monogatari*.
30. Because it was an imperial hunting reserve.
31. Kubota and Yamaguchi, *Roppyakuban utaawase*, p. 195.

poem associates sleet with that mountain's sad aspect, the criticism is unreasonable. Precisely because that poem exists, if one were to say, "In the area of Mt. Utsu, reality . . ." forcibly, it would become a completely unoriginal-sounding poem. Also, if one inquires into places where sleet falls, there are a few examples in the *Man'yōshū*. . . . Going by these examples, the only places where one can write of sleet are Hatano, Tōtsuōumi, Ararematsubara, and Iyahime. What of that? Except these, whatever place one composes a poem about will be subject to the same criticism, that there is no precedent for sleet. Also, what of saying that there is no sleet in the part of *Ise monogatari* where "in the area of Mt Utsu, reality . . ." appears? When someone uses the poetic place names in that *monogatari* to compose about flowers or the moon, must one necessarily seek the same traces?

Kenshō goes on then to give pairs of poems from *Ise* and *Kokinshū* on five poetic places (*utamakura*) that appear in *Ise monogatari*—Kasuga, Mt. Tatsuta, Nunobiki Falls, Mt. Fuji, and Mt. Asama, evidently attempting to demonstrate that multiple associations are possible for each place, and wraps up:

> When one considers these poems, what is one to make of [the criticism] that in the left's poem there is no association to be made between Mt. Utsu and sleet, since sleet does not appear in *Ise monogatari*?[32]

Kenshō's observations about the dearth of places associated with sleet appear quite reasonable, but he appears to have Shunzei's concern backward: the question is not where one may or may not envision sleet, but rather how one must treat Mt. Utsu if one wishes to use it in a contemporary poem. In the same contest, Shunzei praised the following poem by Fujiwara no Yoshitsune as particularly beautiful in conception:

> | *Utsu no yama* | As I follow the traces |
> | *koeshi mukashi no* | of a past crossing |
> | *ato furite* | at Mt. Utsu |
> | *tsuta no kareba ni* | an autumn wind blows |
> | *aki kaze zo fuku* | in the dry leaves of ivy.[33] |

This poem has the advantage not just of preserving the ivy that obstructs the protagonist's path in Section 9 of *Ise monogatari*, an association that would be well established for anyone familiar with *Ise*, but also of

---

32. Ibid., pp. 455–56.
33. Tanaka Maki, "Fujiwara no Shunzei," p. 52.

reflecting specifically upon the protagonist's journey—the "past cross-ing" of the second line—and suggesting decay and the passage of time via the autumn wind in the now-dead leaves. One imagines that Shun-zei would have preferred a sleet poem that eschewed place names alto-gether, given the limited possibilities afforded by classical sources for appropriate associations, as revealed in Kenshō's exploration of the *Man'yōshū*. Shunzei's overriding concern appears to have been the so-called *hon'i* (or *moto no kokoro*, sometimes translated as "poetic essence") of an image or location—something that is inextricably related to associa-tions rooted in the poetry of the *Kokinshū*, the poetry and prose of *Ise monogatari*, and other classical works.[34] Kenshō, on the other hand, seems to value a greater degree of inventiveness in associations. For him the un-pleasantness of falling sleet matches the distress felt by the protagonist in his journey across Mt. Utsu, irrespective of the other specifics of that jour-ney. The pairs of poems from *Ise monogatari* and *Kokinshū* that Kenshō cites to conclude his argument also suggest that he and Shunzei are not on the same page. They do demonstrate that various place names from *Ise* had multiple associations as of the early tenth century, but it does not ap-pear that the *Kokinshū* poems are specifically referring to the *Ise* poems in any way, given that many of them in all likelihood predate the related *Ise* poems. Whether Kenshō is arguing disingenuously or trying to make some other point with these citations is difficult to determine, but in either case they do not really serve to address Shunzei's concerns.

A second example from *Roppyakuban utaawase* gives an even more marked demonstration of Kenshō's taste for unusual associations and his tenacity in philological matters, as well as a hint of the antagonism that existed between the Rokujō family and Mikohidari family during this time of intense competition between poetic houses. The topic of the round is love in association with sea-folk.[35]

---

34. *Genji monogatari* would belong on this list too, judging from Shunzei's remarks elsewhere in *Roppyakuban utaawase* castigating poets who have not read it (Kubota and Yamaguchi, *Roppyakuban utaawase*, p. 187), but *Man'yōshū*, a favorite with Kenshō, ap-pears to have been much less important to Shunzei. Indeed, Teika can be found cau-tioning a student against emulating the *Man'yōshū* in his *Maigetsushō* (1219). See Hashi-moto et al., *Karonshū*, pp. 513–14.

35. *Ama* 海人. Often translated as "fishermen," but, as will become apparent, they do more than fish.

Left (Kenshō)

moshio yaku	It is not the tideland
ama no maku kata	where the seaweed-burning
naranedomo	sea-folk scatter [sand]
koi no someki mo	but there is not much
ito nakarikeri	of the excitement of love.

Right (Ietaka)—winner

omoi ni wa	The sea-folk of Ise
tagui narubeki	who must be like me
Ise no ama mo	in their thoughts of love
hito o uraminu	resent that person
sode zo nurekeru	and wet their sleeves.[36]

The right said: Some say *ama no maku kata* should be *mategata*. How was this decided?

Explanation: We composed this knowing [the correct phrase] to be *maku kata*. In the *Gosenshū* poem the syllables *te* and *ku* are interchanged [that is, the precedent for *mategata* in the *Gosenshū* that seems to be inspiring the right's question is mistaken], but this phrase [*maku kata*, "tideland where they scatter"] accords with the idea of "having no leisure" [*itoma nami*] while making salt. In *Man'yōshū* and *Ise monogatari* as well, there are poems about "making salt and having no time." Also, in Saigū no nyōgo's[37] poem, *maku kata ni ama no kakitsumu moshiogusa* [the seaweed scratched up by the sea-folk where they scatter . . .][38] *mate* does not fit. . . .

The right criticized again: In the *Turtle Mirror Collection* of the Muroyama Novice[39] it is included under *mate*. Also, on a salt beach, do people scatter salt on the tideland?

Again, the left explained: Salt cauldrons are on the beach, and scattering takes place on the tideland. This is the way the natives speak

---

36. *Urami* is a pivot word, meaning both "resentment" and "see the bay."

37. Saigū no nyōgo was a daughter of Emperor Daigo who became the consort of Emperor Murakami after resigning as high priestess. She is one of the thirty-six poetic immortals.

38. Actually, the poem as given in Saigū no nyōgo's personal poetry collection has *mategata* (Kubota and Yamaguchi, *Roppyakuban utaawase*, pp. 412–13, n. 7).

39. A no longer extant privately assembled poetry collection. It is not clear which poem is being referred to here, but perhaps it is the *Gosenshū* poem by Minamoto no Hideakira that will be discussed below.

of it. Also, *mate*[40] are something that they take out of the sand when they see them. They are not something that would cause you to have no leisure.

The right said: It is not limited to *mate*. The various things the sea-folk do cause them to have no leisure, and thus the line, "since [someone] has no leisure" appears in poetry.

The left had no criticism of the right's poem.

The judge said: In the left's poem, beyond using the phrase *ama no maku kata*, "there is not much of the excitement of love," in the lower hemistich does not sound elegant at all. There is no use in my adding comments to this confusion. However, a poem by Lord [Minamoto no] Hideakira in *Gosenshū* says *ama no mategata itoma nami*. In the past, when I was serving Retired Emperor Sutoku, he gave me a text that a certain person[41] had written about things he thought to be difficult points in poetry, and when the emperor said, "Someone says there are many mistakes here. What do you think?" I replied, "When it comes to writing things, even the wise men of the past make mistakes. More recent scholarship goes without saying." Among the various things discussed, he [i.e., a certain person] had given this *mategata* poem, which he seemed to think was a difficult point from *Gosenshū*, and wrote in "*maku*" with no explanation, just leaving it at that. I said, "This should be *mategata*. It appears that he is using a text that has *maku kata* erroneously and he is giving it as a difficult point." Later someone else heard that this person's disciple had been confused by *maku* and brought forth evidence [in support of it]. "Having no leisure" goes particularly well with *mategata*. "Industriously/making salt" and sea-folk having no leisure do not conflict. Both *Man'yōshū* and *Ise monogatari* speak of sea-folk having no leisure. Neither speaks of *maku kata*. Also, when salt is boiled on the beach, surely there is no salt spread on the tideland. There are also many more texts that give Saigū no nyōgo's poem with *mate*. The texts of her collection and of *Gosenshū* that say *maku* are all mistaken. The Nyōgo's poem says,

---

40. Here Kenshō seems to be taking *mate* to be *mategai*—a bivalve mollusk that buries itself in the sand. Later in the exchange, however, Shunzei will take *mategata* to mean "hardworking," following precedents in the *Man'yōshū* where the word is written 両手肩, suggesting working with both hands and shoulders.

41. This person will turn out to be Kiyosuke.

mategata ni	Like the smoke that rises
kakitsumu ama no	from burning seaweed, scratched up
moshiogusa	by hard-working sea-folk:
keburi wa ika ni	"Why break it off?"
tatsu zo to ya kimi	I ask you.[42]

as part of a poetic exchange. Much evidence was brought forth in support of *maku*, but it means just that the sea-folk have no leisure. *Mategata* and *itoma naki koto* are the same thing. In short, it must be as it appears in *Gosenshū*. Hideakira seems to have written few Japanese poems but he was exceptionally accomplished as a writer of Chinese poetry. He would hardly have made mistakes. The right's poem is nothing special, but the left's "there is none of the excitement of love," does not sound elegant even though it uses old words, and there is no evidence for *maku kata*. The right is the winner.[43]

Kenshō's lengthy rebuttal of 1198 begins by quoting the entire exchange from *Roppyakuban utaawase*, then continues:

The poet for the right said that *ama no maku kata* in the poem of the left side should have been *mategata*, and we had an exchange of questions and answers. In the criticism on that occasion, there did not really seem to be a reason for the reading *mategata*. Furthermore, the judge might have been fixated on *mategata* from earlier. And perhaps this was in order to support the usual argument about the disciple. The idea that there is no evidence has been given above [in his citation of the judgment]. I will refute this item by item. Although there might have been such a fear, I have not consulted only my own interpretation. That would be adhering to error. It is not at all a matter of looking down on others' knowledge. It is thinking about principle. First, regarding the text that was given [to Shunzei] by Retired Emperor Sutoku, "a certain person" should not be spoken of again. When the late Kiyosuke wrote the text about *waka* known as *Ōgishō* [Poetic profundities, ca. 1144; the text to which Shunzei had referred], he had doubts about the poem by Captain Hideakira in the *Gosenshū*:

Ise no umi	Like the sea-folk of Ise
ama no maku kata	who scatter [sand] on the tideland,

---

42. In the original poem there is a pun on *tatsu*, referring both to the rising smoke and (possibly) to the breaking off of the relationship.

43. Kubota and Yamaguchi, *Roppyakuban utaawase*, pp. 412–14.

itoma nashi	I have no leisure.
nagaraenikeru	How I resent
mi o zo uramuru	living on this way.[44]

He did not annotate it, but later on, asking a person who was well informed about *ama no maku kata*, he produced a detailed note. It is on a
slip of paper in his own hand, pasted into my text. That interpretation
could not yet be seen [in *Ōgishō*]. It is not at all the work of a disciple. My
view is that when sea-folk make salt fires, they take sand at low tide and
pour it together in a pot where they boil it. Then, after the water is boiled
off, they scatter the sand back on the original tideland, and this is what
is meant by *ama no maku kata*. While the tide is out, they hurriedly scatter the sand. Then, when the tide comes in, the sand is permeated with
salt water, and again, they take the sand, boil it to get salt, and, since in
this way they work constantly, making an association with "having no
leisure," [Hideakira] composed the poem to say, "I have had no time,
and am unhappy not to have been able to call on you for so long. . . ."

A poem in *Ise monogatari*:

Ashinoya no	The salt makers
nada no shioyaki	of the open sea at Ashinoya
itoma nami	have no time
tsuge no ogushi mo	even to dress their hair
sasade kinikeri	with boxwood combs.

Since this poem was composed on having no time because of the same
salt-making activity, and scattering sand is part of making salt, I drew on
this to suggest "having no time," when I composed my poem. Nonetheless, the judge could not understand the reason, and said, "Both
Man'yōshū and *Ise monogatari* speak of having no time. Neither uses the
phrase *maku kata*." If I had cited these poems to support use of the
phrase *maku kata* then he could have spoken this way. They are evidence
that sea-folk have no time when making salt. It is because there are no
examples of poems that use *mategata* to speak of having no leisure. The
poet for the right is deeply attached to a mistaken text that has *mategata*.
This is terribly regrettable for the sake of the Way. When the sea-folk see
a hole left by the shellfish called a *mate*, they make a thing called a *teg-
ushi* and extract it. Or they might dig it out, but this not an activity that
causes them to be busy. It is something they do only once in a while.
Captain Hideakira was a person who was a master of elegant writing. He

---

44. *Gosenshū* has *nami* where Kenshō gives *nashi*.

would not have begun using the phrase *mategata* in the occasional Japanese poems he composed. Poetry is something that is composed using words that sound pleasing, and choosing [appropriate] objects. The word *mategata* sounds thoroughly terrible. It is an exceedingly displeasing-seeming word. And it is also a lowly object. Poetry should not be composed about it. . . .

From what the left has seen, all of the texts of *Gosenshū*, of Saigū no nyōgo's poem, and of Izumi Shikibu's poem say *maku kata*. Some texts happened to have *mategata*, but as has been recorded, according to the right *mategata* appears in all of the poems, so it becomes difficult to resolve, but one should think of this in terms of which of the activities of sea-folk, making salt or digging for shellfish, is what causes them to have no leisure. The poems given in evidence of "having no leisure" must also be considered according to which interpretation they follow. One prepares an interpretation for the purpose of criticism, and measures the criticism against the response, in order to make the meaning clear for both sides and to increase knowledge. What happened here was a matter of being blinded by one's own concerns and contributing to the deterioration of the Way. . . .

What I find regrettable in this question and answer is the right's criticism, "they call it a salt beach; do they really scatter salt on the tideland?" and the judge's words, "They make salt on the beach, and wouldn't scatter salt on the tideland." Although I explained this thoroughly at the time of the judgment, they really must not have understood. . . . [Further descriptions of salt-making follow, the upshot of which is that the workers scatter sand, not salt.] Neither the right nor the judge is able to understand the difference between the beach where the seawater is boiled and the tideland where the sand is scattered. I dare say that if they cannot understand, I should draw a diagram to show them. . . .

A certain native of Ise said, "there are *mate* [shellfish] in that province, but [the sea people] are not responsible for taking them. They take them on occasion, but it is not something that should particularly be composed about in poetry about how busy they are. . . ."

Captain Hideakira's poem, "Because the sea-folk of Ise who spread sand have no leisure . . ." was composed elegantly, and it was splendid that during the awe-inspiring reign of Emperor Murakami, the Five Gentleman of the Pear Pavilion[45] chose it for inclusion in *Gosenshū*. But

---

45. The group of mid-tenth-century courtiers who compiled the *Gosenshū*, among other scholarly activities.

the fact that to this day people thoughtlessly take up mistaken texts that have *mategata*, detestable language for poetry, and use them to make arguments is a troubling thing for the sake of the author. It is distressing to me that the late captain should receive such an injury. How I wish he would appear in people's dreams to give notice that he used the words *maku kata*, and make it known universally. Otherwise, there is no way to trust what anyone says.[46]

Perhaps the kindest thing that can be said for Kenshō's poem, the start of the controversy, is that it is, again, inventive, and inventive in a way that requires a certain erudition to appreciate. A paraphrase of the poem might say simply, "I am not a busy sea-person, but I have no time for love nonetheless." As the poem from Section 87 of *Ise monogatari* attests,[47] the association between sea-people and busyness was already well established via the phrase *itoma nami* ("because they have no leisure," with a pun on the associated word *nami*, meaning "waves"), and was often used in the course of offering a poetic excuse for not calling, but Kenshō, in a move that is hard to view as other than deliberately (or even perversely) obscurantist, avoids this phrase and leaves just *maku kata*, "the tideland where they scatter [sand]" to carry the implications of busyness—an association that seems to have been as hard for his contemporaries to figure out as it is for a modern reader. Shunzei seems to have found Kenshō's use of the word *someki* (excitement) and of the construction *ito . . . nashi* (not very much) even more objectionable for purposes of determining the winner of the round, and Kenshō offers several citations in his rebuttal about these words too, but it is clearly *maku kata* versus *mategata* that is the sore point. It is not clear exactly when the exchange between Shunzei and Retired Emperor Sutoku would have occurred, but given that Kiyosuke's *Ōgishō* was completed by 1144 and the former emperor had been dead for some thirty years by the time of *Roppyakuban utaawase*, we are looking at a dispute of very long standing and one that appears to have excited passions on both sides. Shunzei is operating from the position of strength, both insofar as he is the judge and in view of where he stood in his career at this point compared to Kenshō, and he is delicate enough not to cite Kiyosuke by

46. Kubota and Yamaguchi, *Roppyakuban utaawase*, pp. 472–75.
47. The poem is identified as old in Section 87 of *Ise*. The phrase *itoma nami* also appears in the *Man'yōshū*.

name. Nonetheless, it is quite clear to Kenshō (and no doubt the other participants) whom he is talking about, and the idea that someone would make a claim without evidence of precedents appears to be particularly damning.

Once again, Kenshō and Shunzei appear to be approaching the situation based on divergent principles. It is easy enough to imagine the syllables *te* and *ku* being difficult to distinguish in a manuscript and leading to the existence of variant texts, particularly when neither *maku kata* nor *mategata* seem to have been commonly in use among twelfth-century court poets. For Kenshō, research into the specifics of salt-making and the terminology by which the natives of Ise identify the various parts of their workspace (the *hama* where they boil the combination of sand and seawater versus the *kata* where they scatter what remains after boiling) is sufficient to justify the reading of *maku kata* in *Gosenshū* and other sources, which in turn justifies his use of it in his own poem. The fact that the meaning is obscure to his audience is no obstacle—rather, it creates an opportunity for Kenshō to display his erudition and ingenuity. Shunzei, however, confident that *mategata* is merely a synonym for *itoma nami*, remains unimpressed. Kenshō's frustrated indignation in the rebuttal of 1198 is unmistakable—from the sarcastic comment about drawing a diagram for his opponents, to his accusations that they are destroying the Way of Poetry, to his appropriation of Shunzei's arguments for his own cause (suggesting that *mate* is a lowly object and an unpleasant-sounding word, unsuitable for poetry; insinuating that the whole business is insulting to Hideakira, who would have known better than to use such a word), and above all in his closing wish that Hideakira would return from the dead to settle the dispute since no other authority can be trusted.

Ultimately, the dispute hinges on the question of what constitutes a legitimate, trustworthy source. Shunzei summarily dismisses the texts upon which Kenshō and Kiyosuke base their *maku kata* reading as mistaken, and Kenshō appears no less adamant, though his opening explanation during the contest stating that *te* and *ku* have been switched in *Gosenshū* suggests that he was aware of texts that contained *te* (as, perhaps, does the statement that the judge is "fixated" on *mategata*). The fact that Kiyosuke was not initially able to resolve the problem (in the text of *Ōgishō* that Shunzei discussed with Sutoku-in), and, more important, that the resolution is entirely a matter of hearsay (the mysterious informant from Ise) rather than something rooted in the study of texts, also suggests that Kenshō may have been on wobbly philological ground, but without firm knowledge of the texts of *Gosenshū* and *Saigū no nyōgo shū* in circulation at the time and the methods contemporary scholars used to produce them it is impossible for a modern reader to assess the situation. In the end, what matters is not *how* to determine what constitutes a trustworthy source, but *who* is authorized to make that determination, based on what criteria, and by the 1190s it was the Mikohidari family, not the Rokujō family, that had the poetic capital to back up their selection of authoritative texts and language. The implications are far-reaching: the texts that are used today for all the major poetic anthologies, as well as poetic diaries and *monogatari*, are those handed down from the Mikohidari family.[48]

The Teika Texts of *Ise monogatari* and Their Colophons

In exactly the same way, it was the Mikohidari family that produced what became the most authoritative texts of *Ise monogatari*. What is known of the textual history of *Ise monogatari* is exceedingly complex, a natural outgrowth of the text's episodic form and early writers' penchant for adding to it freely. The texts used by the vast majority of the commentators who figure hereinafter, and those still used today, were produced by Shunzei's son, the great poet and scholar Fujiwara no Teika. Teika copied and collated *Ise monogatari* numerous times in his career, and three slightly divergent Teika texts (known as *Teika-bon*) are of particular importance: the *Tenpuku-bon*, the *Rufu-bon*, and the *Takeda-bon*. The *Tenpuku-bon* is generally thought to be the best, most reliable of the three, closest to Teika's final recension. The earliest surviving exemplar of this lineage is a copy by Sanjōnishi Sanetaka (1455–1537). Though it postdates Teika considerably, it is purported to have been copied faithfully from a no-longer extant text in Teika's own hand, formerly in Sanetaka's possession. The *Tenpuku-bon* has the following colophon:

> On the twentieth of the first month of the second year of Tenpuku [1234], in spite of my blind monk's eyes, amid many consecutive days of wind

---

48. The version of Hideakira's *Gosenshū* poem in *Shin Nihon koten bungaku taikei*, for example, has *mategata*, following Shunzei's interpretation. And when one looks up *mategata* in *Kōjien*, Saigū no nyōgo's poem is given as the lone example.

and snow, finally I copied this in order to give it to my beloved grand-daughter. On the 22nd of the same month, I finished the collation.[49]

The *Rufu-bon* and *Takeda-bon*, meanwhile, are undated, but appear to be among the texts that Teika collated earlier—the title he uses to sign his name to both texts would have been applicable between 1218 and 1227. The *Rufu-bon*, or "circulating text," has numerous variants of dif-fering quality, but they share a colophon in which Teika speculates about the title and authorship of the *monogatari*:

> In the first place, regarding the origins of *Ise monogatari* the explanations of the people of the past do not agree. Some say it was written by the Ariwara Middle Captain [Narihira], etc. Because of this there is humble, self-deprecating language, etc. Others say it is Lady Ise's work. Some say she wrote it when she was a young girl of thirteen, and in the same style as her private poetry collection. Therefore it is called *Ise monogatari*. Considering both theories, it is all the more difficult to decide. The se-crets of [Narihira's] heart and the personal words that arose on the spot would be difficult for someone else to guess at and write down. When you consider this, must it not be said that it is [Narihira's] own writing? However, I have doubts because among its poems in the old style of the *Man'yōshū* there are many that appear in the imperial anthologies, and it roughly records the ritual of the imperial progress of the Ninna era [dur-ing the reign of Emperor Kōkō in 887, seven years after Narihira's death; Section 114]—these things are also dubious. As for Lady Ise's personal poetry collection, the style of the beginning is similar throughout [*Ise monogatari*]. . . . In addition, as for the name of this *monogatari*, if it is not by her, why is it called *Ise*? One explanation says that it has this name because [Narihira] goes to Ise as an imperial huntsman. That explana-tion is difficult to believe. The beginning starts with the words "In the Southern Capital in the village of Kasuga" [Section 1], then adds thoughts of the moon at night at the western wing [Section 4], the snow of Mt. Fuji [Section 9], and the smoke of Musashino [Section 12]; none of these concern the matter of Ise province, yet many regard them as most im-portant to this *monogatari*. There are further doubts about both explana-tions. Ancient matters should just be held up and trusted, but some say that later people replaced the beginning of the text with the matter of the imperial huntsman to accord with the reason for [calling it] *Ise monoga-*

---

49. Ikeda, *Ise monogatari ni tsukite no kenkyū*, p. 138.

tari. The text in question is disordered and suspicious. It is the work of [Sesonji] Koreyuki. We should not use it. The text I copied in recent years was borrowed by someone and lost, and as before I have prepared an authorized text by collating it again.[50]

Teika gives similar opinions in the colophon of the *Takeda-bon*:

I have collated and selected this from many texts, and thus I was able to prepare an authorized text. Recently a text has appeared that places the matter of the imperial huntsman at the beginning of the *monogatari*. Now that I think about it, this must be the work of someone of later ages. It should not be used at all. The views of the people of the past about this *monogatari* are not in agreement. Some say that the Ariwara Middle Captain [Narihira] wrote it himself, and some say it is Ise's work. . . . One should not forcibly seek the author among the people of the past. One should simply enjoy the flowers and leaves of its language.[51]

Although Teika's comments are far from conclusive, they give us some sense of the early thirteenth-century state of the field. The support for Narihira's candidacy as author is the fact that in several spots the narrator tosses out little disparaging comments about the protagonist as a poet, as in Section 101, where the protagonist, identified as Ariwara no Yukihira's brother, tries to demur when asked to compose a poem because he "knows nothing about poetry," or in Section 77, where an "old man" who is director of the Right Imperial Stables composes a poem characterized by the narrator as "not very good." The possibility that this might have been a posture adopted by another writer, or that the depictions of Narihira's secret affairs might have been fictional, is not mentioned, whether because it did not occur to Teika, or simply because the people of the past, whoever they may be, had not advanced such theories. The other candidate, Lady Ise, was an important poet who lived from around 870 to around 940 and served as an attendant to Empress Onshi during the reign of Emperor Uda (887–97). In the *Rufu-bon* colophon, Teika is comparing the opening of her personal poetry collection, which is set in an indeterminate past and in which she is spoken of in the third person ("In

---

50. Ibid., pp. 279–80.
51. Ibid., p. 261.

which reign might it have been? There was a person whose father was in Yamato who served the consort known as the Ōmiyasudokoro")[52] to the phrase "In the past, there was a man" that marks the beginning of most sections of *Ise monogatari*. The "styles" of the two works are thus equally ambiguous with regard to the time frame and the protagonist's identity, but playfully so, given *Ise monogatari*'s various gestures in Narihira's direction, and the fact that Lady Ise is known to be the author of the poetry in her collection despite the misdirection.

Although he opts for cautious agnosticism in the *Takeda-bon* colophon, in the *Rufu-bon* Teika seems to be leaning toward accepting Lady Ise as the author, owing to the neatness with which doing so would solve the question of the title. At the time there were at least three theories in circulation, all of which appear in Kenshō's *Kokinshū chū* (Commentary on the *Kokinshū*, 1185) in his discussion of the poems from Section 69, the story of Narihira's trip to Ise province as imperial huntsman.[53] In addition to the imperial huntsman theory (Kenshō also mentions the dubious texts that start with this section) and the Lady Ise theory, like Kiyosuke, he cites the saying *Isebito no higagoto*, "people from Ise tell tales." Teika may have dismissed this possibility without mentioning it because he desired to distance himself from Kenshō and the Rokujō family.

Although the Old Commentaries pursue their own course without reference to Teika's views, as we will see, the authors of the Transitional Commentaries return to Teika's colophons and analyze them exhaustively for hints about how to answer questions about *Ise monogatari*'s formation.

Early Medieval Esoteric Commentaries

Although the Mikohidari family emerged as the victors in the poetic battles of the twelfth century, within two or three generations of Teika's death, infighting among his heirs led the Mikohidari family to split into three factions—the conservative Nijō, the opposing Reizei, and the relatively short-lived Kyōgoku—each claiming to be the legitimate bearers

---

52. Sasaki Nobutsuna, *Nihon kagaku taikei*, 18:81.
53. Takeoka, *Kokinwakashū zenhyōshaku*, 2:275.

and transmitters of Teika's and Shunzei's legacy. Competition among the factions was fierce, and provided fertile ground for the production of secret teachings and forgeries of various kinds. However, the earliest full-blown commentaries on *Ise monogatari*, the Old Commentaries, emerged from a fourth, less well-known faction led by Teika's grandson Tameaki, a son of Tameie by an unknown lady-in-waiting, whose base of operations appears to have been Kamakura rather than the capital.[54] Susan Klein has linked the often eccentric interpretations put forth in these commentaries to the role they played in poetic initiation ceremonies (*waka kanjō*) within this marginalized school: as transmission of esoteric teachings was a key component of these ceremonies, there was a need to create suitably obscure bodies of proprietary knowledge to transmit.[55] As a result, the sometimes outlandish readings presented in these commentaries, along with the often deliberately falsified evidence used in support of them, became, in effect, a source of distinction for the schools that handed them down, an assurance that they alone possessed a "correct" understanding of the text by which they could differentiate themselves from other schools.

For current purposes, it will suffice to examine the basic approach of the Old Commentaries in order to understand the reaction against them that began in the late medieval Transitional Commentaries. The *Wakachikenshū* (Collection of manifest knowledge about poetry, ca. 1260) and *Reizei-ke-ryū Ise monogatari shō* (Reizei school *Ise monogatari* commentary, a group of closely related *kikigaki*, or notes from lectures, dating mostly from the fourteenth and fifteenth centuries) are the most important Old Commentaries to which subsequent commentaries refer. They proceed as though firmly convinced of *Ise monogatari*'s foundation in the facts of Narihira's life and loves and take the commentator's task to be unearthing the disguised truths that underlie the stories, attempting to identify unnamed characters, to give dates for events, and to reconcile contradictions through allegorical readings. Although *Wakachikenshū* is more circumspect, and much less given to allegorical readings, *Reizei-ke-ryū Ise monogatari shō* goes so far as to make up fictitious sources to support the

---

54. For biographical information on Tameaki, see Klein, *Allegories of Desire*, pp. 100–106.
55. Ibid., p. 29.

"facts" it gives.[56] The last part of its commentary on Section 9 gives an excellent demonstration of the Old Commentaries in action. The target text reads:

> Continuing on as before, they came to a very large river between Musashi and Shimotsufusa provinces. It is called the Sumida River. As they stood in a group on the edge of the river and thought of home, lamenting together about how very far they had come, the ferryman said, "Hurry up and get in the boat. The sun has gone down." About to board the boat and cross the river, they were all wretched, for there was not one of them who did not have someone he loved in the capital.[57]

Reizeike-ryū Ise monogatari shō interprets this as follows:

> "Continuing on as before, they came to a very large river between Musashi and Shimotsufusa provinces," means [the Nijō empress's father] Middle Counselor Nagara was governor of Musashi province and built a house to live in north of the Suita River. [The Nijō empress's brother] Kunitsune was governor of Shimotsufusa and built a house to live in south of the Suita River. This is what is meant by "between Musashi and Shimotsufusa provinces." The Sumida River is the Suita River [in modern Osaka prefecture]. . . .
>
> "They stood in a group" means that in the third year of Gangyō (879) Emperor Yōzei made his first imperial progress to his maternal grandfather Middle Counselor Nagara's estate. The gathering of the courtiers is described as "stood in a group."
>
> "How very far they had come. . . ." This is because they had come to a place separated from the capital.
>
> "The ferryman said, 'Hurry up and get in the boat.'" The meaning is that Narihira was subject to imperial censure, and when he arrived at Middle Counselor Nagara's estate, the current regent [the Nijō empress's other brother] Mototsune came up and said to him, "Emperor Seiwa censured you. Since this is now a new reign, Emperor Yōzei will lift the censure. Live well!"[58] Thus, he is saying "Go into court service."

---

56. Kido, "*Ise monogatari* Reizei-ke-ryū kochū," pp. 10–17, gives a detailed comparison of the two works and their approaches.

57. Citations from *Ise monogatari* are based on the text in Horiuchi and Akiyama, *Taketori monogatari, Ise monogatari*, pp. 79–194.

58. There is a pun here on (*yo o*) *wataru*, combining "ferrying" and "making a living."

"The ferryman" is the regent . . . The sovereign is a boat, and since the regent protects him, he is called the ferryman. . . .[59]
"The sun has gone down" means that Emperor Seiwa has died. The sun is the sovereign. . . .[60]
"They were all wretched," means that everyone thought it was wretched that Emperor Yōzei would pardon Narihira. Since he was a person under censure because of the Nijō empress, everyone was uncomfortable that he would ask her son for pardon, and thus it says everyone was wretched. A certain book says that Yōzei was Narihira's son. When Narihira was secretly visiting the Nijō empress, the emperor did not know that Yōzei was Narihira's son, and made him crown prince. Therefore, in *Yotsugi* too, it says that because Yōzei was Narihira's son, he would be sent out of the royal family and his position was difficult to maintain, so he was driven mad.[61] Therefore, people at the time knew he was Narihira's son. When the emperor too knew Narihira was his parent, everyone observed and felt uncomfortable and wretched.[62]

Needless to say, *Reizei-ke-ryū Ise monogatari shō*'s approach to *Ise monogatari* diverges wildly from the kinds of scholarship practiced in the twelfth century, whether in Kenshō's philological approach or Shunzei's and Teika's concern with aesthetics and the art of composition. Another distinguishing characteristic of the Old Commentaries is the extent to which they embrace the text's eroticism; they go so far as to assert that the "I-se" of the title means women and men, therefore "Tales of relations between the sexes." *Wakachikenshū* states that Narihira is a manifestation of Batō Kannon (Horse-head Kannon, a play on *Uma no kami*, or Director of the Imperial Stables, one of Narihira's titles), and claims he had relations with a total of 3,733 women, motivated by a desire to save them from their attachment to him.[63] Interestingly, both the *Wakachikenshū* and the *Reizei-ke-ryū Ise monogatari shō* con-

---

59. Citations from several sources are offered as support for this reading. One is a quote attributed to the *Shiji* but that cannot be found in that work. The others are from books that cannot be traced at all.

60. Another dubious-sounding source is cited here.

61. This clause is not a fabrication—Yōzei is known to have been mentally unstable.

62. Katagiri, *Ise monogatari no kenkyū, Shiryōhen*, pp. 312–13.

63. See Klein, *Allegories of Desire*, pp. 153–57 and 280–91, and Bowring, "*Ise Monogatari*," pp. 435–39, for details on sex, poetry, tantric Buddhism, and Narihira as a deity in the Old Commentaries.

clude that *Ise monogatari* describes Narihira's relations with twelve specific women. The respective lists differ slightly, but include, for example, the Nijō empress, the Ise priestess, Ki no Aritsune's daughter, and
Ono no Komachi, each of whom comes to be associated with a range of
episodes. In the case of Komachi, for example, although she and Narihira were roughly contemporary (Komachi's dates are not known for
certain), there is no record that they ever met, let alone that they were
romantically involved. However, extrapolating from Section 25, an episode about the protagonist's interaction with a "fickle" woman that jux-
taposes a poem by Narihira with one by Komachi (unrelated apart from
appearing side by side in the *Kokinshū*), every woman whom the text
characterizes as fickle or amorous comes to be identified as Komachi.

Although these commentaries began as secret teachings, by the fifteenth century their content appears to have become widely known—
material from them appears prominently in both Noh plays and *otogizōshi*
that draw on *Ise monogatari* or legends surrounding Narihira.[64] Their
currency in popular culture as well as the vast distance between their
methods and the far more circumspect approach of the poet-scholars of
earlier times go some distance toward explaining the sharp opposition to
them that developed among scholars working after about 1460. But as I
will show in the next chapter, even in scholarship they continued to loom
large, setting agendas and coming to be considered part of the working
knowledge of *Ise monogatari* an aspiring poet was expected to have: they
became part of the baggage carried by a culturally literate person and
contributed enormously to popular perceptions of Narihira. At the same
time, these popular perceptions became ever more important. Although
scholarly production related to *Ise monogatari* (as well as to *Kokinshū* and
Genji monogatari) had been dominated overwhelmingly by courtiers
seeking to impress higher-ranking courtiers or members of the imperial
family in the early medieval period, beginning in the fifteenth century
new classes of people, most notably warriors and *renga* masters, came to
assume key, transformative roles in the production and consumption of
literary scholarship.

---

64. See Bowring, *"Ise Monogatari,"* pp. 455–65, for an overview.

CHAPTER 3

Economies of Secrecy:
Ise monogatari Commentaries after 1460

The age of warfare that ran from the Ōnin War (1467–77) to the early
years of the Tokugawa period (1603–1868) brought as many drastic
changes to the world of scholarship as it did to other facets of Japanese
culture and society. The period was marked by continual violence
and disorder as rival warlords vied among themselves for dominance in
the near vacuum created by the effective collapse of the Ashikaga
shogunate,[1] with constantly shifting alliances and no victories convincing enough to put an end to the chaos. The aristocracy suffered a pre-
cipitous decline in status and great financial hardship as they lost property to fires in the capital and became less and less able to collect
revenues from their estates in the provinces,[2] a situation that led court-

---

1. The shogunate survived until 1573, but the shoguns had little effective control over
other great warrior families after Ōnin.

2. Mary Elizabeth Berry writes: "Many courtiers took rented lodgings (some on
back streets), found shelter in temples or provincial estates, or hid their financial em-
barrassment behind brave fronts. The imperial treasurer, Yamashina Tokitsugu, kept
up his walls and gates but concealed his leaking roofs by borrowing the homes of
friends for formal meetings. . . . The imperial house, which had received income from
as many as 250 land-holdings before the war, collected occasional revenue from no
more than 34 holdings after Ōnin. Aristocrats faced similar constriction and their diaries abound in references to the expediencies they used to make do. Yamashina Tokitsugu pawned not just fine swords but mosquito nets as well. Nobles loaned out precious manuscripts for copying; sometimes they sold the texts (like Sanjōnishi Sanetaka's
medieval copy of *The Tale of Genji*). They suspended major and minor ceremonies; they
even postponed interments." Berry, *Civil War in Kyoto*, p. 62. For a full-length study of

iers with scholarly inclinations to produce commentaries, give lectures, and copy out texts for money. On the consuming end of these transactions were high-ranking warriors who, seeking to elevate and legitimize themselves through association with the courtly literary tradition, began, much as the Ashikaga shoguns had done, to serve as patrons to scholars, poets, and artists, and to amass libraries. The development of *renga* (linked-verse), which required knowledge of classics like *Ise monogatari* and *Genji monogatari*, as a popular pastime in the late medieval period was also instrumental in the expansion of readership, and *renga* masters such as Sōgi (1421–1502) produced commentaries and gave lectures of their own and facilitated exchanges of money and texts between courtiers in the capital and warriors in the provinces. It was in this milieu that the Transitional Commentaries took shape.

The best-known and most frequently cited characteristic of the Transitional Commentaries is their pointed opposition to the Old Commentaries and their methods, in favor of more conservative explication of *Ise monogatari*'s poetry and prose.[3] The first task, accomplished by Ichijō Kaneyoshi (or Kanera, 1402–81), was to wrest the text from the framework of allegorical interpretation that had held sway in the Old Commentaries and resituate it within the larger tradition, as defined by the legacy of Fujiwara no Teika. Commentators of this period point out that in *Eiga no taigai* (Essentials of poetic composition, ca. 1215) Teika had named *Ise monogatari* second only to the *Kokinshū* as a must-read for students of poetry.[4] In contrast to the Old Commentaries, which look at *Ise monogatari* allegorically, or in terms of esoteric religion and sex, Transitional Commentaries consider it vis-à-vis the *Kokinshū*, *Genji monogatari*, and other canonical works and define its nature in terms of them.

However, it would be a mistake to view the commentators of this period as being inimical to secret teachings per se;[5] after Kaneyoshi the

---

the situation of the court and aristocrats from the Ōnin War to the early Tokugawa period, see also Butler, *Emperor and Aristocracy*.

3. See Bowring, "*Ise Monogatari*," pp. 450–53; Klein, *Allegories of Desire*, pp. 293–94.

4. Hashimoto, et al., *Karonshū*, p. 495.

5. Although Richard Bowring suggests that "there are no imprecations on those who might divulge these writings to the wider world, and nothing resembling the secrets of the *Kokinshū*" (Bowring, "*Ise Monogatari*," pp. 453–54), there are in fact admonitions in most of these commentaries, in the colophons, against revealing their

overwhelming majority of mainstream Transitional Commentaries were produced by leaders in the Nijō school of poetry, specifically those who developed and controlled the transmission of the *kokin denju* (secret teachings of the *Kokinshū*). Lewis Cook has linked the *kokin denju* to a reconstitution of the Way of Poetry as a profession and identifies it as "a pedagogical institution based on a curriculum designed not only to preserve and transmit its canon but to teach its proper reading and its use-values, so to speak, as a model for poetic reading."[6] These teachings became a body of knowledge the transmission of which conferred prestige upon its recipient, including, at the highest levels, authority to teach (and to charge for it). Although study of the *Kokinshū* occupied a privileged position in this body of knowledge, the commentators single out *Ise monogatari* as second in importance; it was to be studied after the *Kokinshū*, but preceded the other imperially commissioned poetry anthologies.

Most of these *Ise* commentaries, then, are, in form as well as in content, intimately connected to the process of teaching, which at that point was available to a limited circle of well-placed students. Many of the commentaries record performances: students took notes on teachers' lectures, and teachers then certified clean copies, which might subsequently be lent to others. Conversely, Hosokawa Yūsai's (1534–1610) *Ise monogatari ketsugishō* (Doubting commentary on *Ise monogatari*, 1596), a major commentary that appears at the end of this period and that became the dominant Transitional Commentary in circulation in the Tokugawa period, is a synthesis of earlier commentaries, including some that started as lecture notes, from which Yūsai delivered lectures of his own to Prince Hachijō Toshihito, as a prelude to transmitting the *kokin denju*.

The progress of the Transitional Commentaries describes a neat trajectory from scholar to scholar that follows the transmission of the *kokin denju* (see fig. 3.1 below), but the possible implications of this close association for our understanding of these scholars' work on *Ise monogatari*

---

contents to outsiders. The teachings themselves might have become less outlandish, and might therefore smack less of esotericism, but it is nonetheless important to acknowledge that the Transitional Commentaries arose in a milieu where secret, proprietary traditions were still highly valued.

6. Cook, "Discipline of Poetry," p. 107.

have yet to be examined fully. Insofar as study of *Ise monogatari* took place as part of a graduated curriculum and commentaries were produced in the context of specific social and pedagogical relationships, attention to how and why individual commentaries came into being is indispensable for a grounded understanding of the interpretations they put forth. One goal of this chapter is to consider the extent to which interpretations may have varied with the target audience, both in their presentation and sometimes even in their content.

The first section of this chapter describes the new social networks in which scholarship was produced and circulated in the late medieval period, the complex tangle of relations and transactions among courtiers, warriors and *renga* masters. The second section considers the nature and significance of Ichijō Kaneyoshi's break with the Old Commentaries in his *Ise monogatari gukenshō* (Humble views on *Ise monogatari*, 1460 and 1474). This is followed by an examination in the third section of the methods of Sōgi and members of the Sanjōnishi family, the commentators most closely associated with the Nijō school of poetry and the transmission of the *kokin denju* in this period. While Sōgi and the Sanjōnishi family tend in most instances to reject the Old Commentaries, they also display a tendency to identify sections of *Ise monogatari* as factual or fictitious in order to reframe morally dubious content. Finally, the last section of the chapter examines a corpus of hitherto unstudied secret teachings dating from the early seventeenth century that may explain some of the apparent contradictions to be found in Nijō school scholars' interpretations and that suggest that the mainstream Transitional Commentaries may not tell the full story of those scholars' views of *Ise monogatari*.

New Networks: Courtiers, Warriors, and *Renga* Masters

As Steven Carter has argued, the new social, political, and economic configurations that emerged in the fifteenth and sixteenth centuries led to massive changes in the dynamics of patronage: "Patrons existed wherever there was wealth, and sometimes even where there was little wealth but great prestige or symbolic power," and "the trend throughout the late medieval era was outward and downward on the social scale."[7] The observation holds for the production and consumption of literary schol-

---

7. Carter, "Introduction," p. 14.

arship as much as it does for the literary arts. In earlier times the representative pattern involved courtiers producing literary scholarship for other members of court society. Courtiers' cultural authority continued to be a vitally important component of the new configurations, and courtiers took on roles as teachers or consultants to members of other social groups. But the fact that they were often compensated for their efforts inevitably wrought changes in the power dynamics. Without powerful, wealthy members of the great warrior clans seeking literary knowledge, the scholarship of the period would surely have looked very different, if it had managed to thrive at all.

Courtier diaries and other documents give a vivid picture of the traffic in texts and expertise among courtiers, warriors, and *renga* masters in the late fifteenth and early sixteenth centuries. The following four sets of transactions featuring some of the most prominent players constitute just a small sampling and focus primarily on matters related to *Ise monogatari* and *Genji monogatari* (there were also many exchanges involving poetry collections and poetics texts, as well as *renga*, court kickball, works in Chinese, and so on), but they give ample evidence of warriors' keen interest in classical literature, courtiers' inclination to accommodate those interests, and *renga* masters' pivotal contributing role in creating or disseminating information and texts.

1. Ōuchi Masahiro (1446–95), a warrior whose domain included several provinces in Western Honshū and who was a participant in the Ōnin War, sought to establish a "Little Kyoto" at Yamaguchi, and frequently over the course of many years drew on the expertise and authority of courtiers and *renga* masters, many of whom came to stay in Yamaguchi for extended periods, to assist him. Noteworthy examples include:

1469   While in the capital, Masahiro has Bishop Jikyō of Miidera copy and collate a text of *Ise monogatari* in the hand of poet Shōtetsu (1381–1459), which he later gave to his daughter in response to her earnest request.

1474   Ichijō Kaneyoshi copies out *Kachō kudenshō* (secret teachings pertaining to *Genji monogatari*, a supplement to Kaneyoshi's commentary *Kachō yojō*) for Masahiro.[8]

---

8. Although Kaneyoshi was sharing secret teachings with Masahiro, this work contains only thirteen items withheld from *Kachō yojō*, compared to the fifteen that appear in Kaneyoshi's *Gengo hiketsu*, another compilation of secrets.

1475   Masahiro receives a copy of *Ise monogatari gukenshō* (revised version) in Kaneyoshi's hand.

1476   Masahiro receives a copy of *Kachō yojō* (Kaneyoshi's *Genji* commentary, revised version) from Kaneyoshi. Four years later, Sanjō Kin'atsu (1439–1507), a courtier who had left the capital and taken up residence in Yamaguchi due to losses suffered in the war, borrowed this text to collate it with earlier versions. Kin'atsu worked frequently on other projects for Masahiro as well.

1481   The courtier and poet Asukai Masayasu (1436–1509) finishes copying Teika's *Aobyōshi* text of *Genji monogatari* for Masahiro.

1489   Masahiro has the *renga* master Sōgi, then residing in Yamaguchi, give lectures on *Ise monogatari* and produce *Ise monogatari Yamaguchi shō* (Yamaguchi commentary on *Ise monogatari*, also known as *Yamaguchi ki* or *Sōgi chū*, "Sōgi's notes"), a commentary strictly on the poetry of *Ise monogatari* "for beginners." In the same year, Kin'atsu makes a copy of Sōgi's *Amayo danshō* (Commentary on the rainy night discussion, also known as *Hahakigi betchū*), a commentary on the second chapter of *Genji monogatari* that Sōgi had written in 1485.

1490   Masahiro receives from the priest Ryōchin, Kaneyoshi's son, a copy of the *Kawachi-bon* variant of *Genji monogatari* that Kaneyoshi had copied in 1466. Ryōchin was staying in Yamaguchi at the time.

1490–91 Masahiro has the *renga* master Kensai (1452–1510) compare and take notes on the differences between the *Kawachi-bon* and the *Aobyōshi-bon* variants of *Genji* to create a *Masahiro-bon*, which Kin'atsu copied.[9]

2. Sanjōnishi Sanetaka (1455–1537) was perhaps the most prolific and widely connected scholar of classical literature of the period, lecturing, copying texts, and producing commentaries throughout his long life. He received the *kokin denju* from Sōgi at age thirty, and his family line became the most prominent stewards of Nijō school scholarship for nearly a century. As a complete list of Sanetaka's interactions with others on scholarly matters would run to a great many pages, here we focus

---

9. Time line extracted from Yonehara, *Sengoku bushi*, pp. 581–96. Further discussion of Masahiro's role as a patron and collector, and information about Sanjō Kin'atsu can be found in Carter, "Introduction," pp. 8–10.

just on his exchanges related to *Genji monogatari* with the warrior
Hatakeyama Yoshifusa (1491–1545), lord of the Noto domain (modern
Ishikawa Prefecture). Sanetaka first lectured to Yoshifusa on *Genji* in
1514, and in 1520 sent him a precious text of *Genji* in exchange for 3,000
hiki,[10] plus a copy of a *Genji* genealogical chart and of the *Genji* commentary *Rōkashō*, lecture notes by Sōgi's disciple Botanka Shōhaku
(1443–1527) that had been supplemented by Sanetaka. In 1524 the *renga*
master Sōseki (1474–1533) arrived in Noto bearing three secret *Genji*
teachings from Sanetaka plus old commentaries, and by the end of the
same year Sanetaka had joined forces with Sōseki, Eikan, and Sōboku
(all *renga* masters who traveled back and forth to Noto at various times
on various errands) to produce a new copy of *Genji* in small characters
for Yoshifusa. The next year, Sanetaka requested a cover for this text in
the hand of Emperor Go-Kashiwabara, and he himself provided the
inscription for the box it was to be kept in. Concurrently, Yoshifusa
prepared a volume of questions about unclear points in *Genji* for Sanetaka to address. Yoshifusa's collection of *Genji*-related texts and commentaries came to be extensive and outstanding enough that the
courtier-scholar Konoe Taneie turned to Yoshifusa to borrow a copy of
the fourteenth-century *Genji* commentary *Kakaishō* against which to
collate his own, evidently believing Yoshifusa's to be of better quality
than the ones available to him in the capital. Yoshifusa also played a
role in the formation of *Sairyūshō*, a *Genji* commentary based on notes
taken by Sanetaka's son Kin'eda (1487–1563; a notable scholar in his
own right) on lectures by Sanetaka: Yoshifusa's having lost his copy of
the first version in a fire led Sanetaka and Kin'eda to compile a second,
revised version that went on to exert a great influence on subsequent
Genji scholarship.[11] Although meeting Yoshifusa's demands was clearly
a time-consuming endeavor for Sanetaka and his circle, it also brought
considerable benefits, even aside from the financial benefits of the generous gifts of cash that that Yoshifusa sent regularly.

---

10. Butler, *Emperor and Aristocracy*, pp. 29–32, discusses the difficulties with esti-
mating the value of currency in this period. According to the rough equivalents he
gives for the year 1500, Sanetaka's 3,000 hiki would have equaled roughly six koku of
rice, or enough to feed one person for six years.

11. Further details on these and other interactions can be found in Yonehara, *Sengoku bushi*, pp. 125–33.

3. Konoe Hisamichi (1472–1544), a member of one of the five regental houses who served as both regent and chancellor during his career, was another courtier involved in a variety of scholarly and literary activities with a diverse range of people. As a child, Hisamichi heard lectures by Ichijō Kaneyoshi at Nara, and in 1485 he made his own copy of *Ise mono-gatari gukenshō*. He copied Kaneyoshi's *Kokinshū hishō*, secret teachings related to the *Kokinshū*, for the emperor in 1490, and *Heike monogatari* for the same emperor in 1494. In 1497 and 1498, he heard lectures from Sōgi, sometimes with Sōgi's disciple Shōhaku present, on *Kokinshū*, *Ise monogatari*, *Hyakunin isshu* (One hundred poets, one poem each, early thirteenth century), and *Eiga no taigai*, culminating with his receiving the *kokin denju* from Sōgi, albeit in a less complete form than what Sōgi had transmitted to Sanjōnishi Sanetaka. In 1506 he made a copy of the *Shokugoshūishū* (Continued later collection of gleanings, 1326), the six-teenth of the twenty-one imperially commissioned poetry anthologies, for the shogun Ashikaga Yoshizumi. Starting in 1509 he began lecturing on the *Kokinshū* to other courtiers, sometimes transmitting *kirigami* (memoranda containing secret teachings). He commissioned Shōhaku to give lectures on *Genji monogatari* to an audience of courtiers, warriors, *renga* masters, and doctors in 1510, and the *renga* master Sōseki, another disciple of Sōgi, to do the same for his (Hisamichi's) son Tanemichi (1502–66), again with a mix of courtiers, warriors, and others in attendance. In the 1520s, he presented a copy of the *Kokinshū* to Imagawa Ujiteru, the (warrior) lord of the Suruga domain, and one of *Ise monogatari* to a scion of the Hosokawa warrior clan. He also received secret *Genji* teachings from Sōseki, and lectured on the *Kokinshū*, then transmitted the *kokin denju* to the *renga* master Insei for pay.[12] It is especially useful to consider Hisamichi's activities alongside Sanetaka's. As Kumakura Isao points out, Hisamichi was of higher rank than Sanetaka and in less straitened circumstances: he was able to compensate the *renga* masters he brought in to give lectures, something that Kumakura suggests would have been an extravagance for Sanetaka.[13] But even Hisamichi appears to have been

---

12. Information on Hisamichi extracted from Tsurusaki, "Chūsei kōki koten kenkyū," pp. 338–52, based on entries in Hisamichi's and his father's diaries.

13. Kumakura Isao, "Sanjōnishi Sanetaka, Takeno Jōō," p. 97. Kumakura also gives details about Sanetaka's finances, including amounts received from Hatakeyama Yoshi-ifusa (pp. 97–100).

willing to exploit his literary knowledge for remuneration, and clearly both men sought to be obliging to warriors, the chief power-holders in their world.[14]

4. A final telling example may be found in the movement from hand to hand of a single copy of a single text in this period. In the preface to *Ise monogatari ketsugishō*, Hosokawa Yūsai traces the transmission of the *Takeda-bon* text of *Ise monogatari* in Fujiwara no Teika's hand from Retired Emperor Go-Tsuchimikado (r. 1464–1500) to Retired Emperor Go-Nara (r. 1526–57), to Sanjōnishi Kin'eda, and then to, again, Hatakeyama Yoshifusa. Yoshifusa lost the text in a military disturbance, but it turned up subsequently in the hands of Asakura Norikage (1477–1555), of the warrior family that served as lords of Echizen (northern Fukui Prefecture), passing then to Takeda Nobutoyo (1549–82), warrior of Wakasa (southern Fukui), and to Miyoshi Nagayoshi (or Chōkei, 1522–64), a warrior who controlled the region around the capital and dominated shogunal politics after 1550. Sometime after Nagayoshi's death, the text was found in the town of Sakai (modern Osaka Prefecture) and came into the possession of Yūsai, at last returning to the central lineage of Nijō school scholars. Yūsai states in *Ketsugishō* that he believed this text to be the only one in Teika's hand to have survived to his day; unfortunately it too subsequently disappeared.[15]

Although the foregoing examples are not remotely exhaustive,[16] they should serve to hint at some of the new dynamics in play in scholarship and other forms of cultural production in the late medieval period. Men

---

14. Hisamichi also made a copy of *Kokinshū* for Hatakeyama Yoshifusa: Yoshifusa sent the paper upon which the text was to be inscribed along with the request in 1523 and received the finished product in 1528. He paid Hisamichi ten *ryō* of gold for the task. Yonehara, *Sengoku bushi*, pp. 138–39.

15. For the *Ketsugishō* passage that traces the transmission of the *Takeda-bon*, see Katagiri, *Ise monogatari no kenkyū: Shiryōhen*, p. 730. For other details about the transmission, particularly pertaining to Hatakeyama Yoshifusa, see Yonehara, *Sengoku bushi*, pp. 133–36.

16. Hundreds of pages detailing interactions like this may be seen just in Yonehara, *Sengoku bushi*, and the volumes of Inoue, *Chūsei kadanshi no kenkyū*. In English, see Carter, *Regent Redux* (particularly pp. 180–202) for Ichijō Kaneyoshi's interactions with warriors and *renga* masters; Horton, *Journal of Sōchō*, for examples of the interactions of Sōchō, yet another *renga* master disciple of Sōgi, with both warriors and courtiers; and the essays in Carter, *Literary Patronage*.

like Ōuchi Masahiro and Hatakeyama Yoshifusa clearly saw themselves not merely as eager students, but also as preservers of the classical literary tradition in their own right. Although warriors may in a sense have been the junior partners in this enterprise, dependent upon the expertise and cultural authority of courtiers and *renga* masters to advance their own literary studies, nonetheless the other groups' scholarly activities could not have been conducted as effectively without warriors' participation, given the pervasive, recurring upheaval in this period and the drastically weakened position of the imperial court. Warriors will all but disappear from the discussion below as the focus turns to the content of key *Ise monogatari* commentaries of the period, but it will be helpful to keep in mind the fact that ostensibly court-centered scholarly activities were being conducted with at least some consciousness of the powerful military men in the provinces who formed part of the audience and in large measure held the purse strings.

Ichijō Kaneyoshi and the Longing for Order

The career of Ichijō Kaneyoshi, whose *Ise monogatari gukenshō* is viewed as heralding the beginning of a new age of *Ise monogatari* commentaries, reveals the effects on scholarship of the slide into disorder that took place with the start of the Ōnin War in 1467. Kaneyoshi served three times as regent or chancellor, the highest position in the court bureaucracy, and was very highly esteemed in his time as a scholar, particularly sought after for his knowledge of *yūsoku kojitsu* (court ceremony and etiquette). His library, the best of his day, contained tens of thousands of books. As a poet he was not strictly affiliated with any of the major schools, but rather was on equally good terms with Reizei and Nijō school poets, and was in the unusual position of having access to secret teachings of both schools. Secret texts on the *Kokinshū* that he produced draw on both and add material from sources cited in neither, a mark both of his stature and of his independence of mind.[17] This ability of his to stand both inside and outside the system can perhaps be linked to the confident broad view he displays in producing his pathbreaking commentary on *Ise monogatari*.

---

17. Takei, "<Konton> no jidai," pp. 64–65. For an excellent biography of Kaneyoshi, from which the information given above is drawn, see Carter, *Regent Redux*.

Another factor was his deep interest in *Genji monogatari*. Although *Genji* had also provided fodder for some eccentric secret teachings,[18] mainstream *Genji* scholarship had long been more focused on textual scholarship, the seeking out of historical precedents and sources of allusion, and straightforward explication of poetry and difficult language. *Genji* scholarship had been conducted since the end of the eleventh century but took off in earnest following the collation of would-be authoritative texts by competing families of poet-scholars in the thirteenth century.[19] These new recensions, the *Aobyōshi-bon*, compiled by Fujiwara no Teika, and the *Kawachi-bon*, begun by Minamoto no Mitsuyuki (1163–1244) and completed by his son Chikayuki (d. 1277), and the studies that grew up around them, became a means by which scholars could attract the attention of emperors and higher-ranking nobles, whose lively interest in *Genji* led them to sponsor lectures, discussions, and debates. Though Teika's work was fairly narrowly focused on matters directly related to poetry, commentaries produced by the Kawachi contingent, which remained dominant through the end of the Kamakura period, included wide-ranging research into the trappings of the Heian period and possible historical bases for events and characters in the *monogatari*, in addition to explication of difficult words and passages. As

---

18. For example, secret Nijō school texts inform us that the Uma no kami in the rainy night discussion of the second chapter is Narihira (somewhat reasonable, in that Narihira held the same post and would have been highly qualified to take part in the discussion) and that the Shikibu no jō is Urashima Tarō. Details are also given about the missing "Kumogakure" chapter that supposedly depicted Genji's death—Genji turns out to have been killed by Koremitsu, who got in the way when the Rokujō lady's spirit was attempting to possess Genji and became the unwitting instrument of her ire. Meanwhile, the Reizei tradition offers a date for Genji's death: the fourteenth of the eighth month, 948, and notes that when Genji was in exile in Suma he had a chance to converse with Hitomaro, who was originally a woman but morphed into an old man at age forty-two. See Tsutsumi, *Genji monogatari chūshakushi no kisoteki kenkyū*, pp. 243–44.

19. According to the *Kōan Genji rongi* (1280), *Genji* scholarship began sometime during the reign of Emperor Horikawa (1086–1107), though no specific works from that time have survived. References are made elsewhere to views of Ōe no Masafusa (1041–1111), and Teika's *Okuiri* (ca. 1233) draws upon annotations from lost texts he used to compile the *Aobyōshi-bon*. Sesonji Koreyuki's (d. 1165) *Genji shaku* is the earliest surviving commentary. There also appears to have been considerable *Genji* activity surrounding Kenreimon'in. (Her lady-in-waiting, the well-known poet Kenreimon'in Ukyō no Daibu, was Koreyuki's daughter.) See Cook, "Genre Trouble," for an excellent overview of early *Genji* scholarship.

with commentaries on *Ise monogatari* and the *Kokinshū*, however, the fruits of these scholars' labors did not circulate freely; many of their interpretations were kept as closely guarded secrets, accessible only to select initiates, but widely enough known to shore up the prestige of the house as possessors of special knowledge.[20] Kaneyoshi relied heavily on these commentaries, as well as Yotsuji Yoshinari's *Kakaishō* (1367) to produce his own *Genji* commentary, *Kachō yojō* (1472), and they offered a highly developed alternative to the Old Commentaries on *Ise monogatari* as a precedent for commenting on prose fiction.

Ise monogatari gukenshō exists in two versions, the first written in 1460 when Kaneyoshi was still residing in his mansion in Kyoto, and the second, revised version written in 1474 after Kaneyoshi's home had burned down and he had gone as a refugee to live at Kōfukuji in Nara, where his son was an abbot. The colophon to the first of the two drafts reads:

> At the end of winter in the fourth year of Chōroku [1460], I opened and read this *monogatari*, and wrote out a little of that to which my foolish views were equal. All of it should be hidden at the bottom of a box, and not taken out beyond the threshold. The old man who lives in the Peach Blossom Mansion wrote this for his amusement.

The colophon is brief but gives us some important bits of information. Kaneyoshi is assuming a conventional, humble posture in characterizing his views as foolish; his statement that he writes for pleasure or amuse-

---

20. According to Iwatsubo Takeshi, these secrets were managed by means of clever use of parallel texts. For example, Yotsuji Yoshinari sometimes critiques old interpretations in his more widely circulating *Genji* commentary *Kakaishō* but reserves his own ideas for the parallel *Sankō hishō*; or he gives his own theory in *Kakaishō* but reserves the supporting evidence for *Sankō hishō* (sometimes with *Kakaishō* recording that a secret theory exists); or he puts decoy theories in *Kakaishō* and criticizes them in *Sankō hishō*, or other variations, all of which allow him to be fairly helpful to a reader of *Kakaishō* without giving away the whole game. Kaneyoshi's *Kachō yojō* and *Gengo hiketsu* are related in a similar way. Kawachi-ke affiliates, on the other hand, did not succeed in working out a similar system for themselves in the early stages (i.e., mid-thirteenth century). *Genchū saihishō* was a compilation of secret teachings simply extracted from the more widely circulating *Suigenshō*, which meant, of course, that the teachings were not really secret. Neither were they strictly proprietary—they included the insights of Mikohidari-ke affiliates and others. Later, however, Chikayuki's grandson Gyōa made revisions to *Genchū saihishō*, adding new interpretations, and changing old ones to increase its distance from other more freely circulating texts. See Iwatsubo, "Genji monogatari no nidankai denju ni tsuite."

ment (*fude no susabi*) is similar, though it does suggest that for him the production of a commentary on *Ise monogatari* was not necessarily the sort of almost compulsory act that it became for scholars who followed him, a function, perhaps, of the fact that up until his time the commentarial tradition consisted solely of the very idiosyncratic Old Commentaries. *Ise monogatari* had not yet become the target of what Richard Bowring calls "sober scholarship." Kaneyoshi's request that the commentary be kept hidden safely in a box may be a suggestion that he admits that his endeavor has some value after all or may simply be a continuation of the humble posture.

By the time the colophon of the second version was penned, in the first month of 1474, we find that the circumstances had changed drastically.

> In the last year of Chōroku [1460], after I opened and looked at this *monogatari*, I roughly investigated the errors of the old commentaries, and I wrote a little of the interpretations that came to me. The text in question gradually spread through the world at large. There must be a ring of copyists. After the disturbance in the capital, during the leisure of my retirement in the Southern Capital, again I collated it, but it is not without mistakes. In the same way as before, I dipped my old brush in ink and edited a separate commentary of my own views. It takes the style of "the handsome and elegant old man" [Narihira] to be essential, and also takes Lord Teika's superior explanations as a guide. Overall, the original intentions of old *monogatari* are not lost. . . . The old version was in one volume; now I have divided it in two. If interested parties wish to copy it, they should take this text alone to be the legitimate one.[21]

Now, with his home destroyed and his library looted,[22] he has a more urgent motive—preserving the literature of the past in a way that is

---

21. Katagiri, *Ise monogatari no kenkyū: Shiryōhen*, p. 587.

22. In a work titled (again) *Fude no susabi* 筆のすさび (Amusing myself with my brush), Kaneyoshi wrote of his escape from the capital and the devastation wrought on his home: "In the midst of all this was a hapless old man who had lived long in a place named for its peach blossoms. As his house was located on the border between the two armies, people warned him that he would not be able to stay on there, and so he locked up his weed-bound gate and left like all the rest, taking refuge for a time in a place near Ninth Avenue. When he looked back to the place he had left behind, he saw smoke rising above it, reducing it to a burned-over field. Thanks to its tiled roof and earthen walls, his library escaped the spreading flames, but soon thieves gathered there and, perhaps thinking that the place must contain great treasures, broke in and rifled

faithful to its original meaning. As "old *monogatari*" date from the Heian period, the time that Kaneyoshi's class and his ancestors were at the
height of power and magnificence, we can imagine the poignant nostalgia for those times that contributed to the project. Another indication of
the greater seriousness with which Kaneyoshi approached the second
version is the fact that the colophon is a formal production written in
classical Chinese, rather than the more casual vernacular colophon appended to the first draft. Note too, that despite Kaneyoshi's earlier instructions about keeping the text in a box, the first draft has already
slipped into circulation, and he is concerned with improving the text
and making it available to those who have copies of the older text in order to have corrections made. The two drafts do remain very similar in
scope and intentions, but in addition to correcting small errors, the second draft benefits from the research on *Genji monogatari* with which
Kaneyoshi had been occupied in the intervening years.[23]

The preface to *Ise monogatari gukenshō* gives vital information, directly and indirectly, about Kaneyoshi's project of reclaiming *Ise monogatari* as an object of conventional scholarship:

> Among commentaries on *Ise monogatari*, one called [*Waka*]*Chikenshū* is
> said to be by the major counselor Lord Tsunenobu.[24] It is not the case.
> Also, *Jikkan no shō* [Commentary in ten volumes] circulates widely in
> the world. We do not know whose work it is. In the teachings passed
> down in my family, they are thought of as great secrets. When I looked
> at them covertly, none of the Chinese and Japanese books that are cited
> in their traditions is genuine. Not only do they lose the true meaning of
> old *monogatari*, they cannot become an aid for [understanding] the flow-
> ers and leaves of language. Inexperienced students should never, ever
> trust them. There can be no doubt that they will lead to mistaken paths.
> Next, *Chikenshū* says that Narihira was a manifestation of Batō Kannon
> and that Ono no Komachi was a manifestation of Nyoirin Kannon. And
> everything else about [this text] is dubious too. I think it could be a forg-

---

through every one of the hundreds of boxes of manuscripts left behind, which they
tossed aside like high breakers scattering fish. In the end, there was left not a single
volume of the Chinese and Japanese documents preserved by the family for more than
ten generations. Thus, the old man was like an aging crane without a nest or a blind
man bereft of his cane." Translated by Carter, *Regent Redux*, p. 147.
23. Tanaka Sōsaku, *Ise monogatari kenkyūshi no kenkyū*, pp. 20–21.
24. An important poet who lived from 1016 to 1097.

ery by some amorous person of a later period who borrowed Lord Tsunenobu's name in order to make others partial to this path. If it were really by Tsunenobu, it is impossible that Lord Teika would not have seen it, but starting with Teika's discussion of the title, no mention of it appears. It is all very doubtful. Therefore, these commentaries should absolutely not be used as models.

Regarding the title of this *monogatari*, there is an explanation that [Lady] Ise wrote it. There is also an explanation that the Ariwara Middle Captain [Narihira] himself wrote of matters in his own life as though they were the things of the past. There is not yet any consensus on these two views. The Ninna emperor's imperial progress to Serikawa happened after Narihira's death. When you think about this, it is support for the idea that Ise wrote it. To support the idea that Narihira wrote it himself, some say that the title comes from the fact that the most important part of the story is when Narihira went as an imperial huntsman to Ise province and met the Ise priestess. Because of this there is a text where the matter of the imperial huntsman is placed at the beginning. This was Koreyuki's idea. Lord Teika's colophon says that it should not be used.

It goes without saying that the names of [some of] the women that Middle Captain Narihira visited naturally are given in the *monogatari*. And there are cases where their names are attached to their poems in the various imperial anthologies. However, in [*Ise*] commentaries of the recent past, their names appear in each case and this must be termed very suspicious. Even if they were alive at the same time, it is not to be expected that people far and wide would know of such secret activities. Needless to say, teachings that appear centuries later, guessing about what went on centuries before, are even less to be trusted, even if they are produced by famous sages.

One theory says that Narihira did not go to the East. They say that in this *monogatari* famous places in the East are substituted for Higashiyama [in the capital] or places close to the capital. This is an enormous mistake. The fact that Narihira went to the East is made clear in the *Kokinshū*, the *Gosenshū*, *Yamato monogatari*, and so on, and there should be no need for further evidence. In another theory, when distant places such as Michinoku are mentioned, Narihira did not go there, but wrote as if he composed poems on them. It is said that this follows the customs of fictional *monogatari*. It appears that there is sense to this theory.

Within the *monogatari* there are places where old poems from the *Man'yōshū* and such are included as they are. And in other cases the upper or lower half of the poem is replaced. This is done in order to approach present matters, and when [in China] the feudal lords held banquets for officers of state and composed poems, they said they were making new ones, but they sang the 300 poems of the past [from the *Shijing*], telling of their wishes. When old poems are recited in this *monogatari*, perhaps it is following this practice.

Ariwara no Narihira was the grandson of Emperor Heizei, and the fifth son of Fourth Rank Prince Abo. His mother was Princess Ito, the daughter of Emperor Kanmu. He was born in the eighth month of the second year of Tenchō [825]. His office advanced to Provisional Middle Captain of the Right Bodyguards and Provisional Governor of Mino province, and his rank to Junior Fourth Rank Upper Grade. He died on the 28th of the fifth month of the fourth year of Gangyō [880]. He was fifty-six years old.

In his biography in the national history it says, "Narihira was handsome and elegant in appearance, self-indulgent and unreserved, generally without aptitude for learning and composed Japanese poetry well." In [Ki no] Tsurayuki's preface to the *Kokinshū* it is written that "Ariwara no Narihira['s poetry] contains too much meaning in not enough words. It is like a withered flower whose color is gone but whose fragrance lingers." Now, looking at the poems in this *monogatari*, there are places where the meaning is thoroughly sufficient, and the words do not seem to go far enough. It is as the preface says. This is something that should be attended to carefully and appreciated.[25]

The opening of the preface leaves little doubt as to where Kaneyoshi stands on the Old Commentaries: they are of little value and should in his opinion be discarded, based, variously, on their use of spurious sources, their dubious provenance, their liberal interest in sexual matters, and the outlandish bent of such interpretations as those relying on identification of Narihira with the bodhisattva Kannon.

When Kaneyoshi moves on to questions of title and author, he relies heavily on the views Teika expressed in the colophon to the *Rufu-bon*— again, there is wavering between believing Lady Ise or Narihira to be the author, and a dismissal of the idea that the *monogatari* takes its name from Section 69. There is also the same omission of the old Rokujō family theory that the title comes from the saying, "People from Ise tell tales." Next he turns to issues that Teika never had to deal with, raised

---

25. Katagiri, *Ise monogatari no kenkyū: Shiryōhen*, pp. 505–7.

as they were by the Old Commentaries. Those commentaries held that, although the emperor sent Narihira into exile as a punishment for his behavior with the Nijō empress, one or the other of her close male relatives (different commentaries identify different men) took pity on him and allowed him to stay in hiding with them in or near the capital. The "Azumakudari" sections were then written only to give the impression that he had spent time in the eastern provinces.[26] Kaneyoshi seems willing to entertain the idea that the protagonist never traveled to Michinoku, in the far north of the main island of Japan, but in the case of the "Azumakudari" sections his faith in the reliability of Heian-period sources like the *Kokinshū* convinces him that the journey must have taken place. He concludes with citations of the earliest surviving references to Narihira—the *Sandai jitsuroku* obituary and Ki no Tsurayuki's famous comment in the *kana* preface to the *Kokinshū* on the qualities of Narihira's poetry—and it is these that inform his approach. As he says in the colophon, he wishes to capture the spirit of "the handsome and elegant old man" and asks the reader to savor the surfeit of meaning packed into the slight frame of his poetry rather than trying to figure out which woman is who, and so on.

Having dismissed the Old Commentaries in the preface, Kaneyoshi does not tangle with them in the commentary proper; he begins with a clean slate and devotes most of his attention to glossing difficult vocabulary or phrasing, explaining court customs, and, again, he sticks very close to authoritative texts of the past to support his conclusions. In some cases, as Aoki Shizuko has argued, it may be that he sticks too close.[27] The following, for example, is excerpted from his comment on Section 65, which describes the ill-fated relationship between a court lady and a young "man of the Ariwara clan."[28]

> In the past, there was a woman whom the emperor loved and had taken into his service, and who was allowed to wear the colors.

---

26. See Bowring, "*Ise Monogatari*," pp. 432–33, for details.
27. Aoki, "Ise monogatari kyūchūron jōsetsu," p. 45.
28. See Appendix 2 for a full translation of this section. Note, however, that while the appendix relies on modern scholarship on the *monogatari*, and attempts to render it in legible English as a convenience to the reader, the excerpts that appear as guide phrases in what is translated below are rendered to reflect the difficulties or ambiguities that attract the attention of the commentators.

This woman is Naishi no Suke Fujiwara no Naoiko. She was the cousin of the Somedono empress. Being allowed to wear the forbidden colors means that a court lady whom the emperor found appealing was allowed to wear colored robes with a figured pattern. . . .
At this time, the emperor heard of the affair and sent the man into exile.
Middle Captain Narihira's exile does not appear in the national histories. The text is exaggerating the emperor's slight disapproval. In one interpretation, [Narihira's] seclusion in Higashiyama is spoken of in this way.
He made the woman go to her cousin, his mother, who chastised her by shutting her up in a storehouse.
He made her go to the residence of the Somedono empress, and saying "shutting her up in a storehouse" means placing her in seclusion. A storehouse is a place where one stores objects. "Chastised" means to cause a person suffering.
Like the name of the creature/that lives amid the seaweed/that the fishermen reap/I cry that this is my fault/and I do not blame the world
This poem is by Naishi no Suke Fujiwara no Naoiko, in the fifteenth book of the *Kokinshū*.
Returned every night from the province
This means he came back from the place to which he had been exiled. If he had truly been exiled, he would not have been able to leave that province easily. By this we can know that the incident is made up.
It is because he probably thinks/that we can meet anyway/that it is so sad./He does not know/that I am here and yet not here
The woman recites this [poem] when she is shut up in the storehouse.
Although I went/in vain/only to return again/my desire to see her/lures me back again
This is an anonymous poem from the thirteenth book of the *Kokinshū*. Drawn on by wanting to see that person, he travels back and forth in vain.[29]

Kaneyoshi relies on the *Kokinshū*, which gives the author of one of the poems as the otherwise unknown Fujiwara no Naoiko, to identify the woman in the section, both where the poem appears and as the section opens. In many particulars, this section recalls the Nijō empress story

---

29. Katagiri, *Ise monogatari no kenkyū: Shiryōhen*, pp. 550–52.

as it was presented earlier in the *monogatari*—the mention of Emperor Seiwa, whom she served, and of the Somedono empress (the emperor's mother), who was her cousin, in an interpolated comment at the end of the section (there is no evidence to suggest that Fujiwara no Naoiko was also the Somedono empress's cousin); the unusually direct identification of "a man of the Ariwara clan" (who is, to say the least, self-indulgent and unrestrained); his disgrace and exile, recalling the "Azumakudari" sections; and her stint in a storehouse, recalling Section 6. However unimpeachable the justification for identifying the woman as Fujiwara no Naoiko, given the attribution of the same poem to her in the *Kokinshū*, doing so brushes these parallels aside and removes any opportunity to illuminate the self-referential manner in which *Ise monogatari* progresses. But such considerations seem not to have been of interest to Kaneyoshi. Steven D. Carter's comments on Kaneyoshi's treatment of Section 1 and Section 69 can safely be applied in the case of this section as well, and indeed, to *Ise monogatari gukenshō* as a whole: Kaneyoshi interprets *Ise monogatari* "as a rather straightforward document in court history . . . focusing entirely on the elucidation of customs and problematic expressions (accessible through clarifications gleaned in the commentator's reading of other court classics such as *Nihongi*, *Kokinshū*, and *The Tale of Genji*) and on historical events in the life of Ariwara no Narihira."[30] Although there is a conspicuous emphasis on *Ise monogatari*'s relationship to texts and writers in the poetic tradition, both within the commentary and when Kaneyoshi cites Tsurayuki and Teika in the preface, this too seems to be a matter of fixing the *monogatari* within a particular, specifically courtly, tradition. Kaneyoshi does not generally have much to say about *Ise*'s poetry as poetry, as the sample from Section 65 suggests. Quite unlike the commentators who followed him, he does not tender evaluations of the poetry, examine how the language and rhetorical features produce literary or emotional effects, or suggest how a poet might use the exemplars provided by *Ise monogatari* in his or her own poetic practice. His concern when he comments on poems, beyond identifying the anthologies in which they appear, is in paraphrasing them to make them intelligible

---

30. Carter, "Claiming the Past for the Present," p. 109. Carter also gives a full translation of the commentary on Section 1 on pp. 105–8, and on Section 69 on pp. 109–13.

within the narrative, clarifying who speaks them and how they relate to the situations described in the surrounding prose, an approach that is characteristic of his work on *Genji* as well.

In any case, despite the relatively narrow purview of *Ise monogatari gukenshō*, its repudiation of the methods of the Old Commentaries in favor of the sort of straightforward scholarship that had long been conducted on other works constitutes an important moment in the history of scholarship on *Ise monogatari*. Although the approach of the scholars who followed Kaneyoshi was, as I will show below, shaped by a somewhat different set of concerns, Kaneyoshi's commentary is cited frequently and respectfully by all of them, even when they dissent, as a source of highly reliable information on relevant court customs, difficult language, and other details. Although the break with past interpretations was to be less complete among subsequent commentators, their basic style and approach have enough in common with Kaneyoshi's that his work can quite justifiably be said to have ushered in a new age of commentary on *Ise monogatari*.

Methods and Morals: Sōgi and the Sanjōnishi Family

The most important Transitional Commentaries written between Ichijō Kaneyoshi's *Ise monogatari gukenshō* and the end of the sixteenth century derive from lectures given by the *renga* master Sōgi, the courtier Sanjōnishi Sanetaka, and Sanetaka's heirs to various disciples. The approximate relations among the major players in this period are laid out in figure 3.1. A single-line arrow indicates a lecture or other exchange of information, while the double-line arrows trace the transmission of the main lineage of the *kokin denju*.[31] Kaneyoshi did not formally transmit anything to Sōgi (indeed, there are no records of any lectures by him on *Ise monogatari* at all, though he is known to have lectured on *Genji monogatari*, the *Kokinshū*, and the *Nihon shoki*), but the two came to be on good terms from the 1470s, at which point Sōgi began mediating transactions with warriors in the provinces on behalf of the aged Kaneyoshi.

---

31. In addition to this lineage (the Sanjōnishi-ke *denju*), there were separate lines that passed through Botanka Shōhaku to various *renga* masters (the Sakai *denju*) and through the courtier Konoe Hisamichi to his heirs and other courtiers (the Konoe-ke *denju*).

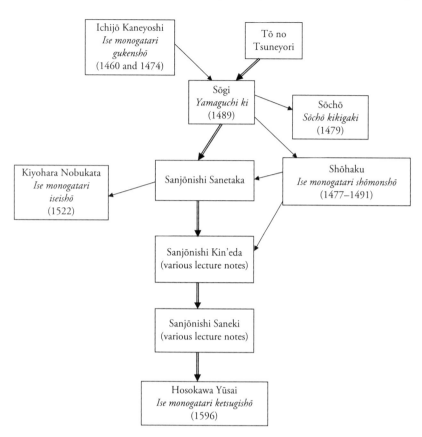

Fig. 3.1 Major *Ise monogatari* Transitional Commentaries: authors and influences, 1460–1596

The most important of the commentaries to come out of Sōgi's activities was *Ise monogatari shōmonshō* (Shōhaku's notes on *Ise monogatari*), notes on lectures that Sōgi gave between 1477 and 1491, taken down by the *renga* master Shōhaku, who was his disciple. Sōgi's own *Yamaguchi ki* (Yamaguchi record, 1489; also referred to as *Sōgi chū*, "Sōgi's notes") deals only with *Ise monogatari*'s poetry and was produced at the request of the warlord Ōuchi Masahiro for the sake of his daughter, but *Shōmonshō* was a more formal production, certified by Sōgi himself, and widely quoted in subsequent commentaries. However, the textual history of *Shōmonshō* is exceedingly complex; Shōhaku revised the text repeatedly in consultation with Sōgi, and there are three main textual lineages, dating from 1477, 1480, and 1491, each with slightly different content.[32]

Sōgi, Shōhaku, and Sōchō, another of Sōgi's disciples who produced a commentary from Sōgi's lectures, all lectured to and otherwise interacted with Sanjōnishi Sanetaka, and Shōhaku went on to interact with Sanetaka's son Kin'eda as well. The major Sanetaka-related commentary, *Ise monogatari iseishō* (Pure thoughts commentary on *Ise monogatari*), derives from notes taken by Kiyohara Nobukata (1475–1550) on lectures Sanetaka gave in 1522. Sanetaka's interpretations of *Ise monogatari* also passed through his son Kin'eda and on to Kin'eda's son Saneki (also known as Sanezumi, 1511–79). Kin'eda's and Saneki's interpretations survive in lecture notes, the latter's most notably in those used by the warrior, poet, and scholar Hosokawa Yūsai to produce *Ise monogatari ketsugishō* in 1596. *Ketsugishō*, which went on to become the dominant Transitional Commentary in the Tokugawa period, also draws very heavily on *Gukenshō*, *Shōmonshō*, and *Iseishō*, the last being particularly prominent owing not only to its close connection to Sanetaka but also to the fact that Kiyohara Nobukata was Yūsai's maternal grandfather. In short, although each of these commentaries has distinctive qualities, the interrelations among them and interpretations put forth in them are exceedingly close. Therefore, for the sake of simplicity, in what follows I will draw principally on *Shōmonshō* as representative of Sōgi's approach and interpretations, and on *Ketsugishō* as representative of the Sanjōnishi family's.

Given that these commentaries grew out of the activities of a group of professional poets plying their trade, it is unsurprising that they devote significantly more attention to *Ise monogatari*'s poetry than Kaneyoshi had done. Consider, for example, *Ise monogatari shōmonshō*'s treatment of the poem in Section 2:

oki mo sezu	After a night that I spent
ne mo sede yoru o	neither awake
akashite wa	nor yet asleep,
haru no mono tote	I spend the day gazing gloomily at the rain
nagamekurashitsu	thinking, "a thing of spring"

---

32. See Ōtsu, *Ise monogatari kochūshaku no kenkyū*, pp. 216–45, for details.

The meaning is simply that he spent a night without being awake and without sleeping, and during the day, again, as is customary in spring, he was in a state of melancholy reverie all day. The meaning that it rained all day is also contained in the word *nagame*. This is the manner of Narihira's poetry. One should consider that the words preceding the poem[33] are well devised. There are unlimited overtones.[34]

Kaneyoshi had written,

Nagame means "long rains" and also "melancholy reverie." It is attached forcibly to *nagamekurashitsu*.[35] Because the rains of spring are something that fall for a long time and become tedious, it says "a thing of spring." This poem is included in book thirteen of the *Kokinshū*, a book of love poetry. It is Narihira's poem.[36]

Kaneyoshi's comments are rather prosaic compared to Sōgi's, limited to the denotation of the words of the poem and its source, whereas Sōgi's, telegraphic though they are, reveal concern with literary qualities, considering the effects of the poem (its "unlimited overtones"), how it relates to the preceding prose context, and the fact that the poem is characteristic of Narihira. *Shōmonshō's* treatment of the same portions of Section 65 discussed above show further noteworthy differences:

In the past, there was a woman whom the emperor thought of.
"The emperor" refers to Emperor Seiwa. "Thought of" means he loved and favored her.
Permitted to wear the colors
It is said that this means someone who has attained the third rank, etc. This person is the Nijō empress. [Kaneyoshi]'s explanation is that it means being allowed to wear the figured robes of a middle-ranking court lady . . .
Shut up in a storehouse
Perhaps a secluded place. "Chastised" means to remonstrate.

---

33. See Appendix 2 for a full translation.
34. Katagiri, *Ise monogatari no kenkyū: Shiryōhen*, p. 594.
35. By "forcibly," perhaps Kaneyoshi means that although *nagamekurashitsu*, meaning "spend the day gazing," is unproblematic, to attach the noun *nagame*, meaning "long rains," to the verb *kurasu* is not grammatically sound.
36. Katagiri, *Ise monogatari no kenkyū: Shiryōhen*, p. 510.

Like the name of the creature/that lives amid the seaweed/that the fishermen reap

The first half of the poem is a poetic preface.[37] The meaningful part of it is "I cry that this is my fault/and I do not blame the world." The place where it says "from me" [my fault] is vitally important to the Way. Where it says "from me," if you think about it, truly there is no reason to think others or society are to blame. Not blaming anyone else is the height of harmony (*wa*). Harmony is the mediator that governs society and oneself. This poem is something people should think about.[38] That this woman thinks back over her own heart and composes that she will not blame the world is a very rare thing.

The man [returned] from the provinces

This again is a fictional story. In our school's interpretation it is decided that he was exiled, but this occurred when he was still in the capital. Because places of exile are established, it says "in the provinces." The interpretation of the Old Commentaries is incorrect.[39]

He sang movingly

He must be singing aloud.

It is because he no doubt thinks[40]

The meaning [of this poem] is that she laments the fact that Narihira probably thinks they can meet, while she herself is not there. It is truly a deeply moving condition.

---

37. I.e., a *jokotoba*, an introductory phrase that is linked to the rest of the poem via wordplay or repetition of sounds.

38. The version of *Shōmonshō* in Takeoka, *Ise monogatari zenhyōshaku*, has this as something poets, rather than people in general, should think about (p. 969). Judging from the colophon (p. 1573), Takeoka's *Shōmonshō* is based on the *Saga-bon* version, collated by Nakanoin Michikatsu in 1609, which, according to Ōtsu, follows the 1477 version of the text (Ōtsu, *Ise monogatari kochūshaku no kenkyū*, p. 230). Katagiri's *Shōmonshō*, meanwhile, is a 1607 manuscript copy of the 1481 version (Katagiri, *Ise monogatari no kenkyū: Shiryōhen*, p. 590).

39. The Old Commentaries claim here, too, that Narihira hid in Higashiyama in the capital rather than going into exile. See *Reizei-ke-ryū Ise monogatari shō*, in Katagiri, *Ise monogatari no kenkyū: Shiryōhen*, p. 360.

40. A line from one of the poems in the section. A literal translation of the full poem might run:

sari to mo to	It is because he probably thinks
omou ramu koso	"Even so"
kanashikere	that it is so sad.
aru ni mo aranu	He does not know
mi o shirazu shite	that I am here yet not here.

Although I went/in vain/only to return again
The meaning is clear. This poem is said to be by Hitomaro.[41] Narihira
applies it to himself and sings it.
In the time of the Mizuno-o emperor
This is Emperor Seiwa. It is said that he secluded himself from the
world at Mizuno-o in Tamba (or Yamaguchi?), etc.[42] There is now a
shrine to him in that place.[43]

Note first that Sōgi ignores *Kokinshū's* attribution of the *"ama no kara"*
poem to Fujiwara no Naoiko and identifies the woman as the Nijō empress. Where Kaneyoshi had identified only references to the man's exile
as a "made up thing" (*tsukurigoto*), Sōgi appears to view the entire section as a "fictional story" (*tsukuri monogatari*); thus there is no need to
have the identity of the woman conform to the *Kokinshū*, and perhaps
the Nijō empress herself can be taken as a fictionalized character here.
Also, where Kaneyoshi had offered the Old Commentaries' view of
Narihira's exile as merely "one interpretation," without commenting on
its legitimacy, Sōgi is more emphatic in his assertion of "our school's"
view and his rejection of the Old Commentaries' Higashiyama theory.
There is still some need for fudging—there is no province that was
designated as a place of exile in the Heian period from which it would
have been possible for the man to return every night to sing to the
woman, and thus Sōgi states that the incident takes place before
the man's exile to the East, while he is still in the capital, reconciling
the disjunctions among the interpretation, historical plausibility, and
what the text actually says with reference to the section's status as fiction. Finally, as before, the treatment of the poems is far more detailed
(Kaneyoshi does not discuss the woman's second poem from the storehouse at all), delving into poetic techniques ("the first lines are a poetic
preface"), emotional effects ("deeply moving"), and even ethical lessons (the passage about harmony), as well as offering an explanation of
the fact that an anonymous poem from the *Kokinshū* is placed in Narihira's mouth.

---

41. This poem is attributed to Hitomaro in *Kokinwaka rokujō*.
42. Katagiri has inserted the words in parentheses from the text of *Shōmonshō*
held by the Imperial Household Agency. Katagiri, *Ise monogatari no kenkyū:
Shiryōhen*, p. 590.
43. Ibid., pp. 624–25.

Ise monogatari ketsugishō's comments on the same passages will serve to illustrate some characteristics of Hosokawa Yūsai's and the Sanjōnishi family's approach.

In the past, there was a woman whom the emperor thought of, and who was permitted colors . . .
Whom the emperor thought of. This is a woman who served Emperor Seiwa and received his favor. *Permitted colors* means she was permitted the forbidden colors. There is a thing called "The Imperial Command about Forbidden Colors." A woman who is permitted colors wears figured robes. *Kinpishō* says that daughters or granddaughters of ministers of state are permitted colors, etc. . . .
At this time, the emperor heard of the affair and sent the man into exile. He made the woman go to her cousin, his mother, who chastised her by shutting her up in a storehouse.
At this time. It was when this was going on that Narihira's exile occurred. The exile does not appear in the national histories. This section is also a fictional story. Perhaps some terrible punishment is given as "sent him into exile"? This distinction also appears in *Gukenshō*. The woman's cousin and the emperor's mother is the Somedono empress. *Made the woman go.* It says that the woman was made to go [to her cousin], but according to one interpretation, previously, because she was distressed [by the man's pursuit of her], she goes back to her family home. This appears to be Lord Nagara's place.[44] Because it says Narihira thought, "If this is the case, it's even more convenient," and visited her at home, [the alternate reading] says she must have been made to leave Lord Nagara's home. I say: because the text goes on to say "The emperor was a handsome man, and when the woman heard him chanting the Buddha's name with great devotion in a noble voice, she wept bitterly," should it not be taken to mean that she returned to the palace? Then, when it says, "she was made to go," her comings and goings would be like this,[45] wouldn't they? *Shut up in the storehouse* must mean she was shut into a *nurigome* [a room divided off from the main room and enclosed, used as a sleeping chamber or a storage room]. *Chastised* means remonstrance.
Like the name of the creature/that lives amid the seaweed/that the fishermen reap/I cry that this is my fault/and I do not blame the world.

---

44. The Nijō empress's father.
45. I.e., she would have returned to court from her father's place, and then been sent to her cousin's.

In *Kokinshū*, Naishi no Suke Naoiko is given as the author. In this collection there are [other] circumstances. This is written as a fictional story. *Like the name of the creature that lives amid the seaweed the fishermen reap.* The first two lines of the poem are a poetic preface. This is [included] in order to say *warekara*, "from myself" and not the fault of others. If one knows this truth, there is no reason to blame other people or society. Not resenting people is the height of harmony. Harmony is the foundation that governs the world and preserves oneself. That this woman thinks back on her own heart and composes that she will not resent the world is a very rare thing.[46] This poem cannot have been composed by the Nijō empress at this time.[47] When she cried like this, the man, who returned every night from the province to which he had been exiled, played his flute very cheerfully, and sang movingly in an elegant voice. Thus the woman, though shut up in the storehouse, could hear that he was there, but they were unable to meet.

Earlier in this section it said he was sent into exile, and this shows the outcome. It sounds as though he went to a nearby province rather than a distant one. Alternately, Narihira was not exiled to any province, but rather hid at the edge of the capital and put up a front of being an exile, and thus it says he returned from the provinces every night. This is the form of a fictional story. Using the appearance that Narihira went to the provinces is an interpretation that values the way of the sovereign. In the headnotes of the imperial poetry collections, etc., it also says that he went to the provinces. . . .

It is because he probably thinks/"Even so,"/that it is sad/He does not know/that I am here and yet not here.

This is a poem that the woman composes while shut up in the storehouse. Its meaning is that Narihira probably thinks that they can meet anyway, while she herself is in a state of being in this world, yet not in it.

As for the man, because he could not meet her, he wandered about in this way, and went back to the provinces, singing this: Although I went/in vain/only to return again/my desire to see her/lures me back repeatedly.

---

46. *Iseishō* has similar content here, stating that the poem should be "held in the hearts of those who would compose poetry," but Yūsai appears to have preferred *Shōmonshō*'s wording.

47. The rationale for this intriguing statement is unclear.

The meaning is clear. This is given as an anonymous poem in the thirteenth book of the *Kokinshū*. However, it is Hitomaro's poem. Perhaps Narihira sang it simply because it was the same as his feelings at the time. He is singing out loud. This must have been during the reign of Emperor Seiwa. The mother of the emperor was the Somedono empress. Or she might have been the Gojō empress.

Here *Ketsugishō* gives a diagram showing the relationships among the three empresses (Gojō, Somedono, and Nijō)[48] and continues:

There is doubt about this note. The Gojō empress is Junshi. The Somedono empress is Meishi, as can be seen in the diagram. Further thought is needed. The Mizuno-o emperor is Emperor Seiwa. Because this emperor was devoted to the Three Jewels [Buddhism], it is said that he secluded himself in a place called Mizuno-o in Yamashiro province. There is now a shrine to him in that place.

Yūsai's commentary is vastly more detailed than those that came earlier, spelling everything out thoroughly in a way that makes the commentary much easier on a reader. One reason for this is that whereas *Shōmonshō* and *Iseishō* were simply certified lecture notes, Yūsai combined material from Saneki's lectures with a perusal of older commentaries in order to produce a text from which he could himself lecture to Prince Toshihito.[49] *Ketsugishō* is thus as much (or more) a writing project as it an im-

48. See Appendix 1 for a more extensive family tree containing the same information.

49. Yūsai explains the full circumstances in his colophon: "Regarding the commentary on this *monogatari*, though I have planned it for some years, I was busy with affairs in the capital and the provinces, and time passed pointlessly. But recently, having several times humbly received the august command of the emperor to lecture to Prince Hachijō [Toshihito] . . . , I looked things up in my notes from lectures the Sankōin Palace Minister [Sanjōnishi Saneki] gave in the past at Nagaoka, where he had family property. Because his command on that occasion was for me to distinguish between the excesses and insufficiencies of *Iseishō*, from the lectures my maternal grandfather, Kansuiken Sōyū [Kiyohara Nobukata], heard given by Shōyōin [Sanetaka], with my foolish wits I pulled them together and marked them. Well, people like Kei'un'in, Daikakuji Junkyō Gishun, Seigoin Junkyō Dosō [members of the aristocratic Konoe family], and extending even to Sōyō, Satomura Jōha [commoner poets], and others besides, were summoned to listen, and, bringing together the various commentaries like *Gukenshō*, *Shōmonshō*, etc., according to [Saneki's] explanations, I made selections for this commentary. In *The Analects* it says 'Hear much and put aside what you are in doubt of, speaking cautiously of the rest, and you will seldom have

mediate record of lectures. Because Yūsai tends to lift things from the other commentaries verbatim, it becomes very easy to see how he wove the three strands of earlier commentary (Kaneyoshi's comments, Sōgi's comments via Shōhaku, and Sanetaka's comments via Nobukata) together, even though he is not conscientious about citing them by name. Much of what remains when the content of these three commentaries is subtracted can be assumed to derive from Saneki's lectures; if Yūsai is giving his own opinion, he marks it clearly, as in the discussion of the Nijō empress's peregrinations. In that case, as elsewhere, Yūsai devotes somewhat more effort to making sense of the broader flow of the narrative, rather than confining himself to the line immediately under discussion. He adds very little that is new to the discussion of the poems in this section, looking back to Sōgi for most of that content, and like Sōgi, he relies on the idea that the section is a "fictional story" to make sense of its contradictions.

The prefaces to these commentaries give further insights into fact-versus-fiction questions as well as how the commentaries operate generally. The following is the preface to *Ise monogatari shōmonshō*:

> In the old commentaries, it says that this *monogatari* is called *Ise* because it is stories about men and women. The reason for this is that the two characters "i-se" can be read as "male" and "female." They construct other interpretations from this. Our school does not use them.
>
> There is an idea that it is called *Ise* because the part when Narihira went to Ise province as an imperial huntsman and met with the Ise priestess is the heart of the *monogatari*. Therefore, it has this name. There is a text where people who believed this placed that story at the beginning. Lord Teika refuted it. In general, the views of the people of the past do not agree about the author of this *monogatari*. Some say that Narihira wrote it himself; in some, we see the statement that the woman named Ise wrote it. Therefore, in Lord Teika's colophon he says the matter is difficult to decide. However, because he says, "If it is not her work, why is it called *Ise*?," his feeling also seems to be that Ise wrote it, and it appears that her name was made the title of the *monogatari*. Because this is the case, our school uses this interpretation.

---

errors.' Therefore, I have given this commentary the name *Ketsugishō* [Doubting commentary]. Will its substance be excessive or insufficient?"(Katagiri, *Ise monogatari no kenkyū: Shiryōhen*, p. 866.)

Even if it is taken to be Ise's work, there is an interpretation that she presented it to Emperor Uda.[50] Our school does not use this interpretation. Ultimately, we should view this as a fictional *monogatari* [*tsukuri monogatari*]. However, it is not like *Genji monogatari*. Within it, words that Narihira wrote himself must be included. Along with the things written about Narihira's life, there are places with a few old poems and such mixed in: all of these are in the method of fictional *monogatari*. The idea that it is a fictional *monogatari* also appears in Ichijō Zenkō [Kaneyoshi]'s commentary. Also, there are sections that tell of things that happened after Narihira's death.[51]

Note first the great consciousness of being part of a school and unquestioning respect for the transmitted teachings, not subjecting those opinions to much scrutiny or supporting them with evidence. The line "our school uses this interpretation" appears scores of times throughout *Shōmonshō* and is taken to be adequate justification for whatever idea is put forth. Second, we see the same return to Teika that marked *Ise monogatari gukenshō*—use of his recension, close examination of his colophons for hints about title, author, etc.—leading this time to the conclusion that Lady Ise had a hand in writing *Ise monogatari* and that this is the source of the title. Teika, of course, had refrained from coming down firmly on Ise's side, but here a pronouncement is made, based not on any new evidence but rather, it seems, on the desire to have a straightforward distinguishing teaching to transmit. The prefaces to *Iseishō* and *Ketsugishō* offer line-by-line commentary on Teika's colophons and place great emphasis on Teika's comment "One should just appreciate the flowers of language and leaves of words," in the *Takeda-bon* colophon, saying that it is "vital to the Way [of Poetry]. This teaching tells us to pay attention to the interesting places in the words and the style, and rely on them for composition."[52] All of these commentators also relied on Teika's *Kenchū mikkan*, his subcommentary on Kenshō's commentary on *Kokinshū*, for interpretations of poems that appear in both *Ise monogatari* and the *Kokinshū*.[53]

The preface to *Shōmonshō* also demonstrates a clear consciousness of *Ise monogatari* as at least partly fictional, a position that neatly disposes

---

50. This refers to *Reizei-ke-ryū Ise monogatari shō*.
51. Katagiri, *Ise monogatari no kenkyū: Shiryōhen*, p. 591.
52. Ibid., p. 731.
53. Ōtsu, *Ise monogatari kochūshaku*, p. 102.

of chronological and other internal contradictions. Although it is described as a *tsukuri monogatari*, it is treated as a hybrid, distinguished from *Genji* in that it tells of some factual things as though they are fiction. *Ketsugishō*, relying partly on *Iseishō*, elaborates on the last section of *Shōmonshō*'s preface as follows:

> According to one explanation, Ise wrote it for the Shichijō empress.[54] We do not use the interpretation that she gave it to Emperor Uda. Ise served the Shichijō empress. She was a person who was very familiar with matters pertaining to Narihira. We should understand that she had something written by Narihira himself, added words to it and made a fictional *monogatari* [*tsukuri monogatari*] of it for the empress. However, it is not a completely fictional *monogatari* like the *Genji monogatari*. It is the life of Narihira rewritten, with old poems and other things added to it. Finally, we settle on this interpretation. In [Teika's] *Eiga no taigai* too, it says that one should learn the *Kokinshū*, *Ise monogatari*, the *Gosenshū* and the *Shūishū*. Because *Ise monogatari* is placed after the *Kokinshū*, and then comes *Gosenshū*, it is natural that we should appreciate it. Therefore in the Nijō school's secret teachings of the *Sandaishū*[55] it says that one should read *Ise monogatari* first. *Genji monogatari* is fiction (*kyo*) written as fact (*jitsu*). This *monogatari* is fact made into fiction. Nonetheless, because fiction is taken as fact in biased interpretations, mistaken interpretations arise. If one takes fact as fact, and views fiction as fiction, there will be no mistakes. This is the orally transmitted teaching regarding this *monogatari*. Things that happened during the span of Narihira's life are written here, and the places that have old poems and things added are the usual way of fictional *monogatari*.[56]

The intrusion of the passage about *Eiga no taigai* into the middle of a discussion of *Ise monogatari*'s fictionality (which, as always, is closely bound up with the question of who wrote it and how it is related to Narihira) appears a little out of place, but perhaps it can be taken to indicate that questions of fact and fiction are as central to the Nijō school's teachings as the order in which canonical texts should be studied in the

---

54. Fujiwara no Onshi, consort of Emperor Uda.
55. I.e., the first three of the twenty-one imperially commissioned poetry anthologies: *Kokinshū*, *Gosenshū*, and *Shūishū*.
56. Katagiri, *Ise monogatari no kenkyū: Shiryōhen*, p. 731.

school's curriculum. Yūsai's statement about the oral transmission—the need to take fact as fact and fiction as fiction—may initially sound almost too circular to be useful, but it too serves as a red flag as one enters the commentary proper. And indeed, it turns out that when one examines any of these commentaries—*Shōmonshō*, *Iseishō*, and *Ketsugishō*—beyond their prefaces, one finds decided idiosyncrasies in their identifications of the various sections as fact or fiction—idiosyncrasies that are more often than not tied up with poetic and moral considerations rather than strictly historical ones.

In the majority of cases, when the Transitional Commentaries encounter a woman whom the Old Commentaries identify as one of Narihira's twelve favorite lovers, the Transitional Commentaries inform us that the woman is "no one in particular" (*dare to mo nashi*), or ignore the matter entirely. For example, of the eighty-eight sections where *Reizei-ke-ryū Ise monogatari shō* identifies a woman,[57] *Shōmonshō*'s, *Iseishō*'s, and *Ketsugishō*'s readings break down as shown in table 3.1.[58] "General comments" include cases where a commentary says, for example, "This woman must be someone of higher rank than Narihira" while declining to specify further. The fact that *Iseishō* and *Ketsugishō* pass over the majority of the Old Commentaries' identifications in silence, while Sōgi comments on a full third, suggests that Sōgi was far more concerned with establishing the views of the Nijō school vis-à-vis those of the Reizei school, and possibly that the effort had been successful enough that by the time *Iseishō* and *Ketsugishō* were compiled (1522 and 1596, respectively) there was less need for overt combativeness in the direction of the Reizei views.

Section 65 has already provided one example of a section identified as a "fictional story." The others in this set include Sections 12, 14, 36, 73, and 115 for *Shōmonshō*, with *Ketsugishō* adding Sections 74 and 76 to those five, and *Iseishō* using the term only in relation to Sections 36 and 76. A perusal of these sections reveals that the term is used in cases where the featured poem is from the *Man'yōshū* (Sections 14, 36, 73, and 74), or

---

57. The remaining thirty-seven sections describe interactions solely among men, show the poet composing a poem to himself, or are ambiguous as to the sex of the man's correspondent.

58. Note that the figures for *Shōmonshō* add up to more than eighty-eight because *Shōmonshō* occasionally makes note of multiple interpretations.

Table 3.1 Transitional Commentaries' responses to Old Commentaries' character identifications

	Shōmonshō	Iseishō	Ketsugishō
No mention	30	67	54
"No one in particular" or rejection of Reizei school identification	30	2	8
General comment	8	4	3
Fictional story	6	2	8
Identification accepted	18	13	15

attributed to another poet or an anonymous poet in the *Kokinshū* (Sections 12, 65, and 115). The term is by no means applied in all cases where the poem cannot be linked to Narihira, but this breakdown gives some indication of what the term meant to these commentators in practice. Its use is particularly prominent in sections that are more than usually outrageous or that contain an especially intractable historical discrepancy,[59] but in most cases the designation comes down to a consideration of the source of the poem. Although the *Shōmonshō* and *Ketsugishō* prefaces seem initially to be setting up the unequivocally fictional *Genji monogatari* as a paradigmatic *tsukuri monogatari*, clearly the statements about "old poems and things added" are closer to the heart of the definition for Sōgi and Yūsai (or Sanjōnishi Saneki). The prefaces suggest that it is the terms *kyo* (falsehood) and *jitsu* (truth) that are more closely linked to absolute fictionality (i.e., something that is made up from whole cloth)

---

59. Of Section 12, for example, where the man is seen abducting a woman in Musashi province and being arrested by the provincial governor, Sōgi says, "This section in particular is a *tsukuri monogatari*." Section 14 depicts the man sleeping with an absurdly rustic woman who composes a slightly altered poem from *Man'yōshū*. Section 115 shows the man bidding farewell to a woman in Michinoku, who responds with a poem by Ono no Komachi. Section 76, meanwhile, includes a poem attributed to Narihira in the *Kokinshū* and addressed to the Nijō empress at the time when she was known as the Mother of the Crown Prince (according to both *Ise* and the *Kokinshū* headnote), but is deemed a *tsukuri monogatari* because Narihira did not yet hold the position in the Imperial Guards that serves to identify him in *Ise* when the Nijō empress was known by that designation. *Ketsugishō* says, "Since this is a *tsukuri monogatari*, anything might be written." (Sōgi also points out the discrepancy but does not use the term *tsukuri monogatari*. Perhaps he had a stricter sense of its application?)

whereas *tsukuri monogatari* often implies a recasting of existing materials.

But it is in the character identifications made by Sōgi, Sanetaka, and Saneki that we find the most conspicuous, and ultimately revealing, idiosyncrasies. As shown in table 3.2, identifications are made of six of the Old Commentaries' twelve lovers: the Nijō empress, the Ise priestess, Aritsune's daughter, Narihira's sister, Narihira's niece, and in one case, Ono no Komachi. In most instances, these identifications are based on evidence offered in the text—in the interpolated notes following the sections, directly in the main part of the prose, or based on links among the sections, such as references to a mansion in the Fifth Ward that occur several times in connection with the Nijō empress—and in all instances they match the identifications made in the *Reizei-ke-ryū Ise monogatari shō*. Where there is no clear justification for making an identification, however, the logic is quite different from that of the Old Commentaries. Section 23 is a case in point. This section begins,

> In the past, a boy and a girl whose parents made their living in the country-side used to go out to the foot of the well to play together, but when they grew up, they became shy of each other. Nonetheless, the boy thought he would win this girl, and the girl continued to have tender feelings toward the boy—though her parents tried to marry her to another, she would not hear of it.

Kaneyoshi had looked at this section and concluded that the story was not even about Narihira, because the boy and girl are described as "children of people who made their living in the country." Even the *Wakachikenshū* had taken this view. The *Reizei-ke-ryū Ise monogatari shō*, meanwhile, names the woman as Ki no Aritsune's daughter, a woman whom the *Kokinshū* identifies as Narihira's wife. In typical fashion, *Reizei-ke-ryū Ise monogatari shō*'s support for the identification derives from a spurious source that confirms Narihira's initiating conjugal relations with the girl when he was five years old.[60] Sōgi, Sanetaka, and Saneki make the same identification, and, perhaps conscious of the extent to which this breaks with normal procedures, offer a justification. "We name this woman as Ki no Aritsune's daughter in order to make known the honor of being a chaste woman." But in Section 19, which is

---

60. Katagiri, *Ise monogatari no kenkyū: Shiryōhen*, p. 332.

Table 3.2 Character identifications in selected commentaries

Section	*Reizei-ke-ryū shō*	*Shōmonshō*	*Iseishō*	*Ketsugishō*	Source of identification
3	Nijō empress	Nijō empress	Nijō empress	Nijō empress	Interpolated note
4	Nijō empress	Nijō empress	No mention	Nijō empress	Mention of Fifth Ward
5	Nijō empress	Nijō empress	Nijō empress	Nijō empress	Interpolated note
6	Nijō empress	Nijō empress	Nijō empress	Nijō empress	Interpolated note
18	Ono no Komachi	Ono no Komachi	No one in particular	No one in particular	
19	Aritsune's daughter	(In *Kokinshū*, Aritsune's daughter)	No mention	No mention	
23	Aritsune's daughter	Aritsune's daughter	Aritsune's daughter	Aritsune's daughter	
26	Nijō empress	Nijō empress	Nijō empress	Nijō empress	Mention of Fifth Ward
29	Nijō empress	Nijō empress	Nijō empress	Nijō empress	"Mother of crown prince"
49	Narihira's sister	Narihira's sister	Narihira's sister	Narihira's sister	"A man observed the beauty of his younger sister. . . ."
65	Nijō empress	Nijō empress	No mention	No mention	Mention of Emperor Seiwa and his mother
69	Ise priestess	Ise priestess (Princess Tenshi)	Ise priestess (Princess Tenshi)	Ise priestess (Princess Tenshi)	Interpolated note
72	Ise priestess	Ise priestess	No mention	Ise priestess	Mention of a lady in Ise
75	Ise priestess	Ise priestess	No mention	Ise priestess	Mention of Ise province
76	Nijō empress	Nijō empress	*Tsukuri monogatari*	*Tsukuri monogatari*	"Mother of crown prince"
79	Narihira's niece	Narihira's niece	Narihira's niece	Narihira's niece	Interpolated note
102	Ise priestess	Ise priestess	Ise priestess	Ise priestess	Interpolated note
107	Narihira's sister	Narihira's sister	Narihira's sister	Narihira's sister	

based on an exchange of poems between Narihira and Aritsune's daughter that appears in the *Kokinshū*, something that would seem to be compelling evidence for making an identification, we are told that Narihira's interlocutor is merely a random woman he met while in the service of the Somedono empress. *Kokinshū* gives the exchange as follows:

[No. 784] During Lord Narihira's marriage to the daughter of Ki no Aritsune, he once became angry with her; he visited her in the daytime but always left in the evening. Finally she sent him the following poem:

amagumo no	Although I see you
yoso ni mo hito no	as before,
nariyuku ka	you have grown distant
sasuga ni me ni wa	as a cloud
miyuru mono kara	in the heavens.

[No. 785] Reply, Lord Narihira:

yukikaeri	That I go and return
sora ni nomi shite	remaining always
furu koto wa	distant as the heavens
wa ga iru yama no	is because the winds are so fast
kaze hayami nari	at my mountain home.[61]

The related section of *Ise monogatari*, meanwhile, runs as follows (note that the second poem is slightly different from *Kokinshū* 785):

A man in the service of an imperial consort once began to see one of her attendants. In no time, the affair came to an end. They served in the same place, and although the woman saw the man, he acted as though she was not there. She sent him this poem:

amagumo no	Although I see you
yoso ni mo hito no	as before,
nariyuku ka	you have grown distant
sasuga ni me ni wa	as a cloud
miyuru mono kara	in the heavens.

He replied:

| *amagumo no* | That I am distant |
| *yoso ni nomi shite* | as a cloud in the heavens |

---

61. Ozawa and Matsuda, *Kokinwakashū*, p. 298–299.

furu koto wa	is because the winds
wa ga iru yama no	are so fast
kaze hayami nari	at my mountain home.

He was saying that another man had been visiting her.

Aoki Shizuko suggests that the decision to identify the woman as Arit-sune's daughter in Section 23 but not in Section 19 derives from the moral implications of the respective sections: it is safe to identify the chaste woman, but one would not want to think of her as dallying with someone besides Narihira in a different section, even when other sources identify the poem as hers.[62] Naturally, Sōgi and Sanetaka knew perfectly well to whom the poem is attributed in *Kokinshū* and mention it in the *Ise monogatari* commentaries.

Even better support for Aoki's view may be found in *Ketsugishō*'s comment on Section 49. The section is as follows:

Long ago a man observed the beauty of his younger sister and composed this poem:

ura wakami	The young grass,
neyoge ni miyuru	that appears so fresh
wakakusa o	and good for sleeping—
hito no musubamu	how regrettable it is
koto oshi zo omou	that someone else will gather it!

She replied:

hatsukusa no	Why do you speak words
nado mezurashiki	rare and amazing
koto no ha zo	as the first grass of spring?
ura naku mono o	I have always loved you
omoikeru kana	quite without reserve.

In the view of most modern scholars, the first poem is an unambiguous expression of thoroughly unbrotherly sentiments. The second is more open to question: some view the sister's statement ("I have always loved you quite without reserve") as meaning "I always felt at ease with you before, but now you are making me uncomfortable," whereas others see it as an indication of reciprocal interest. But *Ketsugishō* says:

---

62. Aoki, "Muromachi kōki," p. 310.

It is said that Narihira was in love with his sister and composed this poem, but this is not the case. He thinks his sister is unfortunate and he pities her. The sister seems to be without impediments as far as he can see, but because people's hearts differ in myriad ways [no one is interested in her and] he is pained to think that she will never achieve some kind of happiness.[63]

Yūsai goes on to note that the "new grass" in the sister's poem indicates novelty and says the sister wishes to convey that she is grateful to him for thinking her happiness so important. Then he cites a passage from the "Agemaki" chapter of *Genji monogatari*, where Prince Niou is feeling attracted to his own sister and recalls this section of *Ise monogatari*, clearly reading the man's poem as an expression of romantic interest and the woman's as one of receptiveness, and continues:

> However, we should not take the intent of the poem this way. In the Nijō school's reading, it is not that way at all. *Ise monogatari, Genji* and others are not based on amorousness. The 300 poems of the *Shijing* also use matters between men and women as a basis for poetry about the way of governing. This is because it is women who harmonize things. There are no songs that we can say are just a model for amorousness. Among the prohibitions in the *Brahmajâla sutra* is one against [relations between] siblings. This section was written for the sake of admonishment. The extent to which one should take care of women, and so on, is the vital point of it. This is said as a teaching. How much the man notices his sister and thinks about her future will be clear later.[64]

Ketsugishō's reading of this section falls somewhat short of being fully convincing. It remains unclear what the analogue is in *Ise monogatari* for the recasting of ostensible love poetry from the *Shijing* as poetry about governing, and the fact that he cites clearly contradictory evidence from *Genji*, then goes on to say that *Genji* is not about amorousness, undercuts the argument about *Ise* rather devastatingly.

The last statement, "How much he thinks about her future will be clear later," is a reference to Section 107, which begins as follows:

> In the past, there was an elegant man. A man named Fujiwara no Toshi-yuki, a secretary, was courting a girl who lived in his house. However, because she was young, she did not excel at writing letters, did not know

---

63. Katagiri, *Ise monogatari no kenkyū: Shiryōhen*, p. 787.
64. A reference to Section 107. See below.

what words to use, and needless to say, could not compose poetry. The master of the house wrote a draft for her and had her copy it.

Ketsugishō comments:

> *An elegant man.* This is Narihira. *A girl who lived in his house.* This is Narihira's younger sister. She is the person who wrote the "first grasses of spring" reply-poem. . . . *Did not excel at writing letters* means the girl was not yet good at writing letters. *Excel* means excellence, control, superiority. It means that she was not yet talented. *Did not know which words to use* means there was no problem with her calligraphy, but she was still a novice with the words of a letter, love letters, etc. *Could not compose poetry.* Previously she composed the "first grasses of spring" reply-poem. It must be that she is not completely unable to compose; rather she does not compose well. *Wrote a draft.* Because Toshiyuki was a calligrapher and poet, thinking she would be looked at with scorn if he let her write a bad poem, Narihira drafts the words of the letter. This is in the manner of the people of the past. The interpretation that Narihira is in love with his sister when he composes the "young grasses that appear good for sleeping" poem is bad. In this section we can hear well that it is not the case. We can see that he is rearing his sister.[65]

Much of this is lifted from *Iseishō*, which is in turn an amplification of *Shōmonshō*. There is no evidence whatsoever in the section as it is written or any other source to support the identification of the girl as Narihira's sister. The commentators appear simply to be accepting the traditional (Reizei school) identification because it meshes so tidily with their safe reading of Section 49: if Narihira was in love with his sister earlier, why would he be helping her secure the attentions of another man now? The fact that she had no problem composing a reply poem before and is characterized here as unable to compose is glossed over by interpreting "did not compose" as "did not compose *well*."

There are similar attempts to neutralize the story of the Ise priestess. Section 69 begins as follows:

> In the past there was a man. When he was dispatched to Ise province as an imperial huntsman, the mother of the high priestess of the Ise Shrine told her daughter to treat him better than she would the usual messengers. Because these were her mother's instructions, she took very good

65. Katagiri, *Ise monogatari no kenkyū: Shiryōhen*, pp. 846–47.

care of him. In the morning she saw him off on his hunting, and when he returned in the evenings she had him stay in her own lodgings. In this way, she treated him very well.

On the night of the second day, the man said quite passionately that he wanted to meet her privately. The woman too was not ill-disposed toward their meeting. However, because there were many prying eyes, they were unable to meet. Because the man was the head of the hunters, he was not lodged far away; he was near the woman's own sleeping quarters. At the first hour of the rat,[66] when everyone had gone to sleep, she came to the man. For his part, the man had been unable to sleep and was lying down looking out into the night when he saw her standing there in the dim moonlight with a little girl before her. The man was overjoyed, and led her into his chamber. She stayed until the third hour of the ox,[67] but before they had talked about anything, the woman returned to her own rooms.

The problematic parts of this for our commentators were first, the fact that the woman is not unwilling to meet the man privately, and second, what exactly Narihira and the priestess were doing for the three hours during which they did not talk about anything. On the first point, *Ketsugishō* says,

> *The woman too was not unwilling to meet.* Because she was the Ise priestess from the time she was young, she did not know the ways of husbands and wives, and understood neither wanting to meet, nor the inappropriateness of meeting. This meaning appears later.[68]

And on the second:

> *Before they had talked about anything.* It is not written that they certainly came together. The style is interesting. However, they must have come together. Thus it is said that members of the Takashina clan, thinking that they are the offspring of the priestess, do not make pilgrimages to the Ise Shrine, etc. It is said that Moronao, the son of Takashina Mineo, was really Narihira's son.[69]

Despite the Ise priestess's lack of amorous inclinations, her innocence appears to have gotten her into trouble. The startling claim about

---

66. Between 11:00 and 11:30 p.m.
67. Between 2:00 and 2:30 a.m.
68. Katagiri, *Ise monogatari no kenkyū: Shiryōhen*, p. 807. The last sentence is a reference to Section 75, discussed below.
69. Ibid., p. 808.

Takashina Moronao's true parentage is attested as early as *Gonki*, the diary of the Heian-period courtier, poet, and calligrapher Fujiwara no Yukinari (972–1027), and even appears in the genealogical charts of *Sonpi bunmyaku*.[70] Given the squeamishness exhibited elsewhere in the commentaries when reputations are at stake (Section 49; Section 23 versus Section 19), it is almost surprising to find a willingness to accept that Narihira and the Ise priestess were intimate here, but it appears that it is prior acceptance of the pregnancy story that necessitates it.

The Ise priestess is identified again in two sections that do not have interpolated notes to provide the rationale. The first is Section 72, which begins, "In the past, there was a man who had been unable to meet a certain lady in Ise, and who was thus extremely resentful as he prepared to depart for another province." This case is not much of a stretch, given how well the details of the opening mesh with Section 69, where the man is prevented from meeting the priestess a second time prior to his departure to continue his imperial huntsman duties in the next province. Section 75, however, begins, "In the past, there was a man who said, 'Come to Ise to live with me,'" then gives two exchanges of poetry in which the woman rebuffs the man's invitation, and closes with the line, "She was indeed a difficult woman to meet." *Ketsugishō* comments on the last line as follows:

> This is in a very interesting style. *Shōmonshō* says: after meeting one time, in the end she was cold to him. Here we see that the Ise priestess was not amorous. That she became pregnant from the vows of one night was perhaps a matter of karma. This is to Narihira's credit. It is evidence that he got through to the gods. Their descendants down to today's Takashina clan do not make pilgrimages to the Ise Grand Shrine. The effect is striking. Now in 1477 [the date *Shōmonshō* was written] already 598 years have passed. It is strange, indeed! From 877 to 1596 [the date *Ketsugishō* was written], it is 719 years.[71]

---

70. It comes up in a conversation between Yukinari and Emperor Ichijō, given as a reason to deny Empress Teishi's son the throne in favor of Empress Shōshi's: as Teishi's mother was a member of the Takashina clan, it is claimed that his appointment as crown prince would result in trouble with the shrine at Ise. See Katagiri, *Tensai sakka*, pp. 55–56.

71. Katagiri, *Ise monogatari no kenkyū: Shiryōhen*, p. 813. The first sentence of this comment is from *Iseishō* and is all that that commentary has to say on the subject.

Again, it is hard to view this interpretation as other than rather opportunistic. In the first place, the only thing in the text itself that evokes the Ise priestess is the mention of the province, described as a place to go, not a place where the woman belongs, but the commentators seize upon even this small opening to turn the section into support for their earlier reading of the priestess's character, while Narihira's vices are once again transformed into virtues. As in the cases of Aritsune's daughter and Narihira's sister, the goal seems to be to manipulate the traditional character identifications, both within sections and across sections, in ways that will defuse suggestions of impropriety, and place Narihira's behavior in the best possible light.

Generic Instability and Secret Teachings

What were Sōgi, Sanetaka, and Saneki doing? Why did they read *Ise monogatari* in this often contradictory, counterintuitive way? Why did they reject the interpretations of the Old Commentaries so unequivocally in the majority of circumstances and adopt some of the same interpretations in others on different but no less slender evidence? Why do they differ so markedly from Kaneyoshi, seeming even to take a step backward from his positivism, when they were obviously familiar with his work and appear in most cases to respect his views?

No evidence that would allow definite solutions to these questions is available, but several sources among the late Transitional Commentaries provide compelling hints. First, the following statement appears in notes taken down by Sanjōnishi Kin'eda on lectures given by his father, Sanetaka, that were put in order in 1547:[72] "It is said that when Tō no Tsuneyori lectured to persons of no consequence, he used the old commentaries to read. For good disciples he read in the proper style, etc."[73] This statement appears to have been considered important, as it is quoted in Emperor Go-Yozei's *Ise monogatari guanshō* (Foolish thoughts on *Ise monogatari*, 1607) and Emperor Go-Mizuno-o's *Ise monogatari gyoshō* (His majesty's commentary on *Ise monogatari*, 1657). Kin'eda's notes state further, "In the past, the old commentaries were used, but Teika made only the *monogatari* the foundation. With beginners, Sōgi too mixed in the old commen-

---

72. Ōtsu, *Ise monogatari kochūshaku no kenkyū*, pp. 266–67.
73. Quoted in Aoki, "Muromachi kōki," p. 313.

taries in his reading." Go-Mizuno-o attributes the same behavior to Sanetaka, Kin'eda, and Saneki.[74] Finally, the preface to *Ketsugishō* contains yet
another similar statement: "In the Nijō school, too, first one reads and
hears lectures based on the old commentaries. For disciples who are devoted to the Way, the old commentaries are abandoned and we read and
transmit according to the interpretations of our school that I am using
now."[75] It becomes tempting, in view of these statements, to suspect that
Sōgi's and the Sanjōnishi family's comments identifying unnamed women
in *Ise monogatari* in the style of the Old Commentaries are introductory
interpretations of the sort attributed to Tsuneyori, that is, interpretations
intended to be disseminated to beginners and outsiders while other
views were reserved for insiders. But the question of what those insider
views might have been remains unanswered.

Ise monogatari kisuishō (Commentary on water in the vessel of *Ise monogatari*), dated 1608, is a twelve-volume compilation of earlier commentaries whose content may serve to shed light on this puzzle, if only indirectly. Only one copy of *Ise monogatari kisuishō* survives, a manuscript
currently owned by Hōsa Bunko in Nagoya and held in the Tokugawa
period by scions of the Owari domain. The box in which the manuscript
is kept has an inscription stating that it was written out by Karasumaru
Mitsuhiro (1579–1638), a courtier and poet who studied with and received the *kokin denju* from Hosokawa Yūsai, but both Ōtsu Yūichi and
Tanaka Sōsaku point out that while a phrase in the *batsubun* (postscript,
an authorizing or informative statement in the colophon of a text) identifies the author as an old man, Mitsuhiro would have been only twenty-
nine years old in 1608. Tanaka speculates that the *batsubun* may have
been composed by Mitsuhiro's father, and the text then copied by Mitsuhiro, and that therefore the commentary may represent a compilation
of *Ise*-related materials in the Karasumaru family's possession. Yamamoto Tokurō, meanwhile, believes that both the date and the attribution are unreliable.[76]

74. Otsu, *Ise monogatari kochūshaku no kenkyū*, p. 267.

75. Katagiri, *Ise monogatari no kenkyū: Shiryōhen*, p. 727. I will suggest below that
this particular statement may involve some dissembling.

76. See Tanaka Sōsaku, *Ise monogatari kenkyūshi no kenkyū*, pp. 58–64; Ōtsu, *Ise monogatari kochūshaku no kenkyū*, pp. 431–36; and Yamamoto, *Ise monogatari ron*, pp.
394–95, for each of these scholars' views.

If *Ise monogatari kisuishō* were a typical compilation-style commentary that simply listed a range of interpretations from major Transitional Commentaries already in existence, the question of who wrote it (and when, and why) might not be a matter for more than idle curiosity. But *Ise monogatari kisuishō* is unusual: beyond the material drawn from better-known commentaries, it records some seventy-seven oral transmissions as well. Who the author might have been and where he obtained these secret teachings appears to be an intractable puzzle. What is indisputable, though, is *Kisuishō*'s close connection to *Ise monogatari shitchū* (Collected commentaries on *Ise monogatari*), which was set down in 1648 by the poet-priest Sairin and published in a woodblock-printed edition in 1652. Both *Kisuishō* and *Shitchū* follow citations of the base text with interpretations derived from *Gukenshō, Shōmonshō, Yamaguchi ki, Iseishō, Ketsugishō*, and a commentary by Kujō Tanemichi (a grandson of Sanjōnishi Sanetaka, 1507–94), as well as views attributed to Sanjōnishi Saneki. Of particular interest, however, are unidentified views that establish connections between *Ise monogatari shitchū* and *Ise monogatari kisuishō*.[77] The overlap between the two texts may be represented as shown in figure 3.2.

Sairin's teacher, and therefore the source of *Kisuishō*'s "A certain commentary," can be identified as Ikkadō Jōa (1526–1614), based on the preface to *Ise monogatari shitchū*:

> As for new commentaries[78] on *Ise monogatari* starting with the *Gukenshō* of Ichijō Kaneyoshi, among the many previous works the one that is most admired nowadays is *Ketsugishō*. When you look at it, mistakes in the copying are numerous, and it also leaves out some of the orthodox transmissions. Therefore, drawing mainly on the secret teachings that my old master Ikkadō Jōa received from His Lordship the Palace Minister

---

77. Two more commentaries that are closely related to this pair were published after *Shitchū* in the seventeenth century and will be discussed in greater detail in Chapter 4. One of them, *Ise monogatari hiketsushō* (1679), compiled by Takada Munekata, includes all of *Kisuishō*'s secret teachings. Unfortunately, because nothing is known about Munekata apart from the fact that he lived in the capital and also wrote commentaries on *Tsurezuregusa* and *Makura no sōshi*, even the existence of *Hiketsushō* sheds no light on the provenance of the secret teachings. Tanaka Yōko, "*Ise monogatari hiketsushō* ni tsuite," pp. 28–29, discusses what is known of Munekata.

78. Sairin's use of this term is of course unrelated to modern use of it to identify early modern commentaries. He uses it for the late medieval Transitional Commentaries.

Ise monogatari kisuishō   *Ise monogatari shitchū*

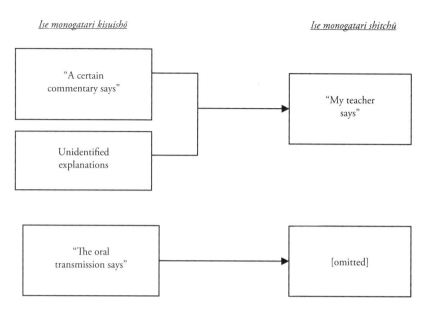

Fig. 3.2 Relationship between *Ise monogatari kisuishō* and *Ise monogatari shitchū*

Sanjōnishi Saneki, and furnishing other commentaries together with it, I have gathered and written them down.[79]

Although the poet and scholar Jōa was sent off by his family to take Buddhist orders at age eight, he was originally a member of the great Takeda warrior family, the son of Takeda Nobutora and brother of Takeda Shingen, and he had close ties as well to the Imagawa warrior family of Suruga province via the diplomatic marriage of his older sister to a head of that family.[80] These connections appeared to have aided him in forging close ties to court scholars of his time. He did not merely study with Saneki and his father, Kin'eda, he was even permitted to receive the *kokin denju*, unlike the commoner *renga* master Satomura Jōha, who also sought to receive it. His association with the Nijō school's teachings in its most authoritative lineage suggests that any *Ise* secrets he and his disciples had access to were likely to have been in some measure orthodox as well.

---

79. Quoted in Yamamoto, *Ise monogatari ron*, pp. 367–68.
80. Detailed biographical information about Jōa can be found in Odaka, *Kinsei shoki bundan no kenkyū*, pp. 206–30.

The preface to *Ise monogatari kisuishō* begins with a section labeled "Contents of House Transmissions on *Ise monogatari*," as follows:

> In this *monogatari*, there are transmissions related to three inner principles and three outer difficulties. The first three transmissions are (1) the matter of the *monogatari's* fictionality and factuality, (2) the god's manifestation,[81] and (3) the capital bird.[82] These are called "inner" because they are not external; they were first written of within this *monogatari*, and therefore they are called "inner." They are called "principles" because they are not superficial matters and were written based on principle. The external difficult matters are (1) *shiojiri*, (2) the Akuta River, and (3) *Ukon no hiori no hi*.[83] These three existed before *Ise monogatari* and became difficult to understand later. Therefore, they are known as the three outer difficulties. These six matters should not be passed on outside our house.

The author goes on to list the seventy-seven oral transmissions pertaining to *Ise monogatari* (the foregoing six, plus seventy-one others).

It turns out that the oral transmissions recorded in *Ise monogatari kisuishō* reveal not just the existence of secret teachings about *Ise monogatari* that diverge in numerous places from what we find in commentaries like *Ise monogatari shōmonshō*, *Ise monogatari iseishō*, and *Ise monogatari ketsugishō*, but also that these teachings account for all of the oddities in the character identifications discussed in the previous section. The first indication of their makeup appears in the commentary to Sections 3 through 6, the sections that form the core of the story of Narihira's relationship with the Nijō empress. Section 3 runs as follows:

> In the past, there was a man. He decided to send something called *hijikimo* [a kind of seaweed] to a woman he was in love with, and composed

> | *omoi araba* | If you loved me |
> | *mugura no yado ni* | surely you would sleep with me |
> | *ne mo shinan* | in a house overgrown with weeds |

---

81. A reference to Section 117, where the god of Sumiyoshi appears and engages in a poetic exchange with the emperor, something *Kisuishō* interprets in terms of the unity between the Way of Poetry and the Way of the Gods.

82. A reference to Section 9.

83. These three are disputed terms (or in the case of the second, a location) that appear in Sections 9, 6, and 99, respectively.

hijikimono ni wa	using just our sleeves
sode o shitsutsu mo	for bedding.

This was when the Nijō empress was not yet serving the emperor, and was still a commoner.

Needless to say, the association of these sections with the Nijō empress springs largely from the interpolated comments that follow Sections 3, 5, and 6. *Ise monogatari ketsugishō* identifies the woman as the Nijō empress at the outset of all four sections based on these interpolations, and the owner of the house in the Fifth Ward that figures in Sections 4 and 5 as the Somedono empress (Fujiwara no Meishi, the Nijō empress's cousin and eventual mother-in-law). He also uses the word *mittsū*, "secret or illicit affair," to characterize the goings-on in the first three of these sections. In all these particulars he follows both *Iseishō* and *Shōmonshō*. All agree further that the interpolated comments emphasize the Nijō empress's status as a commoner, not yet serving the emperor, in order to "help" or "take pity on" Narihira, and minimize his offense, though *Ketsugishō* also points out that the Nijō empress is named in Section 3 in the first place to illustrate Narihira's infamous amorousness.

Ise monogatari kisuishō's comment on the last sentence of Section 3 complicates matters considerably.

> The oral transmission says: for these sections there is a transmission regarding the important matter of distinction between fact and fiction. The reason is that this section is a fictional section. Generally, the places where the Nijō empress's identity is revealed are all fictional. Places where it just says "a woman," and there is no name are fact. Saying that this *monogatari* is fact made into fiction refers to this matter. If it were true that Narihira had an illicit affair with the Nijō empress, surely her name would not have been revealed. People who do not know this teaching assume that there was an example of an illicit affair with the Nijō empress, and make it their companion in amorousness as they enter the way of immorality. Also, the fact that, thinking that this section does not accord with the Way, some cite the rules of *The Book of Rites* . . . and make Lord Narihira out to be the world's most immoral amorous man is because they have not received the fact–fiction teaching (*kyojitsu no narai*) of this *monogatari*. . . . In places where a real name is given, the sections are explained as fiction. This is because fiction is written as if it were truth. And in places where it says just "a woman," the section is

factual. [But] of these too, four out of ten are fictional. This is the custom of fictional *monogatari*. Any place where it says, "This was when she was not yet serving the emperor," etc., is made up. That this section should be viewed as fiction is the transmitted teaching.[84]

The existence of similar oral transmissions is noted briefly after the next two sections as well. The end of the commentary for Section 4 says, "The oral transmission says this section is also fiction."[85] Note that this statement is made despite the fact that the section itself does not actually name the Nijō empress—here the link is via mention of a mansion in the Fifth Ward. Then after Section 5, wherein the protagonist's attempts to visit a woman staying at said mansion are thwarted until he composes a poem moving enough to persuade the owner of the house to relent and permit a meeting, we find, "This too is a fictional section, but it is written in this interesting, open manner. . . . Although the Somedono empress should not excuse this kind of secret affair, this is the custom of fictional *monogatari*."[86]

These comments are startling to anyone familiar with the characteristic haphazard-seeming identifications of characters and moralizing tone of the earlier Transitional Commentaries. The oral transmission pertaining to Section 3 suggests that there might have been more than met the eye in Yūsai's statement, "If one takes fact as fact and views fiction as fiction, there will be no mistakes. This is the oral transmission regarding this *monogatari*"; perhaps he was not giving the substance of the transmission to which he referred (not necessarily identical to the ones that appear in *Kisuishō*), but its framework and intention. The notion that affairs with empresses and Ise priestesses would not likely be commonly known if they had actually happened also meshes neatly with remarks made by Teika in his colophons ("The secrets of [Narihira's] heart and the personal words that arose on the spot would be difficult for someone else to guess at and write down") and by Kaneyoshi in his preface ("It is not to be expected that people far and wide would know of such secret activities. Needless to say, teachings that appear centuries later, guessing about what went on centuries before, are even

84. *Ise monogatari kisuishō*, vol. 2, unpaginated.
85. Ibid.
86. Ibid.

less to be trusted, even if they are produced by famous sages"). What is striking in this formulation is that, although concern with morality definitely persists in the secret teachings—consider the condemnation of those who use the story as a model for their own amorousness—pronouncing a section fictional appears to negate some of the untoward moral implications. Immoral behavior is immoral only if it really happened. The oral transmission appended to Section 5, then, suggests some part of the presumed rationale for fictionalizing fact: it allows things to be written of in a more "interesting" way. Literary value appears to some extent to trump moral value.

The comment on Section 49, the interaction between Narihira and his sister, is even more instructive:

> The oral transmission says: regarding this section there are three layers of meaning. The first layer is what various commentaries note, that Narihira has a feeling of pity for his younger sister, the theory that it is not love. At the second layer, we view it as a feeling of love. The reason is that when you read the sentences of the *monogatari* as they are, without twisting them, the meaning of love is clear. Because it seems like too much that Narihira would be in love with his sister, [the commentaries] twist it and call it pity. Because Murasaki Shikibu also viewed this passage as love, the meaning when it was cited in the "Agemaki" chapter of *Genji monogatari* is also that of love.... As for the third layer, because this *monogatari* is written with fact and fiction mixed together, without knowing these fact–fiction teachings, reading this part is difficult. This section is the most difficult part to understand. People who know the teaching are also rare. Nevertheless, this part is fictional. Narihira was decidedly not in love with his sister. Because it is something that no one in the world would expect, it is written down. This is because it is a fictional *monogatari*. If he had truly had even the slightest such feeling, it would not have been written down. One must consider the circumstances carefully. This is a place where something that could not have happened is written. The oral transmission says that when [a situation] like this appears, one takes fiction as fiction. However, those who do not know the teaching think that when a person's real name is given it is truth, and that when there is no certain name it is fiction. This is not the case. The places that look like fiction are fact. This is what the oral transmission says. In any case, explanations that go according to the first level say that in this section Narihira treats his sister kindly, and she respects him. They say that the relationship

between siblings is one of the Five Relationships. This is the outward interpretation.[87]

Here we find not only evidence that the progenitor of the oral transmission recognized that the "he pities her; she's grateful" reading of Section 49 was rather weak, but also an indication about how the oral transmissions worked: there are levels, the highest of which is accessible only to a few ("people who know it are rare"). Meanwhile, the interpretations at the lowest level serve as the public face of the school's teachings. This leads to a strong implication that commentaries such as *Shōmonshō*, *Iseishō*, and *Ketsugishō*, which reveal only these lowest-level interpretations, also represent only the public face of the teachings.

There are three secret teachings noted in the commentary to Section 69 as well. The first simply echoes the logic we have already seen in the case of the Nijō empress:

> At the highest level of the oral transmissions, it is said that when Narihira went to Ise he took a woman along and put her in the priestess's service. With that in mind, this woman is made out to be the priestess. This is because calling her the priestess makes fact into fiction. Also, the matter of [Narihira's serving as] the imperial huntsman is not included in the national histories, and he must simply have visited Ise. Because this is a fictional story, viewing it as fact is, on the contrary, to turn one's back on its true meaning. The national histories are to be taken as evidence. This is the substance of the secret teaching.[88]

A bit later we find this:

> The oral transmission says: The reading of *Gukenshō* above also makes known the outward face of the *monogatari*. Again, the fact that up to recent times people of the Takashina clan do not go to Ise is because they thought even at that time that this *monogatari* was true, and they did not learn the oral transmission. Hesitating to go to the Ise Shrine, etc., is an ignorant act, but because they had already learned [that they were descendants of Narihira and the priestess], the mistake had true meaning. If they are the offspring of the priestess, they should all the more go to Ise. This should be considered very carefully.[89]

---

87. Ibid., vol. 5
88. Ibid., vol. 7.
89. Ibid.

The *Gukenshō* comment being referred to here is on "before they talked about anything." Kaneyoshi had said, "This means they did not do the real thing. However, it may be that the author isn't entirely frank out of deference to the gods. One theory says that after only one night together, she conceived, becoming pregnant with Moronao. It is impossible to know the truth."[90] (Kaneyoshi also mentions the record of Moronao's parentage in *Sonpi bunmyaku*, claiming that members of the Takashina clan avoid the Ise Shrine, "because they would be the descendants of someone who had violated the virgin and made her pregnant.")[91] Although it is not entirely clear, it appears as though here too there may have been a three-level teaching: at the first level, "they did not do the real thing," and, as in the case of Section 49, the suggestion of immorality is negated, whereas at the second level, they did do the real thing, and Takashina Moronao was the result. But again, at the third, most secret level, the story is simply fiction, and the immoral act is canceled out, apart, that is, from the fact that misguided belief in the story (and/or lack of access to the secret teaching) had real-world effects in the form of causing the Takashina to hesitate to go to Ise Shrine.

The fact that Takashina Moronao is listed as Narihira's child in *Sonpi bunmyaku* presents a lingering problem: we have already been told to trust historical records. But this is resolved in the final transmission associated with Section 69, attached to the interpolated comment that follows the section and identifies the Ise priestess specifically as the daughter of Emperor Montoku and sister of Prince Koretaka:

> The oral transmission says: This phrase is the author's words. Because this section is also fiction, names are revealed. There is an interpretation where the true meaning is that [the priestess] took a woman to Ise with her from the capital. This must be the case. Perhaps a child that that woman bore later came to be known as the priestess's child. [Narihira] never violated the priestess.[92]

Although there is no evidence for the contention made here, the story does have a plausibility that many of the maneuvers performed in *Ketsugishō* and the other commentaries lacked, and it appears to be a

---

90. Carter, "Claiming the Past," p. 112.
91. Ibid., p. 111.
92. *Ise monogatari kisuishō*, vol. 7.

good faith effort to resolve the difficulties, without making an absolute statement about what cannot be supported.

In Section 75, then, the identification of the priestess we saw in *Ketsugishō* becomes unnecessary, and the secret teaching does away with it, while giving insight into a remarkable way in which secret teachings might evolve.

> The oral transmission says: This section does not take place in Ise province. It is set in the capital. When Narihira went to Ise, he invited a woman to come along and reside with him there. . . . It is a mistake to view her as the Ise priestess. . . . The Ise priestess is not mentioned in the prose of this section. However, from the time that someone mistook this woman for the priestess, commentators went along with it. This is the interpretation of the oral transmission. However, they note the surface interpretation and reveal the secret teaching later.[93]

In other words, commentators took advantage of popular misconceptions, propagating the mistaken interpretations for their broader audiences and correcting the mistakes only for students eligible to receive the higher-level teachings.

Aoki Shizuko has examined a pair of little known Sanjōnishi family *Ise monogatari* commentaries and observed, again, conspicuous debts to the Reizei school Old Commentaries. The first, notes from lectures given by Sanetaka, gives the old readings for each section, followed by "our school's" readings for many sections, whereas the second, notes from a lecture by Kin'eda taken down by his second son, Kanenari, notes all the same interpretations without distinguishing those that are "ours" from those that are not, and adds a number of new interpretations in the allegorical style of the Old Commentaries. She remarks that, if the end goal of the Transitional Commentaries was to toss out the Old Commentaries and lecture to good disciples according to "our school's" teachings, it is odd to begin by teaching the Old Commentaries' interpretations as "our school's." She also questions how people like Sōchō and Shōhaku, whose lecture notes contain numerous interpretations from the Reizei school Old Commentaries, could possibly have been considered "beginners" rather than "good disciples" of Sōgi. Her conclusion is that the older interpretations are not in the end diametrically

---

93. Ibid.

opposed to the Nijō school's, that the Old Commentaries and their method of seeking out buried meaning rooted in a metaphorical conceptualization of Narihira's life story precondition the Nijō school's interpretations, and that it is only the specifics of names and dates that the Nijō school rejects.[94] But this conclusion is rather dissatisfying, at odds with the fact that the mainstream Nijō school commentaries do in fact accept a number of random-seeming character identifications, and still more at odds with the tendency to deny or downplay erotic elements in the text that the Old Commentaries embrace and embroider upon. It seems to me that, although it remains speculative, a more compelling explanation is, again, that the mainstream Nijō school commentaries were intended for the late medieval equivalent of a general audience, perhaps including members of the warrior houses with whom Sanetaka, Sōgi, Sōchō, et al. interacted so frequently, while the advanced teachings were transmitted only orally.

Although the oral transmissions recorded in *Ise monogatari kisuishō* cannot be associated firmly with any particular scholar or school, their existence suggests a need to reconsider the mainstream Transitional Commentaries of the Nijō school, and to think twice before we take their assertions and methods at face value. *Ise monogatari*'s generic indeterminacy, its central puzzle, becomes an engine driving the creation of distinguishing teachings that attempt at once to resolve *Ise*'s ambiguities and to be sure that they endure. At first blush, the persistent and unwarranted-seeming identifications of characters found in such mainstream commentaries as *Shōmonshō*, *Iseishō*, and *Ketsugishō* appears to belie an otherwise vigorous rejection of the readings put forth in the Reizei school commentaries, readings that, moreover, had pride of place in popular reception of *Ise monogatari*, as evidenced by the great influence they had in Noh plays and in Muromachi fiction.[95] A closer examination reveals that the inconsistencies of the mainstream Transitional Commentaries arise in specific contexts, that is, in places where extreme improprieties—incest, violations against the throne, even violations against the gods—must be counteracted. And yet, what initially seems

---

94. Aoki, "Sanjōnishi Sanetaka ni okeru Ise monogatari kochū," pp. 76–91, but particularly pp. 90–91.

95. Klein, *Allegories of Desire*, p. 3; as well as Ishikawa, "Muromachi jidai monogatari," esp. pp. 186–205.

to be a profound discomfort with violation of taboos appears in a sense to have been formulated as a protection for those who "can't handle the truth," namely, that provided immoral acts take place in a fictional frame, they need not be a concern, are not models for behavior. This is an important distinction, demonstrating that late medieval scholars' approach to questions of fiction and moral value differs markedly from that of the Confucian scholars who were to follow,[96] despite the resemblances that appear in the commentaries aimed at beginners and outsiders, for whom suitable moral lessons must be extracted even when it is necessary to twist the text as written. For the late medieval Transitional Commentators, detaching the *monogatari* from history allows it to be read with attention to the skill with which it is written, to appreciate poetry composed in circumstances that would in real life be too far beyond the pale to accept, and thereby to return insiders' attention to the matters that were the central concern of the school in the first place.

In the fifteenth and sixteenth centuries the world of scholarship was a small one, a world of lectures and face-to-face meetings, founded on personal ties between those who produced and transmitted knowledge and those who aspired to receive it. Even as simple a thing as access to a text, let alone a secret teaching, depended on a personal relationship with someone who had one, and in such a milieu, controlling and perpetuating a school, in the sense of a tradition of scholarship, was relatively manageable (Kaneyoshi and his ring of copyists notwithstanding). But this little world was about to witness a profound and irrevocable change: in 1608, a scant twelve years after *Ise monogatari ketsugishō* was written and the same year as *Ise monogatari kisuishō*'s colophon, *Ise monogatari* was printed for the first time. Though the shift began slowly, the rise of print, and with it, commercial publishing, eventually wrought radical changes in the way scholarship was produced and circulated. The next chapter will trace those changes and the process by which these late medieval Transitional Commentaries came to lose their authority.

96. See the discussion of Asai Ryōi in Chapter 4 and of Kada no Azumamaro and Goi Ranshū in Chapter 5 for discussion of the Confucian approach.

CHAPTER 4

Commentary Commodified: Ise monogatari *in Print*

The impact of commercial publishing on the reception of classical literature remains an underexplored topic in Japanese literary history. Scholars who study Tokugawa-period print culture have focused more attentively on the wide range of new material that began to be published in the seventeenth century, whereas literary scholars have tended to dismiss printed editions of the classics and popular commentaries on them as insignificant.[1] Nonetheless, the introduction, spread, and diversification of printed texts and commentaries on such works as *Ise monogatari*, *Genji monogatari*, and *Tsurezuregusa* as they found a place in what Mary Elizabeth Berry has called "the library of public information"[2] in the seventeenth and eighteenth centuries constitutes one of the most dramatic developments in the history of these texts' reception and canonization, and they came to constitute a vital, dynamic segment of the market for early modern printed books. *Ise monogatari*, it turns out, was

---

1. As Peter Kornicki aptly notes, "As in other societies, it has been customary for discussions of the book in Japan to omit certain categories of publication. . . . Examples include . . . commercial reprints of classical literature, which are ignored because they have nothing to contribute to the textual tradition, even though they have much to tell us about the circulation and marketing of the classics in the Tokugawa period." Kornicki, *Book in Japan*, p. 4.

2. Berry's initial description of this metaphorical library focuses on the wide-ranging practical information relevant to contemporary life that suddenly became available to the public (*Japan in Print*, pp. 15–18), but she also makes a case for the new status of classical literary works as "collective property" (ibid., p. 191).

not only the first work of vernacular literature to be printed,[3] but also one of the most frequently reprinted throughout the course of the Tokugawa period. In other words, *Ise* was one of Japan's first and most persistent best sellers.

In terms of the history of *Ise* scholarship, the most important effect of this new development was to disrupt the preeminence of the court-associated scholars who had produced the commentaries discussed in the previous chapter. Initially, courtiers themselves were involved in producing old movable-type (*kokatsuji*) editions of *Ise* and its commentaries, despite their vested interest in controlling the spread of information. Once the text and commentaries were out there, however, there was no reining them back in. Unrelated booksellers produced woodblock-printed facsimiles (*fukkokuban*) of the movable-type books. Commoner poets and *kanazōshi* writers of a didactic bent produced for their own purposes new commentaries based on the old court-associated ones; and eventually booksellers themselves solicited popular writers and artists to produce new annotated and illustrated editions. Court scholars continued to lecture on *Ise* and produce commentaries among themselves, but their work had less and less relevance to public reception of the tale as the Tokugawa period progressed.

As indicated earlier, histories of *Ise* scholarship typically parcel commentaries into three groups, with the esoteric Old Commentaries of the Kamakura period and nativists' New Commentaries flanking a group of Transitional Commentaries. This middle group is typically viewed as spanning 250 years, starting with Ichijō Kaneyoshi's repudiation of the Kamakura commentaries in his *Ise monogatari gukenshō*, solidifying shortly thereafter in the work of the Sōgi and Sanjōnishi Sanetaka, being integrated in Hosokawa Yūsai's *Ise monogatari ketsugishō*, and then languishing without significant innovations, the same old interpretations merely being repeated and rearranged with subtle tweaking and amplifications for another hundred years until the appearance of the

---

3. Prior to the 1608 *Saga-bon* version of *Ise*, which is discussed later in this chapter, the *Taiheiki* had been published in 1602 and Hata Sōha's *Tsurezuregusa Jumyōinshō* in 1604, both in movable type, but the former, printed in *kanji* and *katakana*, was at the time viewed more as a historical record than as a work of literature, and the latter, a commentary on *Tsurezuregusa*, included little of the base text. See Ichiko, *Kinsei shoki bungaku to shuppan bunka*, p. 8.

New Commentaries near the turn of the eighteenth century. Although this is not an entirely unreasonable characterization of the progress of the Transitional Commentaries, it is limited in a significant way: it is framed purely in terms of production, in terms of scholars' approach to *Ise*, their attitudes toward evidence and argumentation, the interpretations themselves and how (or if) they evolve. A rather different picture emerges if we ground our examination in the texts as physical objects—if we look at what was circulating and how it circulated, if we include works that have ostensibly little bearing on the evolution of scholarly interpretations or methods, if we examine the deployment of the text on the page. This chapter, therefore, will trace the development of printed editions of *Ise monogatari* from the earliest illustrated, unannotated versions published in movable type in the early seventeenth century, through the woodblock-printed editions published from the mid-seventeenth through the early eighteenth century with increasingly sophisticated apparatus, including not just commentary but also illustrations, introductions, biographies of Narihira and Lady Ise (still assumed to be co-authors), diacritical marks, pronunciation guides, glosses, and stories, illustrations, poetry, or information unrelated to *Ise* itself—designed to render the text accessible and attractive to a new, wider range of readers.

Unfortunately, there are innumerable things that the study of early printed versions of *Ise* or any text cannot tell us. We do not know how large the print runs for these books were and cannot guess how widely they might have circulated. Neither do we know how much they cost and what revenues or profits booksellers might have realized from their sale; the best we can do is to assume that the bookseller would not have made the investment in producing a new edition or reprinting an existing one, whether of the text alone or the text with apparatus, if there were no market for it. Although a handful of catalogs produced between the 1660s and the early eighteenth century, ostensibly for the use of booksellers, do survive, they do not indicate who was publishing what, do not distinguish among editions, and cannot be assumed to give full listings of what was available. Seeing "*Ise monogatari*" in such a list indicates only that some version of it was known to whomever compiled the catalog, without giving a hint as to the contents. Similarly, one quite literally cannot judge these books by their covers—five books titled "*Ise monogatari*" may contain five distinct texts, while five with distinct titles may contain identical texts. Dating of early printed books poses additional problems: some books lack dates and/or the names of the bookseller-publishers that produced them altogether, and even when there are dates, they cannot be assumed to have been updated for printings after the first.[4] And of course, modern lists or catalogs of early printed materials are limited to what has survived, as well as requiring one to examine one by one the books bearing each title in order to determine how or if they are related. There is simply no way to obtain a perfectly comprehensive picture of *Ise*-related printed books in the Tokugawa period.

Nonetheless, such books survive in large enough numbers that a judicious consideration of what we *can* know about them will still shed significant light on the popularization of the classics and the shifts that took place specifically in the *Ise*'s reception and circulation in the seventeenth century, the second half of the period of Transitional Commentaries. Readers and their reading practices or their opinions about what they read are notoriously difficult to get at, and the problem becomes more and more intractable as distance begins to intrude between the producers of texts and their audiences, as is the case with books printed for commercial markets. Even when a reader jots a note in a margin (significant numbers of surviving printed texts of *Ise* contain marginalia), or makes a mention of his/her reading in a diary or letter, conclusions drawn from such bits of evidence cannot necessarily be assumed to extend farther than the individuals who left them behind. Unlike the milieu described in the previous chapter, where small, interrelated groups of people produced handwritten commentaries based on exchanges of knowledge among themselves—a rather homogeneous group engaged in a sense in a single extended project—in an age of commercial print, all who can find and pay for the book may gain access, and, however intently or thoroughly a commentator may attempt to shape the reader's reading of the base text, an anonymous reader is far freer to take or leave what the commentator offers (starting with opting not to bother with a particular commentary at all). Nevertheless, although we cannot survey early modern book buyers to determine their

---

4. Though dates were sometimes updated by cutting the original date out of the block and replacing it with a wooden patch upon which the new date is carved, use of this practice was inconsistent.

needs and how well they were met, provided we view the commercial booksellers as largely rationally self-interested profit seekers, who, again, would not produce (let alone reproduce) inventory that was unlikely to sell, general market trends become clearly discernible in the mass of surviving *Ise*-related books. The delineation of these trends that follows is based on a close examination of approximately 120 distinct printed items,[5] with information about a few dozen others culled from secondary scholarship and exhibition catalogs—enough, I believe, to constitute a representative sampling.

Courtiers' Last Gasps: Early Printed Editions of *Ise monogatari* and Its Commentaries

In 1608 in Kyoto, a small group of men collaborated to bring forth the first piece of illustrated vernacular literature to be printed in Japan, the first *Saga-bon* edition of *Ise monogatari*. For present purposes, the most significant of the collaborators was not Suminokura Soan (1571–1632), the well-heeled Confucian scholar and merchant whose investment made the enterprise possible, nor Hon'ami Kōetsu (1558–1637), the famed calligrapher and artist who is credited with creating the *Saga-bon*'s beautiful calligraphic style, but the third, much less heralded figure—the court poet and scholar Nakanoin Michikatsu (1556–1610), who provided an authorized text, thus planting the seeds of the great changes in *Ise monogatari*'s place in early modern Japanese culture that would sprout and flower over the next century and a half.

It would be difficult to overstate the importance of the *Saga-bon* in the history of Japanese printing. Although printing had existed in Japan for over 800 years, its use through the medieval period was largely limited to Buddhist institutions engaged in woodblock printing of Buddhist texts, along with some Confucian texts and Chinese belles lettres. By the late sixteenth century, movable type had been introduced, on the one hand, from Korea following Hideyoshi's invasions and, on the other hand, via the Jesuits in Kyushu, and came to be used for printing projects undertaken

---

5. In other words, not counting 100 percent identical items as more than one, but counting, say, items that are identical apart from their colophons as two. Approximately two-thirds of the total are held by the University of Tokyo General Library, with the remainder available on microfilm at the Kokubungaku Kenkyū Shiryōkan, also in Tokyo.

by the Tokugawa shogunate as well as by Emperor Go-Yōzei (r. 1586–1617), but these also involved texts written in Chinese. The *Saga-bon* project focused strictly on the vernacular Japanese literary canon, printed in movable type in a mix of *hiragana* and *kanji* in a cursive style that mimicked hand-calligraphed texts, and included, in addition to *Ise monogatari*, editions of such works of prose as *Genji monogatari*, *Hōjōki*, and *Tsurezuregusa*, works of poetry such as the *Hyakunin isshu* and *Sanjūrokkasen* (The thirty-six poetic immortals), and a large selection of Noh libretti of the Kanze school. As this corpus of texts circulated, and was reproduced and expanded upon by other publishers, it exerted an enormous influence over the development of the early modern canon of classical literature. Another important aspect of the *Saga-bon* is the fact that many of the texts incorporated illustrations; the *Saga-bon* comprises the first examples of illustrated vernacular literature in the history of Japanese printing and is thus the starting point for one of the most prominent and distinctive features of printed books in the Tokugawa period.

That the courtier Nakanoin Michikatsu was in a position to provide the text of *Ise monogatari* for the first book to be published as a *Saga-bon* is unsurprising. Perhaps the most distinguished student of Hosokawa Yūsai (he is known particularly for *Mingō nisso*, the massive compendium of earlier commentaries on *Genji monogatari* that he undertook at Yūsai's suggestion), Michikatsu had close familial ties to many other prominent court scholars of the time and of the recent past: he married a granddaughter of Yūsai, his mother was a daughter of Sanjōnishi Kin'eda, therefore a cousin of Kujō Tanemichi, and the *renga* master Botanka Shōhaku was his great grand-uncle. His literary education thus began early—he is recorded as having contributed, at the tender age of five, a poem on a *Genji* chapter title to a sequence commemorating the conclusion of a series of lectures[6]—and, particularly after his exile to Tango province in 1580, following an apparent scandal with a woman at court that earned him the displeasure of the conservative Emperor Ōgimachi (r. 1557–1586), he immersed himself not only in poetry, but also in copying, collating, and commenting on a wide range of texts from the classical tradition, an occupation no doubt encouraged by his

6. Inoue, "Yasokuken," p. 3.

acquaintance with Yūsai, who retired to Tango in 1582. By 1593 the most powerful arbiters of court culture back in the capital, Kujō Tanemichi and Asukai Masaharu (1520–1594), had died, and the influence of Yūsai and Michikatsu increased to the point where young courtiers made the trek to Tango to study with them.[7] By the time Michikatsu returned to the capital in 1599, his reputation was firmly established and his influence immense.

The exact nature of Michikatsu's relation to and interactions with Soan and Kōetsu is obscure, and we do not know how he came to be involved in the *Saga-bon* project, though it is clear that Kōetsu had frequent interactions with people at court. It is probable, however, that an interest in printing developed when, along with many other courtiers, he assisted with Emperor Go-Yozei's so-called Keichō-era printing projects, from 1603 to 1605.[8] The extent to which he was conscious of the possible implications of putting printed texts into circulation is also very much open to question. Perhaps as a result of his experiences outside court circles during his exile, interacting with Yūsai, who was a warrior despite his close ties to court, and numerous commoner poets, he was certainly not an old-school conservative courtier, resolutely holding his knowledge and cultural assets in reserve. For example, he wrote the postscript for the doctor Hata Sōha's commentary on *Tsurezuregusa*[9] and admitted the commoner *haikai* poet Matsunaga Teitoku (of whom more below) to his lectures on the same text, which was just coming into its own as a minor classic at the turn of the century. He is even known to have participated in rather raucous commoners' poetry contests on the commoners' own turf.[10] But at the same time, he was greatly annoyed with Teitoku when the latter went out and gave public lectures on *Tsurezuregusa* and the *Hyakunin isshu* to a group of young doctors. He was, to say the least, ambivalent about the spread of courtly literary knowledge beyond court circles.

---

7. Ibid., pp. 14–15.
8. Kawase, *Zōho Kokatsujiban no kenkyū*, 1:203. Also mentioned in Inoue, "Yasokuken," p. 21.
9. Inoue, "Yasokuken," p. 20.
10. Described in *Taionki*, Teitoku's memoir. Odaka and Matsumura, *Taionki*, pp. 60–62.

In any event, the *Saga-bon* was not itself intended for wide circulation. Constructed impeccably of very rich materials, with methods intended to mimic those used to produce books in the Heian period, these were in large measure art objects rather than casual reading material, and it is easy to imagine the appeal to courtiers and other wealthy or powerful people of owning a familiar classic such as *Ise monogatari* in such a novel and beautifully crafted form. Michikatsu himself gives a hint as to what sort of readership he expected in the colophon to the first edition:

> I have taken the text of Fujiwara no Teika in which his colophon reads, "As for the origins of this *monogatari*, the theories of the ancients do not agree,"[11] and so on, and corrected it using the text of the Tenpuku era that was given to his granddaughter.[12] Still, I am afraid that oversights remain in the collation. Furthermore, the illustrations are based on the contents and divided into two volumes. They are not sufficient to stir a good woman's passions, but will just please the eyes of children.[13]

In short, Michikatsu does not appear to have anticipated for these books the sort of scholarly or poetry-aficionado audience that might have been interested in his hand-copied texts and commentaries, and the reason for it appears to be the presence of illustrations, with their special appeal, in his view, to women and children. The association of picture books with young people is perhaps natural, but there are traces in these comments indicating that he considered the *Saga-bon* to be, again, a diverting novelty rather than something to be taken with the same degree of seriousness as his (and other men's) text-generating activities focused more narrowly on the Way of Poetry. His going out of his way to address possible concerns about the effect of the illustrations on "the passions of women," moreover, is noteworthy. Although some Confucian scholars in the coming decades would take up the question of whether women ought to be exposed to material as licentious and immoral as *Ise monogatari* and *Genji monogatari* with considerable pungency, such rhetoric is not generally heard in the work of courtly scholars of vernacular literature, a natural outgrowth of their desire to preserve the place of these

---

11. I.e., the *Rufu-bon*.
12. The *Tenpuku-bon* of 1234.
13. Quoted in Kawase, *Zōho kokatsujiban no kenkyū*, 1:433

texts at the pinnacle of the canon for poetic studies.[14] Michikatsu is no exception, insofar as he pins possible impropriety not on the sacrosanct words of the *monogatari* but on the added pictures.

The illustrations in the *Saga-bon* fall into a lineage of *Ise* illustrations that goes back at least to the Muromachi period. The *Saga-bon* meshes with that lineage both in the selection of scenes to be illustrated and in the iconography and composition of the scenes. Of particular interest in situating the *Saga-bon*'s illustrations is the *Nara ehon*[15] known as the *Hokuni-Bunko-bon*, one of the few Muromachi-period illustrated *Nara ehon* texts of *Ise* that survive.[16] Although the illustrations of the *Hokuni-Bunko-bon* are extremely crude—they give the appearance of having been copied hastily from another text, dropping or glossing over much detail in the process[17]—and cannot be compared to those of the *Saga-bon* for their artistic merit, the *Hokuni-Bunko-bon* and the *Saga-bon* illustrate exactly the same forty-eight scenes, selected from forty-three sections, and the composition of these scenes in terms of the placement of the human figures and orientation of architectural structures is extremely similar for the vast majority of the illustrations.[18] There is interesting overlap with Michikatsu's colophon here, in that *Nara-ehon* may have played a role in the education of late medieval youngsters, both boys and girls, serving as material for calligraphy practice and as an

---

14. Although, as I showed in Chapter 3, late medieval commentators had definite concerns about the erotic elements of *Ise,* leading them to defuse suggestions of immorality via creative interpretation and manipulation of the line between supposed fact and supposed fiction, none of them go to the length of denouncing it directly. For a detailed account of Confucian scholars' views, see Kornicki, "Unsuitable Books for Women?" pp. 152–62.

15. A medieval hand-calligraphed and illustrated text, in scroll format or codex. *Nara ehon* are most commonly associated with Muromachi short fiction (*otogizōshi*), but a wide variety of kinds were produced in this format, including Noh plays, war tales, *Kōwaka bukyoku,* etc., as well as classical works.

16. Reproduced in its entirety in Itō, *Ise monogatari-e*, gravure, pp. 64–95.

17. See Sayre, "Illustrations of the *Ise-monogatari*," pp. 223–25, for discussion of the style of this text. Itō also discusses it in terms of the likelihood that it was the work of a studio that produced illustrated texts in relatively large quantities (Itō, *Ise monogatari-e*, p. 88).

18. I am not suggesting that the *Saga-bon* is in direct descent from the *Hokuni-Bunko-bon*; only that they may be cousins—perhaps there was some no longer extant parent text or group of texts that the *Saga-bon* follows fairly closely and the *Hokuni-Bunko-bon* fudges.

approachable, enjoyable means to acquire cultural literacy, including knowledge of literary classics and the poetic tradition;[19] thus there is further reason to associate these illustrations in particular with children. In any case, the illustrations of the *Saga-bon* became a conduit through which the lineage was transmitted; it set a standard for the illustrations of *Ise* that appeared over the next century from which deviations were exceedingly rare. And, again, the simple fact of inserting illustrations into the text was enormously influential. Not only do the vast majority of surviving Tokugawa-period printed editions of *Ise* contain pictures, illustrations also became a prominent feature of the contemporary prose works that developed throughout the period.[20]

The *Saga-bon Ise monogatari* was printed five times in 1608, followed by new editions in 1609 and 1610, each of which also went through multiple printings. The former has additional corrections by Michikatsu and a new colophon as follows:

> There are extremely many copies of the newly printed *Ise monogatari* in circulation. I corrected the text of Fujiwara no Teika, whose colophon says, "Regarding the origin of this *monogatari* the theories of the ancients do not agree," and so on, using the text that was given to his granddaughter in the Tenpuku era, but I fear there are still mistakes in the characters, so I have corrected and collated it a little more. Again, the volumes are illustrated according to the content and divided into two

---

19. Ruch, "Chūsei bungaku to kaiga," pp. 295–311.

20. As Ichiko Natsuo notes, in the first half of the seventeenth century there is an interesting divide within the pool of works that we now think of as classical literature, between those that were susceptible to illustration and those that were not. Along with *Ise* (which Ichiko says was always illustrated—this is incorrect; plain woodblock-printed texts dating from the Kan'ei era [1624–43], and 1648 also exist), illustrated editions of *Genji monogatari, Sagoromo monogatari, Hogen monogatari, Heiji monogatari, Soga monogatari,* and the *Gikeiki* were published before 1650. However, editions of such works as *Taketori monogatari, Yamato monogatari, Ima monogatari, Makura no Sōshi, Hōjōki, Tsurezuregusa, Heike monogatari, Jōkyūki, Taiheiki,* and *Hosshinshū* contained no illustrations. War tales exist in both lists; the key is that only those that were printed in *hiragana* have illustrations; the remainder are printed in *katakana* and appear to have been viewed as historical works (though the presence of *Taketori monogatari* in the latter list is a little puzzling if this is the source of the distinction). There are parallels with contemporary tendencies in illustrating *kanazōshi*: among those works, only narratives with a story line are illustrated. See Ichiko, *Kinsei shoki bungaku to shuppan bunka,* pp. 298–99.

volumes, and I think these will give pleasure to the eyes of children. Ah! I am old and weak, and I cannot overlook mistakes in the characters. How can there be no mistakes? If a gentleman of wide learning corrects and amends them, it will be very fortunate.[21]

A significant aspect of this colophon (apart from the glimpse it gives of Michikatsu's fastidiousness, and the fact that he has evidently ceased to be concerned with the effect of the illustrations on women) is the first line, indicating that the *Saga-bon Ise* had achieved considerable popularity. Naturally we do not know how many copies there might have been after the first five printings, nor within what segments of society they might have become numerous. Nonetheless, the numbers were great enough to merit comment and to cause Michikatsu some concern about the quality of the work.

The last edition, of 1610, appeared the month after Michikatsu had died, at age fifty-five. The colophon to this text, thought to be penned by Soan, rehashes the process by which Michikatsu created the text, is unconcerned with the effect of the illustrations on anyone, states that further corrections have been made, and ends by saying, "Again [the book] will be circulated in society."[22] And circulate it did. Shortly after this point other publishers began producing woodblock-printed facsimiles of the *Saga-bon* (*kabusebori*, books created by printing from blocks that had been carved from a tracing of the original text). Because there was no concept of copyright at this early stage, and no regulations governing fledgling booksellers' activities, this need not be viewed as an act of piracy, but undoubtedly one effect of this development was to make copies of *Ise* more widely available. One advantage of the switch from movable-type technology to woodblock printing was that once the investment was made in carving the blocks, new runs of books could be produced quickly and in any quantities; there was no need to painstakingly reset the pages, carve new fonts, and so on.[23]

---

21. Quoted in Kawase, *Zōho Kokatsujiban no kenkyū*, 1:435–36.

22. Ibid, 1:436–37.

23. Note that *kabusebori* books do not always involve creating identical, full copies of the originals. The method was also used to make changes or corrections to existing blocks (or in this case, movable-type books), or simply to replace blocks that had grown worn out from use. For a discussion of the shift from movable type back to woodblock printing, see Kornicki, *Book in Japan*, pp. 134–35.

The first extant copy of *Ise monogatari* to be produced from independently carved blocks (i.e., not *kabusebori*) appeared in 1629. But here too, the debt to the *Saga-bon* is enormous, and the genetic connection is made clear both in the text and by virtue of the fact that this book ends by reproducing the colophon to the 1609 *Saga-bon*—it is not the case, in other words, that independently carved blocks implied an independently assembled text. Figures 4.1 and 4.2 show the two texts for comparison. The 1629 book's illustration of the first section, showing Narihira handing a note written on a strip of cloth torn from his robe to a maid, to be taken in to a pair of sisters (here apparently sitting with an attendant) whom he has encountered in Nara (indicated by the deer), is an extraordinarily faithful copy of the *Saga-bon* illustration—one must look very closely indeed to notice the differences in the pattern of the leftmost sister's robe, in the spots of the deer, and in the women's faces, for example. Equally striking is the partial imitation of the *Saga-bon*'s calligraphy. The *Saga-bon*, printed in movable type, went to lengths to create ligatures between individual characters in an attempt to more faithfully reproduce handwriting—in the first line, which starts with the words *Michinoku no*, for example, the characters *mi* and *chi* are conjoined, as are *no* and *ku*—when it would have been more efficient, requiring the carving of fewer characters of type, to keep them separate. The 1629 woodblock print, on the other hand, reproduces the slight gaps between the characters that is characteristic of movable type (though the hand itself is unlike that of the *Saga-bon*). Both books thus constitute attempts to duplicate existing forms with new technologies. At least thirteen additional dated woodblock-printed editions of *Ise monogatari* (two without illustrations) appeared between 1629 and 1670, some with multiple printings and amended reprintings.[24]

---

24. Several of these reproduce the *Saga-bon* colophon, again indicating a direct connection. These editions date from 1643, 1645, 1646, 1648 (no pictures), 1653 (no pictures), 1654, 1655, 1659, 1660, 1662, 1667, 1669, and 1670, plus one from the Kan'ei era (1624–43). Particularly noteworthy is the 1662 edition, which generated many knockoffs and continued being reprinted as a *fukkokuban* even into the Meiji period (Tesshinsai bunko, *Ise monogatari eiri hanpon*, p. 7). This book reduces the forty-eight illustrations of the *Saga-bon* to thirty, probably in an effort to reduce the cost. As ever, it is impossible to get an accurate count for this period, even if that count is limited to what survives. There are, for example, two versions of the text dated 1646, identical apart from the fact that only one of them gives a publisher—one or the other very likely dates from a different year—and any of the others might also have been printed multiple times

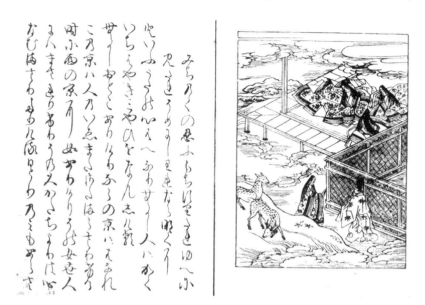

Fig. 4.1 *Saga-bon Ise monogatari*, old movable-type book dated 1608. Courtesy of the Museum of Fine Arts, Boston.

Two commentaries on *Ise monogatari* were also printed in the early seventeenth century. Nakanoin Michikatsu's contribution to the *Saga-bon* project did not end with *Ise monogatari* itself. In 1609 he also prepared for printing the 1477 version of *Ise monogatari shōmonshō*, the commentary discussed in Chapter 3 that grew out of Botanka Shōhaku's notes from lectures by Sōgi. This text is very much the odd man out within the *Saga-bon* corpus; all of the others are works of prose narrative, poetry, or drama. But again, the colophon suggests Michikatsu is driven by his concern with accuracy, wanting to correct errors in the versions of *Shōmonshō* in circulation, in this case amplified by family pride, Shōhaku having been a younger brother of his ancestor.[25] Despite

without the colophons having been changed. Also worthy of note: some of these texts contain the phrase *chūiri*, "with notes," in their titles. However, none of them contain full-blown commentary. The notes in question are limited to a relatively small number of notes Teika made in the *Tenpuku-bon* in *kanbun*, reproduced interlinearly from that text. (None of the texts with Teika's notes have *Saga-bon* colophons, though they persistently base their illustrations on the *Saga-bon*.)

25. Kawase, *Zōho kokatsujiban no kenkyū*, 1:441.

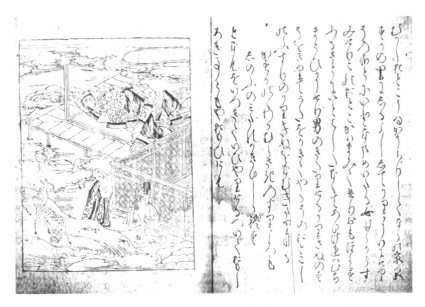

Fig. 4.2 *Ise monogatari*, woodblock-printed book dated 1629. Courtesy of the General Library, the University of Tokyo.

Michikatsu's efforts, however, there is no indication that *Shōmonshō* was reproduced in print after the *Saga-bon* version; only these movable-type texts survive.

The case of Hosokawa Yūsai's *Ise monogatari ketsugishō* could not be more different. As discussed in Chapter 3, *Ketsugishō* was a notably legible synthesis of the interpretations of the principal Transitional Commentaries, produced for the purpose of delivering lectures on *Ise* to Prince Hachijō Toshihito. The lectures took place in 1596, and Michikatsu collated and recopied the text for Yūsai the following year, as the postscript he added indicates. There are four distinct versions of *Ketsugishō* printed in movable type and dating from the Keichō era (1596–1615),[26] the first of which was set and printed by Oyama Niemon, a bookseller who also produced a movable-type *Heike monogatari* and, in 1610, a *setsuyōshū* (a household encyclopedic dictionary).[27] In amusing counterpoint to

---

26. Various indexes, including *Kokusho sōmokuroku*, show a movable-type *Ketsugishō* from 1597, but clearly this is the date of the *batsubun*, not part of the publisher's colophon.

27. Kawase, *Zōho Kokatsujiban no kenkyū*, 1:508–9.

Michikatsu's statement in the postscript that the text should be placed deep in a box and not shown to outsiders, *Ketsugishō* was explosively successful in print, with distinct woodblock-printed editions appearing in 1634, 1642, 1648, 1653, 1658, 1660, 1668, 1704, and 1769, plus a number of undated ones—with the demand for secrecy reprinted intact in every single copy. *Ketsugishō* thus became the dominant Transitional Commentary available in the Tokugawa period.[28]

Figure 4.3 shows the end of the preface and the beginning of the commentary on Section 1 in the 1653 woodblock-printed edition of *Ketsugishō*. The base text (that is, the text of *Ise* itself) is printed flush against the upper border of the page in short fragments with the commentary starting on the next line and indented by one character, a layout identical to that used in earlier manuscripts and movable-type editions. An important thing to note about this text is how very difficult it would be to use it as a means of simply reading *Ise monogatari*. One would be forced to read a few words, scan a lengthy comment, read a few more words, scan some more commentary, and so on. The first citation of the base text on this page, for example, reads simply *mukashi otoko*, "in the past, a man," while the comment runs on a great length about the past being relative—last year is the past of this year, and yesterday the past of today, etc.—the identification of the man with Narihira, and the fact that "in our school," one should pause between the words *mukashi* and *otoko* when reading.

The following example shows *Ketsugishō*'s treatment of the first half of *Ise*'s second section:

> In the past, there was a man. When the capital in Nara had been left behind but before people's houses were established in the present capital, there was a woman in the western part of the city.
>
> When the capital at Nara was moved to the present location, first the Western Capital was opened up, and later the Eastern Capital was opened. It must have been that at that time people's houses were not settled in the Eastern Capital. Emperor Kanmu moved the capital to Nagaoka in Otokuni-gun in Yamashiro province in the eleventh

---

28. Two other late medieval Transitional Commentaries were printed in the Tokugawa period: Ichijō Kaneyoshi's *Ise monogatari gukenshō* in 1673 and 1680, and Sōgi's *Yamaguchi ki* in 1668 and 1788. Although these are listed faithfully in bookseller's catalogs, few copies survive, and neither seems to have enjoyed sufficient demand to merit regular reprinting. These do not remotely approach the popularity of *Ketsugishō*.

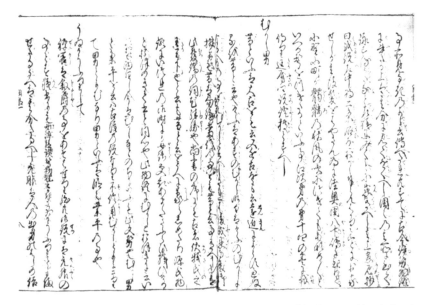

Fig. 4.3 *Ise monogatari ketsugishō*, by Hosokawa Yūsai. Woodblock-printed book dated 1653. Courtesy of the General Library, the University of Tokyo.

month of the third year of Enryaku [784]. In the thirteenth year of the same era [794] he moved it to this Heian capital. This woman is no one in particular. The old commentaries say it is the Nijō empress. We do not use this reading. When the Nijō empress is discussed her name is revealed, but since there is no means of verifying it, speaking like this [i.e., leaving the woman anonymous] is an interesting aspect of this *monogatari*. As I said before, it must be the same as when poetic anthologies say "author unknown." There are people given as "author unknown" who are known but cannot be known on the surface. There are various cases: sometimes they are high-ranking officials, sometimes lowly people, sometimes a respected member of the imperial family, and sometimes the name really is not known. We should think of it as this kind of case.

That woman surpassed other people.

One should insert the character *no* into the word *yohito* "other people" and read it as *yo no hito*. In the text in Lord Teika's hand and in other old texts it is written *yohito*. However, because Retired Emperor Go-Uda's given name was Yohito, it has come to be that we insert the character *no* and read it as *yo no hito*. Also, one can drop the character *yo* and read it just as *hito* "people." When we read the word *kunihito* in the Five Classics as *kunitami*, this too is because Kunihito was the given name of Retired Emperor Go-Saga. Because Emperor Go-Uda lived after Lord Teika, it is natural that it should say *yohito* in the text in Teika's own hand. Saying "she surpassed other people" refers to the rank of her family.

Her mind surpassed even her appearance.

In saying she surpassed other people, her appearance and behavior are being praised more than her family origins, and her mind over her appearance. She is a superior person.

It seemed she was not alone. A serious man pledged his love to her, and returned home—what might he have been thinking?

She has a husband. Therefore, it is unfortunate that he falls in love with her. A serious man pledged his love to her: serious is written with the character 実. Although a serious person should not be amorous, perhaps it is written this way because these are Narihira's own words. Since she is a person who surpasses others it is understandable for even a serious man to fall in love.

It was the last day of the third month, and he sent this to her as a soft rain fell.

Sowofuru may be written as 壮両 or as 添雨. There is a theory that it should be pronounced unvoiced, but it is best if it is voiced.[29]

It is unlikely that one would wish to use this book alone to read through the *monogatari* casually, given the choppy condition of the base text and the sometimes bloated interruptions. It seems much more plausible that a text like this one would be used principally for study or reference, a means for readers to familiarize themselves with mainstream Nijō school interpretations of *Ise*. As the earliest audiences of *Ketsugishō*, composed principally of poets and scholars, would have had *Ise* committed to memory, and thus have had little need for a legible rehash of the base text, this format was no doubt entirely adequate to their needs. This conjecture about the earliest use of the text is supported by the fact that the *Saga-bon* version of *Ise monogatari shōmonshō* appears, judging from the fact that it uses the same typeface, to have been published with a companion plain text of *Ise* (no commentary or illustrations),[30] which readers could use in conjunction with the commentary, and upon which their own notes could

---

29. I.e., it should be pronounced *sōburu* rather than *sōfuru*. The full passage can be found in Katagiri, *Ise monogatari no kenkyū: Shiryōhen*, pp. 736–37.

30. Kawase, *Zōho Kokatsujiban no kenkyū*, 1:439–40.

be written. (Note that *Ketsugishō* also includes a handy blank space at the top for the reader's own notes, a frequent feature of manuscript texts and commentaries as well.) Conservatism is a hallmark of these earliest printed texts: they make no particular attempt to innovate, taking advantage of the possibilities of the new technologies used to create them. Rather, they seek only to duplicate existing texts in their original forms, whether in the *Saga-bon*'s movable-type mimicry of manuscript, the 1629 woodblock-printed edition's mimicry of the *Saga-bon*, or the preservation of the manuscript commentary format in *Shōmonshō* and *Ketsugishō*.

Despite Michikatsu's prominent role in the early history of printed *Ise monogatari*–related texts, courtiers' involvement in the printing of the corpus of texts that had once been their special domain—*monogatari*, poetry, and poetics texts, which were classed together along with related commentaries in booksellers' catalogs as *kasho* (poetry books)—dropped off precipitately after Michikatsu's time, and although such works from the medieval period were taken up and printed by commercial publishers, from the middle of the seventeenth century onward no new work in this area by court scholars appeared in print at all.[31] Among themselves, courtiers remained very active throughout the Tokugawa period in producing commentaries on *monogatari* and poetry, as well as in producing new poetry collections of various kinds, but these circulated only within court circles in manuscript. These scholars were perhaps aware all too concretely that "the technique of reproduction detaches the reproduced object from the domain of tradition"[32] and gave print a wide berth in an effort to preserve the special authoritative "aura" of their work. But the end result of the strategy was to render court scholarship utterly marginal, as commoners jumped in to fill the demand for new publications on the classics in ways that addressed the needs of audiences that extended beyond court circles.

Recentering the Text: Commentaries Intended for Print

Evolution in the format of printed commentaries, reflecting shifts that had been taking place in the market, began in the 1650s. A key figure with connections to this transition was the *waka* and *haikai* poet and

---

31. Ichiko, *Kinsei shoki bungaku to shuppan bunka*, pp. 283–86.
32. Benjamin, *Illuminations*, p. 223.

scholar Matsunaga Teitoku. A commoner who claimed several key court poet-scholars, including Hosokawa Yūsai and Nakanoin Michikatsu, as teachers or mentors, Teitoku had access to some of their works of scholarship and private teachings, but, owing to his non-aristocratic birth, he was never permitted to reach the highest levels: though he wished to receive the secret teachings of the *Kokinshū* himself, Yūsai refused to transmit them to him formally. He did, however, receive a number of lesser secret teachings, and it was through him that the so-called *jige denju* (commoner *denju*) began to be transmitted.[33] Most telling of all, perhaps, is Teitoku's famous participation in a series of public lectures. In 1603, at the invitation of Hayashi Razan, the scholar who subsequently headed the shogunate's Confucian academy, he spoke about *Tsurezuregusa* to an audience of young Confucian scholars and doctors. Despite having confined himself to what was then a minor text—he did not, in other words, go out recklessly revealing orthodox views of the *Kokinshū* or *Ise* to the masses—this act was enough to earn Teitoku an upbraiding from Nakanoin Michikatsu. Many years later Teitoku claimed in his memoir to have been chagrined about this incident,[34] but nonetheless he continued educating people of his own class, many of whom were drawn to him as students not only of court poetry, but also of *haikai*, for the rest of his long life. A new group of commentaries on various classics was produced by Teitoku himself and by members of his school in the mid-seventeenth century, a natural activity given the emphasis in their school of *haikai* on allusions to classical literature. These commentaries no doubt aided many a budding *haikai* poet in gaining familiarity with and a deeper appreciation of texts from the classical tradition.

Although new commentaries on *Ise monogatari* did not appear in print until the 1650s, commentarial activity around *Tsurezuregusa* had flourished in the hands of commoners. Hata Sōha's *Tsurezuregusa Jumyōinshō* (Jumyōin commentary on *Tsurezuregusa*) was written in 1601 and printed in 1604, followed by Hayashi Razan's *Nozuchi* (Field hammer, 1621, first printed sometime between 1634 and 1644). *Nagusamigusa* (Comforting grasses), based on the lectures on *Tsurezuregusa* that Te-

---

33. See Shimamoto, *Matsunaga Teitoku*, pp. 9–32, for a discussion of Teitoku's interactions with various courtiers and his ambivalence toward secret teachings.
34. Odaka and Matsumura, *Taionki*, p. 60.

itoku had continued to give since his outing before the young doctors in 1603, was the contribution of Teitoku's school to this tradition, and the text includes a number of reader-friendly innovations that suggest a great deal about new attitudes toward commentary. It is not known exactly when *Nagusamigusa* was printed, but it appears, like so many commentaries, to have grown out of notes taken at the lectures by a member of Teitoku's school, with corrections, additions, and a post-script by Teitoku himself.[35] The postscript, dating from 1652, at which point Teitoku was eighty-two years old, gives an account of the process:

Nothing is of use before its time comes. The Tale of the Shining Genji appeared at the beginning of the Kankō era [1004–12], but it remained buried for over a hundred years, and became a treasure of the world from the Kōwa era [1099–1104]. Until the Tenshō era [1573–92], people who knew the name of *Tsurezuregusa* were also rare, but from Keichō [1596–1615] it came to be taken up by the world. When I received transmissions from the Nakanoin lay priest [Michikatsu], I heard that he had wrested deep truths from Jumyōin [Hata Sōha] and they had conversed. With me, too, in the course of asking each other "How do you understand this?" "How does that sound?" and with the old Chinese matters he had read about and recalled, and old poems I noticed, we communicated well on many matters. The doctor Jumyōin was also a kind person, and at the Honji'in of Yōhōji, he inquired into unclear points, and for the first time made a commentary, had it printed, and it was spread throughout the world. Around that time, Dharma Seal Dōshun, then still young and known as Hayashi Matasaburō Nobukatsu [Razan], said that, for practice, he would like to try lecturing on the new commentaries on the Four Books. I said it was a fine idea. Dharma Bridge Endō Sōmu lectured on the *Taiheiki*. At that time, the young Confucian scholars and doctors asked me for a reading of this *Tsurezuregusa*. Although I refused, Nobukatsu's father and uncle, Sōmu's grandfather, and others had said, "Since you are just lecturing to young people, even if things are unclear, by all means do it for them." Thus urged after consulting with my dear friends, I read without regard for right and wrong. It was said that these were the first lectures on *Tsurezuregusa* in the world. At that time, I jotted down the "general meaning" of the sections on the back of scraps of paper, and though I spoke of them to no one, the fact that now they have been writ-

35. Odaka, *Matsunaga Teitoku no kenkyū, zoku-hen*, p. 268.

ten into this *Nagusamigusa* is very strange—where could they have been taken from? When I think about it, it must be that someone among those who served me copied them. I have not looked at them again, and will not revise the language, and they are not something that should be showed to others, but now it has spread in the world. Although it is disagreeable to blame someone, since it is not a text that I lent out, there is no way to recover it. Thinking to explain my decision, I have recorded these useless things here for no good reason.[36]

Figure 4.4 shows how *Nagusamigusa* is laid out. The most obvious innovation is the addition of illustrations to the commentary, in this case showing the priest Kenkō, *Tsurezuregusa*'s author, sitting at his reading stand in all his reclusive glory with a pile of books behind him, an illustration of Section 13, which discusses the pleasures of reading. *Nagusamigusa* is the first commentary on any vernacular text to be published with illustrations, and after this point illustrations begin to appear routinely in other texts of *Tsurezuregusa*, with and without commentary. The figure also shows a fragment of base text belonging to the next section—the three leftmost lines. Quite unlike *Ketsugishō*, *Nagusamigusa* keeps the base text for each section of the work together in a single block that can be read without interruption, and equips it with headnotes (*tōchū*) that simply define difficult words and identify references to other texts, content largely imported from earlier commentaries. The most unusual feature, however, is the block of text intervening between the picture and the resumed base text. These give what are called the *tai-i* or "general meaning" of the section they follow. However, they do not merely summarize or give the gist of the sections, nor do they typically offer the sort of factual, research-, or tradition-based commentary that one sees in commentaries like *Ketsugishō*, or in the headnotes to *Nagusamigusa* itself. Instead, they provide a space for Teitoku's personal reflections on the section—his critical insights, stories of his younger days, particularly of his interactions with famous court scholars of the past, ruminations on scholarship and the Way of Poetry, free association, and so on. The "general meaning" for Section 22, for example, reads as follows:

> This section laments the way the speech of courtiers at Kenkō's time had changed from the past. Long ago, when I was learning to read *Genji*

---

36. Yoshizawa, *Tsurezuregusa kochūshaku shūsei*, pp. 999–1000.

Fig. 4.4 *Nagusamigusa*, by Matsunaga Teitoku. Woodblock-printed book published after 1652. Courtesy of the General Library, the University of Tokyo.

monogatari with Kujō [Tanemichi], I read in a straightforward manner, and he laughed, thinking it sounded accented. What he said was, "It's not your fault alone; since Lord [Oda] Nobunaga came up to the capital from Owari, the speech of everyone in the capital, high and low alike, has changed greatly. . . ." When you hear the words the people of the capital say nowadays, sometime they say "dare" instead of "tare" [meaning "who"], or tatta and tata instead of tada [meaning "just," "only"]. There are innumerable examples of this kind. Because it sounds strange even to my ears, how sad the people of the past would find it if they could hear! A person of feeling reading this section would surely be pained. It appears to have been written as a warning to later generations.[37]

Arguably, it was the status of *Tsurezuregusa* as a new classic in the Tokugawa period that permitted Teitoku to write as freely and randomly as he did in these spaces, something that would not have been appropriate for a serious poet-scholar of the time with texts like *Ise* or *Genji*, encrusted as they were with layer upon layer of existing interpre-

37. Ibid., pp. 142–43.

tation and comment that had to be acknowledged and dealt with. At the same time, the *tai-i*, along with the illustrations, provide great added interest for readers, allowing them to hear the voice of this experienced old lecturer in a digressive and contemplative mode as well as in a more strictly edifying one.

The approximately contemporary *Ise monogatari jokai* (*Ise monogatari*, Drawn from the sea), written by Asai Ryōi (d. 1691) and printed after 1655, makes use of very similar innovations. Ryōi is known less as a scholar or poet than as a writer of *kanazōshi*, a rather amorphous category of prose works that are variously didactic, entertaining, or informative in intent. He was among the earliest group of writers to produce stories specifically with the intent of publishing them. Earlier in the century, booksellers had developed books from texts already in existence, and the shift in the case of prose fiction neatly parallels the same shift that was taking place in the case of commentaries. This massive, eight-volume *Ise* commentary is deeply indebted to the still more massive *Ise monogatari shitchū* by the commoner poet Sairin, discussed in Chapter 3. Completed in 1648 and printed four years later, *Ise monogatari shitchū*, as the title suggests, brought together the views of major late medieval Transitional Commentaries, this time including teachings Sairin had received from Ikkadō Jōa. Recall that Sairin's brief preface had situated his work as follows:

> As for new commentaries on *Ise monogatari* starting with the *Gukenshō* of Ichijō Kaneyoshi, among the many previous works, the one that is most admired nowadays is *Ketsugishō*. When you look at it, mistakes in the copying are numerous, and it also leaves out some of the orthodox interpretations. Therefore, drawing mainly on the secret teachings that my old master Ikkadō Jōa received from His Lordship the Palace Minister Sanjōnishi Sanezumi, and furnishing other commentaries together with it, I have gathered and written them down.[38]

Sairin's assessment of *Ketsugishō* makes additional sense when one considers its great success as a printed book, combined with the fact that the process of preparing a manuscript for printing contained enormous potential for introducing errors into a text, then propagating those errors

---

38. Quoted in Yamamoto, *Ise monogatari ron*, pp. 367–68.

more widely and irretrievably than would have been the case with manuscripts, something that early modern scholars can be found lamenting
throughout the period. Yamamoto Tokurō also suggests that in criticizing *Ketsugishō*, Sairin implicitly finds fault with Nijō school's institutions of secret transmissions, both the court version, which had originated with Yūsai, and the commoner version, which Yūsai had passed to
Teitoku.[39]

Ryōi's *Ise monogatari jokai*, then, borrows very heavily from Sairin's
Shitchū, entirely without attribution to him, though he does give the
sources of the individual comments as Sairin did. But again we have a
noteworthy difference in the use of the printed page. Where *Shitchū* was
laid out in a manner resembling *Ketsugishō*, as shown in figure 4.3, Ryōi
adds to his own commentary features very like those that characterized
Nagusamigusa. This book, with illustrations derived from the *Saga-bon*,
is the first *Ise* commentary to have pictures, and also includes *tai-i* giving
the general meaning at the start of each section. Unlike Teitoku's diverse, discursive *tai-i*, however, these have a definite, consistent agenda.
The general comment for Section 3 of *Ise monogatari*, wherein the man
sends an anonymous woman a poem with a gift of seaweed (*hijikimo*),
intended to mobilize a suggestive pun on the word for bedding (*shikimono*), ends with the interpolated comment, "This was when the Nijō
empress was not yet serving the emperor and was still a commoner," is a
good example. Note that this is a short, simple section that rarely provokes much comment compared to the other sections early in the *monogatari*. Ryoi's "general meaning" comment is as follows:

> This section also criticizes amorousness. Together with that, again, it
> hints at the matter of turning one's back on propriety in childrearing.
> The father of the Nijō empress was Lord Nagara. If an empress behaves
> wildly, the offense is slight. When there is negligence in the father's rais-
> ing his child, the offense is not slight. As for why this is so, it is because
> when the empress was not yet serving the emperor and was still a com-
> moner, it was a time when she should have been obeying her father. A
> woman is subject to "the three obediences," such that when she is young
> she obeys her parents, in her prime she obeys her husband, and after she
> is old she obeys her son. A woman cannot stand alone. Within the entire
> span of her life she is entrusted to others, such that she can be compared

---

39. Ibid., p. 372.

to the creeper vines that hang from pine trees. They grow using the pine tree as their strength, and separated from the pine they cannot stand. Classics of both the Confucian and the Buddhist traditions all speak of these three obediences. Also, the rules of the *Li ji* say that from age seven, a girl should not meet her father or her male siblings face to face. A chamber must be constructed elsewhere, divided into inside and outside, where men do not enter and women do not exit. While the parents have not permitted it and wedding gifts have not been brought by an intermediary, she does not meet men. Now, in this case, the fact that both parent and child have turned their backs on propriety, and that the man visits secretly without permission, are being criticized.[40]

Like so many other commentators, here Ryōi takes advantage of *Ise monogatari*'s openness to interpretation to ride roughshod until he finds the message he wants to find: where the line about the Nijō empress having been a commoner when the man sent this poem can safely be taken as the unknown Heian writer's attempt to defend the man against charges of lèse-majesté, here the fact becomes the source of an even graver offense. The heavy-handed Confucianism underlying this comment is extremely typical of Ryōi's appended *tai-i* throughout the text and amounts to an amplification of a similar moralizing tendency in *Ise monogatari shitchū*, in turn an amplification of what we saw in some of the earlier Transitional Commentaries and greatly in keeping with the predominantly Confucian intellectual currents of the time. The decision to put these before rather than after the sections is noteworthy: it suggests a desire to control the reading of the section before the reader even begins.

And yet Ryōi does not actually give the reader a chance to read. Although the base text in *Ise monogatari jokai* is large and prominent compared to the text of the commentary, and also distinctly set off from it, the commentary itself is both verbose and prone to engaging minute details, thereby necessitating impossibly small snippets of guide text. Two full pages of commentary intervene between the words *mukashi otoko* "in the past, a man" in Section 1, and the next phrase, "performed the capping ceremony." If the goal of Sairin's *Ise monogatari shitchū* was to supplant *Ketsugishō* in the public esteem, and part of the goal of Ryōi's

---

40. Asai, *Ise monogatari jokai*, 2:16.

Ise monogatari jokai was to package these views in a format that might attract a wider swath of readers, neither project can be said to have succeeded. Copies of *Ise monogatari jokai* in particular survive in only very small numbers. *Ketsugishō* remained the overwhelmingly dominant Transitional Commentary for the rest of the Tokugawa period and was, as I will show in Chapter 5, the principal jumping-off point for nativist commentators, whether as a source of intermittent borrowing or the butt of aggressive criticism. Nonetheless, *Ise monogatari jokai* gives further evidence of early attempts to draw readers in with the visual appeal of illustrations and the convenience of summaries, tendencies that were to become increasingly sophisticated in the ensuing decades.

Chief among Teitoku's disciples who produced studies of the classics was Kitamura Kigin (1624–1705). Teitoku did not produce an *Ise* commentary himself, but Kigin left *Ise monogatari shūsuishō* (Gathered rice-ears commentary on *Ise monogatari*). Written before 1663 and printed in 1680, *Shūsuishō* was second only to *Ketsugishō* in its influence over the rest of the Tokugawa period. Like *Ketsugishō*, and a number of other Transitional Commentaries produced between the two, it is basically a compendium of earlier scholarship, in this case jumping off from *Ketsugishō*. However, where *Ketsugishō* typically weaves earlier commentators' views together into a synthesized account, picking and choosing from among them without naming the respective sources of the points he makes (though the language generally makes it clear whose work Yūsai is drawing on), in *Shūsuishō* Kigin clearly indicates the original sources of the material, with Teitoku's views and occasionally his own added to the mix.

However, Kigin's commentary is quite unlike *Ketsugishō* in terms of the way it is presented on the printed page. Figure 4.5, which shows the end of the commentary on Section 1 and then the beginning of the base text for Section 2 with commentary, may not initially seem much more approachable than *Ketsugishō*, but in fact it skillfully rearranges the *Ketsugishō* commentary given above, in a way that suggests a different mode of reading and that obviates the need to use two texts at once (unless of course the reader wanted a clean text upon which to record his or her own notes). Kigin's commentary divides the base text into two parcels, the first identical to the first phrase cited in *Ketsugishō* (the last three, larger lines on the left side of the right page in fig. 4.5) and the second combining *Ketsugishō*'s remaining four phrases into one block

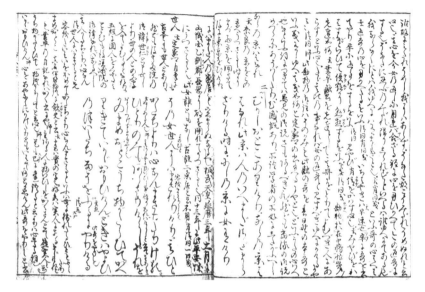

Fig. 4.5 *Ise monogatari shūsuishō*, by Kitamura Kigin. Woodblock-printed book dated 1680. Courtesy of the General Library, the University of Tokyo.

(the six lines in the middle of the left-hand page). To these, Kigin very helpfully adds punctuation to indicate pauses (there is no distinction equivalent to that between commas and periods; both mid-sentence and sentence-ending pauses are indicated by small circles) and marks to indicate voiced consonants as well as numbers at the start of the sections—all features that *Ketsugishō* lacks. The commentary, then, is divided into, on the one hand, a number of moderately lengthy content notes with new, abbreviated guide phrases that frame the text in the form of wrapping headnotes rather than interrupting it, and on the other hand, brief notes dealing quickly with lexical matters or difficult-to-understand phrasings that appear within the blocks of base text as interlinear glosses. Kigin's comment on the first block of text simply quotes Yūsai's (identified with the character 玄 *Gen* from Genshi, Yūsai's Buddhist name), though Kigin stops at "We do not use this reading" and omits the business about anonymity in *Ise* being related to the handling of anonymous poets in the imperial poetry anthologies. He follows this with the observation that *Shōmonshō* (*Shō* 肖) and *Iseishō* (*Sei* 清) say the same thing.

The second block of base text is arranged something like what appears in figure 4.6. The interlinear notes allow the reader to pick up

in her appearance yo no hito
That woman surpassed other people. Her mind surpassed even her

Yūsai: She has a husband. Teacher: since one hesitates to pursue a married woman, he writes
appearance. It seemed she was not alone. A serious man pledged his love

'seemed' and does not mention a husband
to her, and returned home—what might he have been thinking? It was

sent the following poem
the last day of the third month, and he sent to her as a soft rain fell.

> **Other people** Yūsai: One should insert the character *no* into the word *yohito* 'other people' and read it as *yo no hito*. In the text in Lord Teika's hand and in other old texts it is written *yohito*. However, since Retired Emperor Go-Uda's given name was Yohito, it has come to be that we insert the character *no* and read it as *yo no hito*. When we read the word *kunihito* in the Five Classics as *kunitami*, this too is because Kunihito was the given name of Retired Emperor Go-Saga.
>
> **Her heart more than her appearance** *Iseishō*: saying she surpassed other people, her appearance and behavior are being praised more than her family origins, and her mind over her appearance so she sounds like a superior person.
>
> **A serious man** The *mana* text of *Ise monogatari* writes this as 歟夫. Yūsai: serious is written with the character 実 'truth'. Although a serious person should not be amorous, perhaps it is written this way since these are Narihira's own words. Teacher [Teitoku]: to disguise the fact that he pays court to a married woman, it says 'serious man.'

Fig. 4.6 Passage from *Ise monogatari shūsuishō*.

small, vital bits of information (the word should be read "yonohito"; "not alone" is euphemistic; and so forth) while keeping his or her eyes on the text, making for very little interruption in the flow of reading. The headnotes, then, (given below the base text in figure 4.6) can be perused separately, perhaps for a second, more informed reading, and the abbreviated guide phrases make it much easier to find the relevant comments. Despite the fact that Kigin records additional interpretations and sets out the sources of the old ones clearly (note, for example, that the language of the interpretation Kigin attributes to *Iseishō* is almost identical to Yūsai's), he also streamlines Yūsai's comments somewhat, whether because he disagreed, found an alternative more compelling, or simply found the information unnecessary. The end result of the altered format is a more efficient and flexible means of delivering the text to the reader. *Kogetsushō*, Kigin's celebrated commentary on *Genji monogatari* (written 1673, printed 1675), is presented in a very similar format.

Aoki Shizuko has shown that although the printed version of *Shūsuishō* typically sets out impartially the competing theories of earlier scholars and of Kigin's teacher Teitoku, and leaves it to the reader to decide which to follow, the original manuscript is a different matter. According to the colophon (reproduced in the woodblock-printed version), in 1663 the manuscript was presented by Kigin through an intermediary to Retired Emperor Go-Mizuno-o, a devoted scholar of classical literature in his own right who gave lectures to his courtiers and left behind his own commentaries. It turns out that the manuscript contains only the opinions that Kigin identifies as Teitoku's in the printed *Shūsuishō* and also gives interpretations where the printed version says, "There is an oral transmission," suggesting that these were being shared with the emperor in writing.[41] The format differed as well: the manuscript does not include the entire text of *Ise*, only abbreviated phrases to indicate the passages targeted by the notes. In short, the manuscript appears to be a simple transmission of the Teimon school's accepted view of *Ise* and an indication that the school used the same sort of tier system of "correct" interpretations that held sway in the late medieval period. It is quite natural, moreover, that Go-Mizuno-o would have had no need for a rehearsal of the content of the Transitional Commentaries—he was certainly familiar with them and had his own opinions about them—and no need for a conveniently constructed combination of full text plus commentary. The changes made to this manuscript for the woodblock-printed version give a vivid indication of the acute consciousness of audience that marked this commentary and the more deliberate, reader-oriented art that went into the way it is arranged on the page.

Movements at the Margins: The Printed Page and the Pursuit of New Audiences

Between the 1670s and the first decades of the eighteenth century, there occurred a veritable explosion of innovative *Ise* commentaries, clearly directed at popular rather than scholarly audiences. Although the development of texts other than the more scholarly commentaries just examined had been slow earlier in the century—moving from plain texts with illustrations, to texts with section numbers, then with punctuation,

41. Aoki, "*Ise monogatari shūsuishō* no seiritsu," pp. 32–35.

then by the 1660s to texts with the sources of the poetry noted and the brief *kanbun* notes that Teika had left in his Tenpuku-era recension added—thereafter texts began to come fully loaded with helpful apparatus, such that during the decades in question (what one might call a long Genroku era), new unadorned texts were the exception rather than the rule. Although the plainer texts were by no means entirely shunted aside by the new developments—they were reprinted frequently, both with and without emendations to their colophons, and quite often survive with readers' marginalia, demonstrating that students of the tale did in fact use them to take their own selected notes on such full-blown commentaries as *Ketsugishō*, *Shūsuishō*, and eventually the commentaries of nativist scholars—publishers do not appear to have felt much need to tinker with them further until the mid-eighteenth century, and even at that point the investment was in new, eye-catching illustrations in more contemporary styles rather than in adjustments to the text or the presentation of the text on the page.

Table 4.1 provides a rough guide to new publications for each decade of the Tokugawa period after woodblock-printed versions of *Ise monogatari* began to be produced and gives evidence for these trends.[42] The threshold for "newness" in this data set is very low—if a text differs from a predecessor only in its colophon (for instance, a changed date, or the same date with a different publisher), it is counted as a new item. The logic behind the count, as suggested previously, is to seek out clues about trends in demand, or publishers' perceptions thereof, rather than to give a systematic accounting of every single edition, revised edition, and reprint in existence. The table gives, from left to right, the total number of distinct *Ise*-related texts[43] bearing a date in the specified range (those with no date are summarized at the bottom of the table), the number of

---

42. Sources for this table include (1) books I have examined myself, and those described and photographed in (2) Tanaka Sōsaku, *Ise monogatari kenkyūshi no kenkyū*, pp. 319–68; (3) Ikeda, *Ise monogatari ni tsukite no kenkyū*, the third volume of which is devoted to early modern printed texts; and (4) catalogs from exhibitions held at the Tesshinsai Bunko Ise Monogatari Bunkakan in 1992, 1995, and 1999, each featuring printed texts or commentaries on *Ise monogatari*. These four sources I cross-checked to eliminate duplicates and supplemented by further cross-checking against *Kokusho sōmokuroku* and the databases of the Kokubungaku Kenkyū Shiryōkan.

43. They cannot be called "titles," because, again, the titles can vary while the content remains the same.

Table 4.1 New woodblock-printed texts of *Ise monogatari* by decade, 1629–1860s

Period	Total	Traditional commentaries	Popular books (total)	Reprints	Illustrations	Front matter	Annotation	Packaged with other texts	Targeted at women
1629–1639	4	2	2	0	1	0	0	0	0
1640s	8	2	6	≥3	5	0	0	0	0
1650s	12	6	6	≥0	5	1	1	0	0
1660s	10	5	5	≥0	≥4	0	0	0	0
1670s	10	2	8	≥1	8	2	2	0	0
1680s	6	3	3	≥2	3	2	2	0	0
1690s	15	1	14	≥6	14	≥12	≥7	4	0
1700s	11	1	10	≥5	≥9	≥7	3	0	0
1710s	6	0	6	≥2	≥4	≥2	1	2	1
1720s	5	0	5	≥2	≥3	≥2	1	2	2
1730s	3	1	2	2	2	2	2	1	1
1740s	6	0	6	≥2	≥4	≥2	≥1	1–3	3
1750s	10	1	9	≥7	9	≥7	0	0	0
1760s	8	2	6	≥2	≥5	≥3	0–2	2	2
1770s	3	1	2	1	≥1	≥1	0	0	0
1780s	6	1	5	≥3	5	≥3	0	0	0
1790s	7	2	5	≥4	5	5	0	1	0
1800s	5	4	1	1	1	≥1	0	0	0
1810s	4	3	1	≥0	1	0	0	0	0
1820s	3	2	1	1	1	0	0	0	0
1830s	0	0	0	0	0	0	0	0	0
1840s	4	2	2	2	2	0	0	0	0
1850s	1	0	1	1	1	0	0	0	0
1860s	1	1	0	0	0	0	0	0	0
no date	30	5	25	≥17	≥22	≥14	≥13	≥2	≥1
TOTAL	**178**	**47**	**131**	**≥64**	**≥115**	**≥66**	**≥33**	**≥15**	**≥10**

that total that are commentaries in the traditional mold (including, for example, editions of *Ketsugishō*, *Shūsuishō*, *Gukenshō*, Sōgi's *Yamaguchi ki*, and later on the works of nativist scholars), and then the number that remain after traditional, "serious" commentaries are subtracted, identified as "popular books." Both plain, unannotated texts and texts with apparatus are included in the latter category, while parodies and vulgarizations of *Ise* (that is, books that intentionally alter or adapt the base text) are excluded from consideration. Two otherwise "serious" commentaries that contain illustrations, Asai Ryōi's *Jokai*, and the anonymous *Ise monogatari zōsenshō*, are counted as "popular books." It should be noted that the dates cannot be taken as an indication of when the text was actually produced; some of the texts bearing the date 1662, for example, were certainly produced later, with the date left unamended. However, assigning such texts to the period corresponding to their original creation allows us to see something of the movement from newness to satiation, in other words, the date from which a text capable of meeting some aspect of demand was produced. The remaining portion of the table records the number of popular texts (total minus traditional commentaries) with selected attributes. A "reprint" is a text that is identical to another text with an earlier date but for a change to the colophon, or, for example, a change in the size of the book. Taken together with the total number of popular books, this column permits us to see roughly how many of the items assigned to that period are genuinely new. However, because the count is limited to items for which there is conclusive evidence or that I have been able to verify with visual examination, the "greater than or equal to" sign appears frequently.[44] "Front matter" refers to prefaces, biographies, and portraits of the assumed authors, explanations of reading conventions, tables of contents, large captioned illustrations reflecting on *Ise* as a whole rather than illustrating an individual scene, and so on. "Annotation" refers to headnotes or interlinear notes but does not include phonetic glosses attached to *kanji*. Finally, a text is considered to be targeted at women if it has significant content with lessons in feminine deportment or household

---

44. In the case of the "illustrations" column, the number is quite certainly "greater than"—only three distinct texts (2 percent of total) of those I've had direct access to lack them. Two of those are dated before 1660.

Table 4.2 New editions of Traditional Commentaries versus popular books

Period	Total texts	Traditional commentaries	Portion of total	Popular books	Portion of total
1620–1669	34	15	44%	19	56%
1670–1719	48	7	15%	41	85%
1720–1769	32	4	13%	28	87%
1770–1819	25	11	44%	14	56%
1820–1870	9	5	56%	4	44%
No date	30	5	17%	25	83%
Total	178	47	26%	131	74%

management or if it appears in the section of a booksellers' catalog devoted to books for women.[45]

The data reveal several interesting trends. First, as shown in table 4.2, although production of traditional commentaries versus popular texts is fairly even through the mid-seventeenth century, the relative number of popular items shoots up dramatically from the late seventeenth through the late eighteenth century (the point at which the New Commentaries of nativist scholars began to be printed). Table 4.3 shows further that as time passed, an increasing number of the popular books were reprints of older texts—the heyday of innovation was, again, from the 1670s to the mid-eighteenth century, slanted a bit to the earlier part of this period. Apart from illustrations, front matter is the most prominent feature to be added to the texts during this time—most texts begin to have some form of it, though again, as the period progresses an increasing number of these are reprints of older content. Interest in annotation and packaging of *Ise* with other texts also peaks in the Genroku era (1688–1704); very few new popular books with these attributes were produced thereafter, though the old ones apparently continued to circulate. Finally, a trend toward marketing *Ise* as reading for women appears in a concentrated space in the early to mid-eighteenth century, a phenomenon that will be examined in the next section.

45. The count in this category is conservative and likely understated, for reasons that will be discussed below.

Table 4.3 Percentage of popular books with selected features

Period	Popular books	Reprints	With illustrations	With front matter	With annotation	Packaged with other texts	Targeted at women
1620–1669	19	15%	79%	5%	5%	0%	0%
1670–1719	41	39%	95%	61%	37%	15%	2%
1720–1769	28	54%	82%	57%	14%	21%	28%
1770–1819	14	64%	93%	71%	0%	7%	0%
1820–1870	4	100%	100%	0%	0%	0%	0%
No date	25	68%	88%	56%	52%	8%	4%
All	131	49%	88%	50%	25%	11%	8%

The earliest nontraditional *Ise* commentary, known as *Kashiragaki Ise monogatari shō* or *Ise monogatari shushoshō* (both titles mean "*Ise monogatari* with headnotes"), was published in 1674 by the Kyoto bookseller Yamamoto Shichirōbee in conjunction with Kawaseya Hanbee, also of Kyoto, and Hinaya Rokubee in Osaka. Little is known of the author, Sakauchi San'unshi (ca. 1644–ca. 1711?), beyond the works he wrote and fact that he was a *haikai* poet, though there is some speculation, based on his style, that he had ties to Kitamura Kigin.[46] San'unshi produced this commentary in response to a request from the writer and bookseller Yamamoto Hachizaemon, also known as Yama no Yatsu, a member of the same Yamamoto family as the bookseller Shichirobee and several other Kyoto booksellers. Yama no Yatsu is known particularly for the *kōshokumono* (erotic books) he wrote and sold, and evidently his shop did a brisk business in *shunga* (pornographic pictures) as well as in fiction and guides to actors. *Kashiragaki Ise monogatari* is, in short, the product of a very different, far more market-driven environment than the courtly or scholarly milieu in which earlier commentaries took shape. It seems conceivable, moreover, that Yama no Yatsu's move to include an *Ise* commentary among his wares stemmed more from the

46. Noma, "San'unshi," p. 95.

interest his customers might have had in ancient permutations of the *iro-otoko* (amorous man) type than from the text's relation to the study of poetry, though of course either group of readers might find the commentary useful. Figure 4.7 shows the arrangement of *Kashiragaki Ise monogatari shō* on the page. The base text has its own dedicated space, roughly the bottom two-thirds of the page, and is again equipped with section numbering, marks for pauses and voiced consonants, and the anthologies in which the poems appear. The headnotes, meanwhile, are neatly contained within their own territory at the top of the page, with section numbers given in relief, and individual notes separated by small circles. The overall effect is infinitely easier on the eyes and more navigable than *Ketsugishō, Jokai*, and even *Shūsuishō*. At the same time, although the annotations are derived from the more scholarly Transitional Commentaries (this particular one draws mostly on *Ketsugishō*), the notes are stripped down drastically. For example, the headnotes for Section 2, shown in figure 4.7, say simply,

> •*Nara capital left behind*: This must be when, moving from the Nara capital to this capital, this capital was built up from the Western Capital, and in the Eastern Capital people's houses were not settled. •*other people*: This should be read "yo-no-hito" • *not alone* she is a woman with a husband •*serious man*: This is written 実 男 He is a man of truth, so his thoughts are in confusion because her appearance is so beautiful. •*A soft rain fell*: It falls quietly.

There is just enough information to help the reader get the point, nothing that is not immediately relevant, no rehearsals of competing theories, no quibbling about fine points. A final noteworthy feature is the continued inclusion of illustrations, again very closely resembling those in the *Saga-bon*, but in this case the number is cut from forty-eight to just thirty—this reduction combines with the far more efficient use of the page to reduce the cost of the book by saving paper.

Just before the publisher's imprint this text has a note that reads: "There are many editions of *Ise monogatari* in circulation, but because they have mistakes in the characters and in the *kana* usage, these have been corrected, and in order to make the general meaning of this tale known to the young and unenlightened this book has been issued, with reading conventions [*yomikuse*] and notes given at the top." Meanwhile, the frontispiece (fig. 4.8), in addition to creating visual interest when the

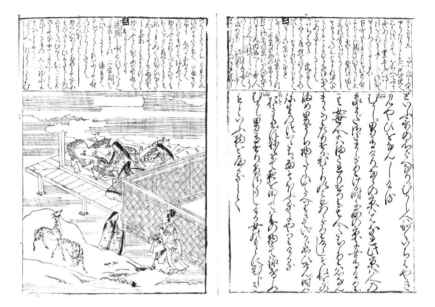

Fig. 4.7 *Kashiragaki Ise monogatari shō*, by Sakauchi San'unshi. Woodblock-printed book dated 1674. Courtesy of the General Library, the University of Tokyo.

book is opened, with its title page and portrait of Narihira, also makes clear to us who the intended audience was not. The note above Narihira's picture reads:

> *Ise monogatari with Headnotes* was made by Sakauchi San'unshi for the sake of beginners. Because this book records the life of Narihira, the publisher has copied a picture of his figure at his coming-of-age and capping ceremony. If those who are deep in the study of poetry find it silly, they should immediately turn the picture to the cover of the book and not look at it.

The book is also equipped with a preface, as follows:

> —There are various interpretations of the title of this *monogatari*. [First, it is called *Ise*] because the characters *I* and *se* should be read "man" and "woman," since the *monogatari* is about men and women.
>
> —It was given this title because the episode where Narihira goes to Ise as an imperial huntsman and meets the Ise priestess was considered interesting.
>
> —After Narihira's death, Lady Ise added to what he had written and offered it to Retired Emperor Uda, or she wrote it when she was a girl of

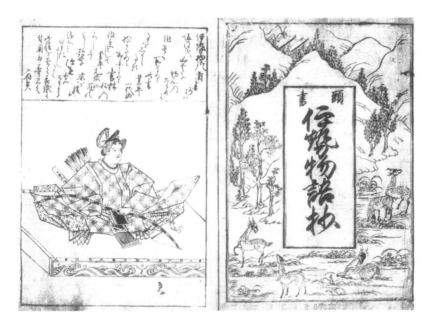

Fig. 4.8 Frontispiece of *Kashiragaki Ise monogatari shō*. Courtesy of the General Library, the University of Tokyo.

thirteen years old. Therefore, it is called *Ise monogatari* because she is thought to be the author.

—There is no doubt that Narihira wrote it himself. The reason is that there is humble language, such as when he speaks of himself disparagingly as a strange old man, etc., or says "because he did not know much about poetry," etc.

Each of foregoing is from the Old Commentaries and our school does not use them. Lady Ise was a lady-in-waiting to the Shichijō empress, and [*Ise monogatari*] is a fictional *monogatari* she wrote it for that empress. The bulk of it is [either] things that were truly from Narihira's life, or things from the *Man'yōshū* and other sources of which Narihira is made the subject. We just view it as a fictional *monogatari*.

—Narihira's life story is written in this *monogatari*. Therefore, it contains everything from his coming-of-age ceremony at the beginning to the evening of his death, and ends with his poem, "I did not know it would be yesterday or today."

—Narihira was the grandson of Emperor Heizei, and the fifth son of Prince Abo. He was born in Nara on the first of the fourth month in the second year of Tenchō [825] during the reign of the fifty-third emperor, Junna.

—His coming-of-age ceremony took place on the eleventh of the third month of the seventh year of Jōwa [840], during the reign of the fifty-fourth emperor, Ninmyō, when he was sixteen years old.

—He died at age fifty-six in on the twenty-eighth of the fifth month of the fourth year of Genkei [880] during the reign of the fifty-seventh emperor, Yōzei.

The preface is for the most part quite clearly derived from one of the mainstream Transitional Commentaries. Its rehearsal of theories about the title proceeds in an order reminiscent of *Shōmonshō*, though the preface to that commentary does not include Narihira's dates and is not reproduced intact. However, despite the stated adherence to the theories of "our school," the author also includes a date for Narihira's coming-of-age that is traceable back to the Old Commentaries and that the Transitional Commentaries cite only to reject.

Another noteworthy aspect of the popular editions is the way they advertise their distinguishing selling points on the cover, as seen in figure 4.9. *Ise monogatari* appears in large print down the middle of the *daisen*, the slip of paper upon which the title is printed, along with little accessory phrases like *shinpan*, "new edition," *eiri*, "illustrated," *shinchū* or *shinshō*, "new notes," *yomikuse tsuki*, "with reading conventions," *kashiragaki*, "with headnotes," and sometimes even, instead of "new commentary," *denju iri*, "with secret teachings" (the content of books labeled "with *denju*" is generally identical to those described simply as "with notes"— there are no particularly deep secrets being revealed here). Reading conventions, a particular obsession of Nijō school scholars, would include such items as the reading of *yohito* as *yo no hito*, or the fact that one should pause between the words *mukashi* and *otoko* ("in the past, a man . . .") rather than reading them together as "the man of the past." In the case of *Kashiragaki Ise monogatari shō* the reading conventions are incorporated into the headnotes, but other editions of the tale give them in one fell swoop as a component of the front matter; a number also follow them up with an announcement in large print stating, "The foregoing reading and voicing conventions are the interpretations of Hosokawa Genshi [Yūsai]." Despite the fact that the annotations themselves consist of little more than warmed-over, readily available *Ketsugishō*, the invocation of "our school," "secret teachings," and Yūsai seems to have

Fig. 4.9 Cover of *Kashiragaki Ise monogatari shō*. Courtesy of the General Library, the University of Tokyo.

been intended to give readers not only the sense that they are engaging with authoritative interpretations but also the small thrill of feeling like they were privy to proprietary knowledge.

In 1679, five years after *Kashiragaki* appeared, an Edo bookseller doing business under the name Shōkai (or Matsue) published a highly derivative edition entitled *Ise monogatari tōshoshō* (*Ise monogatari* with headnotes), shown in figure 4.10.[47] Although different blocks were carved for it, the content of the notes is mostly identical to San'unshi's *Kashiragaki*.[48] Ichiko Natsuo's examination of Shōkai's output reveals that this was a typical activity in the early history of the enterprise: the majority of Shōkai's publications between 1652 and the mid to late 1680s were pirated editions (*jūhan*) of books originally published in Kyoto.[49] A significant change to the original *Kashiragaki* can be found in the illustrations, however. As figure 4.10 shows, these are no longer following the *Saga-bon* strictly; the scene has shifted from the man's sending a poem to the sisters through an intermediary to his initial peeping-tom discovery of them, and the configuration of the scene, with the deer now in the background, has also been changed somewhat. The colophon attributes these new illustrations to Hishikawa Moronobu (ca. 1631–93), the noted Edo artist known for his illustrations of contemporary popular fiction, guides to the pleasure quarters, and prints of kabuki actors. Interestingly, in 1685 there appeared a pair of editions of *Ise monogatari tōshoshō* almost identical to this one but for the publishers (one published by Nishimura Shichirōbee of Kyoto and distributed by Daimonjiya Hanbee in Edo; and the other published by Izutsuya Chūzaemon in Edo

---

47. This particular illustration is from an undated reprint of the 1679 version.

48. Mostow, "Illustrated Classical Texts," pp. 66–67, notes a few amplifications to the later version, but I do not believe the alterations to be substantial or numerous enough to agree with his assessment that the Edo version targeted a significantly more educated audience than the Kyoto version. Readers seeking a serious introduction to *Ise monogatari* scholarship during this period would have turned to *Ketsugishō* or *Shūsuishō*.

49. Ichiko, *Kinsei shoki bungaku to shuppan bunka*, pp. 316–18. In the early days of publishing, the activity was wholly centered in Kyoto and books were produced and sold by single publishers. Subsequently, activity developed in Osaka, and partnerships were established between Kyoto and Osaka booksellers, such as the one among Yamamoto, Hinaya, and Kawase in the case of *Kashiragaki Ise monogatari shō* (Yamamoto owned the blocks and the rights, but the other shops provided additional sales outlets). Eventually, by the late 1680s, three-way partnerships arose among Kyoto, Osaka, and Edo booksellers, but prior to that point booksellers such as Shōkai were pivotal in the dissemination of Kyoto-published books in the east. From the mid-1680s, however, Shōkai largely switched to producing new books and eventually became a designated supplier of books to the shogunate (Kornicki, *Book in Japan*, p. 200).

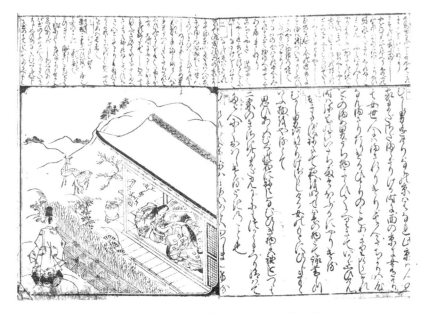

Fig. 4.10 Shōkai-han *Ise monogatari tōshoshō*. Undated woodblock-printed book.
Courtesy of the General Library, the University of Tokyo.

and distributed by Daimonjiya Shichirōbee in Kyoto) and a set of illustrations very close to Moronobu's, but attributed to Yoshida
Teikichi, this time a Kyoto artist famed for his illustrations of contemporary popular fiction, particularly the works of Ihara Saikaku.[50] It is
clear that these commentaries enjoyed great popularity. Speaking
strictly from the point of view of written content, and ignoring changes
to the pictures and recarved blocks, seven *Kashiragaki* variants were
produced between 1674 and 1710 along with numerous undated variants and reprints.[51]

Another popular commentary, published in 1693 by Daimonjiya
Shichirōbee, in conjunction with Izutsuya Chūzaemon of Edo and

50. Matsudaira, "Ehon, eiribon," pp. 266–67.
51. A few of these (again, with no change to the content) are titled *Ise monogatari
denju iri*. There are also cases of otherwise plain texts that lift the preface without including the commentary.

Akitaya Ichibee of Osaka,[52] is titled *Ise monogatari eshō* (*Ise monogatari* with illustrated commentary). This time the jumping-off point is Kitamura Kigin's *Shūsuishō* rather than *Ketsugishō*. The text begins with a two-part preface. Although the title and most of the *furigana* are added for *Eshō*'s version, the remainder is lifted verbatim from the first part of the *Shūsuishō* preface. The compiler, Namura Jōhaku (of whom more below), cuts only a handful of notes in the spots where I have inserted asterisks:

> Theories about the author of *Ise monogatari*
>
> Regarding *Ise monogatari*, an explanation appears in Lord Teika's colophon that, although it is said that it takes its name from the fact that it is the work of Lady Ise, there are various theories and the matter is difficult to decide. The reason is that it has humble and lowly language such as, "although he could not compose poetry," "since from the beginning he did not know much about poetry," "the shabbiness of such a poem!" and so on. Since these are all humble phrases, it is a sign of Narihira's own authorship. Also, the secrets of his heart, such as his visits to the Nijō empress, his meeting with the Ise priestess, etc., are recorded with poems. Since these are things that would be difficult for another to guess at and record, Narihira must have written them himself.[*] Moreover, there is a theory that there was a text of *Ise monogatari* in the Suzaku-in storehouse that was written by Narihira himself.[**] However, in this *monogatari* there is the matter of the Ninna emperor's excursion to Serikawa. This took place after Narihira's death. His brother Yukihira's poem is given there. Moreover this *monogatari* does not just contain Narihira's poems. Many poems from the *Man'yōshū*, etc. are mixed in here and there. Apart from those, since there are many places where old poems are turned into fictional stories, again, it cannot be Narihira's own writing. Therefore, even in the theories of the ancients it is decided that Lady Ise took a book that had first been written by Narihira himself, added her own writing and turned it into a fictional narrative, and gave it to the empress of Retired Emperor Uda, the Shichijō empress Onshi.[***][53]

---

52. Another one dated 1693 omits Akitaya in the colophon but is otherwise identical. See Tesshinsai Bunko, *Ise monogatari eiri hanpon no tenkai*, pp. 40–41. This one is titled *Shinchū eshō Ise monogatari*. Yet another was published by Daimonjiya in conjunction with Izumoji Izuminojō.

53. Namura Jōhaku, *Ise monogatari eshō*, 1:1 recto.

The removed notes from *Shūsuishō* are as follows:

* This much is the gist of Lord Teika's colophon. That colophon is given separately at the end.

** This is the theory in Kenshō's *Shūchūshō*, etc.

*** This is the interpretation in Lord Ichijō's *Gukenshō*, Botanka's *Shōmonshō*, Kansuiken [Kiyowara Nobukata]'s *Iseishō*, Yūsai's *Ketsugishō*, etc.[54]

Although San'unshi did not choose to pirate the lengthy, technical preface from *Ketsugishō* as he did material for the notes in *Kashiragaki*, Kigin's preface to *Ise monogatari shūsuishō*, written as it was for a less expert audience than *Ketsugishō*'s, evidently serves the needs of Jōhaku's projected audience almost as is. Only mentions of other texts, which Kigin himself had subordinated to the rest of the preface in the form of *warichū* (notes written in half-size double lines in line with the main text), are deemed superfluous.

Shūsuishō's preface goes on to give biographies of Narihira and Lady Ise as follows (*Ise monogatari eshō* reproduces the underlined parts of this verbatim):

Narihira was the grandson of Emperor Heizei and the fifth son of Prince Abo. His mother was Princess Ito, the daughter of Emperor Kanmu. It appears in the *Sandai jitsuroku* that he was born in the second year of Tenchō [825] during the reign of Emperor Junna, and that in the third year of the same era, Prince Abo submitted a petition asking that he be granted the surname Ariwara. He assumed duties as Provisional Middle Captain of the Right Bodyguards in the first year of Genkei [877] during the reign of Retired Emperor Yōzei. Since he was the fifth Ariwara son, he is called Zaigo Chūjō. When *Iseishō* refers to "the handsome old man," it means Narihira. His residence was at the intersection of Sanjō-bōmon and Takakura. The fact that the residence had the kind of pillars known as *chimaki* appears in Kamo no Chōmei's *Mumyōshō*.[55] *Sandai jitsuroku* says he died on the 28th of the fifth month of the fourth year of Genkei [880]. His resting place is at the Ariwara Temple at Isonokami in Yamato province. In the *Gyokuyōshū*[56] is the poem

---

54. Full preface of *Shūsuishō* in Takeoka, *Ise monogatari zenhyōshaku*, pp. 1602–4.
55. A collection of poetic lore, dated 1211.
56. The twentieth of the twenty-one imperial poetry collections, completed in 1312.

Composed at Ariwara Temple, by Tameko of the lower third rank

katabakari	In form only
sono nagori to te	do they remain—
Ariwara no	how sad to see
mukashi no ato o	the traces of
miru mo natsukashi	the past of Ariwara

Honchō shinsenden records that one day Narihira rode up the river in Yoshino and his whereabouts are unknown.[57] In *Tsurezuregusa* there is the poem "Admiring the moon, composing poems about flowers," that Jichin[58] wrote at the Iwamoto shrine at Kamo, where Narihira is enshrined.

Ise was the daughter of Tsugikage, the governor of Ise province, and the great-grandchild of the progenitor of their branch [of the Fujiwara clan], Lord Manatsu of Hino. She served as a lady-in-waiting to the Shichijō empress Onshi. Having received the favor of Emperor Uda, she bore Prince Yukiakira. Therefore, she is called Ise no miyasudokoro in the *Gosenshū*, *Yamato monogatari*, etc. This is because a person who bears a prince is called a miyasudokoro. She is also known as Lady Ise. Her residence was at the intersection of Nijō and Higashi no Tōin, and once when the priest Nōin[59] was giving Kanefusa[60] a ride in the back of his carriage, around the intersection of Nijō and Higashi no Tōin, Nōin suddenly got out of the carriage and walked for several blocks. Kanefusa was puzzled, and when he asked about it Nōin said, "These are the remains of Lady Ise's house. A pine tree that she planted is still here. How can I possibly pass it by in a carriage?" As long as he could see the pine tree he did not ride in the carriage, according to Kiyosuke's *Fukurozōshi*. Her grave is in Settsu province. At Kosobe, above Nōin's traces, is a place called Ise Temple. In recent times, Lord Nagai, governor of Hyūga province, renovated it and had Hayashi Razan write an epitaph for the tombstone.[61]

Again, for the most part the indications of sources are edited out, though the information derived from those sources is retained. Most striking,

---

57. No material concerning Narihira appears in extant versions of *Honchō shinsenden*, a late Heian collection of biographies of thirty-seven Japanese personages who became gods or immortals, compiled by Ōe no Masafusa (1041–1111).
58. Better known as Jien (1155–1225), a priest and poet perhaps best known as the author of the historical work *Gukanshō*.
59. Prominent Heian-period poet, born in 988.
60. Fujiwara no Kanefusa, 1001–69, another poet.
61. Takeoka, *Ise monogatari zenhyōshaku*, p. 1603.

however, is the way the author managed the information from the *Shūsuishō* preface that is not underlined above. Between the two parts of *Ise monogatari eshō*'s preface (the "Theory about the author" and the biographical information) there is a two-page spread recapping and bringing to life via illustration some of the anecdotes related to Narihira and Lady Ise that are set out in the biographical portion of *Shūsuishō*'s preface. The right-hand page, devoted to Narihira, shows him riding up the river in Yoshino to a mysterious end (note that this account of Narihira's demise is very much at odds with the text itself, which shows him meeting a much more sedate and poetic end on a conventional deathbed), and depicts the Iwamoto no Miya (with a label) at the upper Kamo Shrine. The blurb written across the top states explicitly that upon riding up the river Narihira became an immortal, this time without referring the reader to *Honchō shinsenden*,[62] and also gives the full text of Jichin's poem. The left-hand page, meanwhile, is devoted to the anecdote about the priest Nōin insisting on walking past the site of Lady Ise's residence, with the text as given in the *Shūsuishō* preface included at the top. The Ise Temple is also represented (with a label) in the corner.

The annotations appended to the base text in *Ise monogatari eshō* are also derived from *Shūsuishō* and utilize a similar division of labor between headnotes and interlinear notes (an approximation of the latter's handling of Section 2 is shown in fig. 4.11), though again, there is a marked tendency to simplify and to omit technical information, reminiscent of the relationship between *Kashiragaki* and *Ketsugishō*. The reading of "other people" as *yohito* is gone, as is Teitoku's little apology

---

62. This is just as well, because a reader who attempts to pursue the story to that text only discovers that it is not there. It seems likely that in making the attribution Kigin was misremembering a passage from the Genji commentary *Kakaishō*, reproduced in his own Genji commentary *Kogetsushō*. The commentary for the nonextant "Kumogakure" chapter, which covers Genji's death, notes: "Generally, among the famous worthies of ancient times, there are many examples where the way they died is unknown, from the Takeuchi Minister on down. This also appears frequently in *Honchō shinsenden*. Furthermore, as for the pioneer of amorousness, Lord Narihira, the story that he went to a cave at the upper reaches of the Yoshino River and passed on at the Tennokawa River appears in the *engi* of that place. This being the case, might [Murasaki Shikibu] have refrained from depicting [Genji's] death with this in mind?" (Kigin, *Genji monogtari kōgetsushō zōchū*, 3:194). The Narihira example does appear immediately after the mention of *Honchō shinsenden* but is clearly derived from a different source.

her appearance was surpassing
That woman surpassed other people. Her mind surpassed even her

She has a husband.   This is Narihira. Written 'honest man'
appearance. It seemed she was not alone. A serious man pledged his love

to her, and returned home—what might he have been thinking? It was

the third month
the last day of the month Yayoi, and he sent to her as a soft rain fell.

Fig. 4.11 Passage from *Ise monogatari eshō,* by Namura Jōhaku.

for the man's morals, while some additional notes ("the third month")
are included. As for *Shūsuishō*'s headnotes, some are converted to interlinear notes (how to write "serious man," the identification of the man
with Narihira) while others are simply discarded. The only headnote for
this section of text that is retained is the one concerning "A soft rain fell,"
which gives a number of Chinese compounds for the word *soufuru.*

The layout, however, has evolved beyond *Shūsuishō*'s, and even beyond *Kashiragaki* (fig. 4.12). Again the headnotes are contained within
their own space at the top of the page rather than intruding into the
base text area, and the guide phrases are made even more prominent by
presenting them in boxes. Most conspicuous, however, is the unusual
use of pictures in this commentary. Most texts give only illustrations
analogous to the illustrations in the *Saga-bon* (forty-eight or fewer), but
this one gives a picture on every page, many of which perform explanatory functions themselves, thereby making up for the reduction in the
quantity of commentary that their inclusion necessitates. The second illustration for Section 6, given in figure 4.13, provides an excellent example. Section 6 tells of the man abducting a woman whose favor he
was unable to win and transporting her to a place called Akutagawa,
where, amid a thunderstorm that obscures her cries, she is eaten by a
demon unbeknownst to the man, who stands guard outside. The section
goes on to record that the man "does *ashizuri*," a gesture that involves
lying on one's back and rubbing one's feet together in the air to express
frustration and unhappiness, and ends with an interpolated note identifying the woman as the Nijō empress, and the supposed demon as her
brothers, who heard her cries and stopped Narihira from taking her

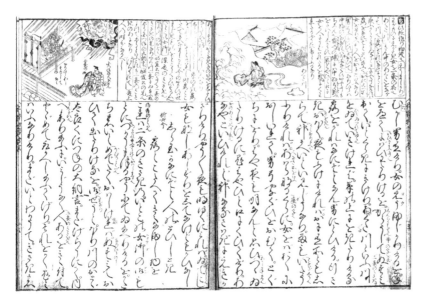

Fig. 4.12 *Ise monogatari eshō*, by Namura Jōhaku. Woodblock-printed book dated 1693. Courtesy of the General Library, the University of Tokyo.

away. The illustration that accompanies the end of Section 6 adopts the more realistic interpretation of the story given in the interpolated comment. In the illustration, the human figures are identified by name—Major Counselor Kunitsune looking rather sternly at the Nijō empress as she weeps into her sleeve, while back in the storehouse, "Narihira does *ashizuri* and cries." This helps to give an image of what the word *ashizuri* means without the author having to devote space to writing about it; *Shūsuishō* had included a lengthy headnote on the subject.[63]

The author-illustrator of *Ise monogatari eshō*, given at the conclusion of the text as Sōdenshi Sankei, has been identified by Ichiko Natsuo as Namura Jōhaku (d. after 1694). Jōhaku started out as a doctor, but eventually became a prolific writer whose output included not just medical and Confucian texts, but also *kanazōshi*, household encyclopedic dictionaries, "treasuries" (*chōhōki*) of practical knowledge directed variously at women, men, and samurai, and also illustrated commentaries

---

63. Note that the creature in the clouds is not the demon, but a thunder god.

Fig. 4.13 Detail from *Ise monogatari eshō*. Courtesy of the General Library, the University of Tokyo.

on *Ise monogatari* and *Tsurezuregusa*. As Ichiko points out, it is noteworthy that although he uses the proper name Jōhaku for the medical texts, Confucian texts, and dictionaries, he chose to apply to the works on *Ise* and *Tsurezuregusa* the pseudonym reserved for his less serious works. Ichiko remarks,

> Although it is usual for commentaries that use headnotes to eat into the base text owing to the insufficiency of the space allocated for the notes, because he divides that space and allocates half of it to illustrations, supporting citations from the various commentaries cannot be expected. The method of applying notes is to equip comparatively difficult vocabulary with a modern translation, and then to supplement insufficiencies with interlinear notes in the base text. He takes a posture of making the base text easier to read by offering simple notes for readers who cannot read it alone but who do not need the sources of or historical investigation into troublesome vocabulary. No scholarly significance can be distinguished, and, though I have not yet confirmed it, the notes them-

selves are probably borrowed from earlier works. In the case of *Tsurezuregusa eshō*, there are no notes at all; the headnote portion is devoted solely to illustrations. There are exceptions, but in general illustrations have been drawn for each section, and some sections have more than one illustration. Efforts have been made to have the illustrations aid in understanding the text, and Jōhaku probably thought that for a text like *Tsurezuregusa* notes were unnecessary. It is emblematic that at the end of both of these texts the author's name is followed by the words "illustrated and captioned by." In short, although these are obvious classics, Jōhaku's signing his name "Sōdenshi," etc., reflects his sense of these productions—that they are not important.[64]

Ichiko's surmise about the provenance of the commentary is of course correct, and his analysis of Jōhaku's use of aliases an intriguing indicator of a shift, or even slippage, in *Ise*'s position in the late seventeenth century. Whereas just a few decades earlier it was still indisputably and unshakably among the most important texts upon which a scholar might comment, in this case it is aligned instead with *kanazōshi* and other such nonserious works. However, this shift appears to have been not so much a reflection on *Ise* itself, as one on the devolution of the commentarial tradition to a place of multiple possibilities, or on the relatively uninitiated readers at whom the new texts were directed. Unlike San'unshi, who appears to have been perfectly content to have his name attached to his commentaries (or, to fragments of Yūsai's commentary) and who even warns away readers of loftier inclinations, Jōhaku appears to have conceived of himself as writing for two distinct audiences— consumers of so-called *mono no hon* (serious works) and consumers of *sōshi* (picture books or light reading). In the case of *Ise monogatari eshō*, although the base text is undeniably part of the high literary tradition— and on this basis even such works as *Eshō* and *Kashiragaki* are included in the lineup with other *Ise* related texts in the category of poetry-related books (*kasho*), a variety of *mono no hon*, in contemporary booksellers' catalogs—the treatment of the text and the anticipated audience for whom that treatment is conceived leads Jōhaku to divorce it from his

64. Ichiko, *Kinsei shoki bungaku to shuppan bunka*, pp. 342–43. However, in his entry on Jōhaku in *Nihon koten bungaku daijiten* he himself dismisses both of these books as being "not particularly noteworthy" owing to their simplicity and the squandering of headnote space on illustrations. Ichiko, "Namura Jōhaku," p. 554.

medical and Confucian oeuvre. Conceivably this divide is as much a matter of effective marketing as it is of Jōhaku's conception of the work as relatively trivial.

A final innovation of this period is in books that package *Ise* together with other works from the classical tradition, represented here by *Ise monogatari taisei*, *Shinchū eiri Ise monogatari kaisei*, and *Kokinwaka Ise monogatari*. Figure 4.14 is a sample of *Ise monogatari taisei*, signed by Namura Shōken (whose relation to Namura Jōhaku is unknown)[65] and published in 1697 by Yamaguchi Mobee of Kyoto in conjunction with Asami Yoshibee and Yoshida Saburōbee. *Ise monogatari* again occupies the bottom two-thirds of the page, but now the space for headnotes is given over to exemplary famous poets and their poems, starting with a full reproduction of the *Hyakunin isshu*. A portrait of each of the one hundred poets with his or her poem from that collection appears on the right side of the upper register of each page, while the left gives commentary on the poem together with a pictorialization. The upper register of figure 4.14 shows Narihira and his poem about red autumn leaves on the Tatsuta River from *Hyakunin isshu*. After all one hundred poems have been exhausted, the text runs through depictions of the thirty-six poetic immortals, followed by the six poetic immortals. Although the text purports to be focused on *Ise* (for each of the work's three volumes, "*Ise monogatari taisei*" appears in large print down the middle of the *daisen*, with the words "Commentary on *Hyakunin isshu*; *Thirty-Six Poetic*

---

65. While *Kokusho sōmokuroku*, for example, takes Shōken to be another of Jōhaku's pseudonyms, Ichiko Natsuo believes, based on a comparison of this text to *Ise monogatari eshō*, that Shōken, also the author of an *ukiyozōshi* and a *Kashiragaki Tsurezuregusa*, is a different person, pointing out that the reading marks and the biographies of Narihira given in the two texts diverge (*Nihon koten bungaku daijiten*, 4:554). However, the biography, which appears at the beginning of the third volume over a picture of Narihira writing, is lifted from *Kashiragaki Ise monogatari shō* or one of its variants, as is the information about Lady Ise given at the beginning of the second volume—the differences between the two need not be attributed to different authors, just to different sources. (Both the *Kashiragaki* biographies and the paraphrased fragment of the *Shūsuishō* preface used in this text take up far less space than those found in *Eshō*; perhaps this is the justification.) The reading marks in the text also appear to be following *Kashiragaki*. In the absence of positive evidence, I will not suggest that Shōken and Jōhaku must be the same person, but in view of the minimal original contributions of the "authors" of these texts, I do not believe that a comparison of *Eshō* and *Taisei* can provide sufficient evidence to negate the possibility.

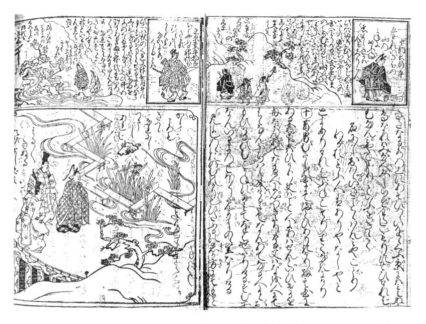

Fig. 4.14 *Ise monogatari taisei*. Woodblock-printed book dated 1697. Courtesy of the General Library, the University of Tokyo.

Immortals; Six Poetic Immortals and Evaluations"[66] beneath it in three lines of much smaller print), apparatus attached to *Ise* itself, in contrast to the full-blown commentary on the *Hyakunin isshu*, has been reduced to punctuation, exceedingly sparse interlinear glosses, and inclusion of poems from the base text within the relevant illustrations. The front matter consists, in the first volume, of a very brief statement about authorship, again similar to *Shūsuishō*, though not identical to it, a large block of reading conventions and a transcription of the *kana* preface to the *Kokinshū*, while the second and third volumes offer depictions respectively of Lady Ise carrying books to Empress Onshi, and of Narihira at his writing desk penning the words "In the past, a man. . . ." These pictures are further equipped with biographies derived from *Kashiragaki Ise monogatari shō* or one of its variants.

---

66. The "evaluations" consist of Ki no Tsurayuki's comments on the six poetic immortals in the *Kokinshū* preface and appear at the beginning of the third volume of the text, along with Narihira's biography.

The second example of this type, shown in figure 4.15, is (*Shinchū eiri*) *Ise monogatari kaisei*, published in 1698 by Daimonjiya of Kyoto in conjunction with Izumoji Izuminojō of Edo in one edition, and with Izutsuya Chūzaemon, also of Edo, in another.[67] This text features one picture from each chapter of *Genji monogatari* with the chapter title and the poem from which the title derives running across the top. When it runs out of these, it goes through the chapters again, showing plants or objects related to the chapter and accompanied by diagrams identifying related varieties of incense;[68] thereafter it runs through thirty-six famous female poets, followed by famous male poets, again in the form of portraits combined with a representative poem.[69] Once more, there is little space left for annotation, and the bulk of the *Ise*-related portion of the book is cobbled together from other sources: the interlinear notes, somewhat heftier than was the case for *Ise monogatari taisei*, derive from those in *Ise monogatari eshō* (belying the "new notes" claim of the cover), as do the biographies of Narihira and Lady Ise that appear with their portraits to begin each volume, while the pictures and captions in the text match those of *Ise monogatari taisei*.

A final example, shown in figure 4.16, is *Kokinwaka Ise monogatari*, published in 1699 by a trio of booksellers in Osaka and reprinted as a smaller book in 1799. This book includes the entire *Kokinshū* in the upper register, and *Waka kimyōdan* (Strange stories about Japanese poetry) in a narrow middle register, with *Ise*, equipped with illustrations, interlinear notes, and a *Shūsuishō*-derived preface, at the bottom.

All three of these texts, *Ise monogatari taisei*, *Ise monogatari kaisei*, and *Kokinwaka Ise monogatari*, move even farther away from the scholarly commentaries by virtue of their drastic reduction in annotation. The

67. The latter forms one of the same duos that published *Ise monogatari eshō* in 1693, suggesting that the pirating in this case may not really have been pirating, as the same firm owned both sets of blocks. All three of these booksellers were large, important publishers with wide-ranging catalogs. There is also another edition with no publication information.

68. See Maeda, "Genji kō," pp. 220–23.

69. Although I have not included *Ise monogatari kaisei* among the editions of *Ise* for women in Table 4.3, Joshua Mostow views the precedence of the female poets over the "coed" poets here as an indication that this book was also aimed at women readers ("Illustrated Classical Texts," pp. 68–72).

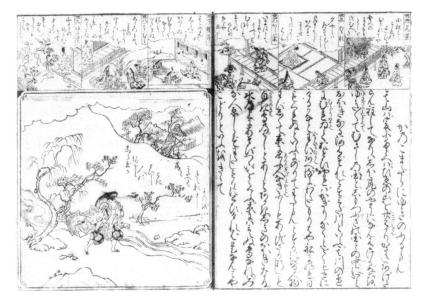

Fig. 4.15 *Shinchū eiri Ise monogatari kaisei*, by Namura Shōken. Woodblock-printed book dated 1698. Courtesy of the General Library, the University of Tokyo.

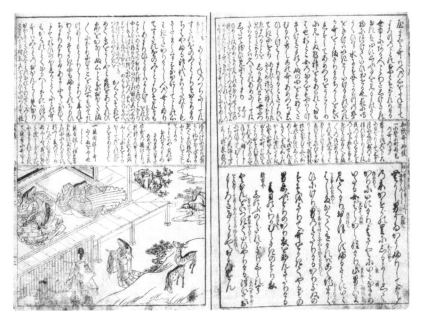

Fig. 4.16 *Kokinwaka Ise monogatari*. Woodblock-printed book dated 1699. Courtesy of the General Library, the University of Tokyo.

"value-added" features they offer in the freed-up space, along with the approach to *Ise* itself, are oriented instead toward giving the reader a general acquaintance with elements of the classical literary tradition, and particularly the poetic tradition, in a pleasurable (given the heavy emphasis on illustrations) and approachable manner. Unlike *Kashiragaki Ise monogatari shō*, which comes close to thumbing its nose at serious poets, these texts all begin by presenting themselves in a decorous manner that invokes the origins of the poetic tradition, thereby suggesting that something of venerable weight is being conveyed: both *Taisei* and *Kaisei* begin with depictions of Sumiyoshi Daimyōjin, Sotoorihime, and Kakinomoto no Hitomaro, the three gods of poetry (the former complete with incense burning before the portraits), while the *Kokinshū* portion of *Kokinwaka Ise* opens with a picture of formally dressed courtiers presenting the completed text to the emperor. The texts thus imply that they are giving the reader access to something quasi-sacred, formerly the exclusive territory of aristocrats. *Ise monogatari*, both a well-established part of the tradition and a text of contemporary interest, provides the anchor for that information. It is striking that in all three cases the added texts are presented parallel to the *Ise* on the page rather than preceding or following it. A hierarchy does remain, given *Ise*'s greater prominence in the titles of the books and in the space allotted to it, but it is not as though *Ise* is to be read prior to *Hyakunin isshu* or the *Genji* poetry, or after it. Rather, the "value-added" bits are arranged to be perused intermittently as the reader is drawn along by *Ise monogatari* (itself a highly interruptable text). Arguably, the effect of this arrangement is to generalize the poetic tradition, to allow the reader to accumulate or confirm a store of broad but (compared to what he or she might take away from a traditional, more scholarly commentary) shallow knowledge, rather than acquiring it in a more programmatic or compartmentalized fashion—again, a pronounced movement away from more orthodox study and scholarship. The prevalence of these books suggests that they were well suited to the needs of the new audiences of less highly educated readers who began to constitute an increasingly large proportion of the demand for reading material in the late seventeenth century.

Ise monogatari as Reading for Women

Although Confucian scholars in the seventeenth century often condemned *Ise monogatari* and *Genji monogatari* as potentially pernicious influences on the morals of women, recent scholarship demonstrates that women's actual reading habits did not necessarily conform to scholars' injunctions,[70] and from the early eighteenth century, evidence of a tendency to market *Ise monogatari* specifically as reading for women begins to appear. Some indication of an association between *Ise* and female readers has already been evident in Michikatsu's colophons; Asai Ryōi as well demonstrated considerable concern with finding strict Confucian lessons for women in *Ise* in his commentary. The discussion of *Ise* and women that appears in the preface to Takada Munekata's *Ise monogatari hiketsushō* (1679), another commentary closely related to Sairin's *Ise monogatari shitchū* but that includes the secret teachings found in *Ise monogatari kisuishō*, discussed in Chapter 3, offers a noteworthy counterpoint to Ryōi's approach.

> Regarding this commentary, I have written out all the reading conventions and oral transmissions about *Ise monogatari* in the words of a lecture because I had a request from a young lady of high rank who, wanting to learn about *Ise monogatari*, had gathered together and looked at the various commentaries but found that their meaning was not apparent and that they were difficult to listen to; she asked that they be written down in lecture style. That is, although I have cited twelve commentaries in a lecture, starting with *Gukenshō* and including all the secret teachings, because the young lady's listening is obstructed by her being at a distance behind her blinds, and it is difficult to grasp the pattern of the lecture, some things she misses, and some things she cannot make out clearly. And sometimes, if she has a question, because she is not face to face with

---

70. Kornicki, "Unsuitable Books for Women?" gives many vivid examples from the writings of scholars on both sides of the debate, as well as mustering evidence from individual women's writings and from illustrations of women reading about what women were actually doing. Joshua Mostow associates the eventual disappearance (or irrelevance) of scholarly debates and the rise of editions of classical texts that appear to have targeted women readers with "the overwhelming desire by members of both the warrior (*buke*) and townsman (*chōnin*) class for their daughters to acquire cultural capital associated with the aristocracy" ("Illustrated Classical Texts," p. 59).

the lecturer she cannot hear and remember the answer as she would like, and the meaning of *Ise monogatari* emerges with difficulty. Still more rare among the women in the four corners of the world who amuse themselves with *Ise monogatari* are those who understand a single a phrase beyond "In the past, a man." To begin with, *Ise monogatari* is fundamental to the Way of Poetry, and though both men and women should make use of it, it is something that women in particular should read. Although this is the case, they simply read the words and do not understand the heart of it. It is like wrapping fine incense in cloth and being unable to smell its fragrance, or hiding gold in a box and not seeing its color. Thus, the fact that they do not look at the colors of spring flowers and express their appearance in the headnote to a poem, or give comfort to their hearts by setting out the sadness of the autumn moon in thirty-one syllables, is because they have not heard lectures on *Ise monogatari*. The reason that sagacious women of the past like Murasaki Shikibu and Sei Shōnagon became poets and remain famous even to this day is that they began by studying *Ise monogatari*. If someone wants to be like them, she should read this commentary. Even without hearing a lecture, and without receiving a teacher's transmissions, nothing about *Ise monogatari* will be unclear. When the high-ranking young lady reclines behind her blinds and has someone read to her, it will be the same as a lecture. And when the lowest of women, while employed in service, amid her bustling, opens and reads this commentary, it will be as though she attends a lecture. Because I have of course noted reading conventions and secret teachings, now it will be like seeing the sun rise in the sky and its light illuminate everything after having traveled falteringly along a path in the dark mountains under the waning moon, where no light shines from between the trees. I have written at length in simple language for the sake of foolish women,[71] and have commented even on things that everyone ought to know in order to produce a handbook for beginners with this *monogatari*. However, because I have included none of my own opinions and have simply revised the wording of the older commentaries, I have called it *Commentary on the Secrets of Ise monogatari*.[72]

Here, of course, we are partly back in the world of the more scholarly commentaries: beyond the fact that Munekata draws on Transitional

---

71. Compared to *Kisuishō*, *Hiketsushō* uses fewer Chinese characters and eliminates references to Chinese works.

72. Takada, *Ise monogatari hiketsushō*, 1:1–2.

Commentaries from *Gukenshō* to *Kisuishō*, there is an assumption that no one, particularly not "foolish women," will be able to handle the text adequately without access to the full commentarial tradition or copious assistance from a teacher who is well versed in it, quite unlike the more optimistic assumptions that underlie the minimally annotated texts examined in the previous section. But conversely there is an assumption that even a rank beginner can learn—or perhaps become a latter-day Murasaki Shikibu—if given access to the necessary resources. Furthermore, Munekata's discussion suggests not just that women should take up *Ise* as an object of study that is particularly suited to them, but that they are already drawn to it, albeit in a way that does not necessarily result in the "heart" of the tale being laid bare to them. Most strikingly, he believes it to be important for ordinary women as well as the highborn, not even reserving the secrets of the commentarial tradition from them. The preface provides a suggestion of how destabilized that tradition was becoming, even by 1679, that its oral transmissions were being printed, and at the same time, a valuable piece of evidence about the perceived breadth of *Ise*'s appeal to contemporary women readers.

Namura Jōhaku's *Onna chōhōki* (Women's treasury), published in 1693, is one of many books produced in the Tokugawa period that were directed specifically at these ordinary women. Its five volumes begin with a brief preface written in the style of a woman's letter that cites *Tsurezuregusa* on the subject of women's innate perversity, self-centeredness, greed, and irrationality,[73] but goes on to offer itself as a corrective, a gathering of necessary information that will enable the expression of women's virtue as well as softening irrationality and perversity.[74] The fourth section of the first volume gives a long list of largely negative things that women purportedly enjoy (talking too much, sleeping late, smoking, attending the theater, behaving unfilially to mothers-in-law, and so on) and about which they should be prudent, followed by a compensatory list of more positive arts to be enjoyed. Fourth on the list, after calligraphy, composing poetry, and studying poetry, is "knowing the meaning of *Genji*, *Ise monogatari*, *Hyakunin isshu*, the *Kokinshū*,

---

73. Section 107 of *Tsurezuregusa*.
74. Nagatomo, *Onna chōhōki, Otoko chōhōki*, p. 10, n. 1.

and the *Manyōshū*,"[75] followed by items such as sewing and weaving, music, drawing, flower arranging, tea ceremony, and board games, and the statement, "Even if you know nothing apart from these, there is nothing lacking."

The early volumes of the text are largely devoted to matters of grooming, marriage, and childbirth, but in the fourth volume Jōhaku turns his attention back to appropriate pastimes, including a section on "Learning to compose poetry, and knowing the authors of poetic texts." Here he gives a list of the twenty-one imperial poetry collections plus the *Man'yōshū*, with dates and compilers, followed by:

> —*Ise monogatari* is the story of Narihira going to Ise province as an imperial huntsman and committing an offense with the Ise priestess, and otherwise peeking in upon captivating women, so it is called *Ise monogatari*. There is also a theory that it is because a woman named Ise wrote the tale.
> —*Genji monogatari* was created by a lady named Murasaki Shikibu when she secluded herself at the Ishiyama Temple in Ōmi province and prayed to Kannon.
> —*Hyakunin isshu* consists of famous poems by one hundred poets which Teika wrote on pieces of paper on the sliding doors of his mountain villa when he lived at Mt. Ogura.
>   Because the foregoing are books that women should amuse themselves with, I have given the authors.[76]

The grouping of *Ise* together with *Genji* and the *Hyakunin Isshu* is, needless to say, reminiscent of the packaging seen in books like *Ise monogatari taisei* and *Ise monogatari kaisei* and reinforces Joshua Mostow's suggestion that those texts too might have been aimed at women readers.[77]

In the eighteenth century, publishers begin tapping this potential market with a number of new editions of *Ise* that make the connection to women and women's education explicit by virtue of a new range of "value-added" material, again printed in the upper register of the page in lieu of headnotes. *Zōho eshō Kaō Ise monogatari* (*Ise monogatari*, the

---

75. Ibid., p. 22.
76. Ibid., p. 128.
77. Mostow, "Illustrated Classical Texts," pp. 68–72.

king of flowers, supplemented and illustrated), published first in 1721 by Kariganeya Shōzaemon of Osaka and reissued in 1738 and 1747 by other publishers (the first in Osaka and the second in Edo), is a particularly striking example. The book was compiled by Hasegawa Senshi (1689–1733), known principally as a writer of plays for the puppet theater, and contains illustrations by Hasegawa Mitsunobu (dates unknown). The note before the publisher's imprint in the 1721 edition reads:

> There are many printed texts of *Ise monogatari* in circulation, but these have quite a few mistakes in the characters and *kana* usage. Now, newly correcting the errors, adding reading conventions and commentary in *hiragana*, and making the heart of the text apparent in Japanese-style pictures, we have added lessons for women and it will be something that will be spread as widely as scattering cherry blossoms.

This note adopts precisely the same ploy as innumerable publishers' notes before it—"there are already many editions of *Ise* out there, but they are wrong and you need this corrected one"[78]—but the emphasis on the notes being written in *hiragana* (an unremarkable fact, as the overwhelming majority of even serious commentaries on the *Ise* are written in *hiragana*), the characterization of the illustrations as *Yamato-e,* and the flowery ending to the note are novel departures.

The text opens with an ornate title page, and again, portraits of Hitomaro and Sotoorihime. The text of *Ise*, with brief interlinear notes and glosses, occupies the bottom two-thirds of the page, while the top third is devoted to a wide array of material thought to be edifying for women. Figure 4.17, for example, shows "Diagram of Ogasawara school methods of paper folding," with a picture of a young girl practicing the method under the watchful eye of an older woman, perhaps her mother or a tutor. Other material includes illustrated explanations of flower arrangements, writing implements, the parts of a samisen, the proper way to store articles ranging from cloth and books to fish, descriptions of seasonal observances, of the six poetic geniuses, and so on. It is worth noting that much of this material closely resembles material found in Namura Jōhaku's *Onna chōhōki.*

---

78. The 1674, 1679, and 1685 editions of *Kashiragaki* each have such a publisher's note, as do illustrated versions of 1697, 1700, 1702, 1713, and various undated editions.

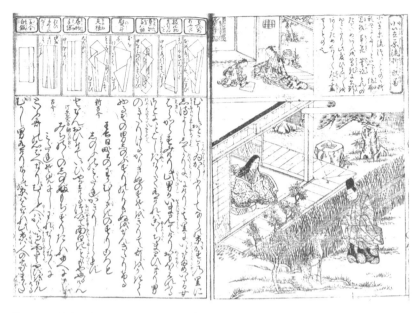

Fig. 4.17 *Zōho eshō Kaō Ise monogatari*, by Hasegawa Senshi. Woodblock-printed book dated 1721. Courtesy of the General Library, the University of Tokyo.

The brief preface gives not just biographical information about Lady Ise, but suggestions about the lessons to be found for women in *Ise monogatari*:

It is because Lady Ise received the favor of Emperor Uda and bore him Prince Yukiakira that she is known as Lady Ise. They say that perhaps it is because she supplemented a text that Narihira had written himself that it is called *Ise monogatari*. From times long past there have been many theories, but they are difficult to adopt. Lord Teika said that without forcibly seeking out the author one should appreciate the language. This is an excellent thing. In the text inside appears the story of Narihira going back and forth to Kawachi. This should be taken as being of great interest to women. Without displaying jealousy about Narihira's going to Kawachi every night, his wife composes the poem, "When the wind blows/and white waves break in the offing," showing concern about his crossing Mt. Tatsuta at night. It says that Narihira allowed that sentiment and gave up his desire to go elsewhere. The Noh play "Izutsu" also praises this lack of jealousy. Jealousy is the first thing a woman should be on guard against.[79]

79. Hasegawa, *Zōho eshō Kaō Ise monogatari*, 1:4–5.

The preface refers to Section 23 of *Ise*, where the man has begun seeing a second woman in Kawachi after his original wife's parents die and he is left without material support. Concerned that his wife's lack of jealousy means that she is involved with someone else, one night he pretends to set out for Kawachi and then hides in the garden, whereupon he sees the first wife recite a poem expressing concern for his safety, and he is so moved that he ceases visiting the second woman. Narihira is otherwise conspicuously absent from this preface, and no biographical information or portraits of him are given anywhere in the book, while a two-page spread again showing Lady Ise carrying books to the empress is placed prominently in the front matter after the pictures of Hitomaro and Sotoorihime. In this way the presentation of the *Ise* itself, despite the dearth of annotation, is just as slanted toward the implied audience of female readers as the bonus material in the upper register.

Additional texts that linked *Ise* to women's education appear in a booksellers' catalogs dating from the mid-eighteenth century: in this case the titles, *Ise monogatari jokunbun* (1747 and 1763) and *Ise monogatari nichiyō bunshō* (1747), both of which appear to use *Ise* as a vehicle to teach writing, as well as *Ise monogatari jokun taizen*, appear directly under the women's education category rather than being classified with poetry texts. Likewise, Yokota Fuyuhiko gives a description of a merchant's well-cataloged private collection that was sold off in 1736: the catalog gives poetry-related texts in one group, *Tsurezuregusa* in another, and lumps *Ise monogatari*, even in plain form, with women's education books. It is impossible to know what sort of edition of *Ise* is being referred to, but this is interesting and suggestive.[80] *Ise* can also be found grouped with educational books for women in booksellers' advertisements, printed in the back of other books, and conversely, plain texts of *Ise* often feature advertisements of books aimed at women. A 1756 illustrated but unannotated edition published by Kichimonjiya of Edo, for example, contains an advertisement that lists picture-book versions of *Genji monogatari*, of the Mt. Tatsuta story from *Ise monogatari*, of poetry-related texts; further titles dealing with writing; a Japanese history for women, a book about Ono no Komachi; and so on. And even a text of *Ise* entirely devoid of apparatus other than lush illustrations,

---

80. Yokota, *Tenka taihei*, p. 325. The list of women's books also includes a Genji-based book. Educational books directed at men are listed elsewhere.

Fig. 4.18 *Ise monogatari*, Kashiwabaraya. Woodblock-printed book dated 1756.
Courtesy of the General Library, the University of Tokyo.

also published in 1756, makes a tacit appeal to women readers by kicking
off with a picture of a young girl and an older woman reading together
(fig. 4.18).

As the eighteenth century wore on, there was a curious drop-off in
production of *Ise monogatari* texts with apparatus other than illustrations, though existing versions continued to be reprinted into the nineteenth century. It is possible that this was related to government inter-
ventions in the Kyōhō period (1716–36) to aid booksellers in suppressing
pirated editions: because new commentaries invariably lifted large
amounts of content from old commentaries, not to mention reproducing
the base text, whoever owned the blocks used to print the earlier text
was in a position to interfere with the publishing of the later one.[81] The

---

81. Ichiko, *Kinsei shoki bungaku*, pp. 20 and 370–71, where he discusses the case of
Tsurezuregusa. Peter Kornicki also observes, for example, that the publisher of a woodblock print edition of the *Kojiki* attempted to block Motoori Norinaga's *Kojiki-den* because its inclusion of the entire text constituted an infringement. See Kornicki, *Book in
Japan*, p. 213.

fact that existing books continued to be reprinted, often by new publishers who formally requested the blocks from the publishers who owned them, suggests that *Ise monogatari* suffered no reduction in popularity. But, particularly in the case of the kinds of books dealt with in this chapter aimed at nonscholarly audiences, where mixing and matching of parts taken from existing texts was standard operating procedure, the new laws must have been devastatingly inhibiting, and publishers no doubt sought out other, more advantageous projects. It would probably be going too far to argue that the early to mid-eighteenth-century tendency to classify *Ise monogatari* as a "women's education" text was solely a function of this need to circumvent the new piracy regulations—the association of *Ise* and women began far earlier than that—but it does seem possible that regulatory as well as marketing considerations were contributing factors.

In conclusion, the first 150 years of printing in Japan sufficed to move reception of *Ise monogatari* into thoroughly new territory. However little the popular books have to contribute to a history of scholarship focused on the evolution of interpretations, they and the arc they trace reveal a great deal about the shifting place of the classics in early modern culture and the changes that took place in the conduct of scholarship. Courtiers continued lecturing, producing commentaries, and transmitting secrets among themselves throughout the Tokugawa period, but owing the sharp aversion to print publication that developed after Michikatsu's time, in effect their work took place in a sealed vacuum. Outside that vacuum, the gradual but drastic stripping down of commentary seen in books published from the late seventeenth century onward is symptomatic of the relative loss of authority of early scholarly Transitional Commentaries and their increasing irrelevance to the way contemporary readers wanted to read. Although the newer books continued to take their basic content from the Transitional Commentaries, they put forth a very different message about *Ise monogatari*—the message not only that anyone, provided he or she had the necessary cash, was entitled to own a piece of the classical tradition and even be privy to supposed "secrets," but also that a well-rounded person (and from the eighteenth century, particularly a well-rounded woman) *should* do so. Aristocratic control of the tradition and access to it had slipped irretrievably. It was in this environment that nativist scholars' New Commentaries, the subject of the next chapter, took shape.

CHAPTER 5

Nativist and Confucian Constructions of Ise monogatari

The preceding chapter examined the shifts in the production and consumption of scholarship on *Ise monogatari* that accompanied the rise of commercial print in the seventeenth century. Although this chapter begins roughly where the last left off, in the Genroku period, we are in effect about to start over, to trace the evolution of a new lineage of *Ise* commentaries from its beginnings in the world of manuscript transmission (which continued to flourish throughout the Edo period), to the point where commentaries of this group too began to be printed and to circulate widely in response to increasing demand.[1] This lineage, which Ōtsu Yūichi dubbed New Commentaries (*shinchū*),[2] is typically viewed as beginning with the work of the Buddhist priest Keichū (1640–1701) and considered to be roughly coextensive with *kokugaku*, or nativism.[3]

---

1. See Kornicki, "Manuscript, Not Print," on manuscripts in the Tokugawa period. Although New Commentaries were being produced before the end of the seventeenth century, they did not start to be published until about a hundred years later.

2. Ōtsu, *Ise monogatari kochūshaku no kenkyū*, p. 25.

3. See Flueckiger, *Imagining Harmony*, p. 233 n. 1, for a discussion of recent efforts by scholars working in English to distinguish between the "*kokugaku*" and "nativism." Flueckiger himself uses the term "nativist" "to indicate those Tokugawa figures who sought to purify Japanese culture of foreign influences, whether or not they belong to what is normally labeled as 'Kokugaku' (which is itself a category with flexible boundaries, defined variously by such factors as these figures' objects of study, scholarly methodology, or institutional affiliation." With the exception of Keichū, who is usually seen

The label "New Commentaries" turns out to have a certain circularity—particular characteristics of the commentaries (supposedly) lead to their categorization, and yet it is the fact that the commentary is already viewed as belonging to the group that causes the gaze to be trained on these characteristics, and not on others. It is useful, therefore, to remember that the category is constructed, just as nativism and its genealogy of "great men"—Keichū, Kada no Azumamaro (1669–1736), Kamo no Mabuchi (1697–1769), Motoori Norinaga (1730–1801)—is itself is a construction.[4] As will be seen below, despite the tendency to view these men as a group with much in common, their work on *Ise monogatari* reveals significant differences in their respective approaches to literature from the classical tradition.

The term "nativism" generally identifies a movement beginning in the eighteenth century to elevate the study of the native tradition vis-à-vis Confucian studies, which enjoyed the official support of the shogunate and formed the curriculum of numerous private academies. In addition to what they saw as misplaced emphasis on Chinese learning itself, scholars identified as nativist were typically hostile to readings of Japanese texts that were driven by "foreign" concepts, meaning Confucian or Buddhist, and they relied in their own work on careful philological methods to recover the meanings of old texts. Ironically, these methods derived in large measure from those of Confucian scholars like Ogyū Sorai (1666–1728), whose *kobunjigaku* (philology of ancient texts) advocated a return to direct examination of the Confucian classics, unmediated by later scholarship and the distortions of *kanbun* renderings of the texts.

But nativist scholars also took aim at medieval scholarship, the conservatism and secretiveness of which they condemned harshly. Although nativism also depended upon master-disciple relationships—nativists operated schools and charged their students fees—Motoori Norinaga, for example, stressed the need for students to speak their minds and

---

as a forerunner to *kokugaku* scholars, and Goi Ranshū, who was a Confucian scholar, all of the scholars discussed in this chapter are typically viewed as both *kokugaku* scholars and nativists.

4. See McNally, *Proving the Way*, pp. 131–78, for a detailed discussion of Hirata Atsutane's role in defining these lineages.

oppose their teachers when they saw something questionable in the teacher's views. In *Tamakatsuma* (A jeweled basket, 1793–1801) he gives the rationale for this view:

> In general, when studying the past, it cannot be expected that one or two people will have the ability to make everything clear. Furthermore, even in the theories of the best scholars, how can there be no mistakes among the many ideas they put forth? It is impossible that there will not be bad things intermixed. A person who comes up with an idea might think to himself, "Now the spirit of the past has been made clear. Apart from this there is no correct idea." But unexpectedly another person might emerge who has a different good idea. As things pass through many hands, they are examined more deeply than in previous thought and our understanding gradually becomes more detailed. So, one should not tenaciously defend a position just because it is the teacher's view. To defend old ideas tenaciously without inquiring into the good and bad of them is a pointless practice that does not advance the way of scholarship. Moreover, revealing the errors of one's teacher may be a fearsome thing, but if one says nothing, the scholars of the world will be confused by those errors, and the time will never come that they recognize a good idea. To know that the teacher's view is bad but to cover it up and not point it out is to respect only the teacher while giving no thought to the Way.[5]

Clearly this is an attitude very unlike that which drove late medieval scholars, who, as we have seen, eschewed direct confrontation with their predecessors and made only gradual, incremental advances over the two hundred years between Ichijō Kaneyoshi and Kitamura Kigin. The "our school uses this reading" approach that pervades the Transitional Commentaries is a fairly clear example of "defending old ideas without inquiring into the good or bad of them," given how infrequently late medieval commentators offer explicit evidence in support of such ideas other than what they can glean from the speculations in Teika's colophons. In contrast, Norinaga suggests that answers to the questions scholars engage with can be found only when they work, in effect, as a community, building on past scholarship and free to criticize each other's ideas openly.

In their *Ise* commentaries, the scholars considered below vary in the way they handle previous scholarship and do not necessarily actualize

---

5. Yoshikawa, et al., *Motoori Norinaga shū*, p. 72.

Norinaga's precepts (which, in any case, postdate all but one of them) to the letter. In *Ise monogatari dōjimon* (A child asks about *Ise monogatari*, 1730s), for example, Kada no Azumamaro is openly contemptuous of Hosokawa Yūsai's views but never faults Keichū for putting forward some of the same views in *Seigo okudan* (Conjectures about *Ise monogatari*, 1692). Kamo no Mabuchi, on the other hand, cites almost no one by name in his *Ise monogatari koi* (The ancient meaning of *Ise monogatari*, 1758), though he occasionally raises earlier theories to disagree with them. Fujii Takanao (1764–1840), Norinaga's student, is the most straightforward of the group considered below, citing Keichū and Mabuchi frequently in his *Ise monogatari shinshaku* (New explication of *Ise monogatari*, 1812) and indicating precisely what he agrees or disagrees with and why. Despite this variation, though, Keichū, Azumamaro, Mabuchi, and Takanao all exhibit great independence of mind, never hesitating to put forward new interpretations and generally basing these on independent research rather than blindly citing the authority of their predecessors. This attitude is taken to be a distinguishing characteristic of the so-called New Commentaries as a group.

Elsewhere in *Tamakatsuma*, Norinaga deplores the practice of secret transmissions and asserts that the key teachings of any art should be disseminated as widely as possible. Keeping the core elements hidden, he suggests, will make the art weak and susceptible to extinction, and in any case, the motivation behind secret teachings is more often the initiates' base desire to retain the art as "private property" and to aggrandize themselves than a genuine concern with preserving the integrity of the art itself.[6] Norinaga states that he himself has never received secret teachings of any kind, and any student who wishes to know his thinking on a subject may simply consult his work, wherein he records everything he has to teach.[7] In this way, he sets himself and his cohorts up as superior to the medieval poet-scholars for whom secret transmissions were a fundamental activity. Thomas Harper has suggested that the nativists' pugnacious attitude toward medieval scholarship stemmed from a sense of disenfranchisement. In the medieval period and into the Edo period, the classical tradition was in a sense "the family property of the nobles whose ancestors

---

6. Ibid., p. 296.
7. Ibid., p. 231.

had written it—or at best the cultural heritage of the aristocratic class. They might deign to initiate certain underlings in its mysteries; what anyone else might have to say about it was not only irrelevant but presumptuous."[8] As a result, nativists were not just marginalized vis-à-vis Confucian scholars, they also had to fight to establish themselves as legitimate interpreters of the native tradition. Their sharp criticism of earlier scholarship, then, is in part fueled by sometimes bitter resentment of the long-standing exclusionary attitude of the elites, and their meticulous examination of old texts in order to support their own arguments becomes part of a strategy to cast doubt on any intrinsic entitlement that might have been claimed for the aristocracy as keepers of the tradition.

This chapter begins with a consideration of the "newness" of the work of Keichū, the figure with whom the New Commentaries are thought to have begun. This is followed by a discussion of Kada no Azumamaro's scathing attack on Hosokawa Yūsai's *Ise monogatari ketsugishō*, an attack that again hinges upon questions of fictionality and moral value, and of his student Kamo no Mabuchi's more nuanced conception of *monogatari* as a genre. In the third section, I turn to *Seigo tsū* (Understanding *Ise monogatari*, 1751), a Confucian commentary on *Ise* written by Goi Ranshū (1697–1762), who employs unusual strategies to neutralize potentially immoral content, but whose sympathy toward Narihira and what he conceived of as the morally sound part of *Ise monogatari* contrasts sharply with Azumamaro's position, and to some extent undermines commonly held notions about distinctions between Confucian and nativist approaches to literary texts. Finally, I discuss the work of Fujii Takanao, the student of Motoori Norinaga through whom the latter's work on Heian literature was continued and who introduced the concept of *mono no aware* into discussions of *Ise monogatari*'s literary and moral value.

The "Newness" of Keichū

The priest Keichū is generally viewed as a forerunner of the nativist scholars, and his *Ise monogatari* commentary, *Seigo okudan*, as the first example of a "New Commentary." One question that arises is how ex-

---

8. Harper, "*The Tale of Genji*," p. 119.

actly Keichū's work is "new" compared to earlier commentaries and how his work compares to the commentaries that followed.

Keichū was born into a samurai family but entered a Buddhist temple, the Myōhōji in Osaka, at age eleven in fulfillment of a vow his parents had made to save his life during a childhood illness. Two years later he took orders and moved to the headquarters of the Shingon sect at Mt. Kōya, where he remained for ten years. He subsequently became head priest at the Mandara-in in Osaka, and then, during the last twelve years of his life, served as abbot at Myōhōji. In his early years Keichū received rigorous training in reading Buddhist scripture, including study of Chinese and Sanskrit; later in his life he turned to study of the Japanese classics.[9] In addition to his magnum opus, the *Man'yō daishōki* (Stand-in's chronicle of the *Man'yōshū*, 1690), a commentary on the *Man'yōshū* that he completed on behalf of his friend Shimokōbe Chōryū (1627–86), and treatises on *kana* usage, Keichū produced commentaries on the *Kokinshū*, the *Hyakunin isshu*, *Genji monogatari*, the *Shinchokusenshū*, and songs from the *Kojiki* and *Nihon shoki*, as well as on *Ise monogatari*.

One aspect of Keichū's background that distinguishes him from the scholars examined thus far is the fact that he remained free of the sort of teacher-disciple ties and school consciousness that constrained late medieval Transitional Commentators. Although he is certainly aware of their work, he constructs his own arguments freely and dissents respectfully but openly when he disagrees with previous commentary. Keichū was also far more philologically and methodologically rigorous than his predecessors, supporting his arguments about the meanings of words in old texts with evidence gleaned as widely as possible from texts as closely contemporary to them as possible.[10]

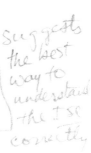

Keichū's final version of *Seigo okudan*, completed in the fall of 1692, opens with an eleven-point preface[11] that gives some insight into

---

9. See Nosco, *Remembering Paradise*, pp. 49–67, for a basic treatment of Keichū's career. There is also a convenient timeline of his career in Hisamatsu, *Keichū den*, pp. 467–84.

10. Hisamatsu, *Keichū den*, pp. 269–75.

11. Extant texts of *Seigo okudan* fall into two groups, a version in five volumes dated spring 1691 and a version in four volumes dated autumn 1692. These were not printed until 1803 and 1802, respectively, but circulated in manuscript in the eighteenth century. The four-volume text, which alone has this preface, can be assumed to be Keichū's

his approach and the degree to which his work alternately resembles and departs from previous commentaries.[12] The first point is as follows:

> This *monogatari* records the events of the life of Ariwara no Narihira. From ancient times, there has never been a clear explanation of the meaning of the title or the author. Lord Teika's colophon [in the *Rufu-bon*] says, "As for ancient matters, one should just look up to [the ancient authorities] and trust them." He also says, "One cannot forcibly find the author among the ancients; one should just take pleasure in the beautiful language." These words are vital. It is right that we should follow them.

Thus far, the preface is almost indistinguishable from late medieval commentaries, asserting that *Ise* is at least loosely biographical (Keichū also routinely identifies the protagonist as Narihira in the commentary proper, much unlike subsequent nativist scholars) and examining Teika's colophons for hints. In the second point, dealing with authorship, however, we see a break with the old style: where the late medieval commentaries had based their decision that Lady Ise wrote the *monogatari* entirely on Teika's comments, Keichū examines other sources to prove that it could not have been completed during Ise's lifetime (her dates are not certain, but she is thought to have been born around 877 and died around 940):

> Someone asked what I think about the theory that this is Ise's work. My answer is as follows. In the matter of the Nijō empress and the matter of the Ise priestess, the *Kokinshū* [compiled in 905] is vague and does not give their names outright, but in this *monogatari* they are written clearly.

---

final version, but copies of the five-volume version in both manuscript and woodblock-printed editions survive in greater numbers. This translation of the preface is based on the four-volume version found in Hisamatsu, et al., *Keichū zenshū*, 9:3–5. The more widely circulating five-volume version can be found in Takeoka, *Ise monogatari zenhyōshaku*.

12. Richard Bowring's discussion of *Seigo okudan* emphasizes its similarities to the Transitional Commentaries. In a note to his discussion of Keichū, he cites Harper's article to support his contention that there is nothing particularly "new" about Keichū's commentary ("*Ise Monogatari*," p. 468, n. 101). However, Harper follows up some initial reservations with an account of the ideological underpinnings of this sense of newness and also cites philological rigor and a sensitivity to the inner workings of the text as concrete manifestations of it. Bowring definitely has a point with regard to Keichū—*Seigo okudan* has enough in common with the Transitional Commentaries that its newness is initially hard to discern. But as I will argue below, in his approach, if not in his conclusions, Keichū does depart from the late medieval commentators in important ways.

Because the Nijō empress was alive until 910, these are not things that should have been spoken of clearly [prior to her death]. Also, because the Nijō empress ceased to be an empress in 896 and was reinstated in 943, wouldn't it have been inappropriate to write "Nijō empress" at a time when she was not empress? In the *Kokinshū* she is identified as the Nijō empress, but this also might be because a later person changed it; although the Biwa Lord [Fujiwara no Tokihira] became Minister of the Left in 938, the author of his poem that begins "At Mount Yoshino/In China" [*Kokinshū* 1049] in the book of humorous poems is given as "Minister of the Left." If you compare the case of the Nijō empress to this, you will understand. If the author wrote "empress" at a time when she was not empress, wouldn't it be turning one's back on imperial commands?

The point here is that Lady Ise would not have been in a position to identify the Nijō empress as an empress by virtue of the timing; only someone amending the text later, as in the case of Tokihira's title as given with his *Kokinshū* poem, could have done so.

Keichū continues with another novel observation:

Is the fact that Narihira is sometimes praised and sometimes demeaned because the author deliberately wrote it to be confusing? Or was the humble language part of Narihira's own writing? The headnotes to Narihira's poems in the *Kokinshū* are detailed and most of them resemble this *monogatari*: Is this because both works derive from the same personal poetry collection or memoir? If this is not the case, then did this *monogatari* copy the *Kokinshū* headnotes and make them more detailed?

Although Keichū hedges here and makes no assertions about things he cannot prove, he considers the relationship between *Ise* and the *Kokinshū* in a way that the Transitional Commentaries had not attempted and suggests for the first time alternatives to the theory that the occasional use of humble language must contain traces of Narihira's own voice, something that late medieval commentators accepted unquestioningly, based again on Teika's comments in the *Rufu-bon* colophon.

Keichū then distinguishes further between *Ise* and the *Kokinshū*, making explicit an assumption that was in place as early as the Kamakura commentaries:

There are differences between this *monogatari* and the *Kokinshū*. Because the *Kokinshū* is an imperial poetry collection it is reliable, and because this is a *monogatari*, there will be things that are left up to the brush.

Finally, Keichū offers a hint about the whys and wherefores of "things being left up to the brush":

> There are places where the dates and the ranks and offices various people held are not reliable . . . It is written in the *Wuzazu*[13] that in China there are also *monogatari* of this kind that mix fiction and fact. The reason must be that they would have no force if they were not written this way. This must be the reason that many things appear in the *monogatari* that are not consistent with an authentic record.

Here it becomes clear that, despite his agreement with late medieval commentaries that *Ise* records Narihira's life story, Keichū has a more subtle and comprehensive notion of what a *monogatari* is. His statement that fact and fiction are mixed in order to give the work more "force" suggests a first step toward appreciating *Ise* as a whole as a narrative, an attitude that becomes more pronounced with Mabuchi and Takanao.[14] Although the preface to *Seigo okudan* is rather underdeveloped by comparison with those of later New Commentaries, it does provide important indications of Keichū's willingness to move beyond past scholarship and hints about his methods.

Another important difference between *Seigo okudan* and late medieval commentaries may be found in Keichū's handling of moral questions. In his analysis of Section 49, the story of Narihira and his younger sister, Keichū is worlds away from the views expressed in the mainstream Transitional Commentaries. After the man's poem about another's hand gathering "the young grasses, so fresh and good for sleeping," Keichū comments:

> Being a little in love with his sister, he composes this poem. Because the text says below that Narihira was his mother's only child [Section 84], perhaps this is his sister by a different mother. In the record of Emperor Ingyō in the *Nihongi*, it says that . . . because it became known that Prince Kinashi Karu and Princess Karu no Ōiratsume had illicit relations, the princess was exiled to Iyo province. This was because Osaka no

---

13. A Ming dynasty miscellany, written by Xie Zhaozhi, that discusses a wide variety of natural and social phenomena. It was published in Japan in 1660.

14. Although the Transitional Commentaries had also included comments here and there about the strategies of "fictional *monogatari*" being employed within *Ise monogatari* to create added interest or aesthetic value, as a rule these comments applied only to individual sections of *Ise*, rather than being applied to the whole.

Ōnakatsuhime was the mother of both of them. Because there are many examples of [emperors'] sisters by different mothers being elevated to empress, it must be that the latter case [i.e., marriage between non-uterine siblings as opposed to uterine siblings] was not viewed as being troubling. According to both Buddhist and Confucian texts there is nothing uncertain about this matter [i.e., relations between siblings are condemned], but this country is founded on the Way of the Gods. Nonetheless, one should not consider this matter recklessly because it was something that existed from the age of the gods. One should not criticize the practices of the past because a thing has become hateful later. At the same time, one should not make the past an example for the present. Some commentaries, forcibly helping Narihira, say that he is not in love with his sister, but if this is the case how can they speak of the Ise priestess and the Nijō empress? Things should just be taken as they are.[15]

Where mainstream Transitional Commentaries had attempted to defuse the scandalous implications of this section by arguing that Narihira's poem indicates pity for the girl in her unmarried state and that her response expresses gratitude for his concern, Keichū unflinchingly accepts the romantic feelings suggested by the brother's poem and seeks out an explanation for the way the situation is presented in the text. In his use of the *Nihon shoki* to make his case, and above all in his contention that Buddhist and Confucian thought are not relevant to Japan, founded on "the Way of the Gods" (Shintō), Keichū's views foreshadow the preoccupations of later nativist scholars. (Recall that Hosokawa Yūsai, by contrast, had rather unconvincingly supported the tamer reading by citing the *Shijing* and the *Brahmajâla sutra*—it seems likely that in this comment Keichū is responding either directly to *Ketsugishō* or to *Shūsuishō* citing the same passage from *Ketsugishō*.)

Keichū has a similarly novel reading of the last section of *Ise*, which contains Narihira's death poem:

In the past, a man fell ill and felt that he would soon die.

tsui ni yuku	I had heard before
michi to wa kanete	that this was a road
kikishikado	we must all travel in the end

---

15. Takeoka, *Ise monogatari zenhyōshaku*, pp. 787–88.

| *kinō kyō to wa* | but I never thought |
| *omowazarishi o* | it would be yesterday or today. |

Keichū says:

> This is an excellent poem for teaching, as it shows a person's true feeling. When people of later ages arrive at the point of death they compose every kind of poem, some about awakening to the [Buddhist] Way, and so on, and they assume an attitude that is not truthful; it is very hateful. At ordinary times, they probably use "wild words and fancy language" [*kyōgen kigo*]; even more at the point when they think death is upon them they return to their true hearts [i.e., feel attached to the world]. In this poem, Narihira expressed the truthfulness of his whole life; people of later ages die expressing the falseness of their whole lives.[16]

Again, Keichū's position foreshadows mainstream nativism. Regarding this passage, Norinaga wrote, "When Keichū said this he did not resemble a Buddhist priest. It is very, very noble: a person with Japanese spirit, even if he is a priest, is like this. Would a Shintoist or scholar of poetry who thought in the Chinese way ever say something like this? The Reverend Keichū taught the world truth; such Shintoists and scholars of poetry teach lies."[17]

However similar Keichū's conclusions may be to those of his predecessors, clearly something is afoot here that must be termed "new." Like Kaneyoshi before him, Keichū is a significant transitional figure who brings a degree of positivism and philological acuity to scholarship on *Ise monogatari* that is remarkable when one considers what was going on in *Ise* studies elsewhere at the time when he wrote; Keichū produced *Seigo okudan* in the same year that *Ise monogatari eshō* was published, in the early years of the decade when popular annotated editions of *Ise* began to flood the marketplace, and when *Ketsugishō* and *Shūsuishō* represented the height of scholarly achievement related to the *monogatari*. However, even though *Seigo okudan* went on to influence subsequent nativist scholars profoundly, society at large does not appear to have been prepared to welcome Keichū's meticulous, detailed approach. The text did circulate among scholars in manuscript, but another 110 years

---

16. Ibid., p. 1582.
17. Yoshikawa, et al., *Motoori Norinaga shū*, pp. 165–66.

passed before it found an audience in print and took its place among readily available nativist commentaries.[18]

Fiction and *Makoto*: Kada no Azumamaro and Kamo no Mabuchi

Kada no Azumamaro descended from a scholarly family who had served as heads of the Fushimi Inari Shrine in Kyoto for over a thousand years. His talents as a poet and scholar led him briefly to a position as a tutor to Prince Myōhōin, a son of Emperor Reigen (r. 1663–87). In his thirties, for reasons unknown, he moved from Kyoto to Edo and set up a school, where he lectured, principally to others who were affiliated with Shinto shrines, on ancient Shinto liturgy, ancient history, and early poetry. Perhaps his greatest claim to fame was his *Sōgakkōkei,* or "Petition to found a school," made to the shogun Yoshimune in 1728 and seeking government support for a school devoted to the study of ancient Japan. Although scholars have questioned the authenticity of this document, and in any event the shogunate did not honor the request, it became the basis for later scholars to trace the origins of *kokugaku* back to Azumamaro.[19]

---

18. In *Tamakatsuma,* Norinaga describes his experience trying to lay hands on Keichū's other commentaries. "Up until 20 or 30 years ago," he says, writing in the 1790s, "neither poets nor Shinto scholars studied the *Man'yōshū.* Through Keichū's work, its importance began to become clear, but still almost no one knew that this guide existed, and copies of Keichū's *Man'yō daishōki* were rare and extremely difficult to come by. Even his *Hyakunin isshu kaikanshō* [1746] was hard to find. When I first borrowed it from someone in Kyoto [during his student days—his teacher Hori Keizan had a copy] I thought I'd like to buy one and went to the bookstore, but there were none there. 'It's been printed. How can you not have one?' I asked, and the bookseller replied, 'There's no one who needs it, so we don't [re]print it.' Eventually, with difficulty I was able to get it, but up to that time it took much effort. Nowadays, however, there are many manuscript copies of *Daishōki,* and the fact that it is not at all difficult to get them is because study of the past has been opened up, and many people have use for them. This is not only true of *Daishōki*—many other books that used to be very hard to get can now be gotten easily, and this is owing to the wonderful, awe-inspiring glory of the reign we live in!" Yoshikawa, et al., *Motoori Norinaga shū,* pp. 67–68.

19. For biographical information on Azumamaro, see Nosco, *Remembering Paradise,* pp. 71–78. See McNally, *Proving the Way,* pp. 152–54, on *Sogakkōkei* and its authenticity, and pp. 147–58 on Azumamaro's place in later views of the lineage of *kokugaku's* "great men," particularly Hirata Atsutane's.

Ise monogatari dōjimon, written by Azumamaro late in his life,[20] is a departure from his Shinto studies, and not, properly speaking, a commentary on *Ise monogatari*, but rather a commentary on commentary. It takes the form of a "child" asking questions about Hosokawa Yūsai's *Ise monogatari ketsugishō*, which, as we have seen, was the most prominent medieval commentary in circulation in the Tokugawa period. However, Azumamaro's opening remarks emphasize *Ketsugishō*'s reputation among scholars irrespective of its broader popularity:

> The child says: There are quite a few commentaries on *Ise monogatari*. However, among them all, scholars of poetry say that none equals the *Ketsugishō* of Hosokawa Yūsai in distinguishing the right and wrong of the various commentaries. Therefore, I will now ask questions based on *Ketsugishō*.[21]

In *Ise monogatari dōjimon*, Azumamaro makes an important break in asserting, repeatedly and vehemently, that *Ise monogatari* is purely fiction, with no trace of Narihira to be found, even where his own poems are included. For example, discussing the first section, Yūsai wrote, "Because this *monogatari* tells of Narihira's entire life, matters running from his coming-of-age to his death are included in it. As a result, it ends with the poem containing the lines 'but I never thought / [my death would come] yesterday or today.'"[22] Azumamaro's child is programmed to ask about Narihira any time Yūsai gives his name, and here he comes through with the requisite question for the first time of many: after quoting Yūsai, the child remarks, "Since [*Ise*] is complete from beginning to end, and since the poem 'but I never thought / it would be yesterday or today' is included in the *Kokinshū* and is without a doubt written by Narihira, isn't this proof [that the man is Narihira]?"

> Answer: No. The "yesterday or today" poem is Narihira's. However, the reason it appears in the made-up things of this *monogatari* as the work of "the man of old" without giving his name is that it is remade into the poem of "the man of old." The *monogatari* is written about "the man of

---

20. The date of *Dōjimon* is uncertain, but Mabuchi mentions in the colophon to one of the texts that Azumamaro wrote it after he had fallen ill. It was probably written in the early 1730s. See Ōtsu, *Ise monogatari kochūshaku no kenkyū*, pp. 570–71.

21. Takeoka, *Ise monogatari zenhyōshaku*, p. 1605.

22. Ibid., p. 55.

old" from his capping ceremony to his death. One should not conclude that it is Narihira. The evidence that it is not Narihira will appear in each place throughout the tale. If the man in the tale were Narihira everywhere, then each time it says "a woman of old" who could we decide it is? Beginning with the words "in the past" means that a specific year and month are not indicated. This is because a fictional *monogatari* is not a historical record. The beginning of *Genji monogatari*, "In a certain reign, among the many consorts and attendants who served the emperor . . ." has the same import as "in the past" in this *monogatari*. Therefore, one should not say that the man is anyone in particular.[23]

So far Azumamaro's critique appears straightforward and reasonable: *Ise* is not a historical record, and it needs to be read in other terms. Elsewhere in the commentary Azumamaro characterizes earlier commentators' habitual equation of the man of old with Narihira as "the first step that leads to a thousand miles of error," and it does sometimes lead to interpretations that strike a modern reader as questionable, as we have already seen in the Transitional Commentaries' "public" approach to Section 49. Azumamaro's determination to separate *Ise* from Narihira, and refutation of corresponding attempts to read the protagonist in terms of some preconceived notion of Narihira's character, whether drawn from different sources or other parts of *Ise* itself, do enable some solid new readings. However, Azumamaro's view of *Ise*'s fictionality is not as simple as it seems at first: it is inextricably entangled with moral questions.

Azumamaro's comments on Section 49 are quite similar to Keichū's. He too sees the man's poem as indicating romantic interest in his sister. Unlike Keichū, however, he does not try to offer any justification for this behavior or read it in terms of what he finds in other early texts: the man is simply immoral, and his poem is an expression of lasciviousness.

> The child asks: In *Ketsugishō*, it says "It is said that Narihira [was in love with his sister and] composed this poem, but this is not the case. He thinks his sister is unfortunate and says it out of pity for her." Is this theory correct?
>
> Answer: No. When we dispose of the usual fallacy of viewing the man of old as Narihira, the theory that he composes the poem because he is in love with his sister must be correct. It must be that as a result of deciding it is Narihira, they made this theory in order to avoid a reading

---

23. Ibid., pp. 62–63.

of love between brother and sister. . . . Since in both the past and the present there are examples of such immorality, although it is written in this *monogatari* as just an exchange of poetry, and it is probably not the intention of the author, we should view it as something that can serve as an admonition to later generations. However self-indulgent and unreserved Narihira's character might have been, if Narihira's spirit is present in the world, will taking such a thing as fact be agreeable to him? Whoever started this groundless rumor is like one dog barking out falsehood and the other dogs calling it truth without perceiving the first dog's lie.[24]

A bit later in the commentary on this section he expands on this charge of immorality as follows:

> When we view both *Ise* and *Genji* as fiction, without regard for traces of facts, they can become somewhat helpful for understanding the good and bad of prose and poetry, and the conditions of their times. If they were true [*jitsuji*], they would not be something a sound hand should take up. From middle antiquity onward, scholars of poetry have come to think of *Genji* and *Ise* as foundational texts, and truly, it reaches the point where the Way of Poetry becomes an agent of lasciviousness. This should be lamented and deplored.[25]

Even when Yūsai acknowledges a section as fiction, Azumamaro criticizes him. The following is his comment on Section 12, in which the man runs off with a girl in Musashi province and is arrested by the provincial governor:

> The child asks: *Ketsugishō* says of this section, "Because this section in particular is a fictional story, it tells of things that did not happen." Isn't this comment correct?
>
> Answer: No. Based on what evidence does he say that only this section is a fictional story? Doesn't he know that if this section is a fabricated, fictional story, then those that come before and after it must also be fictional? If the *monogatari* is factual, then this section should also be viewed as factual. His saying "that section is fact and this section is fiction" stems from the error of viewing everything as Narihira's life. Hesitating to think that Narihira was arrested by the provincial governor as a thief, he says that this section tells of things that did not happen. I cannot accept this. Because previously there was the matter of stealing the Nijō empress away to a place called Akutagawa, if, here in Musashi,

---

24. Ibid., p. 789.
25. Ibid., p. 790.

Narihira had the same desire to steal as before, it is right that he should be arrested. I cannot understand why [Yūsai] avoids in this section what he writes in the previous section, even though this section says, "Even in the provinces, the man did not give up this kind of behavior." If the author of the *monogatari* wrote such a thing in order to expose the shame of amorousness and to serve as an admonition to later generations, then we should allow it. If he unthinkingly wrote such a thing to pique interest, then this *monogatari* is not something that men and women should read. However, when scholars of poetry explain that it is a text one should value, they are making it the foundation of a way of morality. This should be feared. This should be lamented. This should be chastised.[26]

The inflexibility in evidence here, or perhaps insistence on totalizing, such that *Ise* in its entirety must be viewed only in one mode, fact or fiction, is typical of Azumamaro's approach throughout *Dōjimon*. He takes issue in the same way with Yūsai's intermittent characterization of incidents in *Ise* as examples of "*haikai*," comic or vulgar in tone, saying, "If one part is *haikai*, every part must be *haikai*" (implying that therefore no part is *haikai*).[27]

Yūsai's analysis of Section 63 provokes further criticism from Azumamaro, in which he reveals his hand in full. The section is as follows:

In the past a woman who wanted a man to love her thought how she wished she could meet a man of deep feeling. Because she had no way of coming out and saying so, she made up a story about a dream. She called three of her children and told them about it. Two of them made unfeeling responses and dismissed it. The third son said, "It means that a good man will surely come to you," and with that the woman looked very pleased.

Most men are quite without feeling. The son thought he would like to have her meet the Ariwara Middle Captain[28] somehow. He ran into the

---

26. Ibid., p. 296.

27. For a discussion of use of the term *haikai* in commentaries associated with Sōgi, see Yamamoto, *Ise monogatari ron*, pp. 279–91. Yamamoto also takes issue with Azumamaro's view of the Transitional Commentaries' handling of fact and fiction. In Yamamoto's view, the Transitional Commentaries' persistent identification of the protagonist as Narihira, even in sections they view as "*tsukuri monogatari*," does not really involve a contradiction; rather, this is an indication that they recognized the protagonist as a fictionalized Narihira, not a historically accurate Narihira. Azumamaro's definition of *tsukuri monogatari* is simply more extreme, allowing for no middle ground (ibid., pp. 402–5).

28. A position Narihira held at the end of his career. This is the closest the text comes to naming Narihira outright.

Captain when he was out hunting and, taking the bridle of his horse on the road, explained the situation. The Middle Captain pitied her, and went to sleep with her. Then, afterward, because he did not appear again, the woman went to his house and peeped in at him. The man saw her faintly and said:

momotose ni	One year short
hitotose taranu	of one hundred years
tsukumogami	with her thinning hair
ware o kourashi	I see a vision
omokage ni miyu	of one who seems to love me.

Seeing that he looked as if he was about to leave, she returned to her house, bumping against brambles and thorny bushes, and lay down. As the woman had done, the man stood outside looking at her secretly. The woman lamented and started to go to sleep, saying:

samushiro ni	On a narrow mat
koromo katashiki	with a single robe for a cover
koyoi mo ya	again tonight
koishiki hito ni	will I lie here longing for him
awade nomi nemu	but without meeting?

The man was moved, and spent that night with her.

As a rule, people in this world are considerate of those they love and unfeeling toward those they do not love, but this man had a heart that made no such distinctions.

After the first poem, Yūsai writes:

This does not necessarily mean that she is ninety-nine years old. He says this because she is a terribly aged woman who does not appeal to him. However, the fact that he does not abandon her [is because] Narihira pitied people and had a character of deep compassion.

And at the end:

Narihira's character is written about. Although people view desirable and undesirable qualities separately, the author is praising Narihira as a person who shows no such prejudices.[29]

---

29. Takeoka, *Ise monogatari zenhyōshaku*, p. 929.

Azumamaro responds:

> As for praising Narihira's deeply compassionate character, this is idiotic. Things like praising lewdness and immorality as deep compassion are all because of the deterioration of [the Nijō] school. Because they teach and learn that the Way of Poetry is the way of Japan, they use tales of lewdness and immorality to speak of the way. It is discouraging. If *Genji monogatari* and this *Ise monogatari* are viewed as expressing the lewdness and immorality of the men and women of old, and kept to the margins of the teachings, there are things in them that may be allowed. But all the same, one should throw them away, study the book of the *Nihongi* dealing with the age of the gods, which shows the true way, and seek the teaching of "rewarding good and punishing evil" [*kanzen chōaku*] in the deeds of the good and evil deities in the age of the gods. This *monogatari* should be viewed as being like the stories of modern kabuki: those who would look at them should look at them, and those who would avoid them should avoid them. Narihira's debauchery is not at all something that should be praised as a feeling of compassion for people.[30]

The comment on this section and on Section 49 make Azumamaro's position clear. By identifying *Ise* as fiction and then going on to link fiction with amorousness (*kōshoku* or *irogonomi*) and immorality, Azumamaro seeks to discredit medieval Nijō school commentators twice over: first by questioning their ability to handle texts and evidence competently, and second by questioning their judgment in valuing a perniciously immoral text so highly.

The concept that will allow us to unravel this tangle of moral issues, *irogonomi* and fictionality is Azumamaro's notion of *makoto*. *Makoto* might be translated as "sincerity," but it also has affinities with truth, in the sense of fact, in the dichotomy between factual records and things (*jikki, jitsuji*) and fictional *monogatari* (*tsukuri monogatari, tsukurigoto*; also *soragoto*, "fabricated things," or falsehood). In the commentary on Section 111, this association is made explicit. Taking Yūsai to task for privileging *Ise* over *Kokinshū* and *Gosenshū* (Yūsai says that a *Gosenshū*

---

30. Ibid., p. 932. There is more rigidity here as well—according to Azumamaro, because the text is not fictional for Yūsai, et al., if it says the woman is ninety-nine, she must be ninety-nine.

poem involves alterations to lines from an *Ise* poem rather than the other way around), Azumamaro writes:

> Because they forcibly take this *monogatari* as a factual record [*jikki*] and do not use *Kokinshū* and *Gosenshū* when there is evidence that *Ise monogatari* postdates *Gosenshū*, their poetics casts aside the true way and sticks to fabrications [*kyo*] that are not fact [*jitsu*]. . . . The *Kokinshū* is a factual record. Because this is scholarship that does not take up a factual record, and instead considers fabrications to be a factual record, one cannot learn a single thing from Nijō school poetic studies. In a certain text it is written that, discussing the Bishop Henjō's poetry with Retired Emperor Go-toba, Teika said "there is a method that has no *makoto*," so perhaps the teaching of the Nijō school is that the foundation of poetry is a lack of truth [*makoto naki o hon to su*].[31] My poetic studies express *makoto*; I make *makoto* and scholarship the Way of Poetry, but a school that thinks poetry is without *makoto* adheres to this *Ise monogatari*.[32]

Again, the valorization of fiction that Azumamaro perceives in the prominent place the Nijō school poets-scholars assign *Ise* in their studies of poetry becomes a way for Azumamaro to tax the Nijō school with a lack of *makoto*, or sincerity, even though he asserts that the Nijō school failed to acknowledge *Ise* as fiction at all. (One might say that Azumamaro is having his cake and eating it too.)

There is one more twist, one more important aspect of *makoto* as Azumamaro defines it. Like Kamo no Mabuchi after him, Azumamaro associates *makoto* with the poetry of the ancient age, especially the *Man'yōshū*. "All ancient poems contain only truth (*jitsu*); they contain not the slightest fabrication (*kyo*)."[33] Azumamaro also writes that "poetry expresses the *makoto* of human emotion (*ninjō*),"[34] but all human emotions do not participate in *makoto* equally: the preface to Azumamaro's

---

31. Ki no Tsurayuki says in the *kana* preface to the *Kokinshū* that Henjō's poetry lacks *makoto*, "like having one's heart move in vain upon seeing a woman in a painting." Ozawa and Matsuda, *Kokinwakashū*, p. 26.

32. Takeoka, *Ise monogatari zenhyōshaku*, p. 1489.

33. *Man'yōshū hekianshō* (Azumamaro's *Man'yōshū* commentary), quoted in Miyake Kiyoshi, *Kada no Azumamaro*, p. 308.

34. Takeoka, *Ise monogatari zenhyōshaku*, p. 332. From the comment on Section 14, where a rustic woman composes the poem *nakanaka ni/koi ni shinazu wa / kuwako ni zo / narubakarikeru / tama no o bakari*, based on *Man'yōshū* poem *nakanaka ni / hito to arazu wa/kuwako ni zo / naramashi mono o / tama no o bakari*. Azumamaro compares

personal poetry collection, written by one of his disciples, points out that Azumamaro did not compose poetry on the topic of love and therefore did not include a section on love in his collection, because it is "not poetry that expresses *makoto*."[35] In this way we come full circle. Azumamaro's ideal of *makoto* allows room for neither love nor fiction, therefore no room for *Ise* and *Genji* as esteemed texts, or as texts that should be read at all unless as a frivolous entertainment analogous to the contemporary kabuki he discusses so dismissively.[36]

One might be tempted to conclude that with its idiosyncrasies—its rigidity, its moralizing—*Dōjimon* contributes little to the progress of *Ise monogatari* scholarship, but it is important in three ways. First, its extremely confrontational stance highlights the precarious position of early modern nativists trying to establish themselves as rightful interpreters of the native tradition—the need to tear down old scholarship before one could build back up with one's own. Note again that Azumamaro never attacks Keichū, despite clear evidence that he read *Seigo okudan* and was fully aware that Keichū too had an imperfect consciousness of *Ise* as fiction. Azumamaro's derision is reserved solely for the Nijō school (and perhaps by extension court poets of his own time). Second, it serves to show the wide range of views espoused by scholars identified as nativist. Although he very much shares other nativists' concern with the Ancient Way, and a preference for ancient texts, Azumamaro's nativism clearly diverges from other nativists' when it comes to the Heian period. Despite his taking up classical *monogatari* as an object of study, he obviously does not value them in the same way as, for example, Norinaga. He is not finding *mono no aware* or any other redeeming quality in them. In fact, in his emphasis on *kanzen chōaku* and attempts to read "admonitions" into places where they weren't put deliberately by the author, as in the commentary on Section 12, his views are

---

the revised version to the original and says, "Wanting to die of love is not a feeling one should have. There are no examples of it in old poetry."

35. Miyake, *Kada no Azumamaro*, p. 313.

36. Elsewhere he suggests that the anonymity of the author is similar to that of contemporary writers of popular fiction—why would anyone want his name attached to "a fictional monogatari of which no part is an aid to humanity and which must become an inducement to amorousness and immorality?" (Takeoka, *Ise monogatari zenhyōshaku*, p. 1608).

indistinguishable from those of Confucian scholars, precisely the sort of approach that Norinaga would go on to attack in his work on *Genji*.

Third, however limiting Azumamaro's belligerence and inflexibility may have been, his assertion that *Ise* is purely fictitious, with no trace of Narihira to be found, was an important break, an essential foundation for the work of Kamo no Mabuchi and Fujii Takanao.

Richard Bowring has written of *Dōjimon*:

> There is an impatience here that stems not so much from a certainty about [Azumamaro's] own knowledge as a wish to denigrate what had gone before. . . . There is something praiseworthy in the attempt to strip away the layers of previous commentary and open up the basic text again for reexamination. . . . But what is left after the exercise? The feeling remains that he is more concerned with beating down the opposition than in giving the text new life. Neither does there seem to be much concern with the possibility that one was merely recreating the lack of cohesion and structure that had produced all the paint in the first place.[37]

Bowring's views about the nature of Azumamaro's impatience and the effect it had on later commentary (opening up the text for reexamination) are entirely just, but Azumamaro goes well beyond simply failing to give the text new life. His moral stance leads to an outright rejection of *Ise* and *Genji*; he is actively tearing *Ise monogatari* itself down along with Yūsai's commentary.

Azumamaro's student, the prominent waka poet and scholar Kamo no Mabuchi, is considerably more moderate in his *Ise monogatari koi*, completed by 1758. Mabuchi draws on Keichū's and Azumamaro's views, but his main purpose is, as Bowring argues, to make *Ise monogatari* accessible to readers rather than to take issue doggedly with the follies of the past. He explains usage and grammatical points in easy-to-understand terms and gives background information where it will aid in understanding the context. Like Azumamaro, he views the work as fiction, grouping it with *Genji* as a *monogatari* that takes factual things and presents them as fiction, but he says that it differs from *Genji* in that the author "borrows" Narihira's form in order to create an impression of fact. For Mabuchi, unlike Azumamaro, the man of old is "a Narihira

---

37. Bowring, *"Ise Monogatari,"* p. 474.

who is not Narihira," a position that allows him to retain a Narihira-
once-removed as a sort of organizing principle.

The preface to *Ise monogatari koi* consists of eight points. The first of
these, titled "regarding *monogatari*,"[38] gives helpful information about
Mabuchi's understanding of the genre system within which *Ise* existed.

> The reason a work such as this is called a *monogatari* is that it is not like
> a factual record, but collects together in writing things that people have
> said and passed down just as they were said, without regard for whether
> they are true or false; they are like the stories of the past of unknown
> origin that we have today. However, when they are written skillfully,
> they can become a source of diversion without peer. Nonetheless—
> how is it that people of later ages understand the word *monogatari*?—I
> would like to know why they think of this *Ise monogatari*, which is
> particularly composed of falsehoods, as a truthful record. At any rate,
> among *monogatari* there are various kinds. *Taketori monogatari*, the par-
> ent from which earlier *monogatari* sprang, is a tale of a foreign country
> made as though it tells of this country. Because in *Ise monogatari* and
> *Genji monogatari* things that happened here [in Japan] are written about
> in a different way [i.e., different from the way they actually happened],
> they are still fiction. It is difficult to say for certain whether the *Utsuho
> monogatari* and *Ochikubo monogatari* might also have some basis [in
> fact], but they are first of all fiction. Because *Yamato monogatari* and

---

38. The others are: (2) regarding its being called *Ise monogatari*; (3) regarding Lord
Narihira not having written it himself; (4) regarding Lady Ise not having written it;
(5) regarding dates being inaccurate; (6) regarding when it was written; (7) regarding
old texts and recent texts, and also who wrote it; and (8) regarding saying "in the past,
a man." In point (7) we see a striking oddity in Mabuchi's view of *Ise*: as Azumamaro
had before him, Mabuchi believes that the *Mana-bon* version of *Ise monogatari*, written
entirely in *kanji* often used in a deliberately obscure, "playful" manner, is the closest to
the original *Ise*. This preference seems motivated, particularly in Azumamaro's case, by
a desire to create additional distance from the Nijō school by denigrating Teika's texts.
Mabuchi also attempts to use the *Mana-bon* to bolster his argument that Lady Ise
could not have been the author; he views *Ise monogatari* as exhibiting a masculine style
that is best exemplified by the *Man'yōshū*, and reliance on a text written in the "male
hand" is part of a strategy to create distance from the weak, feminine literature of the
Heian period. For more on the *Mana-bon*, see Bowring, "*Ise Monogatari*," pp. 472–76.
For the relevant part of Mabuchi's preface, see Takeoka, *Ise monogatari zenhyōshaku*,
pp. 1612–13. For Mabuchi on ancient "masculine" poetry versus classical "feminine"
poetry, see his remarks in *Kaikō* (Taira and Abe, *Kinsei shintōron*, pp. 355–56) and *Ni-
imanabi* (ibid., pp. 358–61 and 365–68).

Konjaku monogatari are not plotted, but rather record what people said as it was heard, truth and fiction and also very strange things are mixed together. Since *Eiga monogatari* was based on observing the state of the times, sometimes including things from other people's diaries, etc., it consists of truthful things that were given the name *monogatari* after a time. Therefore, leaving *Eiga monogatari* aside, the rest are fiction.

Someone asked, "According to one explanation, *Ise* consists of things that happened written as though they did not, and *Genji* consists of things that did not happen written as though they did. Why is this so different from what you said now?" I replied, "As you say, *Ise* was written thinking entirely about Narihira, but as though it were not about him; furthermore, many things are written in succession that could not have happened. You might say, 'If this is the case, isn't it factual?' but because it is written as though it were not about Narihira, just borrowing his appearance, it is a fictional *monogatari*. As for *Genji*, the author wrote it thinking of the society in which she lived, but she wrote of various things without imitating the appearance of those people clearly. Moreover, she avoids offense by giving the names of emperors from the past, and so on. Therefore, this too is basically fictional.[39]

Mabuchi's taxonomy here may have influenced Norinaga: some of the latter's discussion in *Genji monogatari tama no ogushi* (*Genji monogatari* a small jeweled comb, 1796) of the foundation of *monogatari* in truthful things, sometimes changing names and so forth, is very similar to this. At any rate, much unlike Azumamaro, Mabuchi allows a place for fiction as a valued genre, a position that sets the stage for Takanao, who no longer feels the need to discuss *Ise monogatari's* factuality or fictionality at all.

Mabuchi's analysis of Section 49 is based on Keichū's; some of it is lifted verbatim from *Seigo okudan*. After stating that the sister's poem does not accord with the idea put forth in the Transitional Commentaries that Narihira is not in love with her, he discusses references made to this section in *Genji monogatari* and *Sagoromo monogatari* when male characters find themselves attracted to their sisters. In the case of *Genji*, Niou makes an experimental advance toward his full sister and admires her for rebuffing him, thinking that the sister in *Ise monogatari* was too receptive by comparison. Mabuchi continues:

---

39. Inoue, *Kamo no Mabuchi zenshū*, 16:9–10.

Sagoromo takes this idea and makes it a stepsister, so this was written with an understanding of the customs of the past in our country. Indeed, the *Nihongi* records that in the past in our august land it was considered a great crime to behave indecently with a uterine sibling. Because sisters by different mothers were raised to the position of empress, we can know that that was not taboo. It should not be judged by [the standards of] later ages. Because people in the past in our country were simple, they did not hide their emotions, and although they put broad considerations aside, the reigns were nonetheless well-governed. It seems that sticking to principles and thinking that only Chinese writings are good will not enable us to assess the past here.[40]

He supplements this last remark with a very telling headnote, almost as long as the comment itself.

Someone asked: Isn't it a terrible thing for even half-siblings to behave indecently together? I answered: In these later times when people think the ways of China are the main thing, everyone believes this way. But as a rule all these things are said as principles by which the land should be governed, and here [Japan], from the very beginning when there were only two gods [presumably Izanagi and Izanami] it has been a reasonable thing. However, [relations between children of] the same mother were strongly prohibited, and those between children of different mothers were not. In the ages when it was like this, you should know that all things under heaven flourished, and the country was well governed. Since this is the case, it seems to be good for society for people to act as they feel with few restrictions. We continually hear that in China even people with the same last name may not marry, but that there are many people who commit wickedness. If this is the case, we see that there were rules that were not carried out. Generally over there they have good-sounding words, but really there were no people who used them. It is because of this that the line of the emperors has not continued. People who expound using [Chinese] writings make talking about principles their main point, but it appears as though it is difficult to fathom the workings of heaven, and there are few things that are covered by principles. People like to regulate everything to the four corners of the earth, but there are few people who perform this for themselves. It does no good for there to be a person or two who are like this among all those who do not understand what is good. It is generally best to have light

---

40. Takeoka, *Ise monogatari zenhyōshaku*, pp. 791–92.

restrictions in things. This august land is a straightforward country and in most things does not conform to the ways of China, but there are many people who stick entirely to what is written. Look at how those reigns flourished with such twisted rules! Although it is not that one should now love in such relationships, such things existed in the past, and this is only to make clear the fact that it was not prohibited in those times. Generally, there are many things in old writings that should not be judged based on times before or after them. Also, even regarding things that were good about Chinese people, few of them were put into practice—to think and speak of bringing them here and putting them into practice! It is an extremely foolish thing.

Though this does not have a great deal to do with *Ise monogatari*, it is vintage *kokugaku*, and an important early example of the kind of nationalistic, anti-China rhetoric that became prevalent in subsequent writings.[41]

Although Azumamaro's commentary influenced Mabuchi, it does not appear to have been known to other nativist scholars such as Norinaga and Takanao, and it was not printed until the modern period. Mabuchi's commentary, on the other hand, was prepared for publication by Ueda Akinari (1734–1809) in 1793, the point at which a market for nativist scholarship on the classics had developed, and it came to be very influential in the late Edo period.

Fiction and *Irogonomi* in a Confucian Context: Goi Ranshū's *Seigo tsū*

Goi Ranshū (1697–1762) was a Confucian scholar who served as head instructor and a guiding force in the intellectual life of the Kaitokudō, an academy founded in Osaka in 1726 for the education of townsmen. While many of the instructors at the Kaitokudō had had a personal interest in classical Japanese literature, for example, as *waka* poets, Ranshū went to the length of making a place for it in the curriculum,

---

41. It is worth noting how close some of this is to Mabuchi's *Kokuikō* (Reflections on the meaning of our country, 1765). See Taira and Abe, *Kinsei shintōron*, pp. 378–79 and 387–88; full translation in Flueckiger, "Reflections on the Meaning of Our Country," pp. 211–63. Bowring observes that *Ise monogatari koi* "is almost entirely devoid of the propaganda that was to emerge in the last ten years of his career." (The "*Ise monogatari*," p. 474), but this is a clear exception.

albeit an informal one. His 1758 addendum to the rules of the academy notes:

> Although the lectures will focus on the moral concepts of the Four Books and the Five Classics, to the exclusion of miscellaneous texts, special approval will be given to private seminars and reading groups being held on Chinese literary culture, medicine, and Japanese poetry and literature. Even [Miyake] Sekian [the Kaitokudō's original head instructor] privately taught from medical and poetic texts. Of course, these latter should not be used as the basis of public [*omote muki*] lectures, as previously stipulated in the rules of understanding.[42]

In addition to *Seigo tsū*, his commentary on *Ise monogatari*, Ranshū produced commentaries on the *Man'yōshū*, the *Kokinshū*, and *Genji monogatari*, and compiled reference works on the *Man'yōshū* and *Genji*. Further evidence about the place of the Japanese classics at the Kaitokudō can be found in the preface added by Nakai Chikuzan (1730–1804), Ranshū's student and successor as head instructor, to the last of these, *Gengo ko*, which was pirated, modified, and prepared for publication without attribution some twenty years after Ranshū's death: it is clear that Ranshū's oeuvre related to the Japanese classics continued to be used, copied, and handed down within the academy and was felt to be proprietary, but also that this work was very much subordinate and avocational, therefore that the incident merited only a limited intervention by Chikuzan.[43]

With a handful of noteworthy exceptions, earlier Confucian scholars had had, for the most part, little use for the *monogatari* of the Heian period.[44] Those who were inclined to retain *Ise* or *Genji* as valued texts at all, such as Kumazawa Banzan and Andō Tameakira, were generally forced in the name of *kanzen chōaku* to read troubling, immoral incidents as somehow admonitory, irrespective of how those incidents were presented in the texts themselves, a modus operandi not unlike Azumamaro's in *Ise monogatari dōjimon*. Ranshū, however, rather than condemning the work wholesale, takes advantage of *Ise*'s discontinuous,

---

42. From "Kaitokudō teiyaku fuki," quoted in Najita, *Visions of Virtue*, p. 138. Brackets mine.
43. Nakano, "Aru Genji gochūsho no shuppan sōdō," pp. 20–21.
44. On Banzan, see McMullen, *Idealism, Protest*, pp. 285–407.

fragmentary form to perform a sort of salvage operation, a thoroughly novel reconfiguration of the text's 125 sections on moral grounds.

Ranshū's commentary relies heavily on Yūsai's *Ketsugishō* and Keichū's *Seigo okudan.*[45] He follows Yūsai and other late medieval commentators in assuming that the tale was written partly by Narihira and partly by Lady Ise, though he differs on some of the details, and, in a significant departure, views the interpolated comments that follow some sections as being the work of later writers. (Late medieval commentaries associated with Sōgi view the interpolations as "Ise's words," whereas those associated with Sanetaka, and also Keichū, cite "the author of this *monogatari*" as the source.)

Like Yūsai and Keichū, Ranshū views *Ise monogatari* as being a mixture of fact and fiction, mostly about Narihira's life but with extraneous things added. In the preface to the first volume, he distinguishes between the two types of sections as follows:

> The things written about secret, illicit relations between the sexes are largely made up; they are not factual. There are many examples where a story is created from an existing poem. Although stealing someone else's daughter or visiting someone else's wife [are things that one sees and hears of], above all these matters soil the ears. Nonetheless, because this work was written in the female script, from some point it came to be viewed as something women and girls should amuse themselves with. Because there are improper and immoral things here, I believe that they should be thrown away and not read. Now, using the commentaries of the ancients and adding my own views, I have extracted only that which is true and I call this volume *uchi* [inside]. This I take to be the *Ise monogatari* of my house; I will have my only daughter read it. I desire only to make Narihira's unhappiness with his times and indignation toward society clear, and to rinse away his reputation for amorousness.[46]

---

45. Najita discusses Ranshū's affinity with and admiration for Keichū, a fellow Osakan (*Visions of Virtue*, pp. 138–39). Ranshū even wrote the epitaph for Keichū's gravestone, as Norinaga notes in *Tamakatsuma* (Yoshikawa, et al., *Motoori Norinaga shū*, p. 102).

46. Goi, *Seigo tsū, uchi jō*, p. 2. This edition of the text, published in 1911, consists of two volumes bound in the traditional premodern style but printed in movable type. The two volumes are titled *uchi* and *soto* (inner and outer), and each volume is divided into *jō* and *ge* (upper and lower). All citations that follow are from this text.

Ranshū keeps a scant 47 of the 125 sections for his private *Ise monogatari* and relegates the rest to a second volume, called *soto* (outside). He retains these false ones at all, he says, only because he thinks there are places in them that previous commentators failed to understand and explain correctly.

The association of *Ise*, often paired with *Genji*, with female readers, particularly (though by no means exclusively) among writers of a Confucian bent, was by Ranshū's time a convention of long standing. As discussed in Chapter 4, by the mid-eighteenth century *Ise* was often marketed specifically as a work for female education. However, taking Ranshū's mention of his daughter as the impetus for his writing the commentary at face value, as some scholars do, is misleading. His mentioning her in the third person suggests that the text has some other addressee, as does his having gone to the length of annotating the outer volume, which she supposedly will never see. Moreover, as Yagi Tsuyoshi has pointed out, the manuscript of the text in Ranshū's hand, with its layers of headnotes and interlinear glosses in addition to expository commentary following block quotations (features that the 1911 printed edition lacks), suggests not just that the commentary was used for lecturing to students at the Kaitokudō but that Ranshū might have intended to publish it.[47]

Although the education and moral development of women is, as we will see, a major concern of *Seigo tsū*, there are what we might call masculine concerns at stake here as well. Later in the preface Ranshū elaborates on his view of Narihira as follows:

> I was looking at a commentary on *Genji monogatari*, and it said that Narihira was the pioneer of amorousness.[48] What kind of pioneer could there be for amorousness? This is so outrageous one has to laugh. Narihira probably began to be called an amorous man from the time of this *monogatari* [i.e., *Ise*]. In the national histories, it says just "He was handsome in appearance, self-indulgent and unreserved; generally lacking in aptitude for learning, and composed Japanese poems well." The error [of viewing Narihira as amorous] stems from taking the protagonist of this text to be Narihira everywhere when it says only "a man." As for

---

47. Yagi, "Seigo tsū ni tsuite," p. 31.

48. Such a statement appears in *Kakaishō* (Tamagami, *Shimeishō, Kakaishō*, p. 532) and is quoted in Kitamura Kigin's *Kogetsushō*.

Narihira's character, he was a man who made strenuous, heroic exertions; he lamented the fact that the nation had become different from in the past and the imperial family had shifted to a subordinate position. Therefore, I suppose that there must have been things he thought too much about, and in order to avoid having people suspect him by allowing his talents to show on the outside, he was forced to make a pretext of being amorous.[49]

This is the earliest example I have found of a commentator trying to make broad sense of *Ise monogatari* in terms of Narihira's submerged political frustrations or loyalty to the throne, strategies that recur at the end of the Edo period and again in Meiji.[50] The evidence cited in sup-

---

49. Goi, *Seigo tsū, uchi jō*, pp. 3–4.

50. Ueda Akinari became perhaps the most prominent advocate of this reading. In *Yoshi ya ashi ya*, the volume of his own thoughts on a handful of sections that he appended to *Ise monogatari koi* when he prepared it for publication in 1793, he suggests that Section 124, discussed below, reveals Narihira's indignation with the state of his world, and further, that this is the purpose of *monogatari*. "Generally, when a person who is learned and talented does not conform to the times, he says, 'I have a precious sword,' or composes, 'Even if they don't know [the value of] a pearl, as long as I know . . .'; or his writing becomes indignant, they say, and in this the hearts of people of China and of Japan are no different. There [such writings] are called *yanyi xiaoshuo* and here they are called *monogatari*. The hearts of the people who write and publish them lament their unfortunate positions and, being indignant with the world, they long for the past; or within present society when they see others flourishing like the fragrance of a flower in bloom, they think that it will surely change, or they silently mock people in favor, wondering what their ends will be like; or again, they awaken to the fact that desiring unheard of longevity is as empty as [Urashima Taro's] jeweled box. A crazy person wandering around in search of a difficult-to-obtain jewel, even if he is ashamed, just avoiding the gossip of the world, continuing to write tales that seem not to be blameworthy in untraceable words of the distant past: this is the concern of this kind of text. In this work too, with a tale about a Narihira who is not Narihira as a pretext, to condemn the nonsensical state of the world, still fearing that even a part of his own thoughts should not be divulged, at the end of the text, lamenting with the boast that 'there is no one like me' is something talented people do to give comfort to their own hearts, and restore their lives, I think. Whether this is good or bad, if there is any sense in these countrified words, I leave to others to choose." (Takeoka, *Ise monogatari zenhyōshaku*, p. 1568; see also Burns, *Before the Nation*, pp. 123–25, for a discussion of Akinari's view of *monogatari* as it relates to his nativist thought.) As Akinari and Ranshū were acquainted, and Akinari was an admirer of Ranshū, it is possible that there was some direct influence. A few later texts that pursue similar, overtly political readings include *Ise monogatari sakuhishō* (by the priest Ryūkō, 1819), *Waka no urazurushō* (Motoori Uchitō, 1852), and *Ise monogatari hiun* (Igarashi Atsuyoshi, 1858).

port of these purported frustrations is in part the slow rate at which Narihira advanced in the court bureaucracy, as attested by entries in the *Sandai jitsuroku* and other histories that show him either to have been without an office for a long period of time or to have been demoted briefly.[51]

Ranshū gives further details about Narihira's grievances in his commentary on the "Azumakudari." Late medieval commentators had viewed the "Azumakudari" as an exile without naming the reason for it, while the early medieval commentaries denied that Narihira ever made the journey, asserting that he remained under house arrest close to the capital and suggesting that his troubles arose when his involvement with the Nijō empress came to light. Ranshū rejects both of these views, positing instead a voluntary journey made necessary by Narihira's close association with Prince Koretaka. Koretaka was the first son of Emperor Montoku by Ki no Shizuko, a daughter of Ki no Natora and sister of Ki no Aritsune (Narihira's father-in-law, described in Section 16 as another courtier who had fallen on hard times). The *Gōdanshō* (Excerpts from Ōe's conversations, a late Heian *setsuwa* collection) records that Montoku had hoped to make Koretaka, his favorite son, crown prince, but that he was forced to defer to Fujiwara no Yoshifusa, the powerful Minister of the Right, and bestow the honor on his fourth son, Korehito (later Emperor Seiwa), who was Yoshifusa's grandson. Other sources, such as *Heike monogatari* and *Soga monogatari*, perpetuated this story, and over time Koretaka came to be viewed as a tragic figure whose right to the throne had been unfairly denied.[52] Ranshū gives an account of

Regarding these readings in the Meiji period, see Mostow, "Modern Constructions," pp. 96–119.

51. Some modern scholars believe there are mistakes in the record and neither of these things actually happened. For details, see Katagiri, *Tensai sakka*, pp. 69–74. In addition, the historian Mezaki Tokue has argued that Narihira's ascent to Junior Fourth Rank, Upper Grade was above-average performance at the time for one who, like Narihira, was a member of the imperial family who had been reduced to commoner status. In his view, Fujiwara interference with Narihira's career was unlikely, and, based on the record, the idea that Narihira was uniquely unfortunate is mistaken. See his "Zaigo chūjō to Teiji no mikado," pp. 352–53.

52. According to Katagiri, Koretaka's failure to be named crown prince was not at all unusual for the time. Despite his being the firstborn, his mother's rank was low (*koi* level) and none of her male relatives held ministerial posts, whereas Korehito's mother had extremely powerful backing. Korehito was named crown prince when he was just

the competition between the two princes in his commentary on the "Azumakudari" sections and suggests that Narihira, like many others close to Koretaka (Sections 82, 83, and 85 depict the close relationship between the two), suffered a reversal of fortune after Koretaka was passed over for the succession, a fact that made Narihira weary of society and led him to abandon his position and undertake the trip on his own initiative. Ranshū views various other incidents in the text—the man's travels to nearby provinces (Sections 66–68 and 87) and seclusion in Higashiyama (Section 59)—as symptomatic of the same dissatisfaction.

As in the later examples that pursue this interpretation of Narihira's character, Section 124 is pivotal.

> In the past—what might he have been thinking at the time?—a man composed the following:

> | *omou koto* | I should just keep |
> | *iwade zo tada ni* | my thoughts to myself |
> | *yaminubeshi* | and there let it end |
> | *ware ni hitoshiki* | since there is no one |
> | *hito shi nakereba* | who is like me. |

This section lends itself to strong readings by virtue of its placement directly before Narihira's death poem at the end of the tale; those who are inclined to do so tend to view it as a summing up of all that has gone before. Ranshū writes, "In this poem, Narihira expresses the feeling he has in his own heart. We should be able to guess at what he thought about his whole life from this poem." From the time Ranshū read this poem, he says, he understood Narihira's true character.

> At the time when Narihira was alive there was no one with whom he could spit out the truth of his feelings and discuss them. And not only at that time—even when as long as a thousand years have passed, there is no one who understands. This is because the people who should understand thrust this *monogatari* aside and do not read it carefully. . . . It is a great error to think that Narihira was just an amorous person who composed poetry well.[53]

---

nine months old, at which point Koretaka was seven. See Katagiri, *Tensai sakka*, pp. 47–54.

53. Goi, *Seigo tsū, uchi ge*, p. 21. The Old Commentaries also attached great significance to this section, asserting that Narihira's hidden thoughts have to do with the se-

The commentary on Section 124 also explains Ise's alleged involvement in the text as a product of her sympathy with Narihira. "Even though she was a Fujiwara," Ranshū claims, she was in a position to understand Narihira's hidden unhappiness. In the preface, Ranshū relates that Ise hailed from a different branch of the clan from the one that produced regents, and her family's fortunes had also been in decline. Nonetheless, she secured a position in the service of Empress Onshi, a daughter of Fujiwara no Mototsune. At court, Ise received the imperial favor herself and bore the emperor a child. The kind and gentle Onshi, however, was not jealous and Ise remained in her service, sending the child off to live elsewhere. After Onshi's death, Ise had nowhere to turn, lapsed into poverty and was forced to sell her house. Ranshū sums up:

> She was a talented woman without peer, but she suffered such misfortunes as these. Therefore, she sympathized with Narihira's misfortunes and, taking up the text he had written, she made it known through the world. When Narihira died, Ise was still very young. Though they say the two exchanged poetry, it is hard to believe.[54]

Where the *Wakachikenshū* had justified Ise's involvement by suggesting that she and Narihira were married (despite Ise's having been only twelve years old when Narihira died), and the late medieval commentaries had offered no particular justification other than Teika's colophons, Ranshū tenders a logical explanation—that she and Narihira were, despite not having been romantically or otherwise involved, kindred spirits, fellow sufferers in a world rendered inhospitable by the powerful Fujiwara. Thus, Ranshū's theory of the text's formation, like his understanding of its fictitiousness and his section-by-section commentary, is intermeshed with his image of Narihira.

Ranshū attempts to support his assessment of Narihira's character with evidence from the text. His first move in the commentary proper is to set Narihira up as paragon of Confucian virtue. The inner volume begins with five sections—numbers 84, 83, 41, 46, and 49—taken out of

---

cret, mystical connection between sex, poetry, and salvation. They also hold it up as an admonition against revealing the secret to outsiders. The Transitional Commentaries reject this, saying the point is that Narihira's thoughts cannot be known, thence the line "what might he have been thinking at the time?" Keichū, Azumamaro, and Mabuchi agree with the Transitional Commentaries.

54. Goi, *Seigo tsū, uchi jō*, p. 4.

the usual order found in the *Teika-bon* and the other commentaries.[55] These, it turns out, show Narihira interacting with his mother, with Prince Koretaka, with his wife's sister, with a friend, and with his own sister, demonstrating in rapid succession the five Confucian virtues of filial piety, loyalty to superiors, conjugal affection, faithfulness to friends, and brotherliness.

Needless to say, Ranshū is following Yūsai rather than Keichū in his interpretation of Section 49, the story of the brother and sister, but he includes a few twists of his own. After the man's poem, Ranshū writes:

> "*Ito okashi*" [in reference to the sister] means a person who is reserved and gentle. . . . As for the surface of this poem, the man is thinking that the tips of the leaves of the young grass that comes up in the spring are lovely, and when their roots are fine someone should pluck them up quickly and appreciate them. This is because when months and days have passed they will become hard to the touch. Because this younger sister was brought up well, he is thinking that she should be taken as a wife by someone and not lose the chance to marry. . . . The poem expresses a feeling of affectionate, friendly love for the sister.[56]

And after the second poem:

> This is the sister's reply poem. According to what we see in this poem, in the past Narihira had put aside the matter of his sister's marriage, but now when he addresses this poem to her she is overjoyed, and composes it to say, "What are these words of yours, that you worry about my future in such a novel way? Up to now, I was miserable thinking that you had put aside worrying about how my future would turn out, but it was a mistake!"[57]

As late medieval scholars had done, Ranshū interprets the brother's poem as an expression of concern rather than attraction and the sister's as one of gratitude rather than shock or receptiveness. But Ranshū goes beyond simply neutralizing the suggestiveness of the story; he appears to

---

55. Apart from these five, the sections within each volume follow the order of the *Teika bon*. The first volume runs as follows (with the rest in the second volume): 84, 83, 41, 46, 49, 7–9, 11, 16–17, 29, 33, 38–39, 44, 48, 51–52, 56, 59, 66–68, 76–82, 85, 87–88, 91, 97–98, 101, 104, 106–7, 109, 114, 116–17, 124–25.

56. Goi, *Seigo tsū, uchi jō*, p. 10.

57. Ibid., p. 10.

be molding the section into a focused message for his daughter. To begin with, interpreting the word *okashi* as "reserved and gentle" (*otonashiku yasashiki*) is unique to Ranshū. Ichijō Kaneyoshi, perhaps concerned that the reader might think the sister is "funny," another possible meaning of the word, had said simply that it is a term of praise and carries no bad meaning, a comment that Keichū echoed. (Sōgi, Sanetaka, Yūsai, and Kigin offer no comment.) Modern scholars tend to concur with Kamo no Mabuchi, who defines it as "charming" or "lovely." Ranshū's interpretations of the poems are also much more elaborate than those of his predecessors. As for the first, late medieval commentators had confined themselves to discussing the word *neyoge*, Kaneyoshi pointing out that it means both "good for sleeping" and "good roots," and the others saying that it means "pulling the roots together to sleep on." Ranshū's idea that the grass, and by extension the sister, will cease to be fresh and lovely if not plucked up quickly is new, as is the suggestion following the second poem that "Narihira had put aside the question of his sister's marriage." By fleshing out the situation this way, Ranshū shifts the focus of the section onto the woman's situation and feelings—her fears about her future, her sorrow that her brother had forgotten about her, and her joy and gratitude upon discovering he had not—and transforms the exchange into something with which a young female reader might readily empathize. There is also a suggestion that a young woman who comports herself properly, who is "reserved and gentle," need have no doubt that her older brother will look out for her.

There are lessons to be found elsewhere in the text as well, some of which force Ranshū to make tricky decisions about whether particular sections belong in the inner volume or the outer. For example, he states that someone questioned his inclusion of Section 23 in the outer volume. Section 23 begins as follows:

In the past, a boy and a girl whose parents traveled in the countryside played together at the foot of the well, but when they grew up, both of them grew shy of each other. Nonetheless, the boy thought he would win this girl, and the girl continued to have tender feelings toward the boy; though her parents tried to marry her to another, she would not hear of it. One day the following came from the boy, who lived next door:

tsutsui tsu no   Since last I saw you
izutsu ni kakeshi   my height

maro ga take	seems to have surpassed
suginikerashi na	that of the well-curb
imo mizaru ma ni	where we measured it.

The girl replied:

kurabekoshi	My parted hair
furiwakegami mo	which I compared to yours
kata suginu	now falls past my shoulders.
kimi narazu shite	Who shall tie it up
tare ka agubeki	if not you?

After many such exchanges, they were finally able to marry as they wished.

Ranshū comments, "Someone asked me, 'Why is this not included in the inner volume, when the poem shows the woman's extreme constancy?' Truly, she is constant, but 'refusing to agree when her parents tried to marry her to another' is not the correct path for a person's daughter to follow."[58] This view is at odds with the late medieval commentaries, where, as we have seen, the girl's dedication to the boy was held up as exemplary. Here, a girl's duty to her parents supersedes her duty to a lover, even one who eventually becomes a spouse. Again, Ranshū's desire to educate his daughter properly appears to be the key to the classification of this section.

Conversely, he includes Section 33, an exchange of love poetry that initially appears no different from dozens of others that he rejects, in the inner volume.

In the past, a man was visiting a woman who lived in the Ubara district of Tsu province. Because one day she seemed to think that when he left he would not come again, he composed:

ashibe yori	As the tide floods in
michikuru shio no	ever rising
iyamashi ni	from the reeds at the shore
kimi ni kokoro o	so does my love
omoimasu kana	for you increase.

She replied:

komorie ni	How, like a boatman
omou kokoro o	with his pole, sounding out
ikade ka wa	a hidden inlet

---

58. Goi, *Seigo tsū, soto jō,* p. 18.

| *fune sasu sao no* | can I hope to fathom |
| *sashite shirubeki* | your feelings? |

For a person in the provinces, was this a good poem or a bad one?

About the first poem, Ranshū writes that Narihira is trying to allay the woman's fears that he will not return, and that the exchange must have taken place when he was setting out on his journey to the east. After the second poem we find this:

> The second poem means "It is difficult for me, with my short pole, to fathom your deep feeling." As for Narihira's poem, though he has deep thoughts about something hidden in his heart, thinking that he will not let the woman suspect them, he says just that his feelings for the woman increase. The reply means that the woman sees that Narihira has deep thoughts, but they are not things that a woman or girl can understand.[59]

Although Ranshū does not say so explicitly, his associating this exchange with Narihira's departure on his journey to the east suggests that his deep, hidden thoughts have to do again with his political grievances, the same thoughts he thinks it better not to express in Section 124. This fact, combined with the woman's convenient and proper inability to fathom Narihira's meaning, triggers the inclusion of this section in the inner volume despite its clear depiction of a romantic encounter.

As these examples show, the bases of Ranshū's rather opportunistic separation of fact from fiction, then, are slightly more complicated than what he sets out in the preface. For the most part, the sections break down according to the type of poetry they contain: those that involve exchanges of love poetry are "outer" (often accompanied by discussion of how they betray Narihira's true, non-amorous character), whereas those that include travel poetry, poetry written in connection with public occasions (this group includes many sections that refer to historical figures by name), and poetry exchanged by male friends are "inner." However, sections that support Ranshū's preconceived image of Narihira as a principled man are "inner," even if ostensible romantic content must be squelched, as in his interpretations of Section 49 and Section 33. Finally, sections that serve as object lessons in feminine deportment are "inner," whereas those that undercut such lessons (and must therefore be

59. Goi, *Seigo tsū, uchi jō*, p. 18.

viewed as admonitory) are "outer." It becomes clear that fact and fiction
are not really at issue; deeming something fictitious merely marks it as
being unacceptable or not worthy of consideration. Although Ranshū's
commentary demonstrates that he had considerable exegetical and philological skills, that, like Keichū and Mabuchi, he is quite capable of
delving into other sources to shed new light on the text rather than simply organizing and repeating earlier views, clearly these skills are not
being applied in his assessments of what belongs in the text and what
does not. For example, where earlier commentators often began with the
assumption that sections built around Narihira's poems in the *Kokinshū*
had to be factual because the *Kokinshū* was trustworthy, the sources of
the poems do not figure in Ranshū's separation of the sections between
the two volumes. He includes a full third of Narihira's *Kokinshū* poems
in the outer volume, and a few attributed to poets who flourished well
after Narihira's death in the inner one. "Truth," in other words, is not a
matter of record or historical fact as verified by research, but a matter of
conformity to Ranshū's own fiction, his certainty that he is dealing not
with an amorous man whose passion overflowed the few words of his
poetry, but a serious, faithful man whose poetry bore witness to deep
concerns he could not share with others.

The fact that just over a third of the text is viewed as appropriate for
direct consumption and the degree to which he has to stretch to pull
ideologically sound readings from it suggests that *Ise monogatari* was not
very well suited to Ranshū's aims. But at the same time the effort and
ingenuity he puts into recuperating the text, his going to the length of
creating this strange, divided commentarial form, suggests that he attached considerable importance to it. Nakamura Yukihiko points out
how unusual this stance of Ranshū's was by comparison with other
Confucian scholars of and before his time—although such writers as
Andō Tameakira and Kumazawa Banzan had also found merit in *Genji
monogatari*, Ranshū went to the length of *writing* a Heian-style *monogatari* of his own (a sequel to *Ochikubo monogatari*) and is on record as
having enjoyed the works of Saikaku.[60] The contrast with Azumamaro
is particularly striking: neither scholar has much tolerance for fiction,
and both are at pains to defend Narihira against imputations of immo-

---

60. Nakamura, "Goi Ranshū no bungakukan," p. 191.

rality, but where the nativist scholar's hostility toward depictions of amorousness leads him to reject *Ise* and *Genji* almost completely, the Confucian scholar seeks to extract from the tale what "history" he can.

In Place of Norinaga:
Fujii Takanao and *Ise monogatari shinshaku*

Although he gave lectures on it, Motoori Norinaga never wrote a commentary on *Ise monogatari*.[61] However, he devotes eight sections of his miscellany *Tamakatsuma* to discussion of problems the text presents. In the last, he describes *Ise* as follows:

> Among all the *monogatari* that exist, *Ise monogatari* is delightful and exceptionally well written, and is enjoyed by people everywhere, but there are passages that are strange and difficult to understand mixed in here and there, apparently because of later scribes' miscopyings. However, if someone wants to aid others by explaining the text, instead they end up forcing it. Also, because this is a typical *tsukuri monogatari*, there is no need to find fault with discrepancies in Narihira's or other people's personal circumstances. One should simply take it up and admire how charmingly it is made, and its figurative language, using it as an aid for the study of poetry and a model for writing prose. Occasionally, it includes poems that are more awful than I can say; one should understand this when one looks at them. Among the numerous commentaries, those that should be mentioned are Keichū's *Seigo okudan*, and my teacher's [Mabuchi's] *Koi*, but between them they have both good and bad points, and again, there are not a few places where one wonders what both of them were thinking. There are some passages that I have come to understand, and from an early time I have wanted to record them in detail, but, although I am not a fisherman of Ise cutting seaweed and burning salt fires, I have had no time, and I regret not having brought my desire to fruition. But, I have selected just a few, and have recorded a little of them in the preceding sections.[62]

This is arguably the first time we have seen a scholar display sustained first-person admiration for *Ise monogatari* as a whole (the caution about

---

61. His diary records that he lectured on the entire text twice: once in 1759 and once from 1791 to 1792 (Yoshikawa, et al., *Motoori Norinaga shū*, p. 165). He also appears to have lectured in the capital in 1801 to an audience that included court poets. Yamamoto, "Tesshinsai bunko," p. 33.

62. Yoshikawa, et al., *Motoori Norinaga shū*, p. 165.

the occasional awful poem notwithstanding) without reference to its place in the tradition, its moral value, and so on, and one wishes that Norinaga had found the time to comment on the whole work. But it was left to one of his disciples fill the gap after his death.

Fujii Takanao (1765–1841) was born in Bitchū province into a family that served as hereditary heads of the Kibitsu Shrine, a position that he eventually held himself. He was introduced to Japanese poetry by his father at an early age and studied both Japanese literature and Chinese literature as a youth. In 1793 he traveled to Kyoto to continue his studies and met Norinaga in Matsuzaka at that time, becoming a member of Norinaga's school. Although Takanao returned to Bitchū rather than studying in Matsuzaka, he continued to correspond with Norinaga until the latter's death in 1801 and, soon recognized by his teacher as a promising talent, became the principal disciple through whom Norinaga's studies of Heian literature were continued in the next generation. Takanao associated closely with other nativist scholars, such as Yashiro Hirokata (1758–1841), Hirata Atsutane (1776–1843), and Motoori Ōhira (1756–1833), and worked with them to facilitate the spread of nativism in western Japan. However, Takanao did not fully share the political concerns of some of his contemporaries and concentrated fairly narrowly on literature rather than on studies of the Ancient Way (*kodō*). In addition to *Ise monogatari shinshaku*, an extremely influential commentary regarded as representative of his work, he left unfinished commentaries on the *Kokinshū* and *Makura no sōshi*.

In *Ise monogatari shinshaku*, written in 1812 and printed six years later, Takanao reacts to earlier commentaries much as any commentator before him had, but he moves beyond his predecessors to consider *Ise monogatari* in new terms. Concern with *Ise*'s factuality or fictionality disappears almost entirely, replaced by a sense of the text as something close to an independent literary artifact, a view that necessitates a new role for the commentator. Takanao's preface, though lengthy, deserves to be looked at in full:

> • Because the very elegant style of this *monogatari*, with deep meaning contained in its few words, is without peer, the Middle Counselor Teika said that it should be read after the *Kokinshū* to teach people who are studying poetry. Therefore, from long ago, it has been considered a very valuable work and knowledgeable people of each generation have written to explain its meaning. However, though there are many commentaries, like the [*Waka*]*Chikenshō* and the *Ketsugishō*, because these were written at a time when no

one was studying the past, there are many theories in them that are more juvenile than I can say. Compared to these worthless commentaries, the *Okudan* of the priest Keichū, and the *Koi* written by the Master of Okabe [Mabuchi] are excellent. Since these two commentaries have now been printed and spread through the world, everyone thinks that *Ise monogatari* has been made clear. That is, because these two men have studied the past and are extremely knowledgeable, people judge that the things they say are exceedingly good. However, between them they have both good and bad points, and again, there are not a few places in which both of them are bad. You will understand this if you see what I say in those places.

- There is a commentary called *Shūsuishō*. Because there was no better commentary than this one during the time before *Okudan* and *Koi* were widely known, it was very highly regarded throughout the world, but the reason people do not look at it very much now is because it is incomparably inferior to these two. However, it is not the case that there are no theories in it that should be accepted occasionally. I will draw on it when I think it is good.

- There are various texts of this *monogatari*. The priest Keichū wrote his commentary based on the *kana* text most generally used today [i.e., the *Rufu-bon*], and the Master of Okabe used the *Mana-bon*. Both of these are skewed and bad. This is because between them they have places that differ in quality for some reason. Also, when I spent a year in Edo, I saw a copy of the text in the possession of Yashiro Hirokata called *Suzakuin-nurigome-bon*[63] that was traced from a text written out by Mimbukyō no tsubone.[64] Although there are passages in it that one does not know what to make of, there are some things in it that are particularly excellent. Also, in the same place, because there are a very few good things in the old copy of the *Chikenshō*,[65] I looked at a copy of it made by Shimizu Hamaomi.[66] At this time, looking over all the texts together, I will choose the things that are a little superior for this text.

---

63. This text has 115 sections with 198 poems (compared to the *Teika-bon*'s 125 and 209). Some sections are simply omitted, others combined, and others that are not found in the *Teika-bon* added.

64. Teika's daughter.

65. Takanao refers here to the base text used in the *Wakachikenshū*, not the commentary.

66. Yashiro Hirokata, author of *Sankō Ise monogatari* and *Ise monogatari nango no jō*, and Shimizu Hamaomi, author of *Ise monogatari tenchū*, were, in the concern for

- What I record after the round marks at the end of the comments is limited to discussion of the textual variants.
- When I refer to my teacher's theories, I am taking up the few comments that the master of the Suzunoya [Norinaga] recorded in *Tamakatsuma*.
- As for the title of *Ise monogatari*, what Ueda Akinari says in his *Yoshi ya ashi ya* is good.[67] Also, regarding the fact that Ise did not write it, and the fact that it was written with the dates deliberately mistaken, the explanation in the *Koi* is good. Because these are lengthy, I will not record them here. As for the histories of the various people appearing in the *monogatari*, beginning with Narihira, since these are recorded in the various commentaries, I will omit them. Also, in this commentary I will not write about anything like judging what kind of bird the *miyakodori*[68] is. This is because these are things that have nothing to do with the meaning or style of the *monogatari*.
- Why do people who compose poetry concern themselves with *monogatari* writings? They try to understand, to learn from and imitate, the ancients' knowledge of *mono no aware* and their courtly, elegant character. They also memorize the correct usage of words and use the texts as models for writing prose. Therefore, commentaries should express the intentions that are the main point of the *monogatari*, and should explain and teach the skillful, pleasing writing in passages that novices cannot be expected to understand. However—why is it?—among all of the commentaries from long ago, not one that has this intent has appeared. The commentators

textual variants exhibited in their work, pioneers in textual criticism of *Ise monogatari*. See Vos, *Study of the Ise-monogatari*, p. 111, and Ōtsu, *Ise monogatari kochūshaku no kenkyū*, pp. 639–40 and 647–48.

67. Akinari wrote *Yoshi ya ashi ya* as a supplement to the 1793 edition of *Ise monogatari koi*, which he was responsible for bringing to print. Akinari comments on just a handful of sections, addressing mostly lexical problems, but he includes a preface of moderate length in which he hypothesizes that the original title was *Zaigo chūjō monogatari*, but that people subsequently came to call the work *Ise monogatari* because they were so impressed by Section 69. The theory is based on the observation that in Heian texts *Ise* is identified variously as *Zaigo ga monogatari* (*Genji*, "Agemaki"), *Zaigo chūjō no nikki* (*Sagoromo monogatari*), and *Zaigo chūjō no shū* (*Sarashina nikki*) as well as *Ise monogatari* (*Genji*, "E-awase"). Earlier commentators had been at pains to avoid deriving the title from Section 69 in deference to Teika's comments in the colophons to the *Takeda-bon* and the *Rufu-bon*. See Takeoka, *Ise monogatari zenhyōshaku*, pp. 1614–16.

68. The "capital bird" that appears in Section 9.

say many bothersome, useless things, thinking they want to show others how widely knowledgeable they are; if something is even slightly relevant, they willfully search through even sources from the distant past and write many things in succession. From the time of the Hōgen disturbance [1156] the world was in continuous upheaval, and beginning in the Ōnin era when all the world was in chaos, to an even greater extent no one was able to do things like look at texts in peace. At that time there was no one at all who understood things well, and because it was only Buddhist clerics who were on rare occasions able to study without mingling in society, perhaps worldly people gave up inquiring into things as a result. Therefore, all commentaries on poetry collections and *monogatari*, following Buddhist texts, were called this-or-that-*shō*, and included numerous bothersome things not to be found in the poetry or prose of the works under discussion, all imitating the style of commentaries on Buddhist writings.[69] Although the priest Keichū was a person who surpassed all the world, he was like this all the same. Since on this occasion I will eschew that kind of bad habit, I have titled my work *Shinshaku* [New explication]. However, if people glance at this *Shinshaku*, there will be those who think that it too takes up many things that are not to be found in the poetry and prose. This is because both the poetry and prose of this *monogatari* contain deep meaning in few words and in order to explain that deep meaning there are places which I must accompany with many of my own words. However, because these all relate things that are contained within the poetry and prose, it is not the type of work that includes the kinds of useless things I mentioned.[70]

Takanao is as good as his word: compared to earlier commentaries, *Shinshaku* contains very little historical information that is not immediately related to the passage at hand and little quibbling about the meanings of simple words or *kana* usage. And although there is an undeniable strain of classically nativist thought in his work, such as his locating the "bothersome" qualities of previous commentaries in their affinities with Buddhist commentary and his emphasis on *mono no aware* (of which more below), he never uses the text gratuitously as a soapbox from which to expound theories of the ancient way, as, one

69. This point is one of several appropriated verbatim from *Tamakatsuma*.
70. Fujii, *Ise monogatari shinshaku*, pp. 5–8.

might argue, Mabuchi had done in his analysis of Section 49. Rather, his commentary is solidly grounded in his study of the Heian period and its literature.

Although Takanao mentions *Wakachikenshū* and *Ketsugishō*, the habitual concerns of medieval commentaries have slipped from his purview almost entirely. Instead he takes Keichū and Mabuchi as his jumping-off point, and despite his complimentary remarks early in the preface, he cites them to disagree with them far more often than not, holding up their failure to see through to the true meaning or intention of the *monogatari* as a persistent fault.[71] It should be noted, moreover, that Takanao is extremely direct when he takes issue with his predecessors (including Norinaga); far from the gentle "our school doesn't use this" approach of the late medieval commentators, Takanao favors terms such as "wrong," "bad," "mistaken," "forced," "error," "should not be followed," "should be rejected," and the occasional "what was he thinking?" He also cites the commentaries by name rather than mentioning "a certain commentary" or "one theory" as Keichū and Mabuchi had done. The impression is of an extremely confident man who wants his departures from earlier commentaries, and the significance of those departures in the history of *Ise monogatari* scholarship as it had evolved up to that point, to be very clear to the reader, a concern that is also evident in the care he takes to set out the history of *Ise* scholarship in his preface. Takanao also appears to assume that the reader will be familiar with and have ready access to the various texts he cites.

Takanao's mention of using *Ise monogatari* as a model for prose composition is significant. In *Uiyamabumi* (First Steps into the Mountains, 1798), Norinaga had isolated four fields of study to which aspiring students of nativism should devote themselves: Shinto studies, the study of ancient court practices, the study of historical records, and the study of poetry. For Norinaga, prose fiction was subsumed under poetry, but Takanao viewed vernacular prose as a separate field, which, as was the case with poetry, should be studied both in the interest of appreciating

---

71. Tanaka Sōsaku, *Ise monogatari kenkyūshi no kenkyū*, p. 217, gives a breakdown. Of the 156 times Takanao cites *Okudan*, he is agreeing with Keichū in only 23 of them. Mabuchi fares even worse in percentage terms: 23 out of 200 citations indicate approval of Mabuchi's views. Kitamura Kigin's *Shūsuishō* is raised only 53 times, of which 13 are endorsements.

old texts and in the interest of composing one's own. In a letter to a friend dated 1793, Takanao suggested that poets and Shinto scholars should also pursue prose studies, the former group in order to compose headnotes for their poems, and the latter in order to communicate ideas effectively. While diction and the appropriate use of rhetorical flourishes like *makurakotoba* (pillow words, or poetic epithets) were an important component in Takanao's theory of good prose, the first task for a beginning student was learning to produce a "thread" (*ito*), an argument that the reader can follow. And, although Takanao located the origins of vernacular prose writings in Shinto liturgy and imperial declarations of the ancient age, he emphasized the Heian classics—*Ise, Genji, Makura no sōshi*, and the *Kokinshū* preface—as the best models for contemporary study.[72]

Much of Takanao's *Ise* commentary, then, is devoted to discussing how the language works to further the narrative, both in order to understand the tale itself, the "deep meaning contained in its few words," and to call attention to the expressive techniques it employs. A good example of the first end can be found in his discussion of the opening section:

> In the past, there was a man. Having performed his coming-of-age ceremony, he went to hunt in the village of Kasuga near the old capital of Nara, where he had family property. In that village lived two very captivating sisters. The man peeped in at them through a crack. Much taken aback to have found them in such unbecoming circumstances in the old capital, his feelings were in great confusion.[73]

Commenting on the phrase "sisters lived [in that village]" (*harakara sumu*), Takanao notes:

> Saying 'sisters lived' indicates without saying it that there are no parents, and is skillful. The passage is written [to suggest] how these sisters, living in the desolation of the old capital without parents, are very piti-

---

72. Takanao himself writes lucid, obviously Heian-influenced prose throughout *Shinshaku*. See Kudō, *Fujii Takanao to Matsuya-ha*, pp. 69–74, for more information on Takanao's theory of prose, including quotations from the letter mentioned above.

73. This translation and those that follow use Takanao's base text (which differs from the *Teika-bon*), as pieced together from the text of *Shinshaku* found in Fujii, *Ise monogatari shinshaku*, pp. 10–11. Takeoka includes *Shinshaku* in *Ise monogatari zenyōshaku* as well, but because he does not always transcribe the full base text along with the commentary, it is a bit difficult to follow what Takanao is doing with the texts using Takeoka alone. I will say more about this passage below.

ful, and how one who sees them must take their plight to heart. Seeing such women, the feelings of one who knows *mono no aware* are in confusion. Why is it that Keichū and the [Mabuchi] were unable to see this?[74]

Whether or not one agrees with Takanao completely about the effect of the phrase, this is a genuinely novel approach. In response to the same passage, Keichū, Mabuchi, and the late medieval writers had confined themselves to informing the reader that *harakara* means "siblings," with the late medieval commentators adding a caution that the sisters are no one in particular (early medieval commentators identify them as daughters of Ki no Aritsune), Keichū adding a note that the word is applied to kittens in *Genji*, and Mabuchi suggesting that it applies only to children of the same mother.[75] Takanao, on the other hand, goes beyond the simple denotations of individual words and phrases, seeking out rather the effects of the words, and describing their contributions to the emotional structure of the whole.

Takanao also focuses on what he calls *bunpō*, by which he means less "grammar" than stylistic or rhetorical techniques. For example, he explains a line from Section 6 as follows:

The demon speedily devoured the woman in one gulp. She cried, "Ana ya!" but the man could not hear her above the noise of the thunder.

It appears illogical to say "she cried 'ana ya!'" after the demon devoured her in one gulp, but this is a technique which first describes the general situation, then returns to tell the details.[76]

Takanao comments in the same vein on a sentence in Section 20:

In the past, a man met a woman in Yamato province and took her as his wife. Then, after time passed, since he was a person in court service, when he was on his way back [to the capital] in the third month, he broke off some beautiful colored maple leaves and sent them to the woman from the road.

"After time passed" is connected to "going back." The words in between give the reason for his going back; this is one technique.[77]

---

74. Fujii, *Ise monogatari shinshaku*, p. 10.
75. See Takeoka, *Ise monogatari zenhyōshaku*, pp. 48–76.
76. Fujii, *Ise monogatari shinshaku*, p. 34.
77. Ibid., pp. 87–88.

Elsewhere, Takanao calls attention to and appraises techniques of repetition and parallelism and explains the way the prose and the poetry
echo and support each other. By identifying various phenomena specifically as techniques, or figures (*kotoba no aya*), he provides not only a
scheme for appreciating *Ise monogatari's* use of language, but also a guide
to rhetorical patterns that a student might then use in his or her own
writing.

Takanao makes a major contribution in his belief, apparent in the
commentary on Section 1 quoted above as well as in the preface, that
one reads *Ise monogatari* to learn what it means to "know *mono no
aware*," an idea derived from Norinaga's work on *Genji*. As Norinaga
defines it in *Genji monogatari tama no ogushi*, *mono no aware* is a sponta-
neous eruption of strong emotion in response to an experience or per-
ception. *Aware* covers the entire range of human emotions, from joy to
despair, but because the negative emotions that arise from a frustration
of desire are felt most intensely, they are most likely to be experienced as
aware and are closest to its essence. The experience of love, and most of
all frustrated or forbidden love, produces *mono no aware* more than any
other experience. Underlying Norinaga's formulation is the assumption
that some experiences should give rise to *mono no aware* while others
should not; to feel *mono no aware* indiscriminately or inappropriately is
almost as bad as having no feeling at all. Therefore, one who "knows"
mono no aware recognizes and gives in to the appropriate emotional responses to things.[78]

Takanao takes this to be the main point of *Ise monogatari* and refers to it repeatedly. In his commentary on Section 1 he elaborates as
follows:

> *Monogatari* writings, like poetry, do not discuss the moral principles of
> things. The good and bad of them are judged on the basis of human
> emotions: compassion and pity we consider good, and not having those
> qualities we consider bad. Indeed, even if one knows and adheres to the
> teachings of the Three Histories and the Five Classics, those who are

---

78. These ideas are laid out in detail in the second part of the introduction to *Tama
no ogushi*, titled "*Nao ōmune*" (further generalities). See Nakamura, *Kinsei bungakuron
shū*, pp. 104–13. For a translation of both parts of the introduction, see Harper, "Norinaga's Criticism of *Genji monogatari*." For a more in-depth discussion of Norinaga's
mono no aware ron, see Flueckiger, *Imagining Harmony*, pp. 177–79 and 187–90.

deficient in compassion and who do not know *mono no aware* merely adorn themselves superficially.[79]

The contrast with Azumamaro is striking. Although the two agree that *monogatari* and poetry are not written for moral edification in the Confucian sense of "rewarding good and punishing evil," in places where Azumamaro seethes about lasciviousness and undeserved bad reputations, Takanao seeks out the underlying emotions and takes the characters actions to be rooted in their sensitivity and deep feelings. By filling what Azumamaro perceived as a moral void with a new imperative founded in *mono no aware*, Takanao attempts to secure for *Ise monogatari* a legitimate place at the pinnacle of the canon, in effect rescuing the text from Azumamaro's dismissive association of it with kabuki.[80] Although Takanao does not develop the argument to the extent that Norinaga does, his stance will be familiar to anyone who has read *Tama no ogushi*. In Norinaga's view, the meaning of a work must be found in its internal logic; applying external principles (e.g., Confucianism and Buddhism), unrelated to the author's intention, leads to incorrect interpretations. Norinaga located the moral scheme of a fictional work at the crossroads of how the characters behave and what happens or does not happen to them as a result: good things (worldly success, wealth, physical beauty, etc.) accrue to good people, and in the *Genji monogatari*, good things happen to those who display a sensitivity to *mono no aware*.[81] Takanao would no doubt agree with Norinaga that reading these works in other terms would be "like cutting down a beautiful cherry tree that had been planted for blossom-viewing and using it for firewood."[82]

---

79. Fujii, *Ise monogatari shinshaku*, p. 274.

80. This is not intended to imply that Takanao is responding to Azumamaro directly. There is no evidence that Takanao read him—it seems fairly safe to assume that if he had, he would have said so explicitly in *Shinshaku*. *Dōjimon* circulated only in manuscript during the Edo period and seems not to have been widely accessible to people outside Azumamaro's and Mabuchi's schools. Until the modern period, very few later commentaries refer to it by name. Even in his discussion of the *Mana-bon* in *Tamakatsuma*, for example, Norinaga mentions only Mabuchi's use of it, not Azumamaro's.

81. Nakamura, *Kinsei bungakuron shū*, pp. 99–104.

82. Ibid., p. 117.

A comparison with the late medieval commentaries is also telling. In his commentary on Section 63, the story of the lonely old woman, for example, Takanao explains the last lines ("As a rule in this world, people are considerate of those they love and unfeeling toward those they do not love, but this man had a heart that made no such distinctions") as follows:

> *This person, etc. etc.*: This means that because he is a person of deep compassion who knows *mono no aware*, he does not abandon an unattractive woman. Although within his heart he has those he loves and those he does not love, he has a character such that he does not reveal the division. This is a very, very good personal trait. Genji has such a character too, and what is written in that *monogatari* was learned from this one. As I have said many times already, the import of this *monogatari* may be found in places where a character of this sort appears.[83]

On one level, Takanao's view is almost identical to the late medieval view. When Yūsai wrote, "However, the fact that Narihira does not discard her shows his deep feeling and compassion for others," he was close to acknowledging and valorizing Narihira's knowledge of *mono no aware* in different terms. The crucial difference, however, is in the personalization. In late medieval commentaries, only Narihira possesses this deep feeling and compassion, while Takanao finds *mono no aware* in the responses of other characters as well. At the same time, in keeping with the general tendency of late medieval commentators to deny or downplay erotic elements, Yūsai's comment here as elsewhere in the *Ketsugishō* is rooted more in a desire to absolve Narihira from accusations of amorousness by painting his behavior as something other than amorousness, than in acceptance of the *Ise* protagonist's habitual behavior as sound in itself. Takanao, however, relies on a broader standard of judgment that allows the text to stand almost entirely independent of Narihira, as well as obviating the need to worry about moral questions.

Although modern scholars hold *Shinshaku* in very high esteem for the accuracy of its explications and its pathbreaking emphasis on appreciation of *Ise*'s style, their admiration is tempered by grave reservations about Takanao's approach to the base text. As his comments in the preface

---

83. Fujii, *Ise monogatari shinshaku*, p. 208.

suggest, rather than using a single specific text Takanao in effect produces his own recension, based on the *Teika-bon* but with liberal admixtures of the *Suzakuin-nurigome-bon*, the *Mana-bon*, the *Wakachikenshū* text, and, in the worst cases, things he made up himself.[84] The first sentence of the *Teika-bon*, for example, reads as follows (underscores indicate places where Takanao's text differs):

> In the past a man, having performed his coming-of-age ceremony, <u>left</u> to hunt in the village of Kasuga near the old capital, where he had family property.
> [*Mukashi, otoko uikōburi shite, Nara no kyō Kasuga no sato ni, shiruyoshi shite, kari ni <u>inikeri</u>.*]

Takanao, with the *Suzakuin nurigome bon* as his authority, splits the sentence in order to preserve the typical opening of each section (*mukashi otoko arikeri*), and changes the last word.

> In the past <u>there was</u> a man. Having performed his coming-of-age ceremony, he <u>went</u> to hunt in the village of Kasuga near the old capital of Nara, where he had family property.
> • *There was* (*arikeri*): I have added this from the *Nurigome-bon*. What was said in *Koi*, "Because this is like an introduction, the word '*arikeri*' is not written," is bad. Although the word may be dropped subsequently, should it be omitted at the beginning?[85]

The change from "left" to "went" (*inikeri* to *ikikeri*) is made, Takanao says, simply because he thinks it sounds better. To take another example, in Section 4 of the *Teika-bon* we find the following:

> In the first month of the following year at the height of the plum blossoms, <u>longing for last year and going</u>, he stood and looked, he sat and looked, he looked, but it could not resemble last year.

---

84. Tanaka Sōsaku, *Ise monogatari kenkyūshi no kenkyū*, gives a breakdown on pp. 226–27. Of 498 deviations from the *Teika-bon*, Takanao derives 299 from the *Nurigome-bon*, 53 from the *Mana-bon*, 48 from these two together, 13 from the *Wakachikenshū*, and the rest from miscellaneous sources, including six changes that he makes himself based on no particular text. For in-depth discussion of Takanao's construction of the base text, see Tanaka, *Ise monogatari kenkyūshi no kenkyū*, pp. 219–30, and Kudō, *Fujii Takanao to Matsuya-ha*, pp. 74–80 and 91–94. Tanaka is more critical of Takanao's textual antics than Kudō, who urges the reader to consider *Shinshaku* in terms of Takanao's theory of prose.
85. Fujii, *Ise monogatari shinshaku*, p. 9.

Takanao has the following:

In the first month of the following year when the plum blossoms were at their height, <u>remembering last year, and going to that west wing</u> [where he'd gone before], he stood and looked, he sat and looked, he looked, but it could not resemble last year.[86]

> • *Remembering, to that west wing* (*omoiidete, ka no nishi no tai ni*): The *Nurigome-bon, Mana-bon*, etc. have this, and it is good. Where the *Mana-bon* has "when the plums in front were at their height" [*mae no ume no sakari naru ni*] and "he stood and looked, and went out and looked, but" [*tachite mi idete miredo*] the sentences are awkward and terribly bad. *Koi* says, "this is very good," but I cannot accept this at all. Why was that great master [Mabuchi] so completely unable to distinguish between good and bad writing?[87]

The differences, particularly in translation, may not seem earth-shattering, but for scholars who have been trained to locate the authority of a particular text in its proximity to an original, and to make direct alterations to a text viewed as authoritative only when there is evidence of corruption, Takanao's cavalier picking and choosing from among texts is troubling, and his confident substitution of phrases he devised himself akin to heresy. Takanao himself seems to have recognized that the latter practice was not entirely acceptable—in the original *Shinshaku* he included his own concoctions only a handful of times,[88] and in the revised version he edited them all out. Those inclined to defend him also suggest that the offense is mitigated to some extent by the care he takes to render the collation process transparent by noting his sources and giving the reasons for his selections. Regardless, it is clear that Takanao's approach to his base text is governed by unusual principles: his love of clear, well-crafted prose and his desire to create the best possible model for composition leads him to choose "the things that are a little superior" from among the texts available to him, rather than trying to preserve or advance the authority of a specific text as earlier scholars had done or trying to reconstruct an older form as some modern textual

---

86. Ibid., pp. 23–24.
87. Ibid., p. 24.
88. Tanaka says six, Kudō says four.

critics have done. Takanao does succeed in what he sets out to do; in the example from Section 4, as elsewhere, Takanao's version is certainly easier to understand and probably worthier of imitation than the *Teika-bon* version.[89] But because commentary by its very nature cannot be detached from the text on which it is based, the application of Takanao's work to a (theoretically) unadulterated text like the *Teika-bon*, whose very lack of clarity presents a different set of difficulties from those with which Takanao engages, will inevitably carry problems. In the end, his purporting to unearth the "true meaning" or "true intention" of the *monogatari*, or worse, his rejection of phrases in the least problematic texts available on the grounds that they are "not in the style of this *monogatari*," is at odds with his unwillingness or inability to ground that "truth" and "style" materially in a text with some greater claim to authenticity than being merely pleasing to the ear.

Nonetheless, *Shinshaku* marks a culmination in the progress of the so-called New Commentaries. Taking full advantage of earlier New Commentaries' philological work and their identification of the text as fiction, Takanao's work leaves behind the constraints of traditional interpretation almost entirely, and, in part, paved the way for modern scholarship on *Ise*. Owing to its focus on literary appreciation, its convenient gathering together of earlier scholarship, and its association with Norinaga, *Shinshaku* remained highly respected and influential well into the twentieth century, as evidenced by its having been reprinted numerous times in modern editions. It is also worth noting that, despite its problems, use of Takanao's base text far outstripped use

---

89. Although the motives are a bit different, Takanao's production of a more easily understood text meshes interestingly with innovations in other contemporary commentaries aimed at increased "user-friendliness." Examples include *Ise monogatari zusetsushō* (Saitō Hikomaro, 1801) and *Ise monogatari zue* (Ichioka Takehiko, 1823), both of which use illustrations to supplement verbal explanations; *Ise monogatari tenchū* (Shimizu Hamaomi, 1817) and *Ise monogatari sen* (Tachibana Moribe, 1820), both of which add particles, elided subjects, and other phrases to the text in brackets to make the meaning clearer; and *Ise monogatari rigenkai* (Sasaki Hirotsuna, 1858; [not quite contemporary, and not widely available until the 1880s, but closely related to *Tenchū, Sen*, and *Shinshaku*]), which gives interlinear modern language translations with the text. Tanaka discusses and transcribes samples of some of these (pp. 232–47) and also gives photographic reproductions of samples from manuscripts or early woodblock printings.

of the *Teika-bon* throughout Meiji, Taishō, and early Shōwa. Among the many *Ise monogatari* commentaries and series volumes produced between 1892 and 1950, eighteen, or roughly 60 percent, use Takanao's text, compared to just two or three that use the *Teika-bon*.[90] What effect this might have had on modern *Ise* reception remains open to question.

90. Tanaka Sōsaku, *Ise monogatari kenkyūshi no kenkyū*, pp. 230–31. He gives a list of modern editions and the base texts they use on pp. 248–50. The rest use base texts from other commentaries, most notably *Koi*, *Tenchū*, and *Sankō*.

The Birth of the Poem-Tale: Ise monogatari in the Modern Period

The earliest *Ise monogatari* scholarship of the modern period (1868–present) was in direct descent from New Commentaries of later nativist scholars, but even so, was slow to emerge. Joshua Mostow has noted that *Ise monogatari* was relatively neglected in the early Meiji period, still considered principally in terms of its value in women's education.[1] Arguably, *Ise*'s status had been slipping even earlier than that: apart from Fujii Takanao, who took *Ise* to be a central text both for its representation of what it means to "know *mono no aware*" and for its use as a model of excellent prose writing, the nativist scholars considered in Chapter 5 do not appear to have viewed their work on *Ise* as being as important as their work on poetry or on the Ancient Way. Kada no Azumamaro's *Dōjimon* is essentially a stunt commentary, certainly not founded upon any value Azumamaro found in *Ise monogatari*. Mabuchi's *Ise monogatari koi* was completed for his sponsor Tayasu Munetake, not because it was his own priority. And Norinaga never got around to commenting on *Ise monogatari* at all. Nonetheless, it is highly likely that existing woodblock-printed New Commentaries continued to circulate in the early years of the Meiji period. Fujii Takanao's *Ise monogatari shinshaku* was reprinted as late as 1866. Unfortunately the usual sources (*Kokusho sōmokuroku,* etc.) do not list Meiji-period woodblock reprints, and it is

---

1. Mostow, "Modern Constructions," pp. 99–100.

difficult to get a clear picture, but the modern transition from woodblock-printed editions back to movable type took years to be complete, and in the interim woodblock-printed books continued to be produced and reproduced.[2]

The first prominent new edition of *Ise monogatari* to appear in the modern period was *Tenchū Ise monogatari rigenkai* (Understanding of *Ise monogatari* in common language, with appended comments), by Sasaki Hirotsuna (1828–91). Sasaki had been a student of Ajiro Hironori (1784–1856), who had in turn studied with Arakida Hisaoyu (1746–1804, a student of Mabuchi), Motoori Ōhira (1756–1833, Norinaga's adopted son), and Motoori Haruniwa (1763–1828, Norinaga's eldest son). The preface to *Ise monogatari rigenkai* states that Sasaki wrote it in the Ansei era (1854–60), but it was first published in 1885 by Yanase Kihee as a woodblock-printed book. *Ise monogatari rigenkai* takes its base text and headnotes from *Ise monogatari tenchū* (1817) by Shimizu Hamaomi, the important late Edo-period textual scholar from whom Fujii Takanao obtained a copy of *Wakachikenshū*. To this, Sasaki added interlinear vernacular glosses and, set off in boxes within the base text, particles, subjects, and other grammatical tidbits to aid in reading.[3] As the publisher's advertisement in the back of the book indicates, *Ise monogatari rigenkai* was merely one text in a whole series of classics Sasaki rendered with vernacular glossing: there were *Rigenkai* texts already in existence for *Kojiki*, *Nihon shoki* poems, *Man'yōshū*, *Kokinshū*, *Taketori monogatari*, *Tosa nikki*, *Sarashina nikki*, and *Tsurezuregusa*, with one for *Genji monogatari* forthcoming.[4]

Sasaki's son Nobutsuna (1872–1963), later a prominent national literature scholar and poet, also produced an *Ise* commentary, *Kochū Ise monogatari* (Tales of Ise, collated and annotated), published in modern movable type when he was only twenty years old. But the content of this, too, derives almost entirely from old nativist commentaries—*Seigo*

---

2. For example, as indicated in Chapter 4, the 1662 plain-text woodblock-printed edition of *Ise monogatari* was reprinted twice in the Meiji period.

3. The latter feature proceeds in a manner reminiscent of that employed by Tachibana Moribe (1781–1849) in his *Ise monogatari sen* (1820). Photographic reproduction in Katagiri and Yamamoto, *Tesshinsai bunko Ise monogatari sokan*, vol. 15.

4. Sasaki Hirotsuna, *Tenchū Ise monogatari rigenkai*, unpaginated back matter.

okudan, *Ise monogatari koi*, *Ise monogatari shinshaku*, and again, *Ise monogatari tenchū*.[5]

The first hints of novelty in a modern *Ise* commentary appear the following year, with *Ise monogatari kōgi* (Lectures on *Ise monogatari*, 1893) by Imaizumi Teisuke, a work that is in any event more noteworthy than the preceding two by virtue of its use as a middle school textbook and its longevity in print.[6] In his preface, Imaizumi begins by suggesting that *monogatari* are not unique to the Heian period—they have forebears in stories such as the Urashima legend in *Nihon shoki*. But it is those of the Heian period, he says, that "tell of successes and failures in human life, dramatically reflect human feeling (*ninjō*), and thereby become a way of passing time."[7] He goes on to divide *monogatari* into three types: (1) those that record facts as they are, (2) those that are half factual and half fictional, and (3) those that are completely fictional. In short, Imaizumi continues to make generic classifications on the same fact-fiction axis that goes all the way back to the Old Commentaries. The division is especially reminiscent of Kamo no Mabuchi's in the preface to *Ise monogatari koi*, but for the classification of *Ise monogatari* itself. The first group includes works like *Eiga monogatari* (subsequent writers who use the same scheme include *Ōkagami* here too), the third includes *Genji* and *Taketori*, but *Ise* has in this case been separated from *Genji* to be thrown in with new company in the middle group: *Yamato monogatari* and *Konjaku monogatari shū*. However, while the first group can be classed as historical records, Imaizumi considers both the second and third groups to be "novelistic" (*shōsetsu-teki*) records, insofar as they give insight into the "human feelings and social conditions" (*ninjō setai*) of their times. The language immediately brings to mind Tsubouchi Shōyō's *Shōsetsu shinzui* (1885), which emphasizes precisely these attributes as the central concern of the modern novel. However, for Imaizumi, *Ise monogatari*'s value is principally tied up with its purported factuality, its potential

---

5. Sasaki Nobutsuna, *Kōchū Ise monogatari*, p. 22. Sasaki gives a list of earlier commentaries in which, interestingly, *Seigo tsū* appears, suggesting that it did in fact circulate among nativist scholars, and that perhaps it influenced the reading of *Ise* in terms of Narihira's political grievances that crops up in late Edo-period writings.

6. Fukui, *Uta monogatari no kenkyū*, p. 298. Meiji-period middle school is equivalent to a modern high school. *Ise monogatari kōgi* was reprinted as late as 1920.

7. Imaizumi, *Ise monogatari kōgi*, p. 2.

use as a historical record. The reader is warned repeatedly not to imagine that it is merely the language and style of the *monogatari* that is to be prized (again, the "flowers of language and leaves of words" of Teika's *Takeda-bon* colophon), but rather the depiction of Narihira's deep and sincere antipathy toward the Fujiwara. *Ise monogatari kōgi*, despite its evocation of Tsubouchi Shōyō's then-recent work and classification of *Ise* as a novel, is essentially a conservative text (or, when considered beside *Ise monogatari shinshaku*, perhaps even a regressive one), treading little beyond the approach of late nativist scholars who had revived the idea of *Ise* as a factual work.[8]

Ise monogatari kōgi is also conservative in that it is commentary in the first place. By the start of 1890s, the form had come to the end of its 600-odd years of dominance in *Ise monogatari* studies, and intensive, section-by-section study of the text itself came to persist only in the pedagogical and "classics for the (educated) masses" realm. High-end scholarship began to focus instead on defining the characteristics of a national literature that could take its rightful place among other world literatures, and most of the interesting, groundbreaking theories about *Ise monogatari*'s nature or place in the scheme of things thus began to appear in essays, in sweeping literary histories written in emulation of Western literary histories, and in introductions to new editions of the text. This is a markedly "modern" development, not only because of the influence of the West and the attempts to locate characteristics of the nation in characteristics of the literature, but also because of the privileging of the critic and the historical narrative over the text and the received tradition, a top-down rather than bottom-up approach that would have been unthinkable in premodern scholarly circles.

A watershed step away from the fact-fiction axis that bespoke a new conceptualization of *Ise monogatari*'s generic status was made in 1892, in Ōwada Tateki's *Wabungakushi* (History of Japanese literature), which, according to the preface, was also written as a textbook. Ōwada was the first to propose the *uta monogatari* (poem-tale) category as a suitable classification for *Ise monogatari*. In the section of the text dealing with

---

8. Such as those listed above in Chapter 5, n. 50. Though he cites only premodern sources, here Imaizumi may be vectoring the introduction to the edition of *Ise* that appeared in the series *Nihon bungaku zensho* in 1890 and takes a similar view (see Mostow, "Modern Constructions," pp. 102–3).

the Heian period, he writes that *monogatari* should be familiar to the reader from such children's stories as Momotarō, Kachikachiyama, and so on, texts where spoken words are written down in *kana*.

> This is the origin of *monogatari*. However, the boundaries within which they are carried out are not childish, but adult. They were practiced in the half-child, half-adult society of women, who believed in Buddhism, enjoyed tales of the supernatural, knew about love and observed the evanescence of things. Therefore, in both substance and style they are more refined than Momotarō, and of course they are more finely wrought, but insofar as they copy down spoken words in writing, they are no different.[9]

He then names *Taketori monogatari*, *Ise monogatari*, *Utsuho monogatari*, *Ochikubo monogatari*, and *Yamato monogatari* as the representative works of this period and states, "Of these, because *Ise monogatari* is chiefly in a form like famous poems with lengthy headnotes added, together with *Yamato monogatari*, it is appropriate to call it an *uta monogatari* to distinguish it from continuous *monogatari*."

Although the term *uta monogatari* was not immediately picked up in scholarly works[10]—use of it does not seem to have become widespread until the early Shōwa period—a tendency to look at *Ise* in terms of its position on a poetry–prose axis does become increasingly pronounced from this time, an outgrowth of attempts to adopt the Western separation of genres into poetry, drama, and narrative. Many examples from various kinds of texts might be mentioned. Perhaps the earliest is Mikami Sanji and Takatsu Kuwasaburō's view of *Ise* as being closer to a poetry collection than a novel in their *Nihon bungakushi* (History of Japanese literature, 1890), a designation that serves to devalue it in their scheme, where *monogatari* and novels are privileged.[11]

In 1905, Fujioka Sakutarō returned to the fact-fiction axis in his *Kokubungaku zenshi: Heian-chō hen*. In it, he views *Ise* as a kind of novel that mixes facts of Narihira's life with fiction, and that is therefore not a "pure novelistic fictional *monogatari*" (*junsui no shōsetsu-teki*

9. Ōwada, *Wabungakushi*, p. 176.
10. Fukui Teisuke notes that the early national literature scholar Haga Yaichi (1867–1927) was known to have been fond of the word, and perhaps contributed to its spread, though he did not use it in his written work. Fukui, *Uta monogatari no kenkyū*, pp. 1–2.
11. Mostow, "Modern Constructions," p. 102.

tsukuri monogatari), but he considers the prose–poetry axis too: the prose portions of the texts, he feels, exceed mere prefaces to the poems; they have their own rich quality.[12] He also dismisses the view of Narihira as a patriot.

In the introduction to *Shin'yaku Ise monogatari*, a modern-language translation of *Ise* that appeared in 1912, Ōta Mizuho (1876–1955) characterizes the text as "an autobiography of Narihira's emotional life" and views Narihira as the leader in rescuing Japanese poetry from the obscurity into which it had fallen between the *Man'yōshū* and the ninth century; the decisive figure who established the elegant, emotional style of Heian-period poetry with its themes of love, impermanence, and sadness, and, indeed, the founder of the entire poetic tradition from the Heian period through the medieval period and Tokugawa period. He notes approvingly that Narihira was, as *Ise monogatari* reveals, "a child of emotion, a child of nature, a child of instinct." But, he notes further, he does not intend this praise to absolve Narihira of his "crime" in causing such a limited style as that of the *Kokinshū* to prevail over the whole of remaining Japanese literary history.[13]

One last example is a commentary, *Shinshaku Ise monogatari* (New explication of *Ise monogatari*) by Arima Yotōji, published in 1920. Here we find, on the one hand, *Ise* praised extravagantly for its wide-ranging depiction of human emotions (including the Confucian-sounding duty between lords and retainers, love between parents and children, faithfulness between friends, as well as laughter, weeping, longing for nature, love and passion between men and women, etc.), and on the other, a revival of Imaizumi Teisuke's fact-fiction-based tripartite division of narrative kinds, with *Ise* pronounced to be, again, a mostly factual account of Narihira's frustrated patriotism.

In short, writers in the early part of the modern period seem if anything even less able to decide what to do with *Ise monogatari* than their premodern predecessors had been. The two dominant generic views of *Ise* in the Meiji and Taishō periods—as the deliberately disguised biography-diary of an aggrieved patriot, or as a collection of lyric poetry—in fact have a major thing in common: both views deny or

---

12. Ibid., pp. 309–10.
13. Ōta, *Shin'yaku Ise monogatari*, pp. 2–5.

de-emphasize the presence of fictional elements. In cases where *Ise* is being held up as novelistic in order to force it to lead smoothly to *Genji monogatari* and other premodern "novels," this tendency ends up being rather paradoxical—it becomes the perceived factuality of the text that is closely linked to its portrayal of "human emotions and social conditions," rather than what we would normally think of as the central defining attribute of a novel, its fictionality. At the same time, the majority of the views expressed are more focused on Narihira than on *Ise monogatari*, and it must be said that given how very little is known for certain about Narihira's life, these scholars put themselves in the ironic position (yet again) of producing their own fictions, unacknowledged as such, in order to read *Ise monogatari* as fact. Note that it is much easier to gloss over the difficulties in this view when discussing *Ise* as part of a sweeping literary history than it is when writing a commentary and having to deal with classifying the fact and fiction piece by piece as it comes up. The renewed prevalence of the view of *Ise* as factual can be related to the generic shift that took place in scholarship from commentary to expansive, generalizing essay.[14]

And yet none of this is entirely out of place in a milieu increasingly dominated by what Tomi Suzuki calls "I-novel discourse"[15]—whether Narihira is being read as an imperial loyalist, a champion of indigenous poetry, a child of emotion, nature, and instinct, or a Nestorian priest from Afghanistan, the important point is that *Ise monogatari* is taken to be a direct revelation of Narihira's true self. In a real sense, none of this is terribly distant from viewing Narihira as a manifestation of Batō Kannon. Narihira and *Ise monogatari* itself, its congenial openness to interpretation undisrupted by some 800 years of scholarly activity, merely provide the pretext that allows scholars to expound freely on whatever issues are most meaningful to them, in ways that reflect the intellectual and ideological concerns of their times.

---

14. It is worth noting that most of the late nativist scholars who began reading Narihira as a patriot put their views forth in miscellanies rather than commentaries. And of course, Goi Ranshū had had to scrap over 60 percent of the text to pull it off in a commentary.

15. See Tomi Suzuki, "Gender and Genre," pp. 71–95, for a discussion of this discourse in relation to the canonization of Heian-period women's diary literature, and see her *Narrating the Self* for a more general discussion.

APPENDIX I

Relations among persons who figure in Ise monogatari

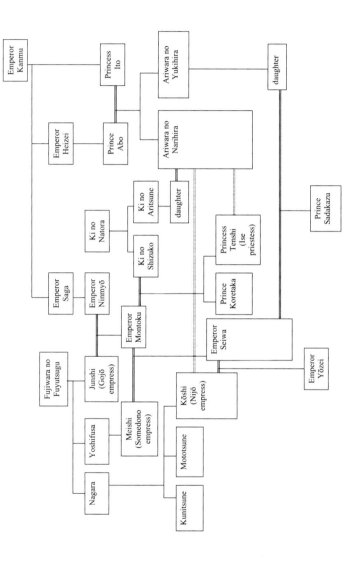

APPENDIX 2

Selections from Ise monogatari[1]

Section 1

In the past, a man came of age[2] and went to hunt in the village of Ka-suga near the old capital of Nara, where he had family property. In that village lived two very charming sisters. The man peeked in at them. Because he was surprised to have found them in such unbecoming cir-cumstances in the old capital, his feelings were in turmoil. The man cut off the hem of the hunting robe he was wearing, wrote a poem on it, and sent it in. He was wearing a hunting robe with a print of tangled hare's-foot ferns.[3]

> *Kasugano no*   Like a patterned robe
> *wakamurasaki no*   dyed with young lavender
> *surigoromo*   from the fields of Kasuga,

1. These translations are based on the text of *Ise* in Horiuchi and Akiyama, *Taketori monogatari, Ise monogatari*, pp. 79–194, which in turn is based on a copy of the *Tenpuku-bon* owned by Gakushūin University. Earlier versions of Sections 1, 2, 4, 9, 12, 23, 63, 65, 69, 82, 101, 107, and 125 appeared in *Traditional Japanese Literature,* edited by Haruo Shirane. Copyright © 2007 Columbia University Press. Reprinted with permis-sion of the publisher.

2. I.e., performed the capping ceremony, in which a youth's hair was cut and he donned adult clothes and a hat for the time.

3. The man's robe is made of cloth on which these ferns had been rubbed, producing a tangled pattern. This cloth was manufactured in the district of Shinobu in Michi-noku province, in the far northern part of Japan.

| *shinobu no midare* | my tangled feelings |
| *kagiri shirarezu* | know no bounds.[4] |

He wrote this rapidly, in a single line.[5] He must have been very pleased with himself. The poem has the same idea as the following:

Michinoku no	Whose fault is it
shinobu mojizuri	that my feelings are tangled
tare yue ni	as the dyed patterns
midare somenishi	on cloth from Michinoku?
ware naranaku ni	Surely not mine. . . .[6]

The people of the past were given to this kind of impetuous elegance.[7]

Section 2

In the past, when the capital in Nara had been left behind but before people were settled into the present capital, there was a woman in the western part of the city.[8] This woman was superior to other people. Her mind surpassed even her appearance. It seemed she was not without lovers. An honest man pledged his love to her, and returned home—what might he have been thinking? It was the last day of the third month,[9] and he sent this to her as a soft rain fell.

| *oki mo sezu* | I spent the night |
| *ne mo sede yoru no* | neither awake |

---

4. *Wakamurasaki* is literally "young gromwell," a plant whose roots were used to make purple dye. In classical Japanese poetry, the color purple suggests affinity; here it represents the sisters. The word *shinobu*, which means "yearning," is a pun referring also to the province in which the cloth was made.

5. The phrase here is ambiguous and may have meant "he wrote with a sophistication belying his youth." Writing "in a single line" would mean that in his eagerness to set the poem down, he did not take time to arrange the graphemes for artistic effects.

6. *Kokinshū* 724, Minamoto no Tōru.

7. The word translated as "elegance," *miyabi*, refers to an urbane sophistication associated with the capital and the aristocracy. Although the word appears only this one time in the text, many modern commentators argue that it is a major theme of *Ise monogatari*.

8. The new capital was established in present-day Kyoto in 794.

9. The last day of spring by the lunar calendar.

akashite wa   nor yet asleep,
haru no mono to te   and the day gazing at the rains
nagamekurashitsu   thinking of spring.[10]

Section 3

In the past, there was a man. He decided to send something called hiji-kimo [a kind of seaweed] to a woman he was in love with, and wrote:

omoi araba   If you loved me
mugura no yado ni   surely you would sleep with me
ne mo shinan   in a house overgrown with weeds
hijikimono ni wa   using just our sleeves
sode wo shitsutsu mo   for bedding.[11]

This was when the Nijō empress was not yet serving the emperor, and was still a commoner.

Section 4

In the past there was a woman living in the west wing of the Grand Empress's[12] mansion in the east Fifth Ward. A man who had deep feelings for her without intending to went there to visit her, but around the tenth of the first month she disappeared. He heard where she was, but because it was not a place where one could go,[13] he grew ever more melancholy. In the first month of the following year, when the plum blossoms were at their height, he longed for the previous year and went back to the west wing. He stood and looked, he sat and looked. He looked, but he could find no resemblance to the year before. Weeping bitterly, he lay down on the rough floor boards until the moon sank, and remembering the last year he wrote:

---

10. *Kokinshū* 616, Narihira. *Nagame* means both "long rains" and "gazing in melancholy."

11. The man appears to choose this particular plant in order to suggest the word for "bedding," *shikimono*.

12. Traditionally identified as Fujiwara no Junshi, who was the aunt of the woman who later became the Nijō empress, Fujiwara no Kōshi. Referring to Junshi here suggests that the woman in the west wing is Kōshi.

13. Some commentators think this place might be court; others suggest the home of a high-ranking person who would not have been sympathetic to the man's visits.

tsuki ya aranu	Is there no moon?
haru ya mukashi no	Is this spring
haru naranu	not the spring of the past?
wagami hitotsu wa	I alone
moto no mi ni shite	am as I was. . . .[14]

When dawn began to break, he went home, still weeping.

Section 5

In the past, there was a man. He had been going very secretly to visit someone in the east part of the Fifth Ward.[15] He wanted to avoid being seen, so could not go in through the gate; instead he went back and forth through a part of the wall that had been crumbled by children's stepping on it. Although it was not a place with many passersby, he visited so frequently that the owner of the house found out, and placed a guard in the man's path every night. Although he went there as usual, he returned home unable to meet his beloved. Then he composed this poem:

hito shirenu	This guard
waga kayoiji no	at the secret place
sekimori wa	where I come and go—
yoiyoigotoni	I wish he would fall asleep
uchimonenanamu	every night![16]

When the woman heard about this, she was distraught, so the owner of the house allowed them to meet again.

Because people had begun to talk about his secret visits to the Nijō empress, her brothers set up a guard, or so it is said.

Section 6

In the past, there was a man. For some years he had been courting a woman whom he could not win, and finally he stole her away and fled into the dark night. When he led her to a place called Akutagawa, she saw the dew on the grass and asked him, "What is that?" When there was still a long way to go, the night was growing late, and because it was thundering and rain was falling heavily, he put the woman in a rundown

---

14. *Kokinshū* 747, Narihira.
15. Suggesting, again, Junshi's residence and that the man is visiting Kōshi.
16. *Kokinshū* 632, Narihira.

storehouse, not knowing that demons haunted the place. He stood guard at the entrance with his bow and quiver. As he was thinking how he wished that dawn would break, a demon swallowed the woman in one gulp. She called out in surprise, but he could not hear her over the noise of the thunder. When dawn broke and he looked in, she was not there. He stamped his feet and wept, but to no avail.

shiratama ka	When she asked me
nani zo to hito no	whether it was a white jewel
toishi toki	or something else—
tsuyu to kotaete	How I wish I had replied,
kienamashi mono o	"It's dew," and vanished!

This was when the Nijō empress was serving her cousin the imperial consort. Because she was so beautiful he stole her away and carried her off on his back, but her older brothers, the Horikawa lord[17] and Major Counselor Kunitsune, were on their way to court (they were still low-ranking officials at the time) when they heard a person crying piteously; they stopped the man and took her back. They were the demons mentioned in the story. It is said that this happened when the empress was still young and just a commoner.

Section 9

In the past, there was a man. Having made up his mind that his position was worthless, he thought that he should live in the east rather than in the capital, and he set out to find a new province where he could reside. He went with an old friend or two. Because none of them knew the way, they wandered about. They arrived at a place called Eight Bridges in Mikawa province. The place is called Eight Bridges because the rivers in which the water flows are branched like a spider's legs and spanned by eight bridges. They dismounted in the shade of a tree at the edge of the marsh there and ate parched rice. In that marsh, the irises [*kakitsubata*] were blooming beautifully. Seeing them, one of the party said, "Make a poem on the subject of travel, placing the five syllables ka-ki-tsu-ba-ta at the beginning of each measure."

karagoromo	Since I have a wife
kitsutsu narenishi	familiar to me as the hem

---

17. Fujiwara no Mototsune (836–891).

tsuma shi areba	of a well-worn robe,
harubaru kinuru	I think sadly of how far
tabi o shi zo omou	I have traveled on this journey.[18]

When he composed this, they all shed tears on their parched rice until it swelled with the moisture.

Moving on, they came to the province of Suruga. When they arrived at Mt. Utsu, they were troubled to find that the road they planned to take was very dark and narrow, with dense growth of creepers and maples. As they were thinking what unexpected and difficult experiences they were having, they met with a pilgrim. "What are you doing on such a road as this?" he asked them, and the man recognized him as someone he had met before. He wrote a letter and asked the pilgrim to take it to the lady he had left in the capital.

Suruga naru	Near Mt. Utsu
utsu no yamabe ni	in Suruga
utsutsu ni mo	I can meet you neither
yume ni mo hito ni	in reality nor even
awanu narikeri	in my dreams.[19]

When they came to Mt. Fuji, they saw that it was very white with falling snow even on the last day of the fifth month.[20]

toki shiranu	The peak of Mt. Fuji
yama wa Fuji no ne	is oblivious to time.
itsu to te ka	What season does it take this to be,
ka no ko madara ni	that the falling snow
yuki no fururamu	should dapple it like a fawn?

---

18. *Kokinshū* 410, Narihira. In addition to fulfilling the condition proposed by his traveling companion, the man's poem contains a large number of puns that could not be incorporated into the translation. *Kitsutsu* means both "coming" and "wearing"; *narenishi* is both "gotten accustomed to" and "grown fond of"; *tsuma* is both "wife" and "hem"; *haru* means "to full [cloth]" and *harubaru* means "distant."

19. The name Mt. Utsu suggests the word for "reality" (*utsutsu*), and the first two lines of the poem are a preface leading to this word. Because people in this period believed that someone who was thinking of them would appear in their dreams, the man's failure to meet his beloved even in his dreams implies that the woman is not thinking of him.

20. I.e., summer.

If we compare this mountain to those here in the capital, it is twenty times the height of Mt. Hiei, and its shape is like a cone of sand used for making salt.[21]

Continuing on as before, they came to a very large river between Musashi and Shimotsufusa provinces. It is called the Sumida River.[22] As they stood in a group on the edge of the river and thought of home, lamenting together about how very far they had come, the ferryman said, "Hurry up and get in the boat. It's getting dark." About to board the boat and cross the river, they were all forlorn, for there was not one of them who did not have someone he loved in the capital. Just then they saw a white bird with a red bill and legs, about the size of a snipe, cavorting on the water and eating a fish. Because this is not a bird one sees in the capital, none of them recognized it. When they asked the ferryman what it was, he said, "Why, that's a capital bird." Hearing this, the man composed a poem:

na ni shi owaba	If you are true to your name
iza koto towamu	then I shall ask:
miyakodori	O capital bird,
waga omou hito no	Is the one I love
ari ya nashi ya to	living or dead?[23]

Everyone in the boat burst into tears.

Section 11

In the past, a man on his way to the east sent this from the road to friends:

Wasuru na yo	Do not forget me!
hodo wa kumoi ni	Though the distance grows as far
narinutomo	as to the clouds above
sora yuku tsuki no	I will meet you again
meguriau made	just as the moon returns to cross the sky.[24]

---

21. *Shiojiri*. The meaning of this word is disputed.

22. The same river that flows through modern Tokyo.

23. *Kokinshū* 411, Narihira. The implication is that a "capital bird" should know what is going on in the capital.

24. This poem is attributed in the *Shūishū* to Tachibana no Tadamoto, who died in 955. It is one of several that postdate Narihira considerably and that give an indication of the late date at which *Ise monogatari* must have been completed.

Section 12

In the past there was a man. He ran off with someone's daughter and led her to the fields of Musashi. Because this made him a thief, he was arrested by the governor of the province. He left the woman in a grassy place and ran away. Some people who came along the road said, "We hear there is a thief in this field," and started to set fire to it. The woman was distressed, and composed the following:

Musashino wa	For today, do not burn
kyō wa na yaki so	this field of Musashi!
wakakusa no	Fresh as young grass,
tsuma mo komoreri	my spouse is hidden here
ware mo komoreri	and I am hidden here too.[25]

When they heard this, they took the woman and led the pair off together.

Section 14

In the past, a man went to Michinoku for no particular purpose. A woman there, perhaps because people from the capital were rare, fell deeply in love with him. She composed:

nakanaka ni	If I'm not
koi ni shinazu wa	to die of love
kuwako ni zo	I would become
narubekarikeru	a silkworm
tama no o bakari	and live only briefly.[26]

Even her poem was rustic. As usual, perhaps because he pitied her, he went and slept with her. Deep in the night as he was leaving, the woman composed:

yo mo akeba	When dawn breaks
kitsu ni hamenade	I'll toss him in the water tank.
kutakake no	That damn rooster

---

25. This poem is a variation on *Kokinshū* 17, anonymous, which gives "the fields of Kasuga" for "the fields of Musashi."

26. This poem is deemed "rustic" because of the unacceptable word "silkworm." It closely resembles a poem in book 12 of the *Man'yōshū*.

| *madaki ni nakite* | crows too soon |
| *sena o yaritsuru* | and sends my man away. |

The man, saying he would return to the capital, replied:

Kurihara no	If the pine tree of Areha
Areha no matsu no	at Kurihara
hito naraba	were one for whom I waited
miyako no tsuto ni	I would say, "Come with me to the capital
iza to iwamashi o	as a souvenir."

The woman was overjoyed. "He must love me!" she said.

Section 16

In the past, there was a man named Ki no Aritsune.[27] He had prospered in the service of three emperors, but times changed with the next reign, and he did not do as well as even ordinary people. He was a man of unusual sensibility and refinement. Even as he grew poorer, he kept up the style and tastes of the days when things had been better, and did not know how to manage his expenses. He had gradually grown estranged from his wife of many years, and at length she became a nun and went to live with an older sister who had preceded her in taking vows. Although they had not been truly intimate, now that she was leaving he was deeply moved, but because he was poor there was nothing he could do for her. Distressed, he wrote to a close friend, "She is leaving, and I cannot do even the slightest thing for her as I send her off." He enclosed this poem:

te o orite	Crooking my fingers
aimishi koto o	I count the years
kazoureba	we were together:
tō to iitsutsu	four times pass
yotsu wa henikeri	as I count to ten.

The friend was very moved when he saw this. He sent a robe and even some bedding, and wrote:

toshi dani mo	The years you passed
tō tote yotsu wa	together
henikeru o	number four times ten—

---

27. Narihira's father-in-law and friend (815–877). He served emperors Ninmyō, Montoku, and Seiwa.

| *iku tabi kimi o* | how many times |
| *tanomikinuramu* | must she have relied on you? |

Aritsune's reply:

kore ya kono	Might this be
ama no hagoromo	the heavenly robe
mube shi koso	of feathers?
kimi ga mikeshi to	A garment such as this
tatematsurikere	is fit only for you.[28]

He was so overjoyed that he also composed:

aki ya kuru	Has autumn come?
tsuyu ya magau to	Or the dew gone astray?
omou made	So I wonder
aru wa namida no	when I see my sleeves
furu ni zo arikeru	wet with tears of joy.

Section 19

A man in the service of an imperial consort once began to see one of her attendants. In no time, the affair came to an end. They served in the same place, and although the woman saw the man, he acted as though she was not there. She sent him this poem:

amagumo no	Though I see you
yoso ni mo hito no	as before,
nariyuku ka	you have grown distant
sasuga ni me ni wa	as a cloud
miyuru mono kara	in the heavens.[29]

He replied:

amagumo no	That I am distant
yoso ni nomi shite	as a cloud in the heavens
furu koto wa	is because the winds
wa ga iru yama no	blow so strong
kaze hayami nari	at my mountain home.[30]

---

28. There is a pun here on *ama*, meaning both heaven of "heavenly robe" and "nun."
29. *Kokinshū* 784, Aritsune's daughter.
30. Slightly altered version of *Kokinshū* 785, Narihira.

He was saying that another man had been visiting her.

Section 23

In the past, a boy and a girl whose parents made their living in the country-side used to go out to the foot of the well to play together, but when they grew up, they became shy of each other. Nonetheless, the boy thought he would win this girl, and the girl continued to have tender feelings toward the boy— though her parents tried to marry her to an-other, she would not hear of it. One day the following came from the boy, who lived next door:

tsutsui tsu no	Since last I saw you
izutsu ni kakeshi	my height
maro ga take	has surpassed
suginikerashi na	that of the well-curb
imo mizaru ma ni	where we measured it.

The girl replied:

kurabekoshi	The parted hair
furiwakegami mo	I once compared to yours
kata suginu	now falls past my shoulders.
kimi narazu shite	Who should tie it up
tare ka agubeki	if not you?[31]

After many such exchanges, they were finally able to marry as they wished.

Several years passed, and the woman's parents passed away. Having lost his support, the man thought there was no use in going on together as they had been, and he began visiting a woman in Takayasu, in Kawachi province. Because in spite of this the first woman saw him off without any evidence of bad feelings, the man began to suspect that she was seeing someone else. When he hid himself in the shrubbery, pre-tending to have gone to Kawachi, the woman carefully put on her makeup and, gazing off sadly, recited

kaze fukeba	When the wind blows
okitsu shiranami	the white waves break in the offing,
Tatsutayama	will you be crossing

---

31. Young boys and girls wore their hair parted in the middle; girls tied theirs up when they came of age.

yowa ni ya kimi ga	Mt. Tatsuta
hitori koyuramu	all alone at night?[32]

When he heard this, his tenderness for her knew no bounds, and he stopped going to Kawachi.

When he did go on rare occasions to look in on the woman in Takayasu, he found that though she had initially made herself out to be refined, now she had become careless. When he saw her take up a ladle herself and pile rice into a serving bowl, he was disgusted and stopped going to see her. The woman gazed off into the distance toward Yamato and said:

kimi ga atari	I shall continue
mitsutsu o oramu	to look in your direction.
Ikomayama	Do not hide Mt. Ikoma,
kumo na kakushi so	O clouds,
ame wa furu to mo	even if it rains.[33]

Finally the man from Yamato said he would come. She waited happily, but after being disappointed several times, she said:

kimi komu to	As each night
iishi yo goto ni	you said you would come
suginureba	passes by
tanomanu mono no	I learn not to trust you,
koitsutsu zo furu	yet my love persists

But the man stopped visiting her.

Section 25

In the past, there was a man. He sent a poem to a woman who would not say whether she would meet him, after it became clear that she would not:

aki no yo ni	My sleeves are more soaked
sasa wakeshi asa no	on a night when I sleep without meeting you
sode yori mo	than on a morning when they part

---

32. *Kokinshū* 994, anonymous. Although the wind and waves do not make a great deal of sense in the translation, they contribute to a play on words in the original: *tatsu*, "break," functions as a pivot word, part of Mt. Tatsuta that also supplies the verb for *shiranami*, the white waves. *Shiranami* may be a euphemism for thieves, who terrorized travelers in the desolate mountain pass. The poem indicates the woman's concern for the man's safety, and with it her continued love for him despite his infidelity.

33. Mt. Ikoma was on the border of Yamato and Kawachi provinces.

| *awade nuru yo zo* | bamboo grass in the autumn fields |
| *hichimasarikeru* | on my way home.[34] |

The flirtatious woman sent back:

mirume naki	Is it because he does not know
wagami o ura to	there is no seaweed on this shore
shiranebaya	that the fisherman comes
karenade ama no	without reaping it
ama no ashi tayuku kuru	until his legs are weary?[35]

Section 29

In the past, when in attendance at a flower-viewing party given by the Mother of the Crown Prince,[36] a man wrote:

hana ni akanu	I have always grieved
nageki wa itsu mo	that I cannot have my fill
seshikadomo	of the cherry blossoms
kyō no koyoi ni	but never so much
niru toki wa nashi	as I do on this night.

Section 33

In the past, a man was visiting a woman who lived in the Ubara district of Tsu province. Because one day she seemed to think that when he left he would not come again, he composed:

| *ashibe yori* | As the tide floods in |
| *michikuru shio no* | ever rising |

---

34. *Kokinshū* 622, Ariwara no Narihira.

35. *Kokinshū* 623, Ono no Komachi. This complex poem contains a number of pivot words (*kakekotoba*) and associated words (*engo*) that can not be captured in translation: *mirume* means "opportunity to see/meet" as well as being the name of a type of edible seaweed; *ura* may mean both "shore" and "disagreeableness"; *karu* is both "cut" or "reap" and "be distant/separated." Thus the poem also asks whether the man persists in approaching because he does not know the woman's cruelty will prevent him from seeing her.

Note that these two poems were not originally composed as an exchange; the author seems to have paired them based simply upon their placement side by side in the *Kokinshū*.

36. A title that again evokes the Nijō empress, who was the mother of Emperor Yōzei. Compare Section 76.

iyamashi ni	from the reeds at the shore
kimi ni kokoro o	so does my love
omoimasu kana	for you increase.

She replied:

komorie ni	How, like a boatman
omou kokoro o	with his pole, sounding
ikade ka wa	a hidden inlet
fune sasu sao no	can I hope to fathom
sashite shirubeki	your feelings?

For a person in the provinces, was this a good poem or a bad one?

Section 41

In the past, there were two sisters. One's husband was low-ranking and poor, and the other had a high-born husband. On the last day of the twelfth month, the one with the low-ranking husband was washing his outer robe, and stretched it out herself to dry. She took great care, but because she was not accustomed to such lowly work, she tore the shoulder of the robe. There was nothing she could do; she just wept and wept. The high-born man heard about this, and, moved to pity, he found a beautiful blue robe[37] and sent it to her with this poem:

murasaki no	When the color of the lavender
iro koki toki wa	is deep, though one gazes
me mo haru ni	into the distance
no naru kusaki zo	one distinguishes nothing else among
wakarezarikeru	the trees and grasses of the field.[38]

He must have been thinking about the poem on Musashino.[39]

---

37. Blue robes were worn by courtiers of the sixth rank.
38. *Kokinshū* 868, Narihira. As in Section 1, lavender suggests affinity, or a strong, deep love. Here it represents the poet's wife; his love for her extends to caring for her sister.
39. *Kokinshū* 867, anonymous.

murasaki no	Because of a single
hitomoto yue ni	lavender plant
Musashino no	I am moved
kusa wa minagara	gazing on all the grasses
aware to zo miru	of the fields of Musashi.

Section 46

In the past, a man had a splendid friend. They were inseparable and thought much of each other. When the friend was posted to another province, they parted sadly. Days and months passed, and the friend wrote in a letter, "Time has passed terribly without our seeing each other. I am in great distress, wondering if you have forgotten me. In this world, it appears that people's hearts are prone to forgetting when they are apart and do not meet." The man sent back this poem:

mekaru to mo	I cannot think
omōenaku ni	that we are apart.
wasuraruru	There is no time
toki shi nakereba	when I forget you;
omokage ni tatsu	your image rises before me.

Section 49

In the past, a man observed the beauty of his younger sister and composed this poem:

ura wakami	The young grass
neyoge ni miyuru	that appears so fresh
wakakusa o	and good for sleeping—
hito no musubamu	how regrettable it is
koto o shi zo omou	that another's hand will gather it!

She replied:

hatsukusa no	Why do you speak to me
nado mezurashiki	in words rare and amazing
koto no ha zo	as the first grasses of spring?
ura naku mono o	I have loved you
omoikeru ka na	without reserve.

Section 59

In the past, a man—what might he have been thinking about the capital?—decided to live in Higashiyama.

sumiwabinu	Living in misery
ima wa kagiri to	and thinking it's the end
yamazato ni	I'll seek lodging
mi o kakusubeki	where I can hide myself
yado motometemu	in a mountain village.

In this way, he became gravely ill, and seemed about to die. People splashed water on his face and he revived.

wa ga ue ni	Dew seems
tsuyu zo oku naru	to fall on me:
ama no kawa	droplets from the oars
towataru fune no	of the boat that crosses
kai no shizuku ka	the River of Heaven.[40]

Section 63

In the past, a woman who wanted a man to love her thought how she wished she could meet a man of deep feeling. Because she had no way of coming out and saying so, she made up a story about a dream. She called three of her children and told them about it. Two of them made unfeeling responses and dismissed it. The third son said, "It means a good man will surely come to you," and with that the woman looked very pleased.

Most men are quite without feeling. The son thought he would like to have her meet the Ariwara Middle Captain Narihira[41] somehow. He ran into the Captain when he was out hunting and, taking the bridle of his horse on the road, explained the situation. The Middle Captain pitied her, and went to sleep with her. Then, afterward, because he did not appear again, the woman went to his house and peeked in at him. The man saw her faintly and said:

momotose ni	One year short
hitotose taranu	of one hundred years
tsukumogami	with her thinning hair
ware o kourashi	I see a vision
omokage ni miyu	of one who seems to love me.

Seeing that he looked as if he was about to leave, she returned to her house, bumping against brambles and thorny bushes, and lay down. As

---

40. *Kokinshū* 863, anonymous. In the *Kokinshū* this poem appears within a sequence of poems composed in connection with the Tanabata festival, when the Herdsman (the star Altair) crosses the Milky Way to meet the Weaver Maid (the star Vega).

41. Narihira held this position at the end of his career. This is the only place where Narihira is named outright.

the woman had done, the man stood outside looking at her secretly. The woman lamented and started to go to sleep, saying:

samushiro ni	On a narrow mat
koromo katashiki	with a single robe for a cover
koyoi mo ya	again tonight
koishiki hito ni	must I lie here alone
awade nomi nemu	without the one I long for?

The man was moved, and spent that night with her.

As a rule, people in this world are considerate of those they love and unfeeling toward those they do not love, but this man had a heart that made no such distinctions.

Section 65

In the past, there was a woman whom the emperor loved and had taken into his service, and who was allowed to wear the forbidden colors. She had a cousin who was the mother of an emperor. A man of the Ariwara clan who served at court was still very young but was on intimate terms with this woman. Because this man was allowed in the women's quarters, he went to where the woman was and refused to budge. When the woman said, "This is most unsuitable. We will surely come to no good. Don't behave this way!" the man composed this:

omou ni wa	My caution
shinoburu koto zo	is quite defeated
makenikeru	by my yearning for you.
au ni shi kaeba	If we can but meet,
sa mo araba are	let happen what may!

The woman retreated to her rooms, but because the man went to her as usual, unconcerned that others saw, the woman was very distressed and went back to her family home. Finding this not a deterrent, but more convenient, the man began visiting her at home. Everyone heard and laughed. When the groundskeepers saw him return to the palace in the mornings, he would take his shoes, throw them in toward the front and enter.[42]

---

42. So that they would not think that he had been out all night. The shoes of latecomers would be farther from the door.

While he was carrying on in this disgraceful way, it occurred to him that he would lose his position and finally be ruined, so he prayed to the gods and buddhas, saying, "Please, somehow, put an end to these feelings!" but his love for her only increased, and his yearning continued to be unbearable. He summoned yin-yang diviners and shamans, made preparations for a ritual ablution that would end his love, and went out to the river. But after the ritual he grew even more despondent, and longed for her even more than before.

koi seji to	The gods
mitarashigawa ni	have not accepted
seshi misogi	the rites I performed
kami wa ukezu mo	here at the sacred river
narinikeru kana	to end my yearning.

The emperor was a handsome man, and when the woman heard him chanting the Buddha's name with great devotion in a noble voice, she wept bitterly. "What an unfortunate fate, and how sad it is to be unable to serve such a lord as this, to be shackled to that man!" she said, and wept. At this time, the emperor heard of the affair and sent the man into exile. He made the woman go to her cousin, his mother, who chastised her by shutting her up in a storehouse. Hidden in the storehouse, she wept.

ama no karu	Like the name of the creature
mo ni sumu mushi no	that lives in the seaweed
ware kara to	reaped by fisherfolk,
ne o koso nakame	I cry, "It is my fault!"
yo o ba uramiji	and I don't blame the world.[43]

When she cried like this, the man, who returned every night from the province to which he had been exiled, played his flute very cheerfully, and sang movingly in an elegant voice. Thus the woman, though shut up in the storehouse, could hear that he was there, but they were unable to meet. She thought:

sari to mo to	How sad that he should still
omou ramu koso	hope we might meet,

---

43. *Ware kara,* which means "due to me," is also the name of a small crustacean that lives in seaweed.

kanashikere	not knowing
aru ni mo aranu	I am here
mi o shirazu shite	yet not here.

As for the man, because he could not meet her, he wandered about in this way, and went back to the provinces, singing this:

itazura ni	I went away
yukite wa kinuru	in vain
mono yue ni	only to return again
mimaku hoshisa ni	my desire to see her
izanawaretsutsu	luring me back.

This must have been during the reign of Emperor Seiwa. The mother of the emperor was the Somedono empress. Or she might have been the empress of the Fifth Ward.[44]

Section 66

In the past, a man who had property in Settsu province took his brothers and friends to visit Naniwa. When they looked out at the beach, they saw that there were boats.

Naniwazu o	At each inlet
kesa koso mitsu no	we saw this morning
ura goto ni	at Naniwa harbor—
kore ya kono yo o	those boats that traverse
umi wataru fune	the rough seas of life.

Moved by this, everyone returned home.

Section 67

In the past, a man went roaming with some friends of whom he was fond to the area near Kisaragi in Izumi province. When they looked at Mt. Ikoma in Kawachi province, the clouds gathered and cleared, rising up then hanging over the mountain in ceaseless movement. In the

---

44. Emperor Seiwa reigned from 858 to 876. His mother, Fujiwara no Meishi, Kōshi's cousin, was known as the Somedono empress. The empress of the Fifth Ward (also mentioned in Section 4) was Kōshi's aunt, but she was also the mother of an emperor (Montoku, Seiwa's father), thence the ambiguity.

morning it was cloudy, and in the afternoon it cleared. The falling snow had left the tree branches very white. Seeing this, one person among the travelers composed:

kinō kyō	The clouds that danced up
kumo no tachimai	to conceal the mountain
kakurou wa	yesterday and today
hana no hayashi o	must have been jealous
ushi to narikeri	of the flowering forest!

Section 68

In the past, a man went to Izumi province. Riding along Sumiyoshi Beach in Sumiyoshi Village in the Sumiyoshi District, because the scenery was very beautiful they dismounted from their horses frequently. A certain person said, "Compose a poem on Sumiyoshi."

kari nakite	There is autumn
kiku no hana saku	when the wild geese cry
aki wa aredo	and the chrysanthemums bloom
haru no umibe ni	but how good to live at the shore in spring
sumiyoshi no hama	at Sumiyoshi beach.[45]

When he composed this, no one could respond.

Section 69

In the past there was a man. When he was dispatched to Ise province as an imperial huntsman,[46] the mother of the high priestess of the Ise Shrine[47] told her daughter to treat him better than she would the usual messengers. Because these were her mother's instructions, she took very good care of him. In the morning she saw him off on his hunting, and when he returned in the evenings she had him stay in her own lodgings. In this way, she treated him very well.

---

45. The place name Sumiyoshi contains a pun on "good for living."
46. "Imperial huntsmen" were sent by the emperor to nearby provinces both to bring back game and to investigate the affairs of the provincial governments.
47. The high priestess was an unmarried princess chosen at the beginning of a new emperor's reign to serve at the Inner Shrine at Ise, dedicated to the sun goddess Amaterasu.

On the night of the second day, the man said quite passionately that he wanted to meet her privately. The woman too was not ill-disposed toward their meeting. However, since there were many prying eyes, they were unable to meet. Because the man was the head of the hunters, he was not lodged far away; he was near the woman's own sleeping quarters. At the first hour of the rat,[48] when everyone had gone to sleep, she came to the man. For his part, the man had been unable to sleep and was lying down looking out into the night when he saw her standing there in the dim moonlight with a little girl before her.[49] The man was overjoyed, and led her into his chamber. She stayed until the third hour of the ox,[50] but before they had exchanged vows, the woman returned to her own rooms. The man, deeply saddened, could not sleep. In the morning he was impatient to hear from her, but it would not have done for him to send her a note, and he was waiting in great distress, when, shortly after dawn the following poem came from the woman, with no other message:

kimi ya koshi	Did you come to me?
ware wa yukiken	Or did I go to you?
omōezu	I cannot tell.
yume ka utsutsu ka	A dream, or reality?
nete ka samete ka	Was I asleep, or awake?[51]

Weeping piteously, the man composed this:

kakikurasu	I have wandered lost
kokoro no yami ni	in the darkness
madoiniki	of my heart.
yume utsutsu to wa	Let us decide tonight,
koyoi sadame yo	dream or reality.[52]

After sending this to her, he went out hunting. He rode through the fields, but he was distracted by thoughts of meeting her even that night, soon after the others went to sleep. But the governor of the province, who also oversaw affairs at the shrine, heard that an imperial huntsman had

---

48. Between 11 and 11:30 p.m.
49. Probably a servant or attendant.
50. Between 2 and 2:30 a.m.
51. *Kokinshū* 645, anonymous.
52. *Kokinshū* 646, Narihira.

come. All night they drank together, and the pair were entirely unable to meet. Because he had to move on to Owari province the next day, the man wept tears of blood,[53] unbeknownst to anyone, but still they could not meet. When the dawn was beginning to break, a poem came from the woman, written on the saucer of a cup of parting. He took it up, and read:

kachibito no	Since ours is a bond
wataredo nurenu	shallow as waters that do not wet
e ni shi areba	the hem of a traveler's robes . . .

She had written this much, but there was no end to the poem. Using charcoal from a pine torch, he wrote the last lines on the saucer:

mata ausaka no	again I will cross
seki wa koenamu	the Meeting Barrier.

At daybreak he crossed to Owari province.

The woman served as high priestess of Ise during the reign of Emperor Seiwa. She was the daughter of Emperor Montoku, and the sister of Prince Koretaka.

Section 72

In the past, a man, unable to meet again with a woman in Ise province, departed for the neighboring province with great resentment. The woman recited:

Ōyodo no	The pine tree of Ōyodo
matsu wa tsuraku mo	is not unfeeling—
aranaku ni	waiting pains me.
uramite nomi mo	It is the waves that turn to go,
kaeru nami kana	ever resentful.[54]

Section 75

In the past, a man said, "Come to Ise to live with me." The woman said,

---

53. "Tears of blood" is a conventional metaphor for extreme grief.

54. There are pivot words in this poem: *matsu* means both "pine tree" and "to wait," while *uramite* is both "resenting" and "seeing the bay." Ōyodo is a bayside location in Ise province.

Ōyodo no	Like the name of the seaweed
hama ni ou chō	that grows, they say,
miru kara ni	on the beach at Ōyodo,
kokoro wa naginu	I am content just to "see" you
katarawanedomo	without further conversation.[55]

Finding this even colder than before, the man replied:

sode nurete	Like the name of the seaweed
ama no karihosu	the fisherfolk harvest,
watatsuumi no	wetting their sleeves,
miru o au nite	you will make do with "seeing"
yamamu to ya suru	and there let it end?

The woman:

iwama yori	Seaweed grows
ōru mirume shi	from between the rocks
tsurenaku wa	as always;
shio hi shio michi	the tide goes out, the tide comes in
kai mo arinan	surely to some avail.[56]

Again, the man:

namida ni zo	As I wring them out
nuretsutsu shiboru	they are drenched again with tears:
yo no hito no	your cruel heart
tsuraki kokoro wa	appears as droplets
sode no shizuku ka	on my sleeves.

She was indeed a difficult woman to meet.

Section 76

In the past, when the Nijō empress was still known as the Mother of the Crown Prince, she went to pay her respects to the ancestral deity of the clan. An old man belonging to the Imperial Guards' Bureau[57] was in

---

55. *Miru* is both the name of a type of seaweed and the verb "to see."

56. The text for this poem seems to be corrupt. A pun on *kai*, meaning both "effectiveness" and "seashells," is not represented in the translation.

57. Another of Narihira's titles, though he did not hold this position when Kōshi was known as the Mother of the Crown Prince.

attendance, and as rewards were being distributed, he drew close to her carriage and recited:

Ōhara ya	On this day
Oshio no yama mo	the god of Mt. Oshio
kyō koso wa	in Ōhara
kamiyo no koto mo	must surely be remembering
omoiizurame	events of the Age of the Gods.[58]

Perhaps she was moved by this, but there is no way of knowing.

Section 82

In the past, there was a prince named Prince Koretaka. He had a palace at a place called Minase, on the far side of Yamazaki. Every year when the cherry blossoms were in full bloom he went to that palace. At such times, he always took along a person who was the Director of the Right Imperial Stables.[59] Because a long time has passed, I have forgotten his name.

Not enthusiastic about hunting, they just drank sake continually, and turned to composing Japanese poetry. The cherry blossoms at the Nagisa residence in Katano, where they were hunting now, were especially beautiful. They dismounted under the trees there, and, breaking off blossoms to decorate themselves with, everyone, of high, middle and low rank, composed poems. The Director of the Stables composed this:

yo no naka ni	If only this world
taete sakura no	were without cherry blossoms,
nakariseba	then might our hearts
haru no kokoro wa	be at ease
nodokekaramashi	in springtime.[60]

Another person composed this:

chireba koso	It is because they fall soon
itodo sakura wa	that the cherry blossoms
medetakere	are so admired.
ukiyo ni nani ka	What can stay long
hisashikarubeki	in this fleeting world?

---

58. *Kokinshū* 871, Narihira.
59. A post held by Narihira.
60. *Kokinshū* 53, Narihira.

When they left the trees to return to Minase it was already dark. The prince's attendants came from the fields with servants bringing the sake. Seeking out a good place to drink it, they came to a place called Amanokawa.[61] The Director of the Stables gave the prince a cup of sake. The prince said, "When you hand me the cup, compose a poem on coming to the banks of Amanokawa after hunting at Katano." The Director of the Stables composed this and handed it to him:

karikurashi	I've spent the day hunting,
tanabata tsume ni	and now will seek lodging
yadokaramu	from the Weaver Maid
ama no kawara ni	for I have come
ware wa kinikeri	to the River of Heaven.[62]

The prince recited this over and over, but could not come up with a response. Ki no Aritsune[63] was attending the prince. He responded:

hitotose ni	She who waits patiently
hitotabi kimasu	for a lord who comes
kimi mateba	but once a year
yado kasu hito mo	will not, I am sure,
araji to zo omou	lodge any other. [64]

They went back to Minase and the prince entered his palace. Until deep in the night they drank and conversed, and then the prince prepared to go to bed, somewhat drunk. As the moon of the eleventh day of the month[65] began to sink, the Director of the Stables composed a poem:

akanaku ni	How can the moon
madaki no tsuki no	hide itself
kakururu ka	before we are satisfied?

---

61. Literally, "River of Heaven," also the name for the Milky Way.

62. *Kokinshū* 418, Narihira.

63. Ki no Aritsune was Koretaka's uncle and Narihira's father-in-law.

64. *Kokinshū* 419, Ki no Aritsune. These poems refer again to the legendary Herdsman (the star Altair) and his wife the Weaver Maid (the star Vega), who were separated by the River of Heaven (the Milky Way) and able to meet only once a year, on the seventh day of the seventh month (celebrated as the Tanabata festival).

65. A waxing moon, about halfway between quarter and full.

| *yama no ha nigete* | I wish the mountain rim would flee |
| *irezu mo aranamu* | so the moon might stay in view.[66] |

In place of the prince Ki no Aritsune replied:

oshinabete	I wish the peaks,
mine mo taira ni	one and all,
narinanamu	would flatten.
yama no ha naku wa	If there were no mountain rim
tsuki mo iraji o	the moon would not hide.

Section 83

In the past, Prince Koretaka, who often visited Minase, went hunting there as he usually did. The old man who was Director of the Imperial Stables came along to attend him. After several days, the prince returned to his palace. The other man saw him back, and though he wanted to leave quickly, the prince gave him sake and gifts and would not let him go. Impatient, the Director of the Stables composed the following:

makura to te	I will not pull up
kusa hikimusubu	and bind the grass
koto mo seji	to make a pillow
aki no yo to dani	while I have not even
tanomarenaku ni	a long autumn night to rely upon.[67]

It was the last day of the third month. The prince passed the whole night without going to sleep.

In this way, the man always attended the prince, but one day, unexpectedly, the prince took the tonsure.[68] In the first month, when the man went to Ono to pay his respects to the prince, the snow was very deep because it was in the foothills of Mt. Hiei. He made his way

---

66. *Kokinshū* 884, Narihira.

67. Binding up grass to make a pillow is associated with traveling, spending the night away from home. The man's poem suggests that if it were autumn, when nights are long, he would want to stay, but because it is spring, when nights are short, he would prefer to return home.

68. Koretaka took the tonsure in 872, at age 28. The act has often been interpreted as an expression of disappointment over having been passed over for the succession, but actually Koretaka's brother had been named crown prince when both were still children.

with difficulty to the prince's hut and when he paid his respects, he found the prince with nothing to do, looking very forlorn, so he stayed somewhat longer than usual and reminisced with him about the past. Although he thought he would have liked to stay longer, he had duties at court and could not linger. Thinking he would leave at dusk, he said:

wasurete wa	When I forget
yume ka to zo omou	I wonder if it might be a dream.
omoiki ya	Could I ever have thought
yuki fumiwakete	that I would make my way
kimi o mimu to wa	through snow to see you?[69]

He went home weeping and weeping.

Section 84

In the past, there was a man. Although he was of low rank, his mother was a princess. She lived in a place called Nagaoka. The man was in court service in the capital, and though he tried to visit her he could not do so frequently. Because he was her only child, she loved him very much. In the twelfth month, he received a letter from her marked "urgent." Alarmed, he opened it, and found a poem:

oinureba	Since they say
saranu wakare no	that growing old
ari to ieba	brings an inevitable parting
iyoiyo mimaku	I long to see you
hoshiki kimi kana	all the more.[70]

Weeping profusely, the son composed:

yo no naka ni	How I wish
saranu wakare no	that in this world
naku mogana	there were no inevitable partings!
chiyo mo to inoru	For the sake of the son
hito no ko no tame	who wishes you a thousand years.[71]

---

69. *Kokinshū* 970, Narihira.
70. *Kokinshū* 900, Princess Itō (Narihira's mother).
71. *Kokinshū* 901, Narihira.

Section 101

In the past, there was a man named Ariwara no Yukihira, who was Commander of the Right Military Guards. Hearing that he had excellent sake at his house, some people from court went there, and that day he gave a banquet with the Controller of the Right Fujiwara no Masachika as the guest of honor. A man of taste, Yukihira had flowers placed in a vase. Among the flowers there was an astounding spray of wisteria [*fuji*] trailing fully three and a half feet. As the company were composing poems using the wisteria as a topic, Yukihira's brother heard there was a party and came by. The company grabbed him and made him compose a poem. Because he had never known much about composing poetry, he tried to refuse, but they forced him, and he composed this:

saku hana no	How many they are
shita ni kakururu	who take refuge in the shade
hito ōmi	of wisteria
arishi ni masaru	greater now
fuji no kage kamo	than ever before.

When they asked him "Why did you compose such a thing?" he said "I composed it thinking of Lord Yoshifusa[72] at the height of his fortunes, and of the amazing success of Fujiwara clan." Everyone stopped criticizing him.

Section 107

In the past, there was an elegant man. Fujiwara no Toshiyuki, a secretary, was courting a girl in his service. However, because she was young, she could not write or speak properly, and needless to say she could not compose poetry. The master of the house wrote a draft for her and had her copy it. Toshiyuki was quite lost in delight, and composed the following:

tsurezure no	Unable to meet you
nagame ni masaru	I can only gaze
namidagawa	on these endless rains

---

72. Fujiwara regent and clan head in the mid-ninth century. Father of Meishi, and grandfather of Emperor Seiwa.

| sode nomi hichite | a river of tears |
| au yoshi mo nashi | drenching my sleeves.[73] |

The first man replied on behalf of the girl:

asami koso	How shallow
sode wa hitsu rame	a river of tears
namidagawa	that wets only your sleeves
mi sae nagaru to	when I hear you are drowning
kikaba tanomamu	I'll trust the depths of your love.[74]

Toshiyuki, completely enchanted, rolled this up and put it in a letter box, which, it is said, he keeps to this day.

Toshiyuki sent a letter (this was after they had begun to meet) saying "I am distressed, seeing that it must rain. If I were at all lucky this rain would not fall." The man sent this reply on the girl's behalf:

kazukazu ni	Since I cannot ask
omoi omowazu	point by point
toigatami	whether you love me or not
mi o shiru ame wa	my tears fall more and more
furi zo masareru	like this rain that will tell my fate.[75]

Having received this, Toshiyuki rushed out flustered, with neither raincoat nor hat, and arrived drenched to the skin.

Section 114

In the past, when the Ninna emperor made a journey to Serikawa,[76] he commanded a man to attend him who had in the past managed the falcon for the hunt, but who now felt such service was unbecoming. On the sleeve of his figured hunting robe, he wrote:

okinasabi	Let no one blame
hito na togame so	this shabby old man
karikoromo	who wears a hunting robe

---

73. *Kokinshū* 617, Fujiwara no Toshiyuki. As above, *nagame* means both "gazing" and "long rains."

74. *Kokinshū* 618, Narihira.

75. *Kokinshū* 705, Narihira.

76. Emperor Kōkō (r. 884–887) made this excursion in 887, seven years after Narihira's death.

| *kyō bakari to zo* | just for today |
| *tazu mo naku naru* | crying like the crane.[77] |

The emperor looked annoyed. The man thought only of his own age, but others who were not young thought of how it applied to them, it is said.

Section 115

In the past, in Michinoku, a man and a woman lived together. The man said, "I am leaving for the capital." The woman, terribly sad, thought she would at least give him a farewell party, and at a place called Capital Island in Okinoite, she gave him sake and composed:

Okinoite	Sadder than if I burned
mi o yaku yori mo	sitting in the embers
kanashiki wa	at Okinoite[78]
Miyakoshimabe ni	is this parting
wakare narikeri	on the shore of Capital Island.

Section 124

In the past—on what sort of occasion might it have been?—a man composed the following:

omou koto	I should end my days
iwade zo tada ni	without saying
yaminubeshi	what I think
ware ni hitoshiki	since there is no other
hito shi nakereba	who shares my feelings.

Section 125

In the past, a man fell ill and felt that he would soon die.

tsui ni yuku	I had heard before
michi to wa kanete	that we all must travel
kikishikado	this road in the end
kinō kyō to wa	but I never thought my time
omowazarishi o	would come yesterday or today . . .[79]

---

77. *Gosenshū* 1077, Ariwara no Yukihira.
78. The *oki* of Okinoite evokes *okihi*, "embers."
79. *Kokinshū* 861, Narihira.

Character List

Abo (prince) 阿保親王
"Agemaki" 総角
Ajiro Hironori 足代弘訓
Amayo danshō 雨夜談抄
Andō Tameakira 安藤為章
Aobyōshi-bon 青表紙本
Arakida Hisaoyu 荒木田久老
Arima Yotōji 有馬與藤次
Ariwara no Narihira 在原業平
Ariwara no Yukihira 在原行平
Asai Ryōi 浅井了意
Asakura Norikage 朝倉教景
Ashikaga Yoshizumi 足利義澄
Asukai Masaharu 飛鳥井雅春
Asukai Masayasu 飛鳥井雅康
"Azumakudari" 東下り
Batō Kannon 馬頭観音
batsubun 跋文
Botanka Shōhaku 牡丹花肖伯
bunpō 文法
chōhōki 重宝記
chūiri 注入り
daiei 題詠
daisen 題簽
dan 段
denju 伝授
denki monogatari 伝奇物語
"E-awase" 絵合

Edo 江戸
Eiga monogatari 栄華物語
Eiga no taigai 詠歌大概
Eikan 栄閑
e-iri 絵入り
Fujii Takanao 藤井高尚
Fujioka Sakutarō 藤岡作太郎
Fujiwara no Akisue 藤原顕李
Fujiwara no Akisuke 藤原顕輔
Fujiwara no Fuyutsugu 藤原冬嗣
Fujiwara no Kiyosuke 藤原清輔
Fujiwara no Kōshi 藤原高子
Fujiwara no Kunitsune 藤原国経
Fujiwara no Meishi 藤原明子
Fujiwara no Mototsune 藤原基経
Fujiwara no Nagara 藤原長良
Fujiwara no Onshi 藤原温子
Fujiwara no Shunzei 藤原俊成
Fujiwara no Tameaki 藤原為顕
Fujiwara no Tameie 藤原為家
Fujiwara no Teika 藤原定家
Fujiwara no Yoshifusa 藤原良房
Fujiwara no Yoshitsune 藤原良経
Fujiwara no Yukinari 藤原行成
fukkokuban 覆刻版
Fukurozōshi 袋草子
Gengo ko 源語詁
Genji ippon kyō 源氏一品経

Genji monogatari 源氏物語
giko monogatari 擬古物語
Gōdanshō 江談抄
Goi Ranshū 五井蘭州
Go-Kashiwabara (emperor) 後柏原
天皇
Go-Mizuno-o (emperor) 後水尾天皇
Go-Nara (emperor) 後奈良天皇
Gonki 権記
Gosen(waka)shū 後撰和歌集
Goshūi(waka)shū 後拾遺和歌集
Go-Tsuchimikado (emperor) 後土御
門天皇
Go-Yōzei (emperor) 後陽成天皇
gunki monogatari 軍記物語
Gukanshō 愚管抄
Gyokuyō(waka)shū 玉葉和歌集
Hachijō Toshihito (prince) 八条宮智
仁
Hahakigi betchū 帚木別注
haikai 俳諧
Hasegawa Mitsunobu 長谷川光信
Hasegawa Senshi 長谷川千四
Hatakeyama Yoshifusa 畠山義総
Hata Sōha 秦宗巴
Hayashi Razan 林羅山
Heian 平安
Heichū monogatari 平中物語
Heike monogatari 平家物語
Heizei (emperor) 平城天皇
hiden 秘伝
hikiuta 引き歌
Hirata Atsutane 平田篤胤
Hishikawa Moronobu 菱川師宣
Hōjōki 方丈記
Hokuni-Bunko-bon 穂久邇文庫本
Hon'ami Kōetsu 本阿弥光悦
Honchō shinsenden 本朝神仙伝
hon'i 本意
honkadori 本歌取り
Hosokawa Yūsai 細川幽斎

Hyakunin isshu 百人一首
Ichijō (emperor) 一条天皇
Ichijō Kaneyoshi 一条兼良
Ihara Saikaku 井原西鶴
Ikkadō Jōa 一華堂乗阿
Imagawa Ujiteru 今川氏輝
Imaizumi Teisuke 今泉定介
Insei 院政
irogonomi 色好み
iro-otoko 色男
Ise monogatari 伊勢物語
Ise monogatari dōjimon 伊勢物語童
子問
Ise monogatari eshō 伊勢物語絵抄
Ise monogatari gyoshō 伊勢物語御抄
Ise mongatari guanshō 伊勢物語愚案
抄
Ise monogatari gukenshō 伊勢物語愚
見抄
Ise monogatari hiketsushō 伊勢物語
秘訣抄
Ise monogatari iseishō 伊勢物語惟清
抄
Ise monogatari jokai 伊勢物語抒海
Ise monogatari jokunbun 伊勢物語女
訓文
Ise monogatari jokun taizen 伊勢物
語女訓大全
Ise monogatari kaisei 伊勢物語改成
Ise monogatari ketsugishō 伊勢物語闕
疑抄
Ise monogatari kisuishō 伊勢物語器
水抄
Ise monogatari kōgi 伊勢物語講義
Ise monogatari koi 伊勢物語古意
Ise monogatari nichiyō bunshō 伊勢
物語日用文章
Ise monogatari sen 伊勢物語箋
Ise mongatari shinshaku 伊勢物語新
釈
Ise monogatari shitchū 伊勢物語集注

Ise monogatari shōmonshō 伊勢物語
  肖聞抄
Ise monogatari shushoshō 伊勢物語首
  書抄
Ise monogatari shūsuishō 伊勢物語
  拾穂抄
Ise monogatari taisei 伊勢物語大成
Ise monogatari tenchū 伊勢物語添註
Ise monogatari tōshoshō 伊勢物語頭
  書抄
Ise monogatari Yamaguchi shō 伊勢
  物語山口抄
Ise no saigū (high priestess) 伊勢の
  斎宮
Ito (princess) 伊都内親王 (also
  given as 伊豆, 伊登, or 伊東)
Izumi Shikibu 和泉式部
Jichin 慈鎮
Jien 慈円
jige denju 地下伝授
jikki 実記
jitsu 実
jitsuji 実事
jōruri 浄瑠璃
Jōsanmi monogatari 正三位物語
jūhan 重版
junkyo 準拠
kabuki 歌舞伎
kabusebori 被せ彫り
Kachō kudenshō 花鳥口伝抄
Kachō yojō 花鳥余情
Kada no Arimaro 荷田在満
Kada no Azumamaro 荷田春満
Kagerō nikki 蜻蛉日記
Kaitokudō 懐徳堂
Kakaishō 河海抄
Kakinomoto no Hitomaro 柿本人
  麻呂
Kamakura 鎌倉
Kamo no Chōmei 鴨長明
Kamo no Mabuchi 賀茂真淵

kanazōshi 仮名草子
Kanmu (emperor) 桓武天皇
kanzen chōaku 勧善懲悪
Karasumaru Mitsuhiro 烏丸光広
kari no tsukai 狩の使
Kashiragaki Ise monogatari shō 頭書
  伊勢物語抄
kasho 歌書
Kawachi-bon 河内本
Keichū 契沖
Kensai 兼載
Kenshō 顕昭
kikigaki 聞き書き
Kimura Takatarō 木村鷹太郎
Ki no Aritsune 紀有常
Ki no Natora 紀名虎
Ki no Shizuko 紀静子
kirigami 切り紙
Kitamura Kigin 北村季吟
Kiyohara Nobukata 清原宣賢
kobunjigaku 古文辞学
kochūshaku 古注釈
kodō 古道
Kofukuji (temple) 興福寺
Kogetsushō 湖月抄
Kojiki 古事記
kokatsuji 古活字
kokin denju 古今伝授
Kokinshū chū 古今集注
Kokinshū hishō 古今集秘抄
Kokinwaka Ise monogatari 古今和歌
  伊勢物語
Kokin(waka)shū 古今和歌集
Kokka hachiron 国歌八論
Kōkō (emperor) 光孝天皇
kokubungaku 国文学
Kokubungaku zenshi: Heian-chō hen
  国文学全史　平安朝編
kokugaku 国学
Konjaku monogatari shū 今昔物語集
Konoe Hisamichi 近衛尚通

Konoe Taneie 近衛種家
Korai fūteishō 古来風躰抄
Korehito (prince) 惟仁親王
Koretaka (prince) 惟喬親王
Koshikibu no Naishi 小式部内侍
kōshoku 好色
kōshokumono 好色物
kotoba no aya 言葉の文
kuden 口伝
Kujō Tanemichi 九条種通
Kumazawa Banzan 熊沢蕃山
kyo 虚
Kyōgoku 京極
kyojitsu no narai 虚実の習ひ
kyūchūshaku 旧注釈
Maigetsushō 毎月抄
makoto 誠, 真, or 実
makurakotoba 枕詞
Makura no sōshi 枕草子
Man'yō daishōki 万葉代匠記
Man'yōshū 万葉集
Matsunaga Teitoku 松永貞徳
Meiji 明治
Mikami Sanji 三上参次
Mikohidari-ke (family) 御子左家
Minamoto no Chikayuki 源親行
Minamoto no Mitsuyuki 源光行
Minamoto no Tōru 源融
Mingō nisso 岷江入楚
mittsū 密通
Miyoshi Nagayoshi (Chōkei) 三好長慶
monogatari 物語
mono no aware もののあはれ
mono no hon 物の本
Montoku (emperor) 文徳天皇
Motoori Haruniwa 本居春庭
Motoori Norinaga 本居宣長
Motoori Ōhira 本居大平
Mumyōshō 無名抄
Mumyōzōshi 無名草子

Muromachi 室町
Nagusamigusa 慰草
Nakai Chikuzan 中井竹山
Nakanoin Michikatsu 中院通勝
Namura Jōhaku 苗村丈伯
Namura Shōken 苗村松軒
Nanbokuchō 南北朝
Nara 奈良
Nara ehon 奈良絵本
Narihira shū 業平集
Nihon bungakushi 日本文学史
Nihongi 日本紀
Nihon sandai jitsuroku 日本三代実録
Nihon shoki 日本書紀
Nijō (emperor) 二条天皇
Nijō-ke (school) 二条家
Nijō no kisaki (empress) 二条后
nikki 日記
ninjō 人情
ninjō setai 人情世帯
Ninmyō (emperor) 仁明天皇
Noh 能
Nozuchi 野槌
Ochikubo monogatari 落窪物語
Ōgimachi (emperor) 正親町天皇
Ōgishō 奥義抄
Ogyū Sorai 荻生徂徠
Ōkagami 大鏡
Ōnin no ran 応仁の乱
Onna chōhōki 女重宝記
Ono no Komachi 小野小町
Ōta Mizuho 大田水穂
otogizōshi 御伽草子
Ōuchi Masahiro 大内政弘
Ōwada Tateki 大和田建樹
Reigen (emperor) 霊元天皇
Reizei-ke (school) 冷泉家
Reizei-ke-ryū Ise monogatari shō 冷泉家流伊勢物語抄
rekishi monogatari 歴史物語

renga 連歌
Rokujō-ke (family) 六条家
Roppyakuban utaawase 六百番歌合
Rufu-bon 流布本
Ryōchin 良鎮
Sadakazu (prince) 貞数親王
Saga (emperor) 嵯峨天皇
Saga-bon 嵯峨本
Sagoromo monogatari 狭衣物語
Saigū no nyōgo 斎宮の女御
Sairin 切臨
Sairyūshō 細流抄
Sakauchi San'unshi 坂内山雲子
Sanbōe 三宝絵
Sanjō Kin'atsu 三条公敦
Sanjōnishi Kin'eda 三条西公条
Sanjōnishi Saneki 三条西実枝
Sanjōnishi Sanetaka 三条西実隆
Sanjōnishi Sanezumi 三条西実澄
Sanjūrokkasen 三十六歌仙
Sarashina nikki 更級日記
Sasaki Hirotsuna 佐々木弘綱
Sasaki Nobutsuna 佐々木信綱
Seigo okudan 勢語臆断
Seigo tsū 勢語通
Sei Shōnagon 清少納言
Seiwa (emperor) 清和天皇
Sesonji Koreyuki 世尊寺伊行
setsuwa 説話
setsuyōshū 節用集
shi 詩
Shi ji 史記
Shi jing 詩経
Shika(waka)shū 詞花集
Shimizu Hamaomi 清水浜臣
Shimokōbe Chōryū 下河辺長流
Shinchokusen(waka)shū 新勅撰和歌
　集
shinchūshaku 新注釈
Shinkokin(waka)shū 新古今和歌集
shinpan 新版 or 新板

Shin'yaku Ise monogatari 新訳伊勢
　物語
Shōkai 松会
Shokugoshūi(waka)shū 続後拾遺和
　歌集
Shokushi (princess) 式子内親王
shōsetsu 小説
Shōsetsu shinzui 小説神髄
Shōtetsu 正徹
Shūi(waka)shū 拾遺和歌集
shunga 春画
Sōboku 宗牧
Sōchō 宗長
Sōdenshi Sankei 艸田子三径
Sōgakkōkei 創学校啓
Soga monogatari 曽我物語
Sōgi 宗祇
Sōgichū 宗祇注
Somedono (empress) 染殿の后
Sonpi bunmyaku 尊卑分脈
soragoto 虚言
Sōseki 宗碩
sōshi 草子
Sotoorihime 衣通姫
Suminokura Soan 角倉素庵
Sumiyoshi Daimyōjin 住吉大明神
Sutoku (emperor) 崇徳天皇
Suzakuin-nurigome-bon 朱雀院塗籠
　本
Tachibana Moribe 橘守部
Tachibana no Tadamoto 橘忠元
tai-i 大意
Taionki 戴恩記
Takada Munekata 高田宗賢
Takashina no Moronao 高階師尚
Takatsu Kuwasaburō 高津鍬三郎
Takeda-bon 武田本
Takeda Nobutoyo 武田信豊
Taketori monogatari 竹取物語
Tamakatsuma 玉勝間
Tayasu Munetake 田安宗武

Teika-bon 定家本
Tenchū Ise monogatari rigenkai 添註
　伊勢物語俚言解
Tenpuku-bon 天福本
Tenshi (princess) 括子内親王
tōchū 頭注
Tokugawa 徳川
Tō no Tsuneyori 東常縁
Tsubouchi Shōyō 坪内逍遥
tsukurigoto 作り事
tsukuri monogatari 作り物語
Tsurezuregusa 徒然草
Tsurezuregusa Jumyōinshō 徒然草寿
　命院抄
Uda (emperor) 宇多天皇
Ueda Akinari 上田秋成
Uiyamabumi うひ山ぶみ
uta awase 歌合わせ
utagatari 歌語り
utamakura 歌枕
uta monogatari 歌物語
Utsuho monogatari 宇津保物語
wa 和

Wabungakushi 和文学史
waka 和歌
Wakachikenshū 和歌知見集
waka kanjō 和歌灌頂
Waka kimyōdan 和歌奇妙談
Waka shogaku shō 和歌初学抄
warichū 割注
Yamaguchi ki 山口記
Yama no Yatsu 山の八
Yamato monogatari 大和物語
Yashiro Hirokata 屋代弘賢
yomikuse 読癖 or 読曲
Yoshida Kenkō 吉田兼好
Yoshida Teikichi 吉田定吉
Yoshi ya ashi ya よしやあしや
Yotsuji Yoshinari 四辻義成
Yōzei (emperor) 陽成天皇
yūsoku kojitsu 有職故実
Zaigo chūjō Narihira hishi 在五中将
　業平秘史
Zōho eshō Kaō Ise monogatari 増補絵
　抄花王伊勢物語
zuihitsu 随筆

Works Cited

Abe Akio, Oka Kazuo, and Yamagishi Tokuhei, eds. *Genji monogatari jō*. Kokugo kokubungaku kenkyūshi taisei 3. Tokyo: Sanseidō, 1960.

Aoki Shizuko. "Muromachi kōki Ise monogatari chūshaku no hōhō—Sōgi, Sanjōnishi-ke-ryū o chūshin ni." In *Taketori monogatari, Ise monogatari*, ed. Katagiri Yōichi. Nihon bungaku kenkyū taisei. Tokyo: Kokusho kankōkai, 1988.

————. "*Ise monogatari shūsuishō* no seiritsu." *Joshidai bungaku, kokubun-hen* 38 (1987): 29–46.

————. "Sanjōnishi Sanetaka ni okeru Ise monogatari kochū—'Igo chōsetsu' 'Shōdan shūkai' ni furetsutsu." *Mozu kokubun* 6 (1987): 76–91.

————. "Ise monogatari kyūchūron jōsetsu—Ichijō Kaneyoshi to Sōgi to." *Joshidai bungaku, kokubun-hen* 37 (1986): 38–52.

Arima Yotōji. *Shinshaku Ise monogatari*. Tokyo: Yūseidō, 1920.

Asai Ryōi. *Ise monogatari jokai*. 12 vols. n.p., after 1655. Osaka University Library.

Asano Akira, Kira Sueo, Taniwaki Masachika, Hara Michio, and Munemasa Isao, eds. *Genroku bungaku no nagare*. Kōza Genroku bungaku I. Tokyo: Benseisha, 1992.

Baswell, Christopher. *Virgil in Medieval England: Figuring the Aeneid from the 11th century to Chaucer*. New York: Cambridge University Press, 1995.

Beebee, Thomas O. *The Ideology of Genre: A Comparative Study of Generic Instability*. University Park: Pennsylvania State University Press, 1994.

Benjamin, Walter. *Illuminations, Essays and Reflections*. Ed. Hannah Arendt and trans. Harry Zohn. New York: Schocken Books, 1969.

Berry, Mary Elizabeth. *Japan in Print: Information and Nation in the Early Modern Period*. Berkeley: University of California Press, 2006.

————. *The Culture of Civil War in Kyoto*. Berkeley: University of California Press, 1994.

Bourdieu, Pierre. *The Field of Cultural Production*. New York: Columbia University Press, 1993.

Bowring, Richard. "The *Ise Monogatari*: A Short Cultural History." *Harvard Journal of Asiatic Studies* 52 (1992): 401–80.

Burns, Susan L. *Before the Nation: Kokugaku and the Imagining of Community in Early Modern Japan*. Durham, NC: Duke University Press, 2003.

Butler, Lee. *Emperor and Aristocracy in Japan, 1467–1680: Resilience and Renewal*. Cambridge, MA: Harvard University Asia Center, 2002.

Carter, Steven D. "Claiming the Past for the Present: Ichijō Kaneyoshi and *Tales of Ise*." In *Rhetoric and the Discourses of Power in Court Culture: China, Europe and Japan*, ed. David R. Knechtges and Eugene Vance. Seattle: University of Washington Press, 2005, pp. 94–116.

———. *Regent Redux: A Life of the Statesman-Scholar Ichijō Kaneyoshi*. Michigan Monograph Series in Japanese Studies 16. Ann Arbor: Center for Japanese Studies, University of Michigan, 1996.

———. "Introduction." In *Literary Patronage in Late Medieval Japan*, ed. Steven D. Carter. Ann Arbor: Center for Japanese Studies, University of Michigan, 1993, pp. 1–17.

Carter, Steven D., ed. *Literary Patronage in Late Medieval Japan*. Ann Arbor: Center for Japanese Studies, University of Michigan, 1993.

Chance, Linda H. *Formless in Form: Kenkō*, Tsurezuregusa, *and the Rhetoric of Japanese Fragmentary Prose*. Stanford: Stanford University Press, 1997.

Chūsei Kuge Nikki Kenkyūkai, ed. *Sengokuki kuge shakai no shoyōsō*. Osaka: Izumi Shoin, 1992.

Cook, Lewis. "Genre Trouble: Medieval Commentaries and the Canonization of *The Tale of Genji*." In *Envisioning* The Tale of Genji: *Media, Gender, and Cultural Production*, ed. Haruo Shirane. New York: Columbia University Press, 2008, pp. 129–53.

———. "The Discipline of Poetry: Authority and Invention in the *Kokindenju*." Ph.D. dissertation, Cornell University, 2000.

Elias, Norbert. "Knowledge and Power: An Interview with Peter Ludes." In *Society and Knowledge: Contemporary Perspectives in the Sociology of Knowledge & Science*, ed. Nico Stehr and Volcker Meja. 2nd rev. ed. New Brunswick: Transaction, 2005, pp. 203–42.

Flueckiger, Peter. *Imagining Harmony: Poetry, Empathy, and Community in Mid-Tokugawa Confucianism and Nativism*. Stanford: Stanford University Press, 2011.

———. "Reflections on the Meaning of Our Country: Kamo no Mabuchi's *Kokuiko*." *Monumenta Nipponica* 63.2 (2008): 211–63.

Frow, John. *Genre*. New York: Routledge, 2006.

Fujii Takanao. *Ise monogatari shinshaku*. 3rd printing. Tokyo: Bunken Shoten, 1929.

Fujioka Tadami, ed. *Fukurozōshi*. Shin Nihon koten bungaku taikei 29. Tokyo: Iwanami Shoten, 1995.

Fukui Teisuke. *Uta monogatari no kenkyū*. Tokyo: Fūbun Shobō, 1986.

Genette, Gerard. *Paratexts: Thresholds of Interpretation*. New York: Cambridge University Press, 1997.

Gerstle, C. Andrew, ed. *Eighteenth Century Japan: Culture and Society*. Paperback ed. Richmond, Surrey: Curzon Press, 2000.

Goi Ranshū. *Seigo tsū*. 2 vols. Osaka: Matsumura Bunkaidō, 1911.

Harper, Thomas J. "*The Tale of Genji* in the Eighteenth Century: Keichū, Mabuchi and Norinaga." In *Eighteenth Century Japan: Culture and Society*, ed. C. Andrew Gerstle. Paperback ed. Richmond, Surrey: Curzon Press, 2000, pp. 106–23.

———. "Norinaga's Criticism of *Genji monogatari*: A Study of the Background and Critical Content of *Genji monogatari tama no ogushi*." Ph.D. dissertation, University of Michigan, 1971.

Harris, H. Jay. *Tales of Ise*. Rutland: Charles E. Tuttle Co., 1972.

Hasegawa Masaharu, Imanishi Yūichirō, Itō Haku, and Yoshioka Hiroshi, eds. *Tosa nikki, Kagerō nikki, Murasaki Shikibu nikki, Sarashina nikki*. Shin Nihon koten bungaku taikei 24. Tokyo: Iwanami Shoten, 1989.

Hasegawa Senshi. *Zoho eshō Kao Ise monogatari*. Kyoto: 1721. General Library, the University of Tokyo.

Hashimoto Fumio, Ariyoshi Tamotsu, and Fujihira Haruo, eds. *Karonshū*. Nihon koten bungaku zenshū 50. Tokyo: Shōgakkan, 1975.

Henderson, John. *Scripture, Canon and Commentary: A Comparison of Confucian and Western Exegesis*. Princeton: Princeton University Press, 1991.

Hisamatsu Sen'ichi. *Keichū den*. Tokyo: Chibundō, 1969.

Hisamatsu Sen'ichi, Tsukishima Hiroshi, et al., eds. *Keichū zenshū*. 16 vols. Tokyo: Iwanami Shoten, 1973–76.

Horiuchi Hideakira, and Akiyama Ken, eds. *Taketori monogatari, Ise monogatari*. Shin Nihon koten bungaku taikei 17. Tokyo: Iwanami Shoten, 1997.

Horton, H. Mack, trans. *The Journal of Sōchō*. Stanford, CA: Stanford University Press, 2002.

Hosokawa Yūsai. *Ise monogatari ketsugishō*. 2 vols. [Kyoto]: n.p., 1653. General Library, the University of Tokyo.

Ichiko Natsuo. *Kinsei shoki bungaku to shuppan bunka*. Tokyo: Wakagusa Shobō, 1998.

———. "Nomura Jōhaku." In *Nihon koten bungaku daijiten*, ed. Nihon Koten Bungaku Daijiten Henshū Iinkai. Tokyo: Iwanami Shoten, 1984, 3:554.

Ikeda Kikan. *Ise monogatari ni tsukite no kenkyū.* 3 vols. Tokyo: Ōokayama Shoten, 1933–34.

Imaizumi Teisuke. *Ise monogatari kōgi.* 3rd ed. Tokyo: Tokyo Shinnodō, 1895.

Inoue Minoru, ed. *Kamo no Mabuchi zenshū.* 27 vols. Tokyo: Zoku Gunsho Ruijū Kanseikai, 1977–92.

Inoue Muneo. *Chūsei kadanshi no kenkyū, Muromachi kōki.* Tokyo: Meiji Shoin, 1972.

———. "Yasokuken Nakanoin Michikatsu no shōgai." *Kokugo kokubun* 40.12 (1971): 1–29.

Ise monogatari kaisei. 2 vols. Kyoto: n.p., 1698. General Library, the University of Tokyo.

Ise monogatari kisuishō. 11 vols. Manuscript, 1608. Kokubungaku Kenkyū Shiryōkan microfilm 48-20-8.

Ise monogatari tōshoshō. 2 vols. n.p., n.d. General Library, the University of Tokyo.

Ishikawa Tōru. "Muromachi jidai monogatari ni okeru *Ise monogatari* kyōju." In *Ise monogatari chū,* ed. Tokue Gensei. Muromachi bungaku sanshū I. Tokyo: Miyai Shoten, 1987.

Itō Toshiko. *Ise monogatari-e.* Tokyo: Kadokawa Shoten, 1984.

Iwatsubo Takeshi. "Genji monogatari no nidankai denju ni tsuite—Kawachi hō to Yotsuji Yoshinari, Ichijō Kaneyoshi o megutte." *Kokugo to kokubungaku* 66.6 (1989): 30–43.

Jameson, Fredric. *The Political Unconscious: Narrative as a Socially Symbolic Act.* Ithaca, NY: Cornell University Press, 1981.

Kamens, Edward. *The Three Jewels: A Study and Translation of Minamoto Tamenori's Sanbōe.* Ann Arbor: Center for Japanese Studies, University of Michigan, 1988.

Katagiri Yōichi. *Tensai sakka no kyozō to jitsuzō: Ariwara Narihira, Ono no Komachi.* Tokyo: Shintensha, 1991.

———. *Ise monogatari no shinkenkyū.* Tokyo: Meiji Shoin, 1987.

———. *Ise monogatari no kenkyū: Shiryōhen.* Tokyo: Meiji Shoin, 1969.

———. *Ise monogatari no kenkyū: Kenkyūhen.* Tokyo: Meiji Shoin, 1968.

Katagiri Yōichi, ed. *Gosenwakashū.* Shin Nihon koten bungaku taikei 6. Tokyo: Iwanami Shoten, 1990.

———, ed. *Taketori monogatari, Ise monogatari.* Nihon bungaku kenkyū taisei. Tokyo: Kokusho kankōkai, 1988.

———, ed. *Ise monogatari, Yamato monogatari.* Kansho Nihon no koten bungaku, vol 5. Tokyo: Kadokawa Shoten, 1975.

Katagiri Yōichi, and Yamamoto Tokurō, eds. *Tesshinsai bunko Ise monogatari sokan.* 15 vols. Tokyo: Yagi Shoten, 1988–2002.

Kawase Kazuma. *Zōho Kokatsujiban no kenkyū.* 3 vols. Tokyo: Nihon Koshosekishō Kyōkai, 1967.

Kido Kuniko. "*Ise monogatari* Reizei-ke-ryū kochū to *Wakachikenshū* to *sono* sōiten o megutte." *Chūko bungaku ronkō* 13. (1992): 10–18.

Kimura Takatarō. *Zaigo chūjō Narihira hishi.* Tokyo: Shunshūdō, 1912.

Kitamura Kigin. *Ise monogatari shūshuishō.* 2 vols. [Kyoto]: n.p., 1680. General Library, the University of Tokyo.

———. *Genji monogtari kōgetsushō zōchū.* Tokyo: Kōdansha, 2001.

Klein, Susan Blakeley. *Allegories of Desire: Esoteric Literary Commentaries of Medieval Japan.* Cambridge, MA: Harvard University Asia Center, 2002.

———. "A Translation of *Ise monogatari zuinō.*" *Monumenta Nipponica* 53.1 (1998): 13–43.

———. "Allegories of Desire: Poetry and Eroticism in *Ise monogatari zuinō.*" *Monumenta Nipponica* 52.4 (1997): 441–65.

———. "Allegories of Desire: Kamakura Commentaries and the Noh." Ph.D. dissertation, Cornell University, 1994.

Knechtges, David R., and Eugene Vance, eds. *Rhetoric and the Discourses of Power in Court Culture: China, Europe and Japan.* Seattle: University of Washington Press, 2005.

Kokinwaka Ise monogatari. 3 vols. Kyoto: n.p.,1699. General Library, the University of Tokyo.

Kokubungaku Kenkyū Shiryōkan, ed. *Ise to Genji: Monogatari honmon no juyō.* Kyoto: Rinsen Shoten, 2000.

Kornicki, Peter F. "Women, Education, and Literacy." In *The Female as Subject: Reading and Writing in Early Modern Japan*, ed. P. F. Kornicki, et al. Ann Arbor: Center for Japanese Studies, University of Michigan, 2010, pp. 7–38.

———. "Manuscript, Not Print: Scribal Culture in the Edo Period." *Journal of Japanese Studies* 32.1 (2006): 23–52.

———. "Unsuitable Books for Women? 'Genji Monogatari' and 'Ise Monogatari' in Late Seventeenth-Century Japan." *Monumenta Nipponica* 60.2 (2005): 147–93.

———. *The Book in Japan: A Cultural History from the Beginnings to the Nineteenth Century.* Leiden: Brill, 1998.

Kornicki, Peter. F., Mara Patessio, and G. G. Rowley, eds. *The Female as Subject: Reading and Writing in Early Modern Japan.* Ann Arbor: Center for Japanese Studies, University of Michigan, 2010.

Kubota Jun, and Yamaguchi Akiho, eds. *Roppyakuban utaawase.* Shin Nihon koten bungaku taikei 38. Tokyo: Iwanami Shoten, 1998.

Kudō Shinshirō. *Fujii Takanao to Matsuya-ha.* Tokyo: Kazama shōbō, 1986.

Kumakura Isao. "Sanjōnishi Sanetaka, Takeno Jōō, and an Early Form of *Iemoto Seido.*" In *Literary Patronage in Late Medieval Japan*, ed. Steven D.

Carter. Ann Arbor: Center for Japanese Studies, University of Michigan, 1993, pp. 95–104.

Kurosaka Katsumi, and Kokushi Taikei Henshū kai, eds. *Nihon sandai jitsuroku*. Kokushi Taikei 3. Tokyo: Yoshikawa Kōbunkan, 1973.

Kuwabara Hiroshi, ed. *Mumyōzōshi*. Shinchō Nihon koten shūsei. Tokyo: Shinchōsha, 1976.

Lurie, David B. "Digesting Antiquity: The Commentarial Tradition and the Emergence of Poetic Philology in the Late Heian Period." Unpublished paper.

Maeda Tomoko. "Genji kō." In *Genji monogatari no hensōkyoku: Edo no shirabe*, ed. Suzuki Ken'ichi. Tokyo: Miyai Shoten, 2003, pp. 220–23.

Makeham, John. *Transmitters and Creators: Chinese Commentators and Commentaries on the Analects*. Cambridge, MA: Harvard University Asia Center, 2003.

Marra, Michele. "*Mumyōzōshi*, Part 3." *Monumenta Nipponica* 39.4 (1984): 409–34.

Matsudaira Susumu. "Ehon, eiribon." In *Genroku bungaku no nagare*, ed. Asano Akira, et al. Kōza Genroku bungaku 1. Tokyo: Benseisha, 1992, pp. 266–74.

Matsunaga Teitoku. *Nagusamigusa*. Kyoto: n.p., n.d. General Library, the University of Tokyo.

McCullough, Helen Craig, trans. *Tales of Ise: Lyrical Episodes from Tenth-Century Japan*. Stanford: Stanford University Press, 1968.

McCullough, William H., and Helen Craig McCullough. *A Tale of Flowering Fortunes: Annals of Japanese Life in the Heian Period*. Stanford: Stanford University Press, 1980.

McMullen, James. *Idealism, Protest and the* Tale of Genji. Oxford: Clarendon Press, 1999.

McNally, Mark. *Proving the Way: Conflict and Practice in the History of Japanese Nativism*. Cambridge, MA: Harvard University Asia Center, 2005.

Mezaki Tokue. "Zaigo chūjō to Teiji no mikado: Kōi keishō, kōshin shisei o megutte." In *Ise monogatari, Yamato monogatari*, ed. Katagiri Yōichi. Tokyo: Kadokawa Shoten, 1975, pp. 349–58.

Miyake Kiyoshi. *Kada no Azumamaro*. Tokyo: Kokumin Seishin Bunka Kenkyūjo, 1942.

Mostow, Joshua. "Illustrated Classical Texts for Women in the Edo Period." In *The Female as Subject: Reading and Writing in Early Modern Japan*, ed. P. F. Kornicki, et al. Ann Arbor: Center for Japanese Studies, University of Michigan, 2010, pp. 59–86.

———. "Modern Constructions of *Ise monogatari*: Gender and Courtliness." In *Inventing the Classics: Modernity, National Identity and Japanese Litera-*

ture, ed. Haruo Shirane and Tomi Suzuki. Stanford: Stanford University Press, 2000, pp. 96–119.

Mostow, Joshua, and Royall Tyler, trans. and commentary. *The Ise Stories: Ise monogatari*. Honolulu: University of Hawai'i Press, 2010.

Murphy, William P. "Secret Knowledge as Property and Power in Kpelle Society: Elders versus Youth." *Africa: Journal of the International African Institute* 50.2 (1980): 193–207.

Nagatomo Chiyoji, ed. *Onna chōhōki, Otoko chōhōki—Genroku wakamono shintokushū*. Tokyo: Shakai Shisōsha, 1993.

Najita, Tetsuo. *Visions of Virtue in Tokugawa Japan: The Kaitokudō Merchant Academy of Osaka*. Honolulu: University of Hawai'i Press, 1997.

Nakamura Yukihiko. "Goi Ranshū no bungakukan." In *Nakamura Yukihiko chojutsushū*, vol. 1. Tokyo: Chūōkōronsha, 1982.

Nakamura Yukihiko, ed. *Kinsei bungakuron shū*. Nihon koten bungaku taikei 94. Tokyo: Iwanami Shoten, 1966.

Nakano Kōichi. "Aru Genji gochūsho no shuppan sōdō—*Gengo ko* to *Gengo tei* to *Gengo ruijūshō*." *Musashino bungaku* 45 (1998): 20–23.

Namura Jōhaku. *Ise monogatari eshō*. 3 vols. Kyoto: n.p., 1693. General Library, the University of Tokyo.

Namura Shōken. *Ise monogatari taisei*. 2 vols. Kyoto: n.p., 1697. General Library, the University of Tokyo.

Nihon Koten Bungaku Daijiten Henshū Iinkai, ed. *Nihon Koten Bungaku Daijiten*. Tokyo: Iwanami Shoten, 1983–85.

Noma Mitsuo, "San'unshi." In *Nihon koten bungaku daijiten*, ed. Nihon Koten Bungaku Daijiten Henshū Iinkai. Tokyo: Iwanami Shoten, 1984, 3:95.

Nosco, Peter. *Remembering Paradise: Nativism and Nostalgia in Eighteenth Century Japan*. Cambridge, MA: Council on East Asian Studies, Harvard University, 1990.

Odaka Toshio. *Kinsei shoki bundan no kenkyū*. Tokyo: Meiji Shoin, 1964.

———. *Matsunaga Teitoku no kenkyū, zoku-hen*. Tokyo: Shibundō, 1953.

Odaka Toshio, and Matsumura Akira, eds. *Taionki, Oritaku shiba no ki, Rantō kotohajime*. Nihon koten bungaku taikei 95. Tokyo: Iwanami Shoten, 1964.

Ōta Mizuho. *Shin'yaku Ise monogatari*. Tokyo: Hakushinsha, 1912.

Ōtsu Yūichi. *Zōteiban Ise monogatari kochūshaku no kenkyū*. Tokyo: Yagi Shoten, 1986.

Ōwada Tateki. *Wabungakushi*. Tokyo: Hakubunkan, 1892.

Ozawa Masao, and Matsuda Shigeho, eds. and trans. *Kokinwakashū*. Shin Nihon koten bungaku zenshū 11. Tokyo: Shōgakkan, 1994.

Parker, Deborah. *Commentary and Ideology: Dante in the Renaissance*. Durham, NC: Duke University Press, 1993.

Radway, Janice A. *Reading the Romance: Women, Patriarchy, Popular Literature.* Chapel Hill: University of North Carolina Press, 1991.

Ruch, Barbara. "Chūsei bungaku to kaiga." In *Jūgo, jūroku seiki no bungaku,* ed. Kubota Jun, et al. Iwanami kōza Nihon bungaku shi 6. Tokyo: Iwanami Shoten, 1996, pp. 295–311.

Sakauchi San'unshi. *Kashiragaki Ise monogatari shō.* 2 vols. Kyoto: n.p., 1674. General Library, the University of Tokyo.

Sasaki Hirotsuna. *Tenchū Ise monogatari rigenkai.* Tokyo: Yanase Kibee, 1885. General Library, the University of Tokyo.

Sasaki Nobutsuna, ed. *Nihon kagaku taikei.* 10 vols. Tokyo: Kazama Shobō, 1956–63.

———. *Kōchū Ise monogatari.* Tokyo: Hakubunkan, 1892.

Sayre, C. Franklin. "Illustrations of the *Ise-monogatari*: Survival and Revival of Heian Court Culture." Ph.D. dissertation, Yale University, 1978.

Scheid, Bernhard, and Mark Teeuwen, eds. *The Culture of Secrecy in Japanese Religion.* New York: Routledge, 2006.

Seidensticker, Edward G., trans. *The Tale of Genji.* New York: Alfred A. Knopf, 1976.

Shimamoto Shōichi. *Matsunaga Teitoku: Haikaishi e no michi.* Tokyo: Hosei Daigaku Shuppankyoku, 1989.

Shinmura Izuru, ed. *Kōjien.* 5th edition. Tokyo: Iwanami Shoten, 1998.

Shirane, Haruo. "*The Tale of Genji* and the Dynamics of Cultural Production: Canonization and Popularization." In *Envisioning The Tale of Genji: Media, Gender, and Cultural Production,* ed. Haruo Shirane. New York: Columbia University Press, 2008, pp. 1–46.

———. "Introduction: Issues in Canon Formation." In *Inventing the Classics: Modernity, National Identity and Japanese Literature,* ed. Haruo Shirane and Tomi Suzuki. Stanford: Stanford University Press, 2000, pp. 1–27.

Shirane, Haruo, ed. *Envisioning The Tale of Genji: Media, Gender, and Cultural Production.* New York: Columbia University Press, 2008.

Shirane, Haruo, and Tomi Suzuki, eds. *Inventing the Classics: Modernity, National Identity and Japanese Literature.* Stanford: Stanford University Press, 2000.

Stehr, Nico. "Knowledge Societies." In *Society and Knowledge: Contemporary Perspectives in the Sociology of Knowledge and Science,* 2nd rev. ed., ed. Nico Stehr and Volker Meja. New Brunswick, NJ: Transaction, 2005, pp. 299–322.

Stehr, Nico, and Volker Meja, eds. *Society and Knowledge: Contemporary Perspectives in the Sociology of Knowledge and Science.* 2nd rev. ed. New Brunswick, NJ: Transaction, 2005.

Suzuki Ken'ichi. *Genji monogatari no hensōkyoku: Edo no shirabe*. Tokyo: Miyai Shoten, 2003.

Suzuki, Tomi. "Gender and Genre: Modern Literary Histories and Women's Diary Literature." In *Inventing the Classics: Modernity, National Identity and Japanese Literature*, ed. Haruo Shirane and Tomi Suzuki. Stanford: Stanford University Press, 2000, pp. 71–95.

———. *Narrating the Self: Fictions of Japanese Modernity*. Stanford: Stanford University Press, 1996.

Taira Shigemichi, and Abe Akio, eds. *Kinsei shintōron, zenki kokugaku*. Nihon shisō taikei 39. Tokyo: Iwanami Shoten, 1972.

Takada Munekata. *Ise monogatari hiketsushō*. 12 vols. n.p., 1679. Osaka University Library.

Takei Kazuto. "<Konton> no jidai." In *Kokinshū no sekai: Denju to kyōju* ed. Yokoi Kaneo and Arai Eizō. Tokyo: Sekaishisōsha, 1986, pp. 49–66.

Takeoka Masao. *Ise monogatari zenhyōshaku—kochūshaku jūnishu shūsei*. Tokyo: Yūbun shoin, 1987.

———. *Kokinwakashū zenhyōshaku—kochū nanashu shūsei*. 2 vols. Tokyo: Yūbun Shoin, 1981.

Tamagami Takuya, ed. *Shimeishō, Kakaishō*. Tokyo: Kadokawa Shoten, 1968.

Tanaka Maki. "Fujiwara no Shunzei no *Ise monogatari* kyōju." *Bunrin* 35 (2001): 47–70.

Tanaka Sōsaku. *Ise monogatari kenkyūshi no kenkyū*. Tokyo: Ofusha, 1965.

Tanaka Yōko. "*Ise monogatari hiketsushō* ni tsuite—Enpō ki no koten kyōju." *Gobun kenkyū* 68 (1989): 26–40.

Teeuwen, Mark. "Knowing vs. Owning a Secret: Secrecy in Medieval Japan, as Seen through the *Sokui kanjō* Enthronement Unction." In *The Culture of Secrecy in Japanese Religion*, ed. Bernhard Scheid and Mark Teeuwen. New York: Routledge, 2006, pp. 172–203.

Tesshinsai Bunko Ise monogatari Bunkakan. *Ise monogatari hanpon no sekai*. Tesshinsai Bunko shozō Ise monogatari zuroku 16. Odawara: Tesshinsai Bunko Ise monogatari Bunkakan, 1999.

———. *Kinsei no shuppan bunka to Ise monogatari chūshaku*. Tesshinsai Bunko shozō Ise monogatari zuroku 9. Odawara: Tesshinsai Bunko Ise monogatari Bunkakan, 1995.

———. *Edo jidai Ise monogatari eiri hanpon no tenkai*. Tesshinsai Bunko shozō Ise monogatari zuroku 2. Odawara: Tesshinsai Bunko Ise monogatari Bunkakan, 1992.

Tokue Gensei, ed. *Ise monogatari chū*. Muromachi bungaku sanshū I. Tokyo: Miyai Shoten, 1987.

Tsurusaki Hiroo. "Chūsei kōki koten kenkyū no issokumen—Konoe Hisamichi no baai." In *Sengokuki kuge shakai no shoyōsō*, ed. Chūsei Kuge Nikki Kenkyūkai. Osaka: Izumi Shoin, 1992, pp. 337–55.

Tsutsumi Yasuo. *Genji monogatari chūshakushi no kisoteki kenkyū*. Tokyo: Ōfūsha, 1994.

Urban, Hugh B. "The Torment of Secrecy: Ethical and Epistemological Problems in the Study of Esoteric Traditions." *History of Religions* 37.3 (February 1998): 209–48.

Vos, Frits. *A Study of the Ise-monogatari*. 2 vols. The Hague: Mouton and Co., 1957.

Yagi Tsuyoshi. "Seigo tsū ni tsuite." *Gobun* 10 (1954): 19–45.

Yamamoto Tokurō. *Ise monogatari ron: Buntai, shudai, kyōju*. Tokyo: Kazama Shobō, 2001.

———. "Tesshinsai bunko no *Ise monogatari* korekushon." In *Ise to Genji: Monogatari honmon no juyō*, ed. Kokubungaku Kenkyū Shiryōkan. Koten kōen shirîzu 5. Kyoto: Rinsen Shoten, 2000.

Yamamoto Tokurō, ed. *Ise monogatari hanpon shūsei*. Tokyo: Chikurinsha, 2011.

———, ed. *Ise monogatari: Kyōju no tenkai*. Tokyo: Chikurinsha, 2010.

Yamamoto Tokurō, and Joshua Mostow, eds. *Ise monogatari: Sōzō to hen'yō*. Osaka: Izumi Shoin, 2009.

Yokoi Kaneo, and Arai Eizō, eds. *Kokinshū no sekai: Denju to kyōju*. Kyoto: Sekai Shisōsha, 1986.

Yokota Fuyuhiko. *Tenka taihei*. Nihon no rekishi 16. Tokyo: Kodansha, 2002.

Yonehara Masayoshi. *Sengoku bushi to bungei no kenkyū*. Tokyo: Ofusha, 1976.

Yoshikawa Kōjirō, Satake Akihiro, and Hino Tatsuo, eds. *Motoori Norinaga shū*. Nihon shisō taikei 15. Tokyo: Iwanami Shoten, 1978.

Yoshizawa Sadato. *Tsurezuregusa kochūshaku shūsei*. Tokyo: Benseisha, 1996.

Index

Reizei-ke (school), 58, 72, 73n, 94, 95, 101, 114, 115

Reizei-ke-ryū Ise monogatari shō (Reizei school *Ise monogatari* commentary), 59–61, 94, 96, 97

Rekishi monogatari (historical tale), 23–24

Renga (linked verse), 64, 67

Renga masters, 26, 62–72 passim, 82n, 83, 107, 122

Rokujō-ke (family), 40, 41, 43, 47, 55, 58, 78

Roppyakuban utaawase (Poetry contest in 600 rounds, 1193), 44–54

Rufu-bon (Circulating text [of *Ise monogatari*]), 55–58, 78, 124, 186, 187, 219, 220n

Saga-bon, 121–30, 133, 134, 140, 151, 156, 162

Sagoromo monogatari (Tale of Sagoromo, 1070s), 37, 38, 39, 126n, 202, 203, 220n

Sairin (b. 1591), 106, 139–41, 171

Sairyūshō (1528; Sanjōnishi Kin'eda), 69

Sakauchi San'unshi (ca. 1644–ca. 1711), 150, 152, 159, 165

Sanbōe (The three treasures, illustrated, 984; Minamoto Tamenori), 35

Sanjō Kin'atsu (1439–1507), 68

Sanjōnishi Kin'eda (1487–1563), 69, 71, 83, 84, 104–5, 107, 117, 122

Sanjōnishi Saneki or Sanezumi (1511–79), 83, 84, 90, 91, 95, 96, 104–7, 139

Sanjōnishi Sanetaka (1455–1537), 55, 63n, 68–70, 82–84, 91, 96, 99, 104–5, 114, 115, 118, 206

Sarashina nikki (Sarashina diary, after 1058), 36, 37n, 220n, 233

Sasaki Hirotsuna, 233

Sasaki Nobutsuna, 233–34

Secret teachings, 11–15, 59, 62–74 passim, 106–16 passim, 131, 135, 139–40, 154, 171, 173, 179, 183. See also *Denju*; *Kokin denju*

Seigo okudan (Conjectures about *Ise monogatari*, 1693; Keichū), 4, 183, 184–90, 199, 202, 206, 217, 219, 222, 233–34

Seigo tsū (Understanding *Ise monogatari*, 1751; Goi Ranshū), 184, 205–16, 234n

Sei Shōnagon, 21, 22, 172

Seiwa (emperor; 850–80), 31, 60–61, 81, 85, 87, 88, 90, 97, 209

Sesonji Koreyuki (d. 1165), 57, 73n, 77

Setsuwa (exempla), 23, 24, 209

Setsuyōshū (household encyclopedic dictionary), 130, 163

Shijing (Book of songs), 78, 100, 189

Shimizu Hamaomi (1776–1824), 219, 233

Shinchokusen(waka)shū (New imperial collection of poetry, 1234), 185

Shinchūshaku. See New Commentaries

Shinkokin(waka)shū (New collection of ancient and modern poetry, 1205), 20

Shinshaku Ise monogatari (New explication of *Ise monogatari*, 1920; Arima Yotōji), 237

Shin'yaku Ise monogatari (New translation of *Ise monogatari*, 1912; Ōta Mizuho), 237

.

Harvard East Asian Monographs
(*out-of-print)

Harvard East Asian Monographs

Harvard East Asian Monographs

Harvard East Asian Monographs

Harvard East Asian Monographs

Harvard East Asian Monographs

Harvard East Asian Monographs